M...
ON
VIDEO

MOVIES ON VIDEO

★★★★★★★★

Roy Pickard

FREDERICK MULLER LIMITED
LONDON

First published in Great Britain, in 1982 by
Frederick Muller Limited, Dataday House,
8 Alexandra Road, Wimbledon, London, SW19 7JU.

British Library Cataloguing in Publication Data

Pickard, Roy
  Movies on video.
  1. Moving-pictures—Catalogs   2. Video
  tape recorders and recordings
  I. Title
  011'.37   PN1998

  ISBN 0-584-11029-4

Phototypeset by Input Typesetting Ltd., London
Printed in Great Britain by Richard Clay (The Chaucer Press) Ltd.
Bungay, Suffolk

CONTENTS

	page
Key to rating systems	6
Introduction	7
A–Z film listing	11
Video companies and distribution	475
Index of 100 top stars	478
Stop press	481

KEY TO RATING SYSTEMS
USED IN THIS BOOK

★★★★ Excellent
★★★ Good
★★ Average
★ Poor

Box-office rentals are set against each film when that film has grossed 4 million dollars or more. These, in turn, are set against an average "top twenty box-office figure" to provide a point of comparison in the year of release.

All Oscars and Oscar nominations won by a film are also set against each title.

If no box-office figure is shown, then that film did not reach the 4 million dollar mark; similarly, no Academy Award data is included if a picture failed to receive any Oscars or Oscar nominations.

INTRODUCTION

You've heard about the video revolution. You've read articles in newspapers and magazines telling you that it's here and that it's one of the fastest growing industries in the country. And, convinced by what you've read, you have chanced your arm and purchased or rented a video machine. Now all you have to do is search around and find those movies you would most like to rent or even buy for your own personal film library.

Finding just what is on offer is rather easier said than done. Monthly video magazines are one source but, because of space restrictions their reviews are inevitably limited. A glance in your local TV showroom will give you an idea of the top selling titles but not much more. So a visit to a video stockist in your nearest big town is probably your best bet, for a specialist will almost certainly carry the widest range of tapes.

But still not wide enough. There is a limit as to what can be displayed on shelves. Hence the need for a guide, a book that can tell you all you want to know about movies on video. This is that book, a detailed guide to not fifty, not a hundred but nearly a thousand top movies.

At first, there seemed to be no need for the book at all, for the video revolution was slow starting with only a handful of movies becoming available in the first few years. But now that trickle has become a flood and a guide is essential if you are to find your way round a market that is at once an Aladdin's cave for genuine movie enthusiasts and fraught with danger for the unsuspecting buyer. For, make no mistake about it, there is an awful lot of rubbish around and it is only too easy to get your fingers burned.

This book therefore tries to separate the good from the bad, the quality movies from those of dubious value, and become an essential reference source for all those film lovers with the technical advantages of video at their fingertips.

So, what is the method of selection? Well, I have tried to confine my entries to films made for the cinema, real movies in other words. I have also raided the catalogues of all the main distributors in this country, those with the highest number of quality films on their lists. Movies of lesser distributors are also included if they are of some value historically or have been popular commercially.

All *genres* are represented – comedies, epics, westerns, thrillers, war films, swashbucklers, horror films, especially the latter which, for some reason best known to psychologists rather than myself, seem to enjoy greater popularity on video than any other kind of film.

Now for the approach. Well, there's no golden rule that says reference books are supposed to be dry and dusty, so with that in mind I have adopted a mostly light-hearted approach (in the case of some of the messy modern day horror films perhaps a vitriolic one) and always tried to keep things entertaining. And, as the book deals with merchandise that you will buy or rent with your own hard-earned money, I have tried to be as objective as possible about the value of each film, its quality, repeatability, and so on.

My own views are represented by a simple *one-to-four* star rating. Already I can hear you groaning: "Oh, no, not another wise guy who thinks he knows more than I do, someone who is going to force his opinions down my throat!"

And I have a great deal of sympathy for those groans for I have uttered a few myself when some knowing critic has not awarded a masterpiece (in my view) a four star rating. But it is simply impossible to prevent personal judgements from creeping into reviews so, for good or ill, the star ratings are there.

But, that having been said, no critic or historian should be allowed to compile a book of this kind without offering his readers some alternative to his judgements. So, as a double insurance, I have adopted a three-way approach to help you decide whether or not a tape is value for money – (1) the star system already referred to (2) a film's success or lack of it at Oscar time and (3) and perhaps most important in that it reflects how popular a film was with the public, how much it took at the box-office.

The star rating is split four ways: *excellent* (four stars), *good* (three stars), *average* (two stars) and *poor* (one star). No star at all indicates total disaster.

The Oscar section is self-explanatory and lists all the Academy Awards and/or nominations won by each film.

It is the third section that needs most explanation, for the "box-office rental figures" are taken from the annual listing published in *Variety* and represent rentals accruing to distributors in the USA and Canada. But, as the American and Canadian markets accurately reflect world trends, the overall popularity of a film can safely be judged from these figures.

To make each rental figure more meaningful, I have also included a comparison figure, compiled from an average of the top twenty grossing pictures of the year of a film's release. In this way it is possible to discover, at a glance, whether a film did good, average or poor business at the box-office.

Deliverance, for instance, took 22,500,000 dollars in 1972 which, when compared with the top twenty average of 17,500,000 puts it high up in the success stakes. *Sleuth*, on the other hand, which was released the same year, took just 5,607,000 dollars, which puts it in the less than successful category.

The system is obviously not infallible but it does give a reasonably accurate reflection of a film's commercial success.

Another important point to remember regarding the box-office figures is that if no figure is shown against a film's title then it can be taken for granted that the film in question did not reach the 4 million dollar mark, the magic figure that automatically gets a film on the *Variety* list with the all-time box-office champions.

So remember, if no figure is shown, a film took less than 4 million dollars.

Similarly with Oscar awards and nominations. If no data is included against a film then the picture did not win any Academy Awards or nominations.

Finally, and to cross a few *t*'s and dot a few *i*'s, here are a few other points to remember when using *Movies On Video*:

1. All movies included in the book are listed in alphabetical order for ease of reference (see also the Stop Press).

2. All running times are the running times of the films when they were originally released in the cinemas.

3. Most films included in this book are available in both the Beta and VHS formats; many are also now available in Video 2000. Check with the tape's distributor for full details.

4. Blue Movies? Not included I'm afraid, for this book is designed strictly for the family audience and not the "dirty mac" brigade.

5. Breakdown of entries. Each film entry is broken down (when applicable) into no fewer than eight different sections:

  1 *Title of film*
  2 *Brief synopsis or theme*
  3 *Money taken at the box-office*
  4 *Average top box-office take in year of release*
  5 *Number of Oscars won*
  6 *Number of Oscar nominations*
  7 *Year of release, director, stars, colour or black and white, running time*
  8 *Name of video distributor*

6. Prices. These are in a constant state of flux, in both the rental and purchasing areas, so it's best if you check out prices with your local stockist. At the time of going to press, however, a two/three-hour cassette can cost anything between £25 and £40 and a three-day rental fee is approximately £5. But do check. And also shop around. Prices will vary depending on the area in which you live.

7. Quality of cassettes. Don't hesitate to return a cassette to your supplier if you think it's faulty. Even review copies supplied to journalists have proved to be faulty on occasion, either through a too grainy appearance or a jumpy print. *You* are paying or renting so be sure to take the tape back if you are not satisfied.

8. Storage. Always store your tapes in an upright position, away from the sun and away from dust.

Finally, happy viewing. This book will provide you with a comprehensive guide to many of the best (and the worst) films available on video. And remember. This is just the first edition of *Movies on Video*. Edition number two is already being prepared.

ROY PICKARD
Spring, 1982

A

Abbott And Costello Meet Captain Kidd

Abbott and Costello met just about everyone during the latter stages of their screen careers, but never anyone as distinguished as Charles Laughton. Quite what Mr. Laughton is doing in a farrago such as this is a bit of a mystery, although he supposedly accepted the role because he wanted to do low comedy. Well, it's low alright and Laughton appears bewildered for most of the time – as well he might, for the zany pair play a couple of 17th century waiters involved in a search for buried treasure on Skull Island. Below par. The 1935 swashbuckler *The Three Musketeers* shares the tape.

1952. Directed by Charles Lamont.
Starring Abbott & Costello, Charles Laughton, Hillary Brooke, Fran Warren, Bill Shirley, Leif Erickson. Colour.
70 minutes.

Kingston Video

Abduction

X-rated thriller with a close affinity to the Patricia Hearst affair in that its heroine is the daughter of a property tycoon who is abducted by a young black revolutionary and his gang, and gradually becomes convinced of the validity of the group's political convictions. The girl's growing self-awareness is well expressed at times, although mostly this is a movie of missed opportunities. Judith-Marie Bergman is the girl; Leif Erickson and Dorothy Malone her parents.

1975. Directed by Joseph Zito.
Starring Judith-Marie Bergman, David Pendleton, Gregory Rozakis, Leif Erickson, Dorothy Malone, Lawrence Tierney, Presley Caton. Colour.
94 minutes.

Picture Time Video
(distributed by VCL)

Absolution

Rigid schoolmaster-priest Richard Burton finds that murder raises its ugly head among the pupils at his rural English boarding school. But, because of the secrets of the confessional, he is unable to do much about it. And to make things even more complicated, does the right voice belong to the right boy in the confessional box? Tricky. Plenty of red herrings and sleuthing around at night in the local woods. Not much in the way of entertainment. The film was on the shelf for a couple of years and it's easy to see why.

1978. Directed by Anthony Page.
Starring Richard Burton, Dominic Guard, Dai Bradley, Andrew Keir, Billy Connolly, Willoughby Gray. Colour.
95 minutes.

Home Video Productions

Accident

A young Austrian student disrupts the lives of some Oxford dons and their wives and brings to the surface a series of petty jealousies, frustrations and prejudices. A very sophisticated piece of film-making made by Joseph Losey during his peak period of the late 60s and one of the most satisfying movies to be found on video. Not as good as *The Go-Between* but not far short. Cleverly constructed with several tricks with time sequences and photographed in the most ravishing colour by Gerry Fisher. Jacqueline Sassard is the cause of all the trouble; Dirk Bogarde, Stanley Baker, Michael York, Vivien Merchant are among those affected by her presence. A gem. Looks even better now than when first released.

1967. Directed by Joseph Losey.
Starring Dirk Bogarde, Stanley Baker, Jacqueline Sassard, Michael York, Vivien Merchant, Delphine Seyrig, Alexander Knox. Colour.
105 minutes.

Thorn EMI Video

Aces High

R. C. Sherriff's famous play *Journey's End* transferred to the skies above the World War I battlefields. Peter Firth is the young pilot who finds that the boy he worshipped as a house captain at school (Malcolm McDowell) has become a drunk and a nervous wreck because of his experiences in the War. The message still hits home effectively, especially when one considers that the life of a young fighter pilot was estimated to be in the region of just two weeks. Good aerial dogfights and quite moving at times.

1976. Directed by Jack Gold
Starring Malcolm McDowell, Christopher Plummer, Simon Ward, Peter Firth, John Gielgud, Trevor Howard, Richard Johnson, Ray Milland. Colour. 114 minutes.

Thorn EMI Video

The Adventure Of Sherlock Holmes' Smarter Brother

A secret document, a music hall singer under the threat of blackmail, Professor Moriarty up to no good as usual and a younger brother called Sigerson Holmes. All the ingredients are there for a successful pastiche of the Sherlock Holmes period. Unfortunately, Gene Wilder who writes, directs and stars, can't bring it all together and one is left with a film made up partly of lavatory humour and partly of slapstick. Uninspired. Worse, unfunny.

Box-office rental	$9,400,000
Average rental (75)	$27,300,250

1975. Directed by Gene Wilder.
Starring Gene Wilder, Madeline Kahn, Marty Feldman, Dom DeLuise, Leo McKern, Roy Kinnear. Colour.
91 minutes.

Twentieth Century-Fox Video

The Adventurers

A cashiered British officer and two Boers set out across the plains of the South African veldt and venture high into the mountains in search of stolen diamonds. Dependable Jack Hawkins does what he can with the material but this is an inferior British production on nearly every level and even Hawkins can't save it. The story is set in the year 1902 shortly after the end of the Boer War.

1950. Directed by David Macdonald.
Starring Dennis Price, Jack Hawkins, Siobhan McKenna, Peter Hammond, Gregoire Aslan, Bernard Lee. Black and White.
86 minutes.

Twentieth Century-Fox Video

The Adventures Of Sherlock Holmes

Sherlock Holmes up against Professor Moriarty, who's out to commit the most daring crime of the century – the theft of the Crown Jewels from the Tower of London. As a sideline, the master sleuth also has to aid frightened little Ida Lupino and put paid to a South American killer who disposes of his victims with a *bolas*, a weapon with three long strands each topped with a leather-covered lead ball. Quite a problem. The main feature on a Sherlock Holmes double-bill. See also *Sherlock Holmes And The Voice Of Terror*.

1939. Directed by Alfred L. Werker.
Starring Basil Rathbone, Nigel Bruce, Ida Lupino, Alan Marshal, Terry Kilburn, George Zucco, E. E. Clive, Mary Gordon. Black and White.
85 minutes.

MGM/CBS Home Video

The Adventures Of Tom Sawyer

1938 version of the Mark Twain classic about a young boy growing up on the banks of the Mississippi during the mid-1800s. Like all Selznick movies made from literary classics, a faithful adaptation with some lovely early Technicolor (James Wong Howe) and some extravagant set designs by William Cameron Menzies, who helped create the huge cavern where Tom and Becky meet up with murdering Injun Joe. Leisurely; pleasing.

Oscars	Nil
Oscar nominations (1)	Best Art Direction

1938. Directed by Norman Taurog.
Starring Tommy Kelly, Jackie Moran, Ann Gillis, May Robson, Walter Brennan, Victor Jory. Colour.
93 minutes.

Guild Home Video

The African Queen

Humphrey Bogart and Katharine Hepburn, a World War I setting, an old tugboat and a wild African river – all for the price of £30 or so. Yes, it's an old and basically thin tale. Just *how* thin becomes apparent when you try to visualise the story without the two stars. But the two stars *are* there and this is a delight of a movie, carried along by Bogart's grizzled skipper and Hepburn's skinny old maid as they travel downriver to blow a German gunboat to smithereens. John Huston directs from a story by C. S. Forester and it's grade 'A' entertainment all the way. Not only the story but also the film's technical quality – colour, sound, etc. – has lasted well. Perfect video entertainment.

Box-office rental	$4,150,000
Average rental (51)	$4,110,450
Oscars (1)	Best Actor (Bogart)
Oscar nominations (3)	Best Actress (Hepburn); Direction; Screenplay

1951. Directed by John Huston.

Starring Humphrey Bogart, Katharine Hepburn, Robert Morley, Peter Bull, Theodore Bikel. Colour.
106 minutes.

Twentieth Century-Fox Video

Africa-Texas Style ★★

English settler John Mills tries to develop wild game ranching in Kenya. Texas cowboys Hugh O'Brian and Tom Nardini lend a hand with a rope; nasty cattle rancher Nigel Green does his best to ruin things. This one's really a Western in an African setting with goodies and baddies and plenty of well-photographed action stuff, including the capture of a charging rhino. OK although a dull script lets it down.

1967. Directed by Andrew Marton.
Starring Hugh O'Brian, John Mills, Tom Nardini, Adrienne Corri, Ronald Howard. Colour.
109 minutes.

Guild Home Video

The Agony And The Ecstasy ★★

It took Michelangelo four years to complete the painting of the Sistine Chapel for Pope Julius II. It takes this movie 140 minutes to tell you how he did it, and very long minutes they are too, full of argument, discussion and Renaissance chit-chat. Still, the splendours of 16th century Italy please the eye and the central performances – Charlton Heston (Michelangelo), Rex Harrison (Julius) – command attention for most of the film's length. The set of the Sistine Chapel cost Fox nine million dollars to reproduce. Based on the novel by Irving Stone.

Box-office rental	$4,000,000
Average rental (65)	$13,881,050
Oscars	Nil

| Oscar nominations (5) | Best Photography; Art Direction; Costume Design; Sound; Music Score |

1965. Directed by Carol Reed.
Starring Charlton Heston, Rex Harrison, Diane Cilento, Harry Andrews, Alberto Lupo, Adolfo Celi. Colour.
140 minutes.

Twentieth Century-Fox Video

Airport 77

Question: What do you do when you have run out of all the disasters that can befall a plane in the air? Answer: Crash it into the sea and keep it underwater with the passengers alive but running out of time and air supply. The *Airport* series almost reached "rock bottom" when this one lurched onto the screen in 1977. Its only really effective scenes were the well-realised plane crash and the submarine rescue attempt. On video, however, even these are reduced to the mundane, and one is left with a kind of cut-price *Poseidon Adventure* and yet another group of motley passengers to contend with. Corny.

Box-office rental	$16,200,000
Average rental (77)	$36,913,348
Oscars	Nil
Oscar Nominations (2)	Best Art Direction; Costume Design

1977. Directed by Jerry Jameson.
Starring Jack Lemmon, Lee Grant, Brenda Vaccaro, George Kennedy, James Stewart, Joseph Cotten, Olivia de Havilland, Christopher Lee. Colour.
114 minutes.

CIC Video

Airport '80 The Concorde

The *Airport* movies always seem as though they can get no worse – then the next one comes along. This was the last (hopefully) in the series and focuses on the numerous disasters that befall the beautiful Concorde *en route* from Washington to Paris. Robert Wagner is the bad guy in this one. He's a millionaire weapons manufacturer who's involved in illegal arms sales and tries to destroy the plane. Alain Delon is at the controls; George Kennedy is once again Joe Patroni. An unintentional laugh-a-minute. Sample passenger: Cicely Tyson carrying a live heart for her son's transplant operation in Paris!

Box-office rental	$8,911,000
Average rental (79)	$31,964,775

1979. Directed by David Lowell Rich.
Starring Alain Delon, Susan Blakely, Robert Wagner, Sylvia Kristel, George Kennedy, Eddie Albert, Bibi Andersson, Martha Raye, Cicely Tyson, Mercedes McCambridge. Colour.
113 minutes.

CIC Video

Alfie Darling

Lacklustre sequel to the 1966 Michael Caine hit (not yet available on video) with Alan Price taking over as the womanizing truck driver Alfie Elkins and including married Joan Collins and cockney gal Sheila White among his conquests. A strained back hampers his sexual performance although he eventually gets (then loses) the one he most hankers for; assistant magazine editor Jill Townsend. If you've seen *Alfie* you'll be disappointed. Even if you haven't, it's doubtful whether you'll think this worth the cash outlay.

1975. Directed by Ken Hughes.
Starring Alan Price, Jill Townsend, Paul Copley, Joan Collins, Sheila White, Annie Ross, Hannah Gordon. Colour.
102 minutes.

Thorn EMI Video

Alice Doesn't Live Here Anymore

Forget (if you can) the foul-mouthed language and dismiss (if you can) the rather squalid surface of this melodrama and you are left with nothing more than an old-fashioned soap opera of the kind Douglas Sirk used to make so well at Universal in the 50s. The saving grace is the performance of Ellen Burstyn, superb as a newly-widowed mother who, in order to cope with the harsh realities of life – supporting both herself and her 12-year-old son – has to take a job as a singer-waitress. Kris Kristofferson as a divorced farmer who tries to win her love is another plus factor and the result is OK video, although not by any means the film it is cracked up to be. More popular in the USA than it was in this country.

Box-office rental	$7,900,000
Average rental (74)	$18,456,150
Oscars (1)	Best Actress (Burstyn)
Oscar nominations (2)	Best Supporting Actress (Ladd); Original Screenplay

1974. Directed by Martin Scorsese.
Starring Ellen Burstyn, Kris Kristofferson, Billy Green Bush, Diane Ladd, Lelia Goldoni. Colour.
112 minutes.

Warner Home Video

Alien

A cross between *Star Wars* and *The Exorcist*; a cleverly calculated piece of cinema merchandise that borrows heavily from the horror flicks of the mid-50s and leaves the crew of a spaceship alone in space with an ever-growing monster. Some eerie and effective scenes early on (especially those set on a barren planet); coarse, routine *Grand Guignol* from then on in. Struck just the right note in the late 70s by earning nearly 40 million dollars from a youth-orientated box-office, but loses much of its effectiveness on video through an over-abundance of dimly lit scenes.

Box-office rental	$39,847,000
Average rental (79)	$31,964,775

| Oscars (1) | Best Visual Effects |
| Oscar nominations (1) | Best Art Direction |

1979. Directed by Ridley Scott.
Starring Tom Skerritt, Sigourney Weaver, Veronica Cartwright, Harry Dean Stanton, John Hurt, Ian Holm, Yaphet Kotto. Colour.
117 minutes.

Twentieth Century-Fox Video

All About Eve

Probably the wittiest and most sophisticated movie to be found on video; Anne Baxter is the Eve of the title, an unscrupulous young actress who worms her way from obscurity to fame by the process of biting every hand that feeds her – including that of Bette Davis as the ageing star she eventually replaces as the toast of Broadway. Davis and George Sanders (as a cynical theatre columnist) take the acting honours in a cast that is well nigh perfect. For those who want to listen to as well as watch great performances this is a must. The movie's 14 Oscar nominations are still a record; its box-office rental figure was just under three million dollars.

| Oscars (6) | Best Film; Supporting Actor (Sanders); Direction; Screenplay; Costume Design; Sound Recording. |
| Oscar nominations (8) | Best Actress (Baxter); Actress (Davis); Supporting Actress (Holm); Supporting Actress (Ritter); Photography; Art Direction; Editing; Music Score |

1950. Directed by Joseph L. Mankiewicz.
Starring Bette Davis, Anne Baxter, George Sanders, Celeste Holm, Hugh Marlowe, Gary Merrill, Gregory Ratoff, Thelma Ritter, Marilyn Monroe. Black and White.
138 minutes.

Twentieth Century-Fox Video

Allegheny Uprising

The year is 1759 and the Yanks are getting fed up with the Brits, especially when military commander George Sanders allows corrupt trader Brian Donlevy to sell goods to the Indians under cover of a government permit. But fearless John Wayne is in the cast, so naturally it's odds on the Yanks having a fighting chance of putting things to rights. Claire Trevor, the "Duke's" girlfriend in *Stagecoach* is again on hand, but this one's a bit slow and cumbersome and certainly doesn't rate as one of Wayne's best. Shares a tape with *Back From Eternity*.

1939. Directed by William A. Seiter.
Starring John Wayne, Claire Trevor, George Sanders, Brian Donlevy, Wilfrid Lawson, Robert Barrat, Moroni Olsen. Black and White.
74 minutes.

Kingston Video

All In A Night's Work

What was pretty young Shirley MacLaine doing in the room of a millionaire publishing tycoon just before he died? Playboy nephew Dean Martin, fearing the company will be blackmailed by the girl in order to keep her liaison quiet, determines to find out. It's all a case of "jumping to the wrong conclusions", but even though this is just a formularised Hollywood comedy, it's considerably more entertaining than most of the material to be found in the video market. And where today can you find a comedy team that can entertain so consistently well as Mr. Martin and Miss MacLaine? The always excellent Jack Weston chips in with a delicious cameo as a house detective. Routine material but neatly handled.

1961. Directed by Joseph Anthony.
Starring Dean Martin, Shirley MacLaine, Charlie Ruggles, Cliff Robertson, Norma Crane, Gale Gordon, Jerome Cowan, Jack Weston. Colour.
94 minutes.

Twentieth Century-Fox Video

All Quiet On The Western Front ★

A great film becomes a dull and uninspired remake. Inevitable perhaps, but one would have thought that director Delbert Mann would have been able to make *something* of the terrifying events of World War 1. Alas, he fails dismally on all counts and the result is no more than a travesty of Erich Maria Remarque's celebrated novel. Richard Thomas appears in the Lew Ayres role as the young German volunteer who outlives all his friends only to be killed by a sniper's bullet just before the Armistice. A plodding, empty shell of a movie, originally made for American TV but shown theatrically in this country. Advice: wait until Milestone's 1930 masterpiece becomes available on video.

1979. Directed by Delbert Mann.
Starring Richard Thomas, Ernest Borgnine, Donald Pleasence, Ian Holm, Patricia Neal, Mark Elliott. Colour.
129 minutes.

Precision Video

All That Jazz

The last few months in the hectic life of Broadway choreographer/film director Roy Scheider as he drives himself into an early grave through overwork. Not the happiest of musicals, but one of the most stimulating and in the "Take Off With Us" number certainly one of the most erotic. Some might find all the bad language and eroticism a bit distasteful but there can be no denying the brilliance with which Bob Fosse handles his material. His staging of the climactic "Bye, Bye Love" is a *tour-de-force*. Partly autobiographical in that Fosse himself suffered a heart attack but luckily survived. Marvellous video but strictly late-night fare.

Box-office rental	$20,000,000
Average rental (79)	$31,964,775
Oscars (4)	Best Art Direction; Costume Design; Editing; Adaptation Music Score
Oscar nominations (5)	Best Film; Actor (Scheider); Direction; Original Screenplay; Photography

1979. Directed by Bob Fosse.

Starring Roy Scheider, Jessica Lange, Ann Reinking, Leland Palmer, Cliff Gorman, Ben Vereen, Erzsebet Foldi, Michael Tolan. Colour.
123 minutes.

Twentieth Century-Fox Video

All The President's Men ★★★

Washington Post reporters Bob Woodward and Carl Bernstein pick up the trail of a small-scale burglary at the Democratic Party's headquarters (the Watergate Building) in Washington and find that the trail leads to corruption in the highest office in the land. The most famous newspaper story of all time and certainly one of the best newspaper *films*, although you need your wits about you to follow the intricacies of the plot. A largish percentage of night scenes don't make video viewing easy but it's worth staying the course. Superior performances from Robert Redford and Dustin Hoffman; an Academy Award – winning one by Jason Robards as Ben Bradlee, editor of the *Post*.

Box-office rental	$30,000,000
Average rental (76)	$22,752,350
Oscars (4)	Best Supporting Actor (Robards); Screenplay; Art Direction; Sound
Oscar nominations (4)	Best Film; Supporting Actress (Alexander); Direction; Editing

1976. Directed by Alan J. Pakula.
Starring Robert Redford, Dustin Hoffman, Jack Warden, Martin Balsam, Hal Holbrook, Jason Robards, Jane Alexander. Colour.
138 minutes.

Warner Home Video

Aloha Bobby And Rose ★

A sort of cut-price *Bonnie And Clyde* with auto-mechanic Paul Le Mat and young divorcee Dianne Hull on the run from the cops after killing a liquor store clerk in a hold-up that was meant to be a joke. Familiar tale of two runaway losers; the pop soundtrack includes songs by Elton John, Emerson Lake & Palmer, Stevie Wonder, etc. Below average video.

Box-office rental	$6,000,000
Average rental (75)	$27,300,250

1975. Directed by Floyd Mutrux.
Starring Paul Le Mat, Dianne Hull, Tim McIntire, Leigh French, Noble Willingham. Colour.
89 minutes.

Picture Time Video
(distributed by VCL)

. . . And Now The Screaming Starts

And it starts when the newly-married Stephanie Beacham moves into the ancestral home of young hubby Ian Ogilvy. It's a bad move. The house is cursed and for the next 90 minutes or so poor Stephanie has to contend with stranglings, arms bursting out of pictures on the wall and rape by a bloody ghost without a hand! And she even finds time off to have a baby! Routine haunted house movie. Peter Cushing, Herbert Lom and Patrick Magee do their best to liven things up in character roles.

1974. Directed by Roy Ward Baker.
Starring Peter Cushing, Herbert Lom, Patrick Magee, Stephanie Beacham, Ian Ogilvy. Colour.
91 minutes.

Guild Home Video

Animal Farm

This was the first full-length cartoon made in Britain, and a very ambitious (and successful) attempt it is too – an animated version of George Orwell's political fable about some farm animals who rise up against the cruelty of a drunken farmer, and then find themselves living under equally terrible conditions when the ruthless pig who helped lead the revolution appoints himself supreme dictator. The theme, of course, is that absolute power corrupts absolutely, which is a message that comes across as well in animated film terms as it does on the printed page. Interesting to note also that cartoon features of this nature hardly date at all. Recommended. 750 scenes, 300,000 drawings; Maurice Denham speaks the voices of all the animals.

1954. Directed by John Halas and Joy Batchelor. Colour.
75 minutes.

Rank Video

Animalympics

Dismal attempt to satirise the Olympic Games by changing all the competitors to animals and having the events staged in Pawprint Stadium. The Z.O.O. network secures the broadcasting rights! Poor animation and an even worse disco score by Graham Gouldman. The funny moments are few and far between.

1979. Directed by Steven Lisberger.
Colour.
79 minutes.

Precision Video

Anna Karenina

Not the Garbo version of 1935 but the rather turgid Korda adaptation of 1948 with Vivien Leigh duly suffering as the aristocratic wife destroyed by her love for a young Russian officer in Tsarist Russia. Ralph Richardson makes something of the woman's dull husband and with Duvivier at the helm there's plenty of convincing atmosphere but the film just plods from one scene to another and is tiresomely overlong. Not producer Korda at his best.

1948. Directed by Julien Duvivier.
Starring Vivien Leigh, Ralph Richardson, Kieron Moore, Hugh Dempster.
Black and White.
110 minutes.

Spectrum
(*distributed by Polygram*)

Annie Hall

This movie is rather like someone opening his private diary and saying to his audience: "Well, here you are, read it, this is how I spent the early 70s in New York with my girlfriend." As the owner of the diary is Woody Allen, it means that it's 93 minutes of wisecracks, cynicism and often fatalistic humour. The time just flies by as Jewish comedian Allen and neurotic girlfriend Diane Keaton fall in love, live together, cook lobsters together, go to movies and parties together, but go solo when they visit their respective analysts. Very enjoyable; fine New York locations.

Box-office rental	$18,093,000
Average rental (77)	$36,913,348
Oscars (4)	Best Film; Actress (Keaton); Direction; Original Screenplay
Oscar nominations (1)	Best Actor (Allen)

1977. Directed by Woody Allen.
Starring Woody Allen, Diane Keaton, Tony Roberts, Carol Kane, Paul Simon, Shelley Duvall, Janet Margolin, Colleen Dewhurst, Christopher Walken. Colour.
93 minutes.

Intervision

Antony And Cleopatra

Respectful but laborious piece of filmed Shakespeare that emerges as uninspired entertainment and stodgy video. Charlton Heston directs himself as Antony; Hildegard Neil looks good enough to eat but her acting hardly suggests a queen with enough erotic passion to bring about the downfall of the strongest men. Dull; even a sea battle is poorly rendered. A 162-minute tape of the Royal Shakespeare production with Richard Johnson and Janet Suzman is available on Precision Video.

1972. Directed by Charlton Heston.
Starring Charlton Heston, Hildegard Neil, Eric Porter, John Castle, Fernando Rey, Juan Luis Galiardo, Carmen Sevilla, Freddie Jones. Colour. 160 minutes.

Video Unlimited

Any Which Way You Can

If you liked *Every Which Way But Loose* (see page 163) then this should also be up your street for it's practically a re-run with fighting truck driver Clint Eastwood forced back into action when some mobsters kidnap his girlfriend. As bad (or as good) as number one. The only surprise is that talents such as Ruth Gordon, Harry Guardino and Geoffrey Lewis should lend themselves to such uninspired knockabout stuff as this. Be warned. It all takes 115 minutes.

Box-office rental	$39,500,000
Average rental (80)	$30,086,027

1980. Directed by Buddy Van Horn.
Starring Clint Eastwood, Sondra Locke, Geoffrey Lewis, William Smith, Harry Guardino, Ruth Gordon. Colour.
115 minutes.

Warner Home Video

Arabian Adventure

Christopher Lee imprisoned in a magic mirror; Milo O'Shea transformed into a toad; a flying carpet attack on a mountain palace; Oliver Tobias daring all for the hand of a beautiful princess! It should all add up to just the right kind of fantasy fare for the kids. That it doesn't is because it lacks the vulgar exuberance that Hollywood used to bring to this kind of nonsense and because its effects are no more than passable. Good sets are an asset, however.

1979. Directed by Kevin Connor.
Starring Christopher Lee, Milo O'Shea, Oliver Tobias, Emma Samms, Puneet Sira, Mickey Rooney. Colour.
98 minutes.

Thorn EMI Video

Arch Of Triumph

Version of Erich Maria Remarque's novel about the love of fugitive German doctor Charles Boyer for lovely tramp Ingrid Bergman in the period just prior to the Nazis marching into Paris in World War II. Very heavy going and tedious. Even Charles Laughton as a nasty Nazi doesn't manage to liven things up. Louis Calhern as a philosophical Russian doorman does slightly better but it's all very dreary and desperate. 1½ rating.

1948. Directed by Lewis Milestone.
Starring Ingrid Bergman, Charles Boyer, Charles Laughton, Louis Calhern.
Black and White.
120 minutes.

Intervision

Are You Being Served?

Dreadful spin-off from the long-running BBC TV series in which the staff of the Grace Brothers department store take a holiday in Costa Plonka and find their hotel attacked by revolutionary forces. Mrs. Slocombe's Union Jack knickers, an inflatable brassiere and German tourists are among the subjects for the so-called jokes.

1977. Directed by Bob Kellett.

Starring John Inman, Mollie Sugden, Frank Thornton, Trevor Bannister, Wendy Richard, Arthur Brough, Nicholas Smith, Arthur English. Colour. 95 minutes.

Thorn EMI Video

Ash Wednesday

Whoops, a right *dog* of a movie with Elizabeth Taylor as a once-beautiful woman deciding to have cosmetic surgery from top to bottom in order to try to recapture the love of bored hubby Henry Fonda. Those with a macabre interest in the intricacies of such surgery might find that the film has certain qualities (much of the operation is shown in close-up); those with an ear for a really bad script will fall about uncontrollably when a desperate and newly-transformed Liz makes a last play for Henry's affections: "Look at these breasts, aren't they beautiful!"

1973. Directed by Larry Peerce.
Starring Elizabeth Taylor, Henry Fonda, Helmut Berger, Keith Baxter, Maurice Teynac, Margaret Blye. Colour.
99 minutes.

Home Video Productions

The Asphyx

The Asphyx of the title is the Spirit of Death. It appears if people are photographed at the time of their demise and shows up as a black smudge on the print. Psychical researcher Robert Stephens decides that if he can separate the spirit from his body he will become immortal. Wrong? No, right for a change, although the cost is high! An intriguing theme but even a goodish cast and the lensing of Freddie Young can't prevent this one from becoming a static exercise in Victorian melodrama. A disappointment.

1972. Directed by Peter Newbrook.

Starring Robert Stephens, Robert Powell, Jane Lapotaire, Alex Scott, Ralph Arliss, Fiona Walker. Colour.
99 minutes.

Intervision

Assault On Precinct 13

Small-scale thriller about a Los Angeles police station which finds itself under an all-night attack from a gang of vengeful youths. Really no more than an exercise in tension but very well put together and containing some of the virtues of the old-style Hollywood crime movies of the 40s and 50s. Made by John Carpenter, whose no-nonsense approach to his material also recalls the work of film-makers such as Hathaway and Fleischer. Brisk, efficient, violent. No names in the cast but none needed. Keeps you on the edge of your seat. 2½ rating.

1976. Directed by John Carpenter.
Starring Austin Stoker, Darwin Joston, Laurie Zimmer, Martin West, Tony Burton, Charles Cyphers, Nancy Loomis. Colour.
91 minutes.

Media Video
(*distributed by Video Programme Distributors*)

Asylum

Four little horror stories all set within the confines of a Gothic asylum and each recounted to a young doctor (Robert Powell) who has just applied for a job there. Some interview! Among those indulging in the nasty goings-on: Richard Todd, who chops up his wife into little pieces and wraps her in paper parcels; necromancer Peter Cushing who tries to reanimate his dead son; Charlotte Rampling as a drug addict with a split personality; and Herbert Lom who constructs miniature dolls and makes 'em walk at his command. *Grand Guignol* at its most flamboyant. Not the most brilliant entertainment in the world but it never flags.

1972. Directed by Roy Ward Baker.

Starring Patrick Magee, Robert Powell, Barbara Parkins, Sylvia Syms, Richard Todd, Peter Cushing, Britt Ekland, Charlotte Rampling, Herbert Lom. 2½ rating. Colour.
88 minutes.

Guild Home Video

Atlantic City U.S.A.

Having explored the brothels of New Orleans in *Pretty Baby* (see page 342) Louis Malle now takes a look at modern-day Atlantic City, where ageing numbers runner Burt Lancaster suddenly makes it to the big time when he has to commit a double murder to protect his young girlfriend. Sounds grim. Surprisingly it's not; more a wry, affectionate portrait of a loser approaching old age who is suddenly brought to life again by unexpected good fortune. Quite one of the best movies available on video. This and *Pretty Baby* make up a superb double bill if you can afford the outlay. Beautifully observed backgrounds of the gaudy run-down city with its pleasure palaces and slum apartments; music by Michel Legrand.

Oscars	Nil
Oscar nominations (5)	Best Film; Actor (Lancaster); Actress (Sarandon); Direction; Original Screenplay

1980. Directed by Louis Malle.
Starring Burt Lancaster, Susan Sarandon, Kate Reid, Michel Piccoli, Hollis McLaren, Robert Joy. Colour.
105 minutes.

Home Video Productions

At The Earth's Core

Eccentric Peter Cushing invents a giant mechanical mole that takes both him and rugged American Doug McClure to the centre of the earth. Is their journey worthwhile? Not really, for all they find is a prehistoric land inhabited by monsters and feuding tribes. In fact, it's the usual "monsters and feuding tribes" type movie with Cushing grabbing what few good lines there are around: "A rhamphorhynchus of the Middle Eolithic. But gad how enormous!"

1976. Directed by Kevin Connor.
Starring Doug McClure, Peter Cushing, Caroline Munro, Cy Grant, Godfrey James, Sean Lynch. Colour.
90 minutes.

Thorn EMI Video

Autobiography Of A Princess

A quite exquisite film about the exiled daughter of an Indian maharajah who, each year, on the occasion of her father's birthday, invites his former English tutor/secretary to tea in her Kensington flat. Together they reminisce about old times, study old photographs and home movies and remember India as it was under the Raj. Just 59 minutes in length but as perfect a piece of atmospheric cinema as you could hope to find. Not only for specialists. Everyone will enjoy this. James Mason plays the tutor, Madhur Jaffrey the princess.

1975. Directed by James Ivory.
Starring James Mason, Madhur Jaffrey, Keith Varnier, Diane Fletcher, Timothy Bateson, Johnny Stuart, Nazrul Rahman. Colour.
59 minutes.

Home Video Productions

Autumn Sonata

Famed concert pianist Ingrid Bergman and daughter Liv Ullmann tear each other apart when they meet for the first time in seven years at the daughter's house in Norway. A *tour-de-force* of emotional acting, but you have to be in the mood for Ingmar Bergman (here directing Ingrid for the first time) and this one, although brilliant, is full of anguish, regret and self-pity and is not a little depressing. Providing you *are* in the mood, it's a fascinating chamberwork about how lack of care and understanding can have a devastating effect on a human being.

| Oscars | Nil |
| Oscar nominations (2) | Best Actress (Bergman); Screenplay |

1978. Directed by Ingmar Bergman.
Starring Ingrid Bergman, Liv Ullmann, Lena Nyman, Halvar Bjork, Arne Bang-Hansen, Gunnar Bjornstrand. Colour.
92 minutes.

Precision Video

The Awakening

Archaeologist Charlton Heston breaks into the tomb of evil Egyptian Queen Kara at the very moment his wife gives birth to their daughter. Eighteen years later he finds he's got quite a problem on his hands, for his daughter turns out to be the 3,800-year-old queen reincarnated and is about to embark on a life of havoc around London. This is the usual "mummy-revived-type" movie (based on this occasion on Bram Stoker's 1903 novel *The Jewel Of Seven Stars*) but it's none too efficiently handled and even the usually reliable Mr. Heston is off form. Some graphic horror scenes will interest ghoulish *devotees* and Jack Cardiff's Technicolor location work is splendid as always. But this one's mediocre when it should have been interesting.

| Box-office rental | $4,250,000 |
| Average rental (80) | $30,086,027 |

1980. Directed by Mike Newell.
Starring Charlton Heston, Susannah York, Jill Townsend, Stephanie Zimbalist, Patrick Drury. Colour.
105 minutes.

Thorn EMI Video

B

Back From Eternity

An airliner crashes in the South American jungle. It's headhunter country, which causes not a little panic among the assorted passengers, especially when it's learned that Hollywood's scriptwriters have decreed that the plane can only take off if three of the passengers are left behind. Ho, hum ... Enduring the various moments of terror, hysteria and relief are Rod Steiger, Anita Ekberg, Robert Ryan and others. The film shares a double-bill video tape with *Allegheny Uprising*.

1956. Directed by John Farrow.
Starring Robert Ryan, Anita Ekberg, Rod Steiger, Phyllis Kirk, Gene Barry, Keith Andes, Beulah Bondi. Black and White.
97 minutes.

Kingston Video

Back To Bataan

The setting: the Philippines shortly after the fall of Bataan to the Japanese in World War II. The theme: the comeback of a guerrilla army made up of stranded American troops and Philippino freedom fighters. The man who organises things: American colonel John Wayne. The result: no more than routine unfortunately, but with some ferocious battle scenes and efficient direction by Edward Dmytryk as plus factors. Supported by *Roadblock* on a double-feature video tape.

1945. Directed by Edward Dmytryk.
Starring John Wayne, Anthony Quinn, Beulah Bondi, Fely Franquelli, Richard Loo. Black and White.
97 minutes.

Kingston Video

Badlands

This picture has been described as "one of the finest literate examples of narrated cinema since the early days of Welles and Polonsky". It's stylish certainly, but when you get right down to it, it's no more than a violent folk tale about a teenage girl and a young garbage collector who take off across America leaving a trail of murder in their wake. She's 15, he's 25 but it don't amount to a hill of beans. Routine.

1973. Directed by Terrence Malick.
Starring Martin Sheen, Sissy Spacek, Warren Oates, Raymon Bieri. Colour.
95 minutes.

Warner Home Video

The Ballad Of Joe Hill

Interesting story of Joseph Hillstrom, a young Swede who emigrated to America in 1902 in search of equality and opportunity, but found instead prejudice and corruption and helped form the organisation Industrial Workers Of The World. Some brilliant passages of immigrant life in New York at the turn of the century and rather an intriguing film to find on video. Well worth seeking out if you want something a bit unusual and an evening away from the cops and robbers stuff.

1971. Directed by Bo Widerberg.
Starring Thommy Berggren, Anja Schmidt, Evert Anderson, Cathy Smith, Kelvin Malave. Colour.
114 minutes.

Thorn EMI Video

The Baltimore Bullet

The escapades of ageing pool hustler James Coburn and his young protégé Bruce Boxleitner, as they wander across America and plan for a supermatch with suave kingpin Omar Sharif. Which means that if you've seen *The Hustler* or *The Cincinnati Kid* you won't want to buy or rent this one, for it's practically a reprise of those two fine movies and way, way below their high standard. If by any chance you haven't seen them you might just find it passable.

1979. Directed by Robert Ellis Miller.
Starring James Coburn, Omar Sharif, Ronee Blakley, Bruce Boxleitner, Jack O'Halloran, Michael Lerner. Colour.
103 minutes.

Rank Video

Barbarella

Just being allowed to gaze at the lovely frame of Jane Fonda – rigged out in the most elaborate and scanty of sci-fi outfits – should be value enough for your £5 video rental fee. If not (and you must be a hard man to please) there are plenty of other things to enjoy as Miss Fonda – cast as a 40th century astronaut – zips around the Universe seeking out adventures that invariably include a touch of perversion and sado-masochism. And when they're in short supply there's always a one-eyed lesbian to encounter or a female narcotic called "Essence Of Man" to enjoy. Bizarre comic book stuff but highly viewable.

Box-office rental	$5,500,000
Average rental (68):	$14,411,950

1968. Directed by Roger Vadim.
Starring Jane Fonda, John Phillip Law, Anita Pallenberg, Milo O'Shea, David Hemmings. Colour.
98 minutes.

CIC Video

The Bat

The Bat of the title refers to a hooded killer who gets his kicks by clawing at his victims' jugular veins. So you won't be surprised to learn that Vincent Price is involved in events, most of which are set in a gloomy old mansion in which is hidden a million dollars embezzled by a crooked banker. Agnes Moorehead appears as a writer of mystery stories. Low budget thrills; strictly off the Hollywood conveyor belt.

1959. Directed by Crane Wilbur.
Starring Vincent Price, Agnes Moorehead, Gavin Gordon, John Sutton, Lenita Lane. Black and White.
78 minutes.

Rank Video

Battle Beyond The Stars

The Magnificent Seven in outer space with Richard Thomas recruiting mercenaries willing to fight for a planet threatened with extinction by evil warlord John Saxon. George Peppard as a Space Cowboy, Steve Davis as a primitive warrior and Robert Vaughn (one of the original seven!) as an outlawed troubleshooter are among those on the payroll. Intriguing idea but let down by the script and mediocre special effects.

1980. Directed by Jimmy T. Murakami.
Starring Richard Thomas, Robert Vaughn, John Saxon, George Peppard, Darlanne Fluegel, Sybil Danning, Sam Jaffe, Steve Davis. Colour.
103 minutes.

Warner Home Video

Battle For The Planet Of The Apes

Number five in the *Planet Of The Apes* films with the story just about back to where it was in movie number one i.e. with the apes supreme and the humans reduced to living primitively in the wild. The end result – after several skirmishes between the apes themselves – is more optimistic however. Routine monkey cowboy stuff, a long way from the inventive brilliance of *Planet Of The Apes*. John Huston (as The Lawgiver) is among those skulking behind the ape masks.

Box-office rental $4,027,000
Average rental (73) $22,271,150

1973. Directed by J. Lee Thompson.
Starring Roddy McDowall, Claude Akins, Natalie Trundy, Severn Darden, Lew Ayres, Paul Williams, John Huston. Colour.
86 minutes.

Twentieth Century-Fox Video

The Battle Of The Bulge

This was originally produced for the Cinerama screen which will probably give you some idea of how much it loses on video. It's about the Germans' last offensive of World War II in December, 1944, when the brilliant tactics of a Nazi panzer commander stopped the Allies in their tracks in the Ardennes. Robert Shaw is the Nazi genius and watch out for Telly Savalas, 13th in the cast list as an army sergeant. Plenty of epic battle scenes if that's what you want for your cash. Little else.

Box-office rental $5,100,000
Average rental (65) $13,881,050

1965. Directed by Ken Annakin.
Starring Henry Fonda, Robert Shaw, Robert Ryan, Dana Andrews, George Montgomery, Ty Hardin, Charles Bronson. Colour.
162 minutes.

Warner Home Video

Battlestar Galactica

Lorne Greene, the commander of a futuristic aircraft carrier the size of a small city, picks up the survivors of several doomed planets and leads them in the direction of the distant planet Earth. Watered-down *Star Wars* type adventure and OK for undemanding kids. But what on earth are Lew Ayres, Ray Milland and Wilfrid Hyde White doing in something like this?

| Box-office rental | $7,100,000 |
| Average rental (78) | $39,443,850 |

1978. Directed by Richard A. Colla.
Starring Richard Hatch, Dirk Benedict, Lorne Greene, Ray Milland, Lew Ayres, Jane Seymour, Wilfrid Hyde White. Colour.
122 minutes.

CIC Video

The Beast In The Cellar

Two sweet old ladies – Flora Robson and Beryl Reid – keep something nasty, not in the woodshed but in the cellar. The trouble is that the "something nasty" keeps on escaping and committing hideous murders in the woods nearby. What is it? Well, if this sort of thing is your cup of tea, try the movie and find out. But, to be frank, it's not up to much despite the presence of Miss Reid and Miss Robson. In fact, in one scene Beryl is required to push a clawed eyeball back into its socket. OK for starters?

1971. Directed by James Kelly.
Starring Beryl Reid, Flora Robson, Tessa Wyatt, John Hamill, T. P. McKenna. Colour.
87 minutes.

Guild Home Video

Beat The Devil

Screenwriter Harry Kurnitz once said of this film: "No matter where you come in during the running, you seem to have missed half the picture." And he's right. The remark applies even if you watch the movie from the beginning! Humphrey Bogart is an American fortune hunter mixed up with some international crooks (plus Gina Lollobrigida and Jennifer Jones) in some shady uranium dealings in British East Africa. It seems as though it was made up as they went along, but John Huston and Truman Capote are credited with a screenplay so presumably some thought went into it all. Good fun; the stars carry it.

1954. Directed by John Huston.
Starring Humphrey Bogart, Jennifer Jones, Gina Lollobrigida, Robert Morley, Peter Lorre, Edward Underdown, Ivor Barnard. Black and White.
93 minutes.

Twentieth Century-Fox Video

The Beggar's Opera

Anyone with a liking for cinematic curiosities might just find this movie of interest, for it's an abbreviated version of John Gay's 1728 ballad opera about the exploits of dashing highwayman Captain Macheath in 18th century London. And with Laurence Olivier acting *and* singing the role of Macheath, the result should have been intriguing. Not so. Even cineastes will probably find this disappointing and regard it as no more than an interesting experiment that failed. It's certainly a dubious video buy. The colour is garish to say the least.

1953. Directed by Peter Brook.
Starring Laurence Olivier, Stanley Holloway, Dorothy Tutin, Daphne Anderson, Mary Clare, George Devine, Athene Seyler. Colour.
94 minutes.

Thorn EMI Video

Behave Yourself

Farley Granger and Shelley Winters find themselves mixed up in murder and a two-million dollar hijack plot when Granger brings home a stray dog. Early 50s attempt to repeat the success of MGM's *Thin Man* films which doesn't come off, mainly because Granger and Winters ain't no Powell and Loy. Good supporting cast, which might make it of interest to film buffs. And something of a rarity.

1951. Directed by George Beck.
Starring Farley Granger, Shelley Winters, William Demarest, Francis L.

Sullivan, Margalo Gillmore, Lon Chaney Jr, Hans Conried, Elisha Cook Jr.
Black and White.
81 minutes.

21st Century Video
(distributed by VCL)

Being There

Peter Sellers as a feeble-minded gardener who is let loose on the outside
world when his benefactor dies, and through a series of accidents becomes a TV personality and an advisor to the President, who hangs on
his every word. A thin joke over-extended, although there are some witty
comments on the American way of life in today's television age. Seems
very long on video. Shirley MacLaine adds sparkle in a delicious scene
when she tries for kinky sex whilst all Sellers is interested in is the TV.

Box-office rental	$10,804,296
Average rental (79)	$31,964,775
Oscars (1)	Best Supporting Actor (Douglas)
Oscar nominations (1)	Best Actor (Sellers)

1979. Directed by Hal Ashby.
Starring Peter Sellers, Shirley MacLaine, Melvyn Douglas, Jack Warden,
Richard Dysart, Richard Basehart, Ruth Attaway. Colour.
130 minutes.

MGM/CBS Home Video

The Belstone Fox

An abandoned fox cub grows up with a young puppy and becomes
something of a legend because of its ability to outwit and outrun the local
hunt. When it leads the hounds into the path of a train, however, huntsman
Eric Porter vows revenge and sets out for the kill. A rather disquieting
film, and for those against blood sports certainly one to stay away from,
even though the screenplay hints that it's against them from time to time.
Difficult to sum up, for it's an uneasy mix of lovely countryside, bloody

incident and one or two rather nasty people. It does have one thing in its favour, however. The fox is still alive at the end.

1973. Directed by James Hill.
Starring Eric Porter, Rachel Roberts, Jeremy Kemp, Bill Travers, Dennis Waterman, Heather Wright. Colour.
103 minutes.

Rank Video

Beneath The Planet Of The Apes

The inevitable follow-up to *Planet Of The Apes* (see page 337) with Charlton Heston discovering there *is* more intelligent life on Earth – a race of mutants who live in the ruins of the New York underground and worship a god, a live atomic bomb! The aggressive apes, intent on destroying the deformed race, raid their subterranean dwelling with the net result that everyone goes up in smoke yet again. All, that is, except three. This film misses the chilling prophetic doom of its predecessor but on a comic book adventure level it gets by easily enough.

Box-office rental	$8,600,000
Average rental (70)	$16,881,800

1970. Directed by Ted Post.
Starring James Franciscus, Charlton Heston, Kim Hunter, Maurice Evans, Linda Harrison, Paul Richards, Victor Buono, James Gregory, Jeff Corey. Colour.
94 minutes.

Twentieth Century-Fox Video

Bengazi

Three adventurers set out from Bengazi to search for a fabulous treasure hidden in a mosque. When, eventually, they come up trumps, their joy is short-lived. Some brutal tribesmen drop by, trap them in the desert shrine and allow them the choice of giving up the treasure and staying alive, or . . . The choice for video buyers is simpler. Forget it. Shares a tape with the Alan Ladd Western *Guns Of The Timberland*.

1955. Directed by John Brahm.
Starring Richard Conte, Victor McLaglen, Richard Carlson, Mala Powers, Richard Erdman. Black and White.
78 minutes.

Kingston Video

Berlin Express

One of those "see-it-where-it-happened" espionage stories so popular in the immediate post-war era. On this occasion, the setting is the war-shattered town of Frankfurt where a group of Allies (Ryan, Oberon, Korvin, etc.) search for a German statesman kidnapped by a gang of underground Nazis. The reason for the kidnapping? The Nazis want to thwart the statesman's plans for the reunification of Germany. Impressive performances and sinister atmosphere; the main feature on a good value double tape. Making up the double bill: the Val Lewton horror flick, *Isle Of The Dead*.

1948. Directed by Jacques Tourneur.
Starring Merle Oberon, Robert Ryan, Charles Korvin, Paul Lukas, Robert Coote. Black and White.
86 minutes.

Kingston Video

Best Of The Badmen

Former Union colonel Robert Ryan organizes a gang of outlaws, including the James and Younger brothers, to help him seek revenge on the man who sent him to jail on a false charge. Coventional Western with an above-average cast; shares a double-feature video tape with *Sealed Cargo*.

1951. Directed by William D. Russell.
Starring Robert Ryan, Claire Trevor, Jack Buetél, Robert Preston, Walter Brennan, Bruce Cabot, John Archer, Lawrence Tierney. Colour.
84 minutes.

Kingston Video

The Beyond ★

Tale of a New York girl who arrives in Louisiana to inherit an old hotel but finds that it once belonged to a Satanist and stands on one of the seven gateways to hell. And once those gates are opened the zombies shall walk the earth. Despite all the muggings, the girl should have remained in New York! Ends in hell itself. Gruesome Italian horror flick.

1981. Directed by Lucio Fulci.
Starring Katherine McColl, David Warbeck, Sarah Keller, Antoine Saint John, Veronica Lazar. Colour.
86 minutes.

Vampix
(*distributed by Videomedia*)

Beyond A Reasonable Doubt ★★

A Fritz Lang movie with an interesting theme about a journalist who plants false evidence against himself in a murder case in order to prove the fallibility of circumstantial evidence. Unfortunately, the newspaper publisher who is to cover him with an alibi is killed in an auto-accident and the writer finds himself in a bit of a jam. Watch out for a twist ending. On the same video tape as *Flying Leathernecks*

1956. Directed by Fritz Lang.
Starring Dana Andrews, Joan Fontaine, Sidney Blackmer, Philip Bourneuf, Barbara Nichols, Shepperd Strudwick. Black and White.
80 minutes.

Kingston Video

Beyond The Poseidon Adventure

That liner is still floating upside-down in the Atlantic Ocean but, before it finally goes to the bottom, salvage-tug skipper Michael Caine makes a grab for the jewels in the ship's safe and arms dealer Telly Savalas goes after the missile and other weapons stored in the hold. A piece of cinematic rubbish that's not worth ten minutes of anyone's time.

1979. Directed by Irwin Allen.
Starring Michael Caine, Sally Field, Telly Savalas, Peter Boyle, Jack Warden, Shirley Knight, Slim Pickens, Shirley Jones, Karl Malden. Colour. 114 minutes.

Warner Home Video

Beyond The Valley Of The Dolls ★

If you thought *Valley Of The Dolls* was bad, wait until you see this piece of junk which has nothing at all to do with the first film but which repeats its basic premiss – three girls trying to break into show biz. Only this time the girls are female rock stars and the city is Los Angeles and not New York. The ingredients? Blackmail, drug-taking, suicide attempts, mass murder and sex. Which is, after all, what you would expect from skin-flick king Russ Meyer. Along with *Myra Breckinridge* one of the worst movie mistakes Twentieth Century-Fox ever made.

Box-office rental	$7,000,000
Average rental (70)	$16,881,800

1970. Directed by Russ Meyer.
Starring Dolly Read, Cynthia Myers, Marcia McBroom, John La Zar, Michael Blodgett, David Gurian, Edy Williams. Colour. 106 minutes.

Twentieth Century-Fox Video

The Bible . . . In The Beginning ★

The first 22 chapters of the book of Genesis in something close to three hours of video entertainment that will probably bore you right out of your skull. Producer Dino De Laurentiis was originally going to make this movie with several directors, each of them contributing one episode. Orson Welles, Visconti, Fellini and Bresson were among those mentioned. In the end, it finished up in the hands of John Huston and a depressingly bad job he makes of it too. He jollies it up a little with a personal appearance as Noah but, for all his faults and crudity, DeMille would have been a better bet as director. He certainly would have made it more entertaining. The trouble is he'd been dead for some years when this was made so he never got the chance! Not a good buy despite its box-office figure.

Box-office rental	$15,000,000
Average rental (66)	$8,826,100
Oscars	Nil
Oscar nominations (1)	Best Music Score

1966. Directed by John Huston.
Starring Michael Parks, Ulla Bergryd, Richard Harris, John Huston, Stephen Boyd, George C. Scott, Ava Gardner, Peter O'Toole. Colour. 175 minutes.

Twentieth Century-Fox Video

The Big Combo

Dark little thriller with zealous cop Cornel Wilde obsessed not only with bringing racketeer Richard Conte to book but also rescuing beautiful young society woman Jean Wallace from the mobster's clutches. Quite tough (and erotic), this one got a bit lost among all the biggie movies of 1955 but it still holds up well, as do many of the films of underrated director Joseph Lewis. A raw, deliberately crude piece of work; the torture scenes when hit men Lee Van Cleef and Earl Holliman torment Wilde with amplified sound still pack a punch. Something of a lost movie and well worth a glance on video.

1955. Directed by Joseph Lewis.
Starring Cornel Wilde, Richard Conte, Brian Donlevy, Jean Wallace,

Robert Middleton, Lee Van Cleef, Earl Holliman, Helen Walker. Black and White.
89 minutes.

Video Unlimited

The Big Land

A group of cattlemen and wheat farmers join together to build a railroad link to Texas and put a stop to the activities of some ruthless cattle buyers. Run-of-the mill Western with Alan Ladd sorting things out in his usual fashion in the usual climactic showdown. Some parallels with *Shane* but a long, long way from the standard of that great movie. Hardly a value for money buy. On the same tape: the 1932 William Wellman epic *Pioneer Builders*.

1957. Directed by Gordon Douglas.
Starring Alan Ladd, Virginia Mayo, Edmond O'Brien, Anthony Caruso, Julie Bishop, John Qualen. Colour.
92 minutes.

Kingston Video

The Big Red One

Cult director Sam Fuller's first film for many years, a combat diary about the lives of five men serving in the US Army's famous infantry division, "The Big Red One". The action takes the men from North Africa to Sicily then to the Normandy beaches, and makes for one of the more interesting war films of recent times, although whether it is quite the masterpiece some critics claim it to be is rather open to question. One can also argue that one has already seen much of this sort of stuff before in films like *A Walk In The Sun*. Still, it has its moments and indeed some brilliant passages. Lee Marvin leads the squad.

1980. Directed by Samuel Fuller.

Starring Lee Marvin, Mark Hamill, Robert Carradine, Bobby Di Cicco, Kelly Ward, Stephane Audran. Colour.
113 minutes.

CIC Video

The Big Sky

Two Kentucky mountaineers join a French keelboat in St. Louis and journey a thousand miles up the treacherous and uncharted Missouri river to trade furs with Indian tribes. Given the subject, this one should have been exciting but, despite director Howard Hawks throwing in some hostile Indians and confrontations with rival trappers, the result is as slow and tedious to the video viewer as the original journey must have seemed to the pioneers. The quickie *Code Of The West* makes up an all-Western video double bill.

Oscars	Nil
Oscar nominations (2)	Best Supporting Actor (Hunnicutt); Photography

1952. Directed by Howard Hawks.
Starring Kirk Douglas, Dewey Martin, Elizabeth Threatt, Arthur Hunnicutt, Buddy Baer, Steven Geray. Black and White.
122 minutes.

Kingston Video

The Big Sleep

Anyone who tries to update and move to England Raymond Chandler's classic tale of blackmail and murder must have thought it a good idea at the time. That it was a complete miscalculation is sadly evident in this travesty of a thriller, which has Robert Mitchum (second time out as Chandler's private-eye Philip Marlowe) simply going through the motions and blinking wearily at a supporting cast that deserves rather better material than it gets here. A total lack of atmosphere completes a miserable video experience. Oh for Los Angeles and Bogart and Bacall!

1978. Directed by Michael Winner.
Starring Robert Mitchum, Sarah Miles, Richard Boone, Candy Clark, Joan Collins, Edward Fox, John Mills, James Stewart, Oliver Reed. Colour.
99 minutes.

Precision Video

The Big Steal

This unpretentious little RKO thriller, vintage 1949, runs for not much more than an hour, but contains one of the most exciting "prior-to-*Bullitt*" car chases put on film. The director responsible is Don Siegel, then in the early stages of a distinguished career. The stars he puts through their paces: Robert Mitchum as an army officer framed for the theft of a payroll; William Bendix and Patric Knowles as the two men who set him up; and lovely Jane Greer. Excellent Mexican landscapes; sharing the same tape, Jane Russell in *Underwater*.

1949. Directed by Don Siegel.
Starring Robert Mitchum, Jane Greer, William Bendix, Patric Knowles, Ramon Novarro. Black and White.
71 minutes.

Kingston Video

Billy Liar

A kind of revamping of James Thurber's Walter Mitty idea. A hero indulges in fantasies in order to escape from his routine and rather mundane existence. In this case the dreamer is a young undertaker's clerk (Tom Courtenay) living with his parents in a suburb in the North of England. In his effort to escape from reality he imagines himself a dictator, a soldier, a novelist, a cripple, but at the final count, when a real-life opportunity presents itself and allows him the chance to break free from his chains, he backs away and retreats into the safety of his dreams. Very amusing at times but ultimately rather a sad movie. Mona Washbourne and Wilfred Pickles are perfection as Courtenay's long-suffering parents and John

Schlesinger's observations of suburban life remain wickedly funny. Good video value.

1963. Directed by John Schlesinger.
Starring Tom Courtenay, Julie Christie, Wilfred Pickles, Mona Washbourne, Ethel Griffies, Finlay Currie, Rodney Bewes. Black and White.
98 minutes.

Thorn EMI Video

The Birds

One of the slowest-starting of all contemporary Hitchcock films (nearly an hour goes by without anything of note happening on screen) but which then picks up steam rather quickly as thousands of birds attack, without any apparent reason, a small community on the Pacific coast. Could it be the bomb? Could it be some other strange reason? Hitchcock gives no answers. Instead, he offers several of his most terrifying set pieces, including the one in which Tippi Hedren sits quietly in a playground whilst hundreds of ravenous crows build up behind her as they wait for the children to leave school. Like most Hitchcock movies, this one looks better now that it did at the time of its release and as video viewing makes a chilling after-dinner experience. Ingeniously advertised when it first appeared, with the seemingly incorrectly-phrased advertising slogan, "The Birds Is Coming".

Box-office rental	$5,000,000
Average rental (63)	$8,360,900
Oscars	Nil
Oscar nominations (1)	Best Special Visual Effects

1963. Directed by Alfred Hitchcock.
Starring Rod Taylor, Tippi Hedren, Suzanne Pleshette, Jessica Tandy, Charles McGraw. Colour.
120 minutes.

CIC Video

The Birth Of A Nation

D. W. Griffith's 165-minute epic, tracing the story of the American Civil War from the early years of the conflict to the bitter aftermath, when negro factions rose to power and the Ku Klux Klan was formed in the South. Quite bigotted in many of its views (Griffith was accused of anti-negro bias), but spectacular and historically important as being the film that turned the medium from an entertainment to an art form practically overnight. Raoul Walsh, later a top director, has a role as Lincoln's assassin, John Wilkes Booth; Erich von Stroheim appears fleetingly in a bit part.

1915. Directed by D. W. Griffith.
Starring Lillian Gish, Mae Marsh, Henry Walthall, Miriam Cooper, Mary Alden, Ralph Lewis, George Seigmann, Walter Long, Robert Harron. Black and White.
165 minutes.

Spectrum
(distributed by Polygram)

The Bitch

Or, the further adventures of man-eating jet-setter Joan Collins, first introduced in *The Stud* (see page 406) and here setting her cap at crooked gambler Michael Coby. Sister Jackie's story line includes a nude bathing party and 20 more disco songs. Virtually indistinguishable from its predecessor. Ian Hendry offers a portrait of a Mafia chief.

1979. Directed by Gerry O'Hara.
Starring Joan Collins, Michael Coby, Kenneth Haigh, Ian Hendry, Carolyn Seymour, Sue Lloyd, Mark Burns. Colour.
94 minutes.

Brent Walker Video
(distributed by Videospace)

Blackbeard The Pirate

Robert Newton giving a variation of his Long John Silver role in *Treasure Island*, this time as the infamous buccaneer who pillaged his way across the high seas of the Caribbean in the early years of the 18th century. William Bendix is his first mate, Linda Darnell his lovely hostage. Newton delivers such lines as "What've ye done with the boodle, me beauty?" and finishes buried up to his neck in the sand, watching apprehensively as the tide rolls slowly towards him. Routine pirate yarn. Should have been better with Raoul Walsh at the helm. Supported by three shorts: *Fish Feathers*, *The Fireman* and *Pal's Adventures* with Edgar Kennedy.

1952. Directed by Raoul Walsh.
Starring Robert Newton, Linda Darnell, William Bendix, Keith Andes, Richard Egan, Irene Ryan. Colour.
99 minutes.

Kingston Video

Black Beauty

The most recent screen version of Anna Sewell's classic about a luckless horse, who is parted from a young farm boy and passes from squire to tinker to circus owner to soldier, and so on, before returning to his original owner and a well-deserved retirement. Pleasantly photographed video entertainment for all children with a love of horses; adults might find the predictable and sentimental events rather hard going. Walter Slezak features among the supporting cast as the circus owner.

1971. Directed by James Hill.
Starring Mark Lester, Walter Slezak, Peter Lee Lawrence, Uschi Glas, Patrick Mower, John Nettleton. Colour.
106 minutes.

Hokushin

The Black Hole

Walt Disney's rather belated attempt to jump on the *Star Wars* bandwagon and not a very good one at that, despite an intriguing opening when a survey ship, lost some twenty years before, is found circling a black hole in outer space. On board is madman Maximilian Schell. Under his command are humanoid figures who obey his every whim. Or are they humanoids? After that the movie goes down the drain very fast, despite some excellent effects which are still impressive on the small screen but nowhere near as breathtaking as they were in 70mm. In some ways a reworking of *20,000 Leagues Under The Sea* in outer space.

Box-office rental	$25,000,000
Average rental (79)	$31,964,775
Oscars	Nil
Oscar nominations (2)	Best Photography; Visual Effects

1979. Directed by Gary Nelson.
Starring Maximilian Schell, Anthony Perkins, Robert Forster, Joseph Bottoms, Yvette Mimieux, Ernest Borgnine. Colour.
98 minutes.

Walt Disney Home Video

Blackmail

A bit of a museum piece this – no pun intended, in that the climactic chase takes place across the dome of the British Museum – but because it was the very first British sound movie, made way back in 1929. There's some inventive early Hitchcock stuff, including the use of the word "knife" as a symbol of guilt, plus a clever story of a detective's girlfriend who accidentally kills an artist and then finds her boyfriend investigating the case. But the long pauses between the sentences tend to amuse rather than thrill and the picture remains of interest more to historians than the average video viewer.

1929. Directed by Alfred Hitchcock.

Starring Anny Ondra, Sara Allgood, John Longden, Charles Paton, Donald Calthrop, Cyril Ritchard. Black and White.
78 minutes.

Thorn EMI Video

The Black Panther

Any movie that recreates the hideous activities of Donald Neilson so quickly after he had received a life sentence for his crimes (particularly the brutal murder of 15-year-old Lesley Whittle) smacks of opportunism. And it would probably have been better for all concerned if this one had not been made. As it stands, however, it is *not* a sensationalistic account of the events, more a documentary retelling, and as such it is not uninteresting. But entertainment?

1977. Directed by Ian Merrick.
Starring Donald Sumpter, Debbie Farrington, Marjorie Yates, Sylvia O'Donnell, Andrew Burt, Ruth Dunning. Colour.
98 minutes.

Intervision

The Black Pirate

Silent swashbuckler and an excellent example of the two-colour Technicolor process used by film-makers during the early 20s. Douglas Fairbanks stars as a young Spanish nobleman who vows vengeance on the pirates responsible for marooning him on a desert island and causing the death of his father. Great swordplay and many acrobatic feats from Fairbanks; good value for *devotees* of silent cinema. Piano music score.

1926. Directed by Albert S. Parker.
Starring Douglas Fairbanks, Billie Dove, Donald Crisp. Colour.
83 minutes.

Spectrum
(Distributed by Polygram)

The Black Torment

Old-fashioned but passably entertaining horror flick, vintage 1964, about the rather nasty events that befall an English lord and his young bride when they return to their country estate. The period is 1780 and murder is the order of the day, although witchcraft, rape, ghosts, insanity, even an apparition on horseback all figure in the course of events. Corny but not unlively.

1964. Directed by Robert Hartford-Davis.
Starring Heather Sears, John Turner, Ann Lynn, Peter Arne, Norman Bird, Raymond Huntley. Colour.
85 minutes.

Vampix
(*Distributed by Videomedia*)

Blazing Saddles

If you're a Mel Brooks fan, you'll probably have your own views as to which of his films is the most amusing, but this spoof Western, one of the few to successfully satirise the *genre*, must rank very highly and was enormously popular back in 1974, the year of its release. Cleavon Little is the black sheriff of the unfriendly 1870s town of Rock Ridge; Gene Wilder is a once-legendary gunman turned alcoholic. Together they help clean up the town and save it from unscrupulous speculators. The theme song, sung by Frankie Laine, satirizes the *High Noon* type of ballad heard so often in Westerns back in the 50s.

Box-office rental	$45,200,000
Average rental (74)	$18,456,150
Oscars	Nil
Oscar Nominations (3)	Best Supporting Actress (Madeline Kahn); Best Editing; Song

1974. Directed by Mel Brooks.
Starring Cleavon Little, Gene Wilder, Slim Pickens, Madeline Kahn, David Huddleston, Dom DeLuise. Colour.
93 minutes.

Warner Home Video

Bless This House

An attempt to transfer TV's hit comedy series into a successful movie. The attempt fails simply because thirty minutes of this sort of thing is about all you need. When spread out to three times that length the scriptwriters need to have a few aces hidden up their sleeves – which in this case they haven't. The "plot" is built around the continuing battles between the Abbotts (Sid James and Diana Coupland) and their new next-door neighbours, Terry Scott and June Whitfield.

1973. Directed by Gerald Thomas.
Starring Sidney James, Diana Coupland, Terry Scott, June Whitfield, Peter Butterworth, Sally Geeson, Robin Askwith. Colour.
89 minutes.

Rank Video

The Blob

Minor sci-fi quickie of the late 50s about a gelatinous mass that falls from a meteor and quickly grows to the size of a house as it devours the population of a small American town. Worthy of attention only because it was the first movie in which the late Steve McQueen had a starring role. He plays a teenager who runs around rather helplessly in search of help.

1958. Directed by Irvin S. Yeaworth Jr.
Starring Steve McQueen, Aneta Corseaut, Earl Rowe, Olin Howlin. Colour.
86 minutes.

Mountain Video

Blood And Black Lace

Flashy Italian horror flick about a mad killer who goes round bumping off fashion models in contemporary Rome. Mario Bava is the director so devotees of the *genre* will know what to expect – plenty of blood and gore and cinematic bravado. But just another horror movie, nothing more.

One time sex symbol Eva Bartok features as the wealthy owner of the fashion salon.

1965. Directed by Mario Bava.
Starring Eva Bartok, Cameron Mitchell, Thomas Reiner, Arianna Gorini, Mary Arden, Franco Ressel. Colour.
90 minutes.

Iver Films

Blood And Sand

A 1941 remake of the silent classic, with Tyrone Power cast this time as the ill-fated matador who finds himself torn between the love of two women – Madrid aristocrat Rita Hayworth and childhood sweetheart Linda Darnell – before being torn apart in the bullring. It's all a bit trite and tedious, although the colour camerawork of Ray Rennahan and Ernest Palmer pleases the eye even if the performances do not.

Oscars (1)   Best Photography
Oscar nominations (1)   Best Art Direction

1941. Directed by Rouben Mamoulian.
Starring Tyrone Power, Linda Darnell, Rita Hayworth, Nazimova, Anthony Quinn, J. Carrol Naish, Lynn Bari, Laird Cregar. Colour.
123 minutes.

Twentieth Century-Fox Video

The Blood Beast Terror

An obsessed entomologist creates monster moths which go around killing and clawing people "something 'orrible". So who plays the villain of the piece? Well, despite the fact that Peter Cushing is in the cast, not he. Best to let you find out for yourself, although be warned, this is a very low-grade horror offering and hardly worth your time and attention. Roy Hudd as a mortuary attendant offers light relief.

1968. Directed by Vernon Sewell.
Starring Peter Cushing, Robert Flemyng, Wanda Ventham, Vanessa Howard, David Griffin. Colour.
88 minutes.

Vampix
(*Distributed by Videomedia*)

Blood On Satan's Claw

Question: What do you do when you uncover a gruesome skull (with one eye still intact) when ploughing a field in 17th century England? Answer: Run like mad and, above all, pray, for there's little else you can do when a Devil's claw sets off on the rampage and causes some village children to be caught up in a Satanic cult. Passable horror fare with some strong scenes.

1971. Directed by Piers Haggard.
Starring Patrick Wymark, Linda Hayden, Barry Andrews, Avice Landon, Simon Williams. Colour.
93 minutes.

Guild Home Video

Blood Relations

A virginal young nurse arrives at a small town hospital, joins the local blood-drinking set and does her best to bring the town's vampire inhabitants to their senses. Instead, she gets her big toe bitten off and becomes a full blooded vampire herself. Daft little horror thriller not unfunny at times. Eddie Constantine is a priest unable to do much about events.

1977. Directed by Wim Lindner.
Starring Maxim Hamel, Sophie Deschamps, Gregoire Aslan, Robert Dalban, Jacqueline Huet, Eddie Constantine. Colour.
90 minutes.

Home Video Productions

Blood Relatives

Donald Sutherland as Ed McBain's famous 87th Precinct cop Steve Carella trying to discover who stabbed a 17-year-old girl to death in the streets of Montreal. The direction is by French thriller master Claude Chabrol, which means the result should have been intriguing. But despite a promising start and a strong supporting cast, the film quickly descends to the level of a routine whodunnit. None of Carella's 87th Precinct colleagues feature in the movie. Mediocre.

1977. Directed by Claude Chabrol.
Starring Donald Sutherland, Aude Landry, Lisa Langlois, Laurent Malet, Stephane Audran, Donald Pleasence, David Hemmings. Colour.
95 minutes.

Picture Time Video
(*distributed by VCL*)

Blow-Up

What on earth is this all about? Good question. The trouble is, "What's The Answer?" And more to the point, "Is It Worth Finding Out?" Best to judge for yourselves perhaps, as you follow fashion photographer David Hemmings on his rounds and discover with him that he has accidentally taken a photograph of a murder being committed in a London park. It's great up to this point, but then the whole thing becomes obscure and meaningful and, eventually, a bore. Some sexy model gals please the eye in the first half and Antonioni's portrait of London in the Swinging Sixties brings about a nostalgic glow.

Box-office rental	$6,350,000
Average rental (66)	$8,826,100
Oscars	Nil
Oscar nominations (2)	Best Direction; Story & Screenplay

1966. Directed by Michelangelo Antonioni.
Starring David Hemmings, Vanessa Redgrave, Sarah Miles. Colour.
110 minutes.

MGM/CBS Home Video

Blue Blood

Stately home charades of the most unpleasant kind with drug-addicted young master Derek Jacobi upstairs and sinister, menacing butler Oliver Reed on the rampage downstairs. Reed triumphs in a coarse, repellent movie that includes a drunken orgy and a dose of black magic to bolster up its weak story line. Easy to ignore.

1973. Directed by Andrew Sinclair.
Starring Oliver Reed, Fiona Lewis, Anna Gael, Derek Jacobi, Meg Wynn Owen. Colour.
86 minutes.

Intervision

Blue Hawaii

Financially the most popular of all the Elvis Presley musicals; a 1961 opus, with Elvis trying to readjust after a couple of years in the army and deciding to work as a tourist guide rather than in the profitable pineapple business of his parents. Agreeable enough of its sort, handsomely photographed in Technicolor and with an extra bonus in the form of Angela Lansbury as Elvis' mom. If you're an Elvis *devotee* this one is probably the most enjoyable of the lot, with 14 songs including "Rock-A-Hula Baby", "Beach Boy Blues" and the popular title song.

Box-office rental	$4,700,000
Average rental (61)	$8,103,100

1961. Directed by Norman Taurog.
Starring Elvis Presley, Joan Blackman, Nancy Walters, Roland Winters, Angela Lansbury, John Archer. Colour.
101 minutes.

Twentieth Century-Fox Video

The Blue Lagoon

Made once before (in 1948) with Jean Simmons and Donald Houston, this tale of two Victorian children who are shipwrecked and grow up together on a desert island has its attractions even if they are primarily of a visual nature – the beautiful scenery, handsome photography, the "man appeal" of the lovely Brooke Shields. Unfortunately, 101 minutes is a bit long with only two characters for company although Leo McKern (as the ship's cook) does his best to enliven the early scenes before expiring and turning into a skeleton.

Box-office rental	$28,456,000
Average rental (80)	$30,086,027
Oscars	Nil
Oscar nominations (1)	Best Photography

1980. Directed by Randal Kleiser.
Starring Brooke Shields, Christopher Atkins, Leo McKern, William Daniels, Elva Josephson, Glenn Kohan. Colour.
101 minutes.

RCA/Columbia International Video

The Blue Max

World War I flying drama with George Peppard as a young German pilot with two ambitions in life – to shoot down twenty enemy planes and earn the Blue Max medal, and to lay down beautiful young countess Ursula Andress. He succeeds on both counts but gets his come-uppance because Ursula's hubby, Prussian aristocrat James Mason, would prefer him out of the way. Great in the air and not so bad on the ground when Peppard and Andress get to grips. Otherwise a bit flat and two-dimensional. Mason and the planes (photographed by Douglas Slocombe) just get it through. 2½ video rating.

Box-office rental	$7,275,000
Average rental (66)	$8,826,100

1966. Directed by John Guillermin.

Starring George Peppard, James Mason, Ursula Andress, Jeremy Kemp, Karl Michael Vogler, Anton Diffring, Harry Towb. Colour.
156 minutes.

Twentieth Century-Fox Video

The Blues Brothers

Two hoodlum brothers decide to search for redemption. And how to do it? By raising money to save the orphanage in which they were raised from closing down. And how to do that? By bringing together members of their now defunct rhythm and blues band. And once that's accomplished? Well, from then on in it's mayhem and noisy destruction all the way. Much liked for its monumental car chase, this one tends to give the impression that film comedy has regressed fifty years – at least! But a lot of people enjoyed it. Look at those box-office figures.

Box-office rental	$31,000,000
Average rental (80)	$30,086,027

1980. Directed by John Landis.
Starring John Belushi, Dan Aykroyd, Kathleen Freeman, James Brown, Henry Gibson, Armand Cerami, Cab Calloway. Colour.
133 minutes.

CIC Video

Bob & Carol & Ted & Alice ★★

Sophisticated young married couple Natalie Wood and Robert Culp try to convince their best friends, Elliott Gould and Dyan Cannon, that "natural spontaneous behaviour", that is, enjoying extra-marital sex without any recriminations from either side, is the best way to ensure a happy married life. But on a holiday trip to Las Vegas things don't quite work out as planned. It all seemed bright, witty and original when first released but it's rather dated now. Finishes up with all four performers in the same bed.

Box-office rental	$14,600,000
Average rental (69)	$13,660,950
Oscars	Nil
Oscar nominations (4)	Best Supporting Actor (Gould); Supporting Actress (Cannon); Story & Screenplay; Photography

1969. Directed by Paul Mazursky.
Starring Natalie Wood, Robert Culp, Elliott Gould, Dyan Cannon, Horst Ebersberg, Lee Bergere. Colour.
105 minutes.

RCA/Columbia International Video

Body And Soul

Of all the movies that have explored the murkier aspects of American boxing, this one (along with Robert Wise's *The Set-Up*) holds up the best. John Garfield is the young Jewish boy from New York who becomes corrupted on the way to the championship and sacrifices friends, family, and love. Abraham Polonsky's intelligent screenplay probes quite deeply into the perversion of moral values; Hazel Brooks offers a stand-out cameo as a gold-digging night club floozie. Memorable theme tune.

| Oscars (1) | Best Editing |
| Oscar nominations (2) | Best Actor (Garfield); Original Screenplay |

1947. Directed by Robert Rossen.
Starring John Garfield, Lilli Palmer, Hazel Brooks, Anne Revere, William Conrad, Joseph Pevney, Canada Lee. Black and White.
104 minutes.

Intervision

The Body Stealers

Sad to think that George Sanders once gave one of the screen's most sophisticated performances as drama critic Addison DeWitt in *All About*

Eve, but was eventually reduced to appearing in rubbish like this. In this one, dear old George is a NATO commander involved in the testing of a new parachute. Imagine his surprise when the parachutists all disappear in a red mist on the day of the jump and he discovers that aliens have taken 'em over. Weak and feeble.

1969. Directed by Gerry Levy.
Starring George Sanders, Maurice Evans, Patrick Allen, Neil Connery, Hilary Dwyer, Robert Fleming. Colour.
91 minutes.

Guild Home Video

The Boldest Job In The West ★

Continental (Spain-France-Italy) Western of the usual inane variety about treachery among a gang of thieves after they have robbed a supposedly impregnable bank near the Canadian border. Bleak and dismal to look at; bleak and dismal as video fare.

1971. Directed by José Antonio de la Loma.
Starring Mark Edwards, Carmen Sevilla, Fernando Sancho, Charly Bravo, Piero Lulli. Colour.
101 minutes.

Intervision

Bonnie And Clyde

Arthur Penn's lyrical and folksy treatment of the activities of Clyde Barrow and Bonnie Parker, who murdered some eighteen people during a three-year killing spree in the early years of the Depression. Caused much controversy when it was first shown because of its violence and sympathetic approach to its leading characters; now looks considerably less innovative than it did at the time of its release. Plus factors: the death-in-slow-motion climax which remains a *tour-de-force* of film technique and the stunning camerawork of Burnett Guffey.

Box-office rental	$22,700,000
Average rental (67)	$13,081,250
Oscars (2)	Best Supporting Actress (Parsons); Photography
Oscar nominations (8)	Best Film; Actor (Beatty); Actress (Dunaway); Supporting Actor (Hackman); Supporting Actor (Pollard); Direction; Story & Screenplay; Costume Design

1967. Directed by Arthur Penn.
Starring Warren Beatty, Faye Dunaway, Michael J. Pollard, Gene Hackman, Estelle Parsons, Denver Pyle, Gene Wilder. Colour.
111 minutes.

Warner Home Video

Bon Voyage, Charlie Brown

The Peanuts gang embark on their first international jaunt – to France, where Charlie Brown, Linus, Peppermint Patty and Marcie, all of whom have been chosen as exchange students, are joined by Snoopy and Woodstock in their usual complex adventures. About par for the Charlie Brown course!

1980. Directed by Bill Melendez.
Colour.
75 minutes.

CIC Video

Borderline

Routine Charles Bronson actioner not shown in British cinemas and first released in this country on video which may indicate what ITC thought of its chances with a mass audience. Bronson's a border patrol officer in search of the immigrant smugglers who have murdered his police colleague. Conveyor belt stuff, set on the Mexican border. Fairly dismal.

1980. Directed by Jerrold Freedman.
Starring Charles Bronson, Bruno Kirby, Karmin Murcelo, Michael Learner, Ed Harris. Colour.
97 minutes.

Precision Video

The Boston Strangler

Journalistic account of the tracking down of Albert DeSalvo who, between June 1962 and January 1964, raped and murdered some thirteen women and turned the city of Boston into a place of terror. Gripping, if macabre, entertainment with Tony Curtis surprisingly effective as DeSalvo. The film slows towards the final reels and loses much on video because of director Fleischer's obsession with split screen techniques. But still above average.

Box-office rental	$8,000,000
Average rental (68)	$14,411,950

1968. Directed by Richard Fleischer.
Starring Tony Curtis, Henry Fonda, George Kennedy, Mike Kellin, Hurd Hatfield, Murray Hamilton, Jeff Corey, Sally Kellerman, William Marshall. Colour.
114 minutes.

Twentieth Century-Fox Video

The Boys From Brazil

Gregory Peck, as the notorious war criminal Dr. Josef Mengele, plans to build a new race of Hitlers (94 cloned kids made from the tissue of the Fuehrer's body) and looks like succeeding until ageing Jewish Nazi hunter Laurence Olivier interferes with his plans. A bizarre story that just manages to hold credibility during its first hour but then collapses into a mishmash of outrageous clichés and a laughably improbable (and prolonged) climax. The constantly changing locations – Europe, South America, etc – work in the film's favour and Henry Decae's colourwork is stunning. But don't watch if you're afraid of dogs. Mr. Peck meets a very nasty end at the teeth of some Doberman Pinschers. 2½ rating.

Box-office rental	$10,165,000
Average rental (78)	$39,443,850
Oscars	Nil
Oscar nominations (3)	Best Actor (Olivier); Editing; Music Score

1978. Directed by Franklin Schaffner.
Starring Gregory Peck, Laurence Olivier, James Mason, Lilli Palmer, Uta Hagen, Steven Guttenberg, Denholm Elliott, Rosemary Harris, John Dehner. Colour.
125 minutes.

Precision Video

The Boys In The Band

Straightforward film version of Mart Crowley's stage play about a homosexual's birthday party which starts out brightly enough, but soon turns into a set piece of pain, hatred and tears and gradually reveals the hidden thoughts and fears of the various guests. Carefully done; based on a one-set play, which tends to make the whole thing rather overpowering at times. Works better on video than it did on the big screen.

1970. Directed by William Friedkin.
Starring Leonard Frey, Kenneth Nelson, Cliff Gorman, Frederick Combs, Reuben Greene. Colour.
120 minutes.

MGM/CBS Home Video

Breaking Away

Director Peter Yates (*Robbery*, *Bullitt*) again obsessed with wheels but this time cycle wheels, as four teenagers from the wrong side of the tracks take on and defeat a University team in a 200-lap cycle race. But that's only the climax. Before that there's an in-depth study of the kids as they uncertainly embark on their adult lives after high school. Doesn't sound particularly exciting but it is, a *sleeper* that deserved more Academy Awards than it actually received. Set in small town Indiana. Could have done with a better title.

Box-office rental	$9,876,000
Average rental (79)	$31,964,775
Oscars (1)	Best Original Screenplay
Oscar nominations (4)	Best Film; Direction; Supporting Actress (Barrie); Adaptation Music Score

1979. Directed by Peter Yates.
Starring Dennis Christopher, Dennis Quaid, Daniel Stern, Jackie Earle Haley, Barbara Barrie, Paul Dooley. Colour.
101 minutes.

Twentieth Century-Fox Video

Breaking Glass

The oh-so-familiar tale of the rise and fall of a punk rock singer who starts from humble beginnings, becomes a top star then cracks up through ruthless exploitation, drugs and overwork. Composer-singer Hazel O'Connor leads the anarchic rebellion; *Breaking Glass* is the name of her band. Fans of the pink-haired Miss O'Connor will probably find this noisy tape worth the expense. Others less enamoured with her personality and the film's overall portrait of present-day London might find the proceedings rather less than exciting.

1980. Directed by Brian Gibson.
Starring Hazel O'Connor, Phil Daniels, Jon Finch, Jonathan Pryce, Peter-Hugo Daly, Mark Wingett. Colour.
104 minutes.

Picture Time Video
(*distributed by VCL*)

A Bridge Too Far

You could well have ear-ache plus a migraine by the time this one comes
to a close. It takes 175 minutes to retell the story of the fateful Battle Of
Arnhem – a battle which took place in September 1944 and resulted in
a humiliating defeat for the Allies, after they had parachuted into Holland
and tried to bring World War II to an early close by capturing six vital
bridges. An all-star cast helps you keep abreast of things: Robert Redford
gets his men across a river under heavy fire; Ryan O'Neal breaks his
back in the jump; Sean Connery is in there somewhere. So too are Dirk
Bogarde and Michael Caine. And Edward Fox offers another of his
well-known caricatures, this time of Lt. Gen. Brian Horrocks. But it's all
very long-winded and could well have benefited from being an hour
shorter. At the final count it emerges as a mosaic of destruction and
rather pedestrian video. 2½ rating.

Box-office rental	$21,000,000
Average rental (77)	$36,913,348

1977. Directed by Richard Attenborough.
Starring Dirk Bogarde, James Caan, Michael Caine, Sean Connery, Ed-
ward Fox, Elliott Gould, Gene Hackman, Anthony Hopkins, Hardy Kruger,
Laurence Olivier, Ryan O'Neal, Robert Redford, Maximilian Schell, Liv
Ullmann. Colour.
175 minutes.

Intervision

Brief Encounter

A man and a woman meet by chance at a railway station. He is a happily
married doctor; she is a happily-married suburban housewife. Without
quite realising it they fall in love. After spending a few furtive afternoons
together, they realise they have no chance of happiness and agree to
part. That's it. Just 86 minutes of video but a superb example of British
craftsmanship (it was the first movie in which David Lean was really given
his head as a director) and one of the most adult British films of the 40s.
Now much parodied by comedians, it looks terribly dated at times but
just adapt the situation into the 80s and you'll see what a clever and
enduring piece of work this is. Developed by Noel Coward from his own
one-act play. Trevor Howard and Celia Johnson play the hapless couple.

| Oscars | Nil |
| Oscar nominations (3) | Best Actress (Johnson); Direction; Screenplay |

1945. Directed by David Lean.
Starring Celia Johnson, Trevor Howard, Stanley Holloway, Joyce Carey, Cyril Raymond, Everley Gregg. Black and White.
86 minutes.

Rank Video

Note: They did update the film into a 1975 TV movie with Richard Burton and Sophia Loren but unfortunately didn't make a very good job of it. Still, the remake is available on Precision Video if you want to compare the two versions.

Brighton Rock

To claim that a film is not as good as the novel upon which it is based is always a little unfair, but Graham Greene's portrait of underworld life in a seedy and sordid prewar Brighton was so evocative and convincing that this film version tends to pale in comparison. Nonetheless, it *is* superior to most other British films of its period and contains one of Richard Attenborough's finest portrayals as Pinkie, a teenage razor hoodlum who murders a rival gangster and then tries to do the same to the 16-year-old waitress he has married to keep quiet. Realistic location work; notable support from William Hartnell, Wylie Watson and Nigel Stock as Attenborough's gangland friends.

1947. Directed by John Boulting.
Starring Richard Attenborough, Hermione Baddeley, William Hartnell, Carol Marsh, Nigel Stock, Wylie Watson, Harcourt Williams, Alan Wheatley. Black and White.
92 minutes.

Thorn EMI Video

Bringing Up Baby

It's amazing how many of Cary Grant's movies bear watching today. This one is no exception, for it's among the fastest and funniest Hollywood comedies of the late 30s. He's a staid professor who has been building the skeleton of a dinosaur for four years; Katharine Hepburn is the thorn in his flesh who involves him in a hunt for a tame leopard, a search for a bone, a weird household of Connecticut nuts and a crazy sheriff! Smashing stuff. It runs just over 100 minutes and crams an awful lot in during that time.

1938. Directed by Howard Hawks.
Starring Cary Grant, Katharine Hepburn, Charles Ruggles, Walter Catlett, Barry Fitzgerald, May Robson. Black and White.
102 minutes.

Thorn EMI Video

Bronco Billy

Not quite the type of Clint Eastwood movie his fans have come to expect, more a Frank Capra type comedy about a wandering urban cowboy (and ex-jailbird) who struggles to keep his tatty little Wild West Show on the road against all the odds. Runaway New York heiress Sondra Locke helps him in his quest. Pleasant, affable entertainment. Geoffrey Lewis is outstanding as Locke's opportunistic boyfriend. Above average. 2½ rating.

Box-office rental	$14,100,000
Average rental (80)	$30,086,027

1980. Directed by Clint Eastwood.
Starring Clint Eastwood, Sondra Locke, Geoffrey Lewis, Scatman Crothers, Bill McKinney, Sam Bottoms, Dan Vadis. Colour.
116 minutes.

Warner Home Video

The Brood

Hideous alien children – manifestations of the rage of a mentally disturbed woman – run around killing people before their creator dies from strangulation. A nauseating piece of rubbish that takes the cinema one step nearer the final frontier. Samantha Eggar (who once played Anna in a TV version of *The King And I*) is the mother of the brood; Oliver Reed plays a doctor.

1979. Directed by David Cronenberg.
Starring Oliver Reed, Samantha Eggar, Art Hindle, Cindy Hinds, Nuala Fitzgerald. Colour.
91 minutes.

Alpha Video
(*distributed by Intervision*)

Brubaker

Newly appointed warden Robert Redford poses as a prisoner and gets a close-up look at the workings of his jail from the inside. He doesn't like what he sees and sets out on a programme of reform. He also exposes the collusion of prison officers, the prison board and local businessmen in exploiting free labour. Very grim especially during its first thirty minutes; ultimately let down by a phoney upbeat ending. Based on fact.

Box-office rental	$19,000,000
Average rental (80)	$30,086,027
Oscars	Nil
Oscar nominations (1)	Best Screenplay

1980. Directed by Stuart Rosenberg.
Starring Robert Redford, Yaphet Kotto, Jane Alexander, Murray Hamilton, David Keith, Morgan Freeman. Colour.
130 minutes.

Twentieth Century-Fox Video

The Brute

The unpleasant experiences of fashion model wife Sarah Douglas at the hands of her brutal husband who beats her, chases her half-naked through the house and threatens to brand her while making love. Nice chap! Nasty film though which despite pretending to look at the very real problem of wife-beating succeeds only in coming across as a glossy piece of movie porn. The camera and the script leave nothing to chance. You see and hear it all!

1977. Directed by Gerry O'Hara.
Starring Sarah Douglas, Julian Glover, Bruce Robinson, Jenny Twigge, Suzanne Stone, Peter Bull, Charlotte Cornwell. Colour.
90 minutes.

Brent Walker Video
(*distributed by Videospace*)

Buck Rogers In The 25th Century

Buck Rogers, frozen in space for 700 years, returns to Earth and finds much of his beloved planet reduced to rubble and dust. Tongue-in-cheek science fiction that never takes itself too seriously although that, unfortunately, doesn't make it value for money. Pamela Hensley as a scantily-clad and quite gorgeous princess from another galaxy momentarily makes you feel that you haven't quite wasted your cash.

Box-office rental	$12,010,000
Average rental (79)	$31,964,775

1979. Directed by Daniel Haller.
Starring Gil Gerard, Pamela Hensley, Erin Gray, Tim O'Connor, Henry Silva, Joseph Wiseman. Colour.
89 minutes.

CIC Video

The Buddy Holly Story

Hollywood bio-pic of the 50s rock 'n roll performer who burned brightly for a few years before meeting a premature death in a plane crash at the age of 22. Gary Busey's look-alike performance earned him a rather surprising Oscar nomination. He also sings all of Holly's songs instead of miming the originals, which might disappoint Holly fans. The songs include "That'll Be The Day", "Peggy Sue", "Chantilly Lace", and "Words Of Love", but it all amounts to no more than standard rags-to-riches stuff and not unlike a small group version of *The Glenn Miller Story*.

Box-office rental	$5,900,000
Average rental (78)	$39,443,850
Oscars (1)	Best Adaptation Score
Oscar nominations (2)	Best Actor (Busey); Sound

1978. Directed by Steve Rash.
Starring Gary Busey, Don Stroud, Charles Martin Smith, Conrad Janis, William Jordan, Maria Richwine, Amy Johnston. Colour.
114 minutes.

Hokushin

Bugsy Malone

Quite why this movie is held in such high regard remains something of a mystery to this reviewer. It's original certainly – an all-child cast re-enacts a musical spoof of the American gangster movie of the 30s – but after the initial novelty of the idea has worn off it all becomes a bit too coy and cute and needs some good musical numbers to fill out some decidedly tedious passages. Paul Williams' score – despite its Oscar nomination – doesn't even come close. The kids are all excellent but the film is not exactly one to watch again and again and is only an average video purchase.

Oscars	Nil
Oscar nominations (1)	Best Original Song Score

1976. Directed by Alan Parker.

Starring Scott Baio, Jodie Foster, Florrie Dugger, John Cassisi, Martin Lev, Paul Murphy. Colour.
93 minutes.

Rank Video

Bullitt

Ruthless assistant DA Robert Vaughn hires conscientious cop Steve McQueen to guard a vital witness whose testimony will help smash a crime syndicate. But the witness is murdered and as the hunt for the killers begins the tension between Vaughn and McQueen begins to mount. The car chase in this thriller can be watched again and again and still you don't get bored. The question remains, however: "Is it the best car chase ever filmed or is the one in *The French Connection* its equal?" Well, both movies are available on video so you have the chance to compare the two.

Box-office rental	$19,000,000
Average rental (68)	$14,411,950
Oscars (1)	Best Editing
Oscar nominations (1)	Best Sound

1968. Directed by Peter Yates.
Starring Steve McQueen, Robert Vaughn, Jacqueline Bisset, Don Gordon, Robert Duvall, Simon Oakland, Normal Fell. Colour.
114 minutes.

Warner Home Video

Bus Stop

Marilyn Monroe out to prove she's a serious dramatic actress. And a pretty good job she makes of it too, as a tinselled floozie who sings in an Arizona cafe and finds that a naive young Montana cowboy (Don Murray) wants her for his wife – despite her dubious past. It's a static movie, set mostly in a roadside diner during a snowstorm, but the acting, especially of character performers Arthur O'Connell, Betty Field and Eileen Heckart, proves that lack of action need not necessarily be a fatal drawback. Based on the stage play by William Inge.

Box-office rental	$4,250,000
Average rental (56)	$8,814,900
Oscars	Nil
Oscar nominations (1)	Best Supporting Actor (Murray)

1956. Directed by Joshua Logan.
Starring Marilyn Monroe, Don Murray, Arthur O'Connell, Betty Field, Eileen Heckart. Colour.
96 minutes.

Twentieth Century-Fox Video

Butch And Sundance: The Early Days ★★

The sequel, sorry prequel, depicting how Butch and Sundance first got together and began their outlaw careers. Look-alikes Tom Berenger and William Katt do well with the leading roles (especially when one considers they are living in the shadows of such famous names) and Richard Lester takes pains to get some of the real West on the screen. But, inevitably, it's all a bit of a let-down. Jeff Corey as Sheriff Bledsoe is the only actor to appear in both films.

Oscars	Nil
Oscar nominations (1)	Best Costume Design

1979. Directed by Richard Lester.
Starring William Katt, Tom Berenger, Jeff Corey, John Schuck, Michael C. Gwynne, Peter Weller, Brian Dennehy. Colour.
112 minutes.

Twentieth Century-Fox Video

Butch Cassidy And The Sundance Kid ★★★★

Everyone's favourite Western? Probably, although as much for the fact that Redford and Newman are together as for any historical interest in the Old West at the turn-of-the-century. For the record, the film follows the last months in the lives of the two outlaws when they find their violent way of life (robbing trains and banks) rather difficult to sustain and head for new adventures – and death – in Bolivia. The handling is so light and easy that one forgets until the very end that this is a sad film. Poetic bicycle riding by Newman; a dubious cliff jump by Redford; a sexy striptease by Katharine Ross. Perfect.

Box-office rental	$46,039,000
Average rental (69)	$13,660,950
Oscars (4)	Best Story & Screenplay; Photography; Music Score; Song ("Raindrops Keep Falling On My Head")
Oscar nominations (3)	Best Film; Direction; Sound

1969. Directed by George Roy Hill.
Starring Paul Newman, Robert Redford, Katharine Ross, Strother Martin, Henry Jones, Jeff Corey, George Furth, Cloris Leachman. Colour.
110 minutes.

Twentieth Century-Fox Video

C

Cabaret ★★★★

Musical version of Christopher Isherwood's stories about an immoral show girl caught up in the rise of Nazism in prewar Berlin. Hardly the most uplifting of musicals, in fact in terms of content probably the most frightening musical ever made. Certainly no more malignant a character has ever been put on screen than Joel Grey's Master Of Ceremonies of the Kit Kat Klub. But still brilliant cinema and, together with the very different and much more gentle *My Fair Lady*, probably the most successful musical adaptation of a straight original ever put on stage or screen. Stunning video. Songs include "Money, Money", "Maybe This Time I'll Be Lucky", "Tomorrow Belongs To Me" and "Cabaret". (See also *I Am A Camera*.)

Box-office rental	$20,250,000
Average rental (72)	$17,543,950
Oscars (8)	Best Actress (Minnelli); Supporting Actor (Grey); Direction; Photography; Art Direction; Sound; Editing; Scoring Of A Musical
Oscar nominations (2)	Best Film; Screenplay

1972. Directed by Bob Fosse.
Starring Liza Minnelli, Michael York, Helmut Griem, Joel Grey, Fritz Wepper, Marisa Berenson. Colour.
123 minutes.

Rank Video

Caddyshack

Witless *Animal House*-type movie revolving around a high school senior who takes a vacation job as a golf caddy at an American country club and finishes up actually playing in a vital $40,000 golf match. One of the jokes revolves around a bar of chocolate being found in a swimming pool and being mistaken for a turd. Funny? There's plenty more where that came from.

Box-office rental	$20,000,000
Average rental (80)	$30,086,027

1980. Directed by Harold Ramis.
Starring Chevy Chase, Rodney Dangerfield, Ted Knight, Michael O'Keefe, Bill Murray, Sarah Holcomb. Colour.
98 minutes.

Warner Home Video

California Suite

Four Neil Simon vignettes all based at the Beverly Hills Hotel and ranging from the good – actress Maggie Smith in town with reluctant hubby Michael Caine for the Oscar ceremonies – to the mundane – Richard Pryor and Bill Cosby as two doctors nearing the end of an exhausting vacation. Jane Fonda catches fire for a few moments as a hardbitten New York lady out to reclaim her teenage daughter. Uneven but witty, very civilized and *very* entertaining. Ear-catching music score by Claude Bolling.

Box-office rental	$29,200,000
Average rental (78)	$39,443,850
Oscars (1)	Best Supporting Actress (Smith)
Oscar nominations (2)	Best Screenplay; Art Direction

1978. Directed by Herbert Ross.
Starring Alan Alda, Michael Caine, Bill Cosby, Jane Fonda, Walter Matthau, Elaine May, Richard Pryor, Maggie Smith. Colour.
103 minutes.

RCA/Columbia International Video

The Call Of The Wild

Jack London's classic tale of a man and his dog adventuring during the Klondike gold rush. It's a great story on the printed page but in this version at least not of any great quality on the screen. Five countries had a hand in its production and it shows. The Norwegian locations are a plus factor.

1973. Directed by Ken Annakin.
Starring Charlton Heston, Michele Mercier, Raimund Harmstorf, George Eastman, Maria Rohm, Juan Luis Galiardo. Colour.
105 minutes.

Guild Home Video

Camelot

Guenevere (Vanessa Redgrave) flirts with Lancelot (Franco Nero) in the mythical kingdom of Camelot whilst King Arthur (Richard Harris) looks on morosely and sings "How To Handle A Woman." Harris and the sets are splendid but this is a long, long haul and at times makes you feel as though you have been sitting in front of the screen forever. The lovely Lerner & Loewe songs – "Take Me To The Fair", "If Ever I Would Leave You", "What Do The Simple Folk Do?", etc – just about make it worthwhile but only just. The rest is uninspired. Director Logan's frequent use of close-ups benefits video viewing.

Box-office rental	$14,000,000
Average rental (67)	$13,081,250
Oscars (3)	Best Art Direction; Costume Design; Scoring Of Music
Oscar nominations (2)	Best Photography; Sound

1967. Directed by Joshua Logan.
Starring Richard Harris, Vanessa Redgrave, Franco Nero, David Hemmings, Lionel Jeffries, Laurence Naismith, Estelle Winwood. Colour.
180 minutes.

Warner Home Video

Canadian Pacific

If anyone can ensure that the Canadian Pacific Railroad gets built it's rough-tough surveyor and troubleshooter Randolph Scott. Still, there are a few who don't believe he can make it, among them villainous Victor Jory, a trapper who whips the Indians up against the rail pioneers. Standard Hollywood Western, filmed in the Rockies. Dreadful Cinecolor.

1949. Directed by Edward L. Marin.
Starring Randolph Scott, Jane Wyatt, J. Carrol Naish, Victor Jory, Nancy Olson. Colour.
95 minutes.

Intervision

Can-Can

Not one of Hollywood's most successful attempts at transferring a stage musical to the screen. In fact, rather a limp and tepid exercise with Parisian lawyer Frank Sinatra trying to persuade judge Maurice Chevalier to stop the gendarmes closing down the nightclub of his girl-friend Shirley MacLaine. Bouncing Shirl is at her best when she's high-kicking the Can-Can. So is the film. Frank Sinatra cashes in with three Cole Porter standards that weren't in the original show: "Let's Do It", "Just One Of Those Things" and "You Do Something To Me". Most of the other songs were dropped. The period is the 1890s.

Box-office rental	$4,200,000
Average rental (60)	$6,787,500
Oscars	Nil
Oscar nominations (2)	Best Costume Design; Scoring Of A Musical

1960. Directed by Walter Lang.
Starring Frank Sinatra, Shirley MacLaine, Maurice Chevalier, Louis Jourdan, Juliet Prowse, Marcel Dalio. Colour.
131 minutes.

Twentieth Century-Fox Video

The Candidate

Idealistic young lawyer/civil rights worker Robert Redford agrees to run for the Senate only when he is assured by the Democratic Party that he has no chance of winning and that he can speak his own mind on important issues. But the plan backfires. He doesn't lose, he wins and finds himself on the way to the Senate, not a little bewildered and asking in desperation, "What do we do now?" What *you* could do now is to take a peek at this neat little movie which shows what a dirty game American politics really is. And if that doesn't grab you as a subject there's always the boyish charm of Mr. Redford to carry you along.

Oscars (1)	Best Story & Screenplay
Oscar nominations (1)	Best Sound

1972. Directed by Michael Ritchie.

Starring Robert Redford, Melvyn Douglas, Peter Boyle, Don Porter, Allen Garfield, Karen Carlson, Quinn Redeker. Colour.
110 minutes.

Warner Home Video

A Candle For The Devil

Sexual frustration, religious mania and grisly goings-on (murder by meat cleaver, axe, knife, etc.) in a Spanish village hotel run by Aurora Bautista and her sister. Formula horror stuff and certainly nothing to get worked up about. Judy Geeson is the only well-known name in the cast and one of the few survivors.

1973. Directed by Eugene Martin.
Starring Judy Geeson, Aurora Bautista, Esperanza Roy, Vic Winner, Lone Fleming. Colour.
84 minutes.

Vampix
(distributed by Videomedia)

Can't Stop The Music

But oh, oh, if only they could! This is a perfect example of promotion before story, exploitation before thought and of a movie being made to further the career of a pop group rather than entertain its audience. "Give 'em this and they'll accept anything" appears to be the thinking behind this mish-mash about an aspiring young composer who rounds up a group of Greenwich Village singers to help promote his music. From then on it's downhill all the way. "This is the music of the 80s" claims the hero. Roll on the 90s or, preferably, bring back the 40s and 50s. The one star is for colourful art direction.

1980. Directed by Nancy Walker.

Starring The Village People, Valerie Perrine, Bruce Jenner, Steve Guttenberg. Colour.
124 minutes.

Thorn EMI Video

Capricorn One

Three astronauts become national heroes when they land on Mars and their pictures are transmitted back to Earth via satellite. But are they really up there? Where is the tangible proof? Is it all a hoax? And what has an air base hidden away in the desert got to do with it all? An intriguing premiss and one that is built up quite cleverly in the opening reels of this movie. Then invention flags and the whole thing disintegrates into just another action flick full of plane crashes, helicopter chases, cars careering out of control, etc. In the end just another movie. Some good opportunities missed, for this could have been a really chilling thriller.

Box-office rental	$12,000,000
Average rental (78)	$39,443,850

1978. Directed by Peter Hyams.
Starring Elliott Gould, James Brolin, Brenda Vaccaro, Sam Waterston, O. J. Simpson, Hal Holbrook, Karen Black, Telly Savalas. Colour.
124 minutes.

Precision Video

Captain Apache

For *devotees* of the Continental Western; Lee Van Cleef has the title role, an Indian serving with the U.S. Army and assigned to track down the killers of an Indian Commissioner. A corrupt sheriff, a gold-digging adventuress, much brutality by all concerned and even two songs sung, believe it or not, by Lee Van Cleef, are what you get for your money. Need one say more!

1971. Directed by Alexander Singer.

Starring Lee Van Cleef, Carroll Baker, Stuart Whitman, Percy Herbert, Tony Vogel. Colour.
94 minutes.

Cinema Features
(*distributed by VCL*)

Caravan To Vaccares

Most of Alistair MacLean's novels have reached the screen, some more successfully than others. This one falls into the "also ran" category, and features David Birney as a footloose American who is hired to escort a mysterious Hungarian to New York. Why? The Hungarian has worked out a formula for a fuel substitute and some crooks want to prevent him from delivering it to the United Nations. Cliché-ridden stuff; Charlotte Rampling provides glamorous relief.

1974. Directed by Geoffrey Reeve.
Starring Charlotte Rampling, David Birney, Michel Lonsdale, Marcel Bozzuffi, Michael Bryant. Colour.
98 minutes.

Derann Video

Carefree

Not by any means top-grade Astaire/Rogers – he's a psychiatrist, she's a songstress who goes to him for treatment – but with the usual moments of charm and of course many Irving Berlin numbers, among them "Change Partners And Dance"; "I Used To Be Colour Blind"; "The Yam" and "The Night Is Filled With Music". On the same video double-bill: *Easy Living*.

Oscars	Nil
Oscar nominations (3)	Best Art Direction; Song ("Change Partners And Dance"); Music Scoring

1938. Directed by Mark Sandrich.

Starring Fred Astaire, Ginger Rogers, Ralph Bellamy, Luella Gear, Jack Carson. Black and White.
83 minutes.

Kingston Video

Carnal Knowledge

Much underrated Mike Nichols movie about the frustrations and sexual obsessions of two men, from their life in college in the mid-40s to a despairing middle age. Pessimistic but very truthful in its observations of how men can drift into a depressing conformity. Bachelor Jack Nicholson and Art Garfunkel whose marriage ends in failure are the two men; Ann-Margret is a knockout as Nicholson's kittenish mistress. The final memory of a beautiful skater circling on the ice leaves you emotionally shattered. Worth a look. Highly erotic.

Box-office rental	$12,351,000
Average rental (71)	$13,465,850
Oscars	Nil
Oscar nominations (1)	Best Supporting Actress (Ann-Margret)

1971. Directed by Mike Nichols.
Starring Jack Nicholson, Candice Bergen, Art Garfunkel, Ann-Margret, Rita Moreno, Cynthia O'Neal, Carol Kane. Colour.
96 minutes.

Twentieth Century-Fox Video

Carquake

Back on the *Death Race 2000* circuit with David Carradine once more behind the wheel and after the $100,000 prize in the no-holds-barred Grand Prix Motor Race across America. Plenty of fatal accidents, crashes at 175 miles per hour, etc. There's also an all-girls team. Roger Corman guests in a cameo part as a district attorney. Martin Scorsese is another director who puts in an appearance. Known as *Cannonball* in the States.

1976. Directed by Paul Bartel.
Starring David Carradine, Bill McKinney, Veronica Hamel, Gerrit Graham, Robert Carradine, Judy Canova. Colour.
91 minutes.

Picture Time Video
(distributed by VCL)

Carrie

Poor little misfit Sissy Spacek is mocked by her high-school classmates, who pay the penalty when they realise too late that she is possessed of telekinetic powers and can blast 'em all to smithereens. Which she does. A frightening Brian De Palma movie, but as crude and flashy as they come and with scarcely a hint of subtlety in its entire running time. Piper Laurie as Carrie's mom finishes up a victim when she is crucified by flying kitchen knives; John Travolta also ends up on the casualty list when Sissy decides enough is enough and utterly destroys the school prom. Watch out for a scarey last scene.

Box-office rental	$15,000,000
Average rental (76)	$22,752,350
Oscars	Nil
Oscar nominations (2)	Best Actress (Spacek); Supporting Actress (Laurie)

1976. Directed by Brian De Palma.
Starring Sissy Spacek, Piper Laurie, Amy Irving, William Katt, John Travolta, Nancy Allen. Colour.
98 minutes.

Intervision

Carrington V.C.

Courtroom drama with army major David Niven facing a charge of embezzling mess funds and up for court-martial. Actually, he's only swiped the cash because the army hasn't come up with some back pay and because neurotic wife Margaret Leighton is always on the nag. Terribly British and terribly decent movie, now a little on the quaint side, although thanks to the skilful handling of Anthony Asquith still quite watchable. Based on a play by Dorothy and Campbell Christie. 2½ rating.

1954. Directed by Anthony Asquith.
Starring David Niven, Margaret Leighton, Noelle Middleton, Laurence Naismith, Clive Morton, Mark Dignam, Allan Cuthbertson, Victor Maddern. Black and White.
105 minutes.

Twentieth Century-Fox Video

Carry On Abroad ★★

The Carry On team off on a package holiday to a Mediterranean island where they find their hotel only half built, staffed by just three people and lacking private bathrooms. Kenneth Williams is the courier. Sample joke: "Please Miss Plunkett, you're squashing my itinerary!" You know what to expect. Average entertainment, probably four star video if you revel in the double-innuendo.

1972. Directed by Gerald Thomas.
Starring Sidney James, Kenneth Williams, Charles Hawtrey, Joan Sims, Kenneth Connor, Peter Butterworth, Jimmy Logan, Barbara Windsor, June Whitfield, Hattie Jacques, Bernard Bresslaw. Colour.
88 minutes.

Rank Video

Carry On At Your Convenience ★

If one assumes that the Carry On movies have a standard then this one is strictly below par. Sid James, Charles Hawtrey, Joan Sims and co. are all involved in working at a lavatory factory named W. C. Boggs and Sons and find themselves on a one-day strike because of a dispute over tea breaks. This was Number 22 in the series and it shows.

1971. Directed by Gerald Thomas.
Starring Sidney James, Kenneth Williams, Charles Hawtrey, Joan Sims, Hattie Jacques, Bernard Bresslaw, Kenneth Cope. Colour.
90 minutes.

Rank Video

Carry On Behind

One of the better Carry On movies with archaeologist Kenneth Williams and sexy Russian assistant Elke Sommer at large on a dig behind a holiday caravan site. Plenty of sight gags and farce situations and almost a reprise of *Carry On Camping*. But no Sid James on this occasion.

1975. Directed by Gerald Thomas.
Starring Elke Sommer, Kenneth Williams, Joan Sims, Bernard Bresslaw, Jack Douglas, Windsor Davies, Kenneth Connor, Liz Fraser, Peter Butterworth. Colour.
90 minutes.

Rank Video

Carry On Camping

Sid James and Bernard Bresslaw take girlfriends Joan Sims and Dilys Laye to a holiday camp in Devon. End of story but beginning of smutty situations, for the camp is teeming with just about everyone in the Carry On crowd including Kenneth Williams and Hattie Jacques as two teachers in charge of a young ladies finishing school called Chayste Place.

1969. Directed by Gerald Thomas.
Starring Sidney James, Kenneth Williams, Joan Sims, Charles Hawtrey, Bernard Bresslaw, Terry Scott, Barbara Windsor, Hattie Jacques, Peter Butterworth, Dilys Laye. Colour.
88 minutes.

Rank Video

Carry On Cleo

This isn't exactly history, but then you wouldn't expect it, would you, with Sid James as Marc Antony, Kenneth Williams as Julius Caesar and Amanda Barrie as Cleopatra. Kenneth Connor is also in there somewhere as an inventor called Pod who is working on a square wheel. And then there's Sheila Hancock as his wife Senna Pod . . . Oh, well!

1965. Directed by Gerald Thomas.
Starring Sidney James, Kenneth Williams, Kenneth Connor, Charles Hawtrey, Joan Sims, Jim Dale, Amanda Barrie, Sheila Hancock. Colour.
92 minutes.

Thorn EMI Video

Carry On Emmannuelle

The Carry On team head for the X-certificate market (not quite, the movie was AA in the cinemas) as French ambassador's wife Suzanne Danielle seduces her way through what is left of the old gang. Kenneth Connor, Jack Douglas and Peter Butterworth are among her victims; Kenneth Williams is the French ambassador and spends most of the movie in his boxing shorts.

1978. Directed by Gerald Thomas.
Starring Suzanne Danielle, Kenneth Williams, Kenneth Connor, Jack Douglas, Joan Sims, Peter Butterworth, Beryl Reid. Colour.
88 minutes.

Picture Time Video
(distributed by VCL)

Carry On Henry

The casting gives you some idea of what to expect from this Carry On offering: Sid James as Henry VIII, Kenneth Williams as Thomas Cromwell, Terry Scott as Cardinal Wolsey ... The whole thing revolves around

Henry's discovery that his garlic-loving queen has been made pregnant by her lover. Characteristically lewd; not very funny.

1970. Directed by Gerald Thomas.
Starring Sidney James, Kenneth Williams, Joan Sims, Charles Hawtrey, Terry Scott, Barbara Windsor, Kenneth Connor. Colour.
89 minutes.

Rank Video

Carry On Matron

Sid James, convinced he can make a fortune by selling contraceptive pills abroad, disguises his son as a nurse and sends him to a maternity hospital to obtain a steady supply. The rest is chaos. The alternative titles that appear during the film's credits include "From Here to Maternity" and "Womb At The Top". At one point during the proceedings Sid also has to adopt a medical alias – Doctor Zhivago!

1972. Directed by Gerald Thomas.
Starring Sidney James, Kenneth Williams, Hattie Jacques, Charles Hawtrey, Barbara Windsor, Terry Scott, Joan Sims, Kenneth Cope, Bernard Bresslaw, Kenneth Connor. Colour.
87 minutes.

Rank Video

Carry On Nurse

Hattie Jacques as the hospital matron; a long series of blue jokes (although not nearly as blue as some of those employed later in the series); and a motley collection of patients who include Kenneth Connor, Kenneth Williams, Charles Hawtrey and Leslie Phillips. During the movie they decide to carry out their own operation for a bunion removal. The mind boggles! Quite good fun for its level and the top British moneymaker of 1959. The second in the long-running Carry On Series.

1959. Directed by Gerald Thomas.

Starring Kenneth Connor, Kenneth Williams, Charles Hawtrey, Terence Longdon, Shirley Eaton, Bill Owen, Leslie Phillips, Hattie Jacques, Joan Sims. Black and White.
86 minutes.

Thorn EMI Video

Carry On Up The Jungle ★

The Carry On team (without Kenneth Williams but with Frankie Howerd as a replacement) set out into a Pinewood studio jungle to search for the rare Oozulum bird of Africa. Sid James plays a white hunter, Bernard Bresslaw his assistant native tracker Upsidasi!

1970. Directed by Gerald Thomas.
Starring Frankie Howerd, Sidney James, Charles Hawtrey, Joan Sims, Terry Scott, Kenneth Connor, Bernard Bresslaw. Colour.
89 minutes.

Rank Video

Carry On . . . Up The Khyber ★★

The setting: India, 1895. Sid James is the governor of the Northwest Frontier. Up against him is his deadly enemy – Kenneth Williams as the Khasi of Kalabar. On Sid's side: the feared Highland regiment, The Third Foot and Mouth. Supporting Ken: The Burpa tribesmen. Hardly a masterpiece but, on its level, one of the best of the Carry On team's ribald excursions into history.

1968. Directed by Gerald Thomas.
Starring Sidney James, Kenneth Williams, Charles Hawtrey, Roy Castle, Joan Sims, Bernard Bresslaw, Petter Butterworth, Terry Scott. Colour.
88 minutes.

Rank Video

Casablanca

What is there left to say about *Casablanca* that hasn't already been said? Bogie and Bergman rekindling a love they lost in Paris; Conrad Veidt hunting down resistance leader Paul Henreid; Sydney Greenstreet idly swatting flies; Claude Rains as a Vichy official running with the wind. And, of course, Dooley Wilson singing "As Time Goes By". An unrepeatable cast and unrepeatable value. Perhaps it wouldn't seem as effective if they still made movies like it today. But they don't!

Oscars (3)	Best Film; Director; Screenplay
Oscar nominations (5)	Best Actor (Bogart); Supporting Actor (Rains); Photography; Editing; Music Score

1943. Directed by Michael Curtiz.
Starring Humphrey Bogart, Ingrid Bergman, Paul Henreid, Claude Rains, Conrad Veidt, Sydney Greenstreet, Peter Lorre, S. Z. Sakall. Black and White.
102 minutes.

Intervision

The Cassandra Crossing

A terrorist carrying a deadly plague virus boards a train at Geneva and everyone on board finds themselves in danger of contamination. Neurosurgeon Richard Harris (with a little help from Sophia Loren) tries to take care of the passengers; intelligence officer Burt Lancaster wisely directs operations from afar. The further *you* can get away from this preposterous movie the better!

Box-office rental	$4,184,000
Average rental (77)	$36,913,348

1977. Directed by George Pan Cosmatos.
Starring Sophia Loren, Richard Harris, Ava Gardner, Burt Lancaster, Martin Sheen, Ingrid Thulin, Lee Strasberg, John Phillip Law, Ann Turkel, O. J. Simpson, Lionel Stander. Colour.
129 minutes.

Precision Video

The Cat And The Canary

Abysmal remake of John Willard's classic old house tale about some greedy relatives who gather to hear the reading of the will of an eccentric millionaire on the twentieth anniversary of his death. Made twice before (in 1927 and 1939) and on both occasions with some style. Not this time. Despite the usual cinematic old house trickery – sliding panels, secret torture chambers and the like – this one comes over with a dull thud. The cast looks promising. Don't be fooled.

1978. Directed by Radley Metzger.
Starring Honor Blackman, Michael Callan, Edward Fox, Wendy Hiller, Olivia Hussey, Beatrix Lehmann, Carol Lynley, Daniel Massey, Peter McEnery, Wilfrid Hyde White. Colour.
98 minutes.

Video Unlimited

Cat Ballou

Spoof Western that hasn't survived the test of time too well, although Lee Marvin's Oscar-winning portrait of a drunken gunfighter (and also that of his vicious twin Silvernose) still manages to tickle the ribs from time to time. Plot has lovely schoolteacher Jane Fonda turning outlaw to avenge the death of her rancher father. Nat King Cole and Stubby Kaye accompany the action as a kind of minstrel chorus. 2½ rating.

Box-office rental	$9,300,000
Average rental (65)	$13,881,050
Oscars (1)	Best Actor (Marvin)
Oscar nominations (4)	Best Screenplay; Editing; Scoring Of Music; Song ("The Ballad Of Cat Ballou")

1965. Directed by Elliott Silverstein.
Starring Jane Fonda, Lee Marvin, Michael Callan, Dwayne Hickman, Nat King Cole, Stubby Kaye. Colour.
96 minutes.

RCA/Columbia International Video

Caught

A good example of the type of well-made melodrama that used to creep out of Hollywood in the 40s and get lost among all the bigger budget movies that received greater publicity. Thanks to director Max Ophuls, this one has style and quite a few emotional complexities as it unfolds a tale of a young woman (Barbara Bel Geddes) who finds unhappiness and brutality at the hands of her tycoon husband (Robert Ryan) and understanding from a young doctor (James Mason). A minor treasure hidden away on the video lists.

1949. Directed by Max Ophuls.
Starring James Mason, Barbara Bel Geddes, Robert Ryan, Frank Ferguson, Curt Bois, Natalie Schafer. Black and White.
88 minutes.

Intervision

Cauldron Of Blood

Cheap horror flick with Boris Karloff as a blind sculptor whose wife provides him with skeleton bones in order to help him with his work. Sounds neighbourly. Trouble is that the skeletons all belong to people she has murdered and that poor old Boris is blind because she tried to murder him! Not a nice person to have around. Not a very satisfactory movie.

1967. Directed by Edward Mann.
Starring Jean-Pierre Aumont, Boris Karloff, Viveca Lindfors, Rosenda Monteros, Milo Queseda. Colour.
101 minutes.

Vampix
(distributed by Videomedia)

Centrefold Girls

A psychotic killer believes that girls who take their clothes off and appear nude in men's magazines are sick. So he takes off on a murder rampage and works his way through quite a few girls before getting a dose of his own medicine at the hands of one of his would-be victims. Hardly cosy entertainment; exploits sex and violence to the full.

1974. Directed by John Peyser.
Starring Andrew Prine, Jaime Lyn Bauer, Janet Woods, Jennifer Ashley, Kitty Carl. Colour.
91 minutes.

Intervision

The Champ

Can drunken ex-boxer Jon Voight come out of retirement and make enough money to keep his small son out of the clutches of former wife Faye Dunaway, who deserted them both years before but now wants her little boy back? Big question, soggy answer. This one's so wet that you become knee-deep in tears before half-an-hour has elapsed. And although you are bound to say at the close, "What a load of . . .", my hunch is that you won't turn off. And that's mainly what this kind of entertainment's all about. Beautiful colour effects as always from Zeffirelli.

Box-office rental	$12,600,000
Average rental (79)	$31,964,775
Oscars	Nil
Oscar nominations (1)	Best Music

1979. Directed by Franco Zeffirelli.
Starring Jon Voight, Faye Dunaway, Ricky Schroder, Jack Warden, Arthur Hill, Strother Martin, Joan Blondell. Colour.
121 minutes.

MGM/CBS Home Video

Champion

The film that made Kirk Douglas a star. The story of a young boxer who determines to fight his way to the top no matter what the cost to all those around him – his wife, his crippled brother, his long-suffering manager, and so forth. Familiar? Yes, the story has since become a movie cliché but, despite the advent of the *Rocky* films, the boxing sequences remain as realistic as ever and there's always Marilyn Maxwell, Lola Albright and Ruth ("white bathing suit") Roman to soften the effect of the ferocious Mr. Douglas.

Oscars (1)   Best Editing
Oscar nominations (5)   Best Actor (Douglas); Supporting Actor
                              (Kennedy); Screenplay; Photography; Music

1949. Directed by Mark Robson.
Starring Kirk Douglas, Marilyn Maxwell, Arthur Kennedy, Paul Stewart, Ruth Roman, Lola Albright. Black and White.
99 minutes.

Spectrum
(distributed by Polygram)

Chariots Of Fire

Quality movie that gives rise to the hope that British films might once again reach the standard of the late 40s and early 50s when David Lean and Carol Reed dominated the scene. The story is of two athletes, both outsiders and both running for a cause in the 1924 Olympics in Paris – Jewish Harold Abrahams, who runs to overcome the prejudice he experiences at Cambridge University and missionary's son Eric Liddell, who runs for the greater glory of God. A remarkable all-round achievement that is served well by the video process, so much so that it might have been made for TV. Which is a converse way of saying that it is very good indeed and in the *Tinker, Tailor, Brideshead Revisited* class.

Oscars (4)   Best Film; Original Screenplay; Costume
                              Design; Music Score

Oscar nominations (3)   Supporting Actor (Holm); Direction; Editing

1981. Directed by Hugh Hudson.
Starring Ben Cross, Ian Charleson, Nigel Havers, Nicholas Farrell, Daniel Gerroll, Cheryl Campbell, Alice Krige, John Gielgud, Lindsay Anderson, Nigel Davenport, Ian Holm. Colour.
121 minutes.

Twentieth Century-Fox Video

Charley-One-Eye

An on-the-run negro soldier teams up with a lone Indian after deserting from the Union Army during the Civil War. Together they try to make a new life for themselves on the Mexican border. A ruthless bounty hunter tracks them down however and makes sure that they are not left in peace. Spanish-made Western with the usual locational deficiencies but, of its kind, fairly respectable and not without its moments of interest. Richard Roundtree and Roy Thinnes also manage to make something of their roles as soldier and Indian respectively.

1972. Directed by Don Chaffey.
Starring Richard Roundtree, Roy Thinnes, Nigel Davenport, Jill Pearson, Aldo Sambrell. Colour.
96 minutes.

Intervision

Charlotte's Web

A lonely and unhappy piglet is horrified to learn that pigs are raised for the sole purpose of turning them into ham and bacon. Charlotte, a friendly spider, decides to save him from that fate by spinning a magic web. Average feature-length cartoon version of E. B. White's classic fantasy; should have been more imaginative considering it comes from the studio of Hanna and Barbera who, between them, were responsible for the great Tom and Jerry cartoons of the 40s. Debbie Reynolds (Charlotte), Agnes

Moorehead and Martha Scott are among the star names lending their voices to the characters.

1973. Directed by Charles A. Nichols and Iwao Takamoto.
Colour.
96 minutes.

Home Video Productions

Charly

Surely one of the most moving experiences on video; the heartbreaking tale of a mentally retarded 30-year-old who is turned into a superbrain after experimental surgery, falls in love with his teacher, and then reverts back to his former self when the effects of the experiment begin to wear off. Great acting from Robertson in the title role and warm, sympathetic support from Claire Bloom as the teacher. Split screen techniques irritate video viewing but it's a five-handkerchief experience all the way.

Box-office rental	$7,260,000
Average rental (68)	$14,411,950
Oscars (1)	Best Actor (Robertson)
Oscar nominations:	Nil

1968. Directed by Ralph Nelson.
Starring Cliff Robertson, Claire Bloom, Leon Janney, Lilia Skala, Dick Van Patton, William Dwyer. Colour.
103 minutes.

Rank Video

Children Shouldn't Play With Dead Things

A group of actors mess about trying to raise the dead on a lonely burial island off the East Coast of the United States. A little annoyed at being woken from their slumbers, the dead emerge as zombies and wreak vengeance on the meddlers, the last of whom is eaten alive. Serves 'em right. On a rating of one to ten this one barely gets past the figure two.

1974. Directed by Benjamin Clark.
Starring Alan Ormsby, Anya Ormsby, Valerie Mamches, Jane Daly, Jeffrey Gillen. Colour.
87 minutes.

Intervision

The China Syndrome

Jane Fonda has the knack of appearing in topical movies and she couldn't have been more up-to-the minute than with this one, which was released just a matter of weeks before the atomic power disaster on Three Mile Island in Pennsylvania. No matter which way you look at it – exposé movie or thriller – it works beautifully, as TV reporter Fonda discovers a cover-up at a Californian nuclear plant and supervisor Jack Lemmon spills the beans about some faulty equipment. Terrifying if you think about it too much but great video entertainment. And very fast-moving.

Box-office rental	$26,073,700
Average rental (79)	$31,964,775
Oscars	Nil
Oscar nominations (4)	Best Actor (Lemmon); Actress (Fonda); Screenplay; Art Direction

1979. Directed by James Bridges.
Starring Jane Fonda, Jack Lemmon, Michael Douglas, Scott Brady, James Hampton, Peter Donat, Wilford Brimley, Richard Herd. Colour.
122 minutes.

RCA/Columbia International Video

Chinatown

This one needs following carefully for it's in the Hammett/Chandler tradition, which means that if you lose the thread for an instant you'll never pick it up again. The whole thing revolves around matrimonial private-eye Jack Nicholson who becomes entangled in a series of nasty goings-on in prewar Los Angeles when a man is found dead in the city sewers. Nicholson looks puzzled for much of the time, which is not surprising since he's trying to discover why Faye Dunaway is such a double-crosser, why vicious little thug Roman Polanski insists on ripping open his nose with a flick-knife and why malevolent landowner John Huston delights in eating his fish with their heads still on. Try and stay with this one if you can. Video slows it down quite a bit but it's in the classic mould and already they don't make movies like this anymore.

Box-office rental	$12,400,000
Average rental (74)	$18,456,150
Oscars (1)	Best Original Screenplay
Oscar nominations (10)	Best Film; Actor (Nicholson); Actress (Dunaway); Direction; Photography; Art Direction; Costume Design; Sound; Editing; Original Score

1974. Directed by Roman Polanski.
Starring Jack Nicholson, Faye Dunaway, John Huston, Perry Lopez, John Hillerman, Darrell Zwerling, Diane Ladd, Roman Polanski. Colour.
131 minutes.

CIC Video

Chisum

Cattle baron John Wayne up against corrupt businessman Forrest Tucker who is buying land in New Mexico at the time of the Lincoln County War. Standard Western fare, which has a vigorous climactic fistfight and a rousing score by Dominic Frontiere as two of its attributes. One good scene has a Mexican rustler trying to sell back some cows he has stolen from Wayne. Says he: "Did you bring some gold with you?" Replies Wayne curtly: "No." Persists the Mexican: "Silver?" Wayne shakes his head: "No, just lead!" You know the rest.

Box-office rental $6,000,000
Average rental (70) $16,881,800

1970. Directed by Andrew V. McLaglen.
Starring John Wayne, Forrest Tucker, Christopher George, Ben Johnson, Bruce Cabot. Colour.
110 minutes.

Warner Home Video

Chitty Chitty Bang Bang

Inventor Caractacus Potts hits the jackpot when he comes up with a magical flying car that transmits him and his children to the mythical kingdom of Vulgaria, where all children are declared illegal. Sounds like a good idea (the latter part anyway) but it's a case of missed opportunities all the way along the line, and a film that should have run for 90 minutes is padded out to a tedious 145. The end result has you looking anxiously for the closing titles and the "off" switch. Poor special effects and a *Mary Poppins*-type score don't exactly help things either, although Anna Quayle as a wicked baroness and Robert Helpmann as the official child-catcher liven things up a bit towards the end.

Box-office rental $7,075,000
Average rental (68) $14,411,950
Oscars Nil
Oscar nominations (1) Best Song ("Chitty Chitty Bang Bang")

1968. Directed by Ken Hughes.
Starring Dick Van Dyke, Sally Ann Howes, Lionel Jeffries, Gert Frobe, Anna Quayle, Benny Hill, James Robertson Justice, Robert Helpmann. Colour.
145 minutes.

Intervision

The Circus

Charlie Chaplin's optimistic little tramp finds a job in a circus where he becomes a top clown and also, in one superb scene, a stand-in tightrope walker. Not Chaplin's best-known or most accomplished work; although as always, the pathos and slapstick are perfectly blended and the gags impeccably timed. Won Chaplin a special Oscar for "his versatility and genius in writing, acting, directing and producing *The Circus*". Supported on this video tape by a 1919 Chaplin two-reeler, *A Day's Pleasure*.

1928. Directed By Charles Chaplin.
Starring Charles Chaplin, Myrna Kennedy, Betty Morrissey, Harry Crocker, Allan Garcia, Henry Bergman, Stanley J. Sanford. Black and White.
72 minutes.

Spectrum
(distributed by Polygram)

Circus World

John Wayne as a circus manager; Rita Hayworth as a frumpish ex-acrobat who has left the trapeze and gone on the bottle; Claudia Cardinale as her pretty spitfire daughter. Or, if you prefer, a turn-of-the-century circus story that plods from one scene to the next with an ominous predictability. Director Henry Hathaway should have been able to come up with something better than this, although he handles a big top fire with some assurance. OK but only just.

1964. Directed by Henry Hathaway.
Starring John Wayne, Rita Hayworth, Claudia Cardinale, Lloyd Nolan, Richard Conte. Colour.
135 minutes.

Intervision

Citizen Kane

The life and death of a newspaper tycoon, told in flashback and pieced together by a newsreel reporter as he interviews those most closely connected with the magnate during his lifetime. Generally considered to be the greatest film of all time and ideal video entertainment in that it can be watched again and again and always comes up fresh and exciting. The dramatic lighting of Gregg Toland adds immeasurably to the film's effectiveness as does the screenplay of Herman Mankiewicz, who worked on the script with the young Orson Welles. But it is Welles' film from first to last. He is credited in the acting, direction and writing categories but he had a hand in just about everything. Great film and great video.

Oscars (1) Best Original Screenplay
Oscar nominations (8) Best Film; Actor (Welles); Direction;
Photography; Art Direction; Sound
Recording; Editing; Music Score

1941. Directed by Orson Welles.
Starring Orson Welles, Dorothy Comingore, Joseph Cotten, Everett Sloane, George Coulouris, Ray Collins, Ruth Warrick, Erskine Sanford, Agnes Moorehead, Paul Stewart. Black and White.
119 minutes.

Thorn EMI Video

City Lights

Celebrated Charlie Chaplin film about the little tramp's efforts to restore the sight of a pretty young flower-seller. The usual Chaplin mixture of pathos, slapstick and mime with Charlie's hilarious boxing match with Hank Mann as the standout sequence. Made in 1931 but silent, despite the fact that Chaplin halted production halfway through to consider re-shooting in sound. Watch out for the young Jean Harlow as an extra in a night-club sequence.

1931. Directed by Charles Chaplin.

Starring Charles Chaplin, Virginia Cherrill, Harry Myers, Hank Mann, Florence Lee, Allan Garcia, Henry Bergman. Black and White.
81 minutes.

Spectrum
(distributed by Polygram)

City On Fire

A fire sweeps across an American city destroying all before it, including the credibility of the viewer. Dullsville all the way despite the mandatory all-star cast which has Henry Fonda as the city's fire chief and Ava Gardner as a TV news presenter hooked on the bottle. Oh for the day when stars such as these appeared in real movies!

1979. Directed by Alvin Rakoff.
Starring Barry Newman, Susan Clark, Shelley Winters, Leslie Nielsen, James Franciscus, Ava Gardner, Henry Fonda. Colour.
106 minutes.

Rank Video

Clash By Night

Torrid Clifford Odets tale about disillusioned drifter Barbara Stanwyck, who returns to her home town to settle down with Monterey fisherman Paul Douglas but finds that his best pal, cynical Robert Ryan, has the sex appeal she most craves for. Very different from the original play, which ended in murder, but meaty stuff nonetheless and which still holds the attention – not least for the fact that Marilyn Monroe (in tight jeans and black bikini top) comes in at number four on the cast list as "a fish cannery worker".

1952. Directed by Fritz Lang.

Starring Barbara Stanwyck, Paul Douglas, Robert Ryan, Marilyn Monroe, J. Carrol Naish, Keith Andes, Silvio Minciotti. Black and White. 105 minutes.

21st Century Video
(distributed by VCL)

Clash Of The Titans

Laurence Olivier, Claire Bloom, Ursula Andress and company feature as the immortals of Greek Mythology and do their best to compete with the monsters of Ray Harryhausen. Not surprisingly they fail as Harryhausen comes up with the winged horse, Pegasus, the mighty sea monster, The Kraken and, best of all, Medusa, complete with piercing eyes and a head full of swirling snakes. He also pays homage to *Star Wars* by creating a mechanical owl called Bubo. Harry Hamlin (as Perseus) is the one who has to face them all. So-so adventure, rather on the slow side and hampered by murky photography.

Box-office rental	$15,632,341
Average rental (81)	$32,180,110

1981. Directed by Desmond Davis.
Starring Laurence Olivier, Claire Bloom, Maggie Smith, Ursula Andress, Harry Hamlin, Judi Bowker, Burgess Meredith, Sian Phillips. Colour. 118 minutes.

MGM/CBS Home Video

Cleopatra

The most notorious epic of the post-war years, reduced in effectiveness by the small screen and, in any case, released on video in a much shortened version of 176 minutes. When you consider that the film once ran to 243 minutes, that means an awful lot finished up on the cutting-room floor. What remains is a good first half dealing with Cleopatra's relationship with Caesar and a poor second when Marc Antony gets twisted around her little finger. One great spectacular moment: Cleopatra's entry into Rome mounted on a giant sphinx.

Box-office rental	$26,000,000
Average rental (63)	$8,360,900
Oscars (4)	Best Photography; Art Direction; Costume Design; Special Visual Effects
Oscar nominations (5)	Best Film; Actor (Harrison); Sound; Editing; Music Score

1963. Directed by Joseph L. Mankiewicz.
Starring Elizabeth Taylor, Richard Burton, Rex Harrison, Pamela Brown, George Cole, Hume Cronyn, Cesare Danova, Kenneth Haigh, Andrew Keir, Martin Landau, Roddy McDowall. Colour.
176 minutes.

Twentieth Century-Fox Video

The Clones

This one predates *The Boys From Brazil* by several years in its story of a research scientist who finds himself on the run in California because he's discovered the government's into cloning. What is more, they're into cloning scientists and setting them up in teams to gain world domination through control of the weather! Believe this one and you'll believe anything. Still, it does have the courage to send itself up, and that's something in its favour!

1973. Directed by Paul Hunt and Lamar Card.
Starring Michael Greene, Otis Young, Gregory Sierra, Susan Hunt, Stanley Adams, Alex Nicol. Colour.
94 minutes.

Intervision

Close Encounters Of The Third Kind ★★

Overrated sci-fi spectacular with ambitious special effects that fail dismally on video and make you wonder what all the fuss was about. Basically, it's a 2¼-hour version of a plot that is no longer than a short story: friendly beings from other worlds make contact with Earth people and take a dozen or so off with them into the Universe. That's about it. With the effects so devalued there's not enough good acting or writing left to carry the rest. This one's the special edition with some original material cut out and some new sequences added. Mediocre.

Box-office rental	$77,000,000
Average rental (77)	$36,913,348
Oscars (2)	Best Photography; Sound Effects Editing (Special Award)
Oscar nominations (7)	Best Supporting Actress (Dillon); Direction; Art Direction; Sound; Editing; Music Score; Visual Effects

1977. Directed by Steven Spielberg.
Starring Richard Dreyfuss, Francois Truffaut, Teri Garr, Melinda Dillon, Cary Guffey, Bob Balaban. Colour.
132 minutes.

RCA/Columbia International Video

Code Of The West ★

Minor Western with James Warren up against a baddie out to deprive honest settlers of their claim. Derived from a short story by Zane Grey, it supports Howard Hawks' *The Big Sky* on a double-feature video tape.

1947. Directed by William Berke.
Starring Raymond Burr, James Warren, Debra Alden, Steve Brodie. Black and White.
57 minutes.

Kingston Video

The Colditz Story

The place is Colditz Castle, a POW camp in Germany in World War II. The challenge is to escape, for the castle is supposed to be escape-proof. So can any of the Allied prisoners make it to the outside? You bet they can, especially with Eric Portman in charge of escape operations and John Mills, Bryan Forbes, Ian Carmichael, Lionel Jeffries, Richard Wattis and co. willing and rarin' to go. A terribly solid piece of British cinema, effective enough in its conventional run-of-the-mill way but hardly doing justice to the real-life POWs who tried for freedom. The famous TV series came later.

1954. Directed by Guy Hamilton.
Starring John Mills, Eric Portman, Christopher Rhodes, Lionel Jeffries, Bryan Forbes, Ian Carmichael, Richard Wattis, Frederick Valk, Anton Diffring. Black and White.
97 minutes.

Thorn EMI Video

College

Silent Buster Keaton comedy with Buster working his way through college and vying with bone-headed athlete Harold Goodwin for the favours of girlfriend Ann Cornwall. Outstanding sequence: Keaton coxing a boat with the rudder tied to his behind and trying to emulate – with disastrous results – the college champion in all the major sporting events. Very funny; co-directed by James W. Horne who later went on to make many of the Laurel and Hardy pictures.

1927. Directed by Buster Keaton and James W. Horne.
Starring Buster Keaton, Ann Cornwall, Harold Goodwin, Snitz Edwards, Florence Turner. Black and White.
65 minutes.

Spectrum
(distributed by Polygram)

Coma

Pretty young surgeon Genevieve Bujold becomes suspicious when a friend slips into an irreversible coma after a relatively minor operation. Investigating the matter, she finds there have been other similar such cases and inadvertently opens a whole can of worms (or rather spare parts) as she discovers that the hospital is deliberately killing off patients and selling their organs to those rich enough to be able to afford them. Nasty! And incredible! Or is it? Goodish thriller and often quite tense, although it could and should have been better.

Box-office rental	$14,600,000
Average rental (78)	$39,443,850

1978. Directed by Michael Crichton.
Starring Genevieve Bujold, Michael Douglas, Elizabeth Ashley, Rip Torn, Richard Widmark, Lois Chiles. Colour.
113 minutes.

MGM/CBS Home Video

The Comeback

Jack Jones' father once sang "The Donkey Serenade" in *The Firefly*. His son's a good singer too, so why he should have thought it necessary to appear in this mish-mash is difficult to fathom. He's an American singer who returns to England to record a new album, but finds that his recording sessions are somewhat marred by the murder of his wife, some rotting corpses, a transvestite, an axe murder, a girl walled up in the attic, etc. Drivel.

1978. Directed by Pete Walker.
Starring Jack Jones, Pamela Stephenson, David Doyle, Bill Owen, Sheila Keith, Holly Palance, Richard Johnson. Colour.
100 minutes.

Derann Video

Coming Home

This one's different from most movies about the Vietnam War in that it concentrates on the effects of the war on both men *and* women, and also on the problems they had to face both during the conflict and after the war when they had to come to terms with a new set of values. It revolves around lonely wife Jane Fonda, who helps out in a veterans' hospital and finds herself caught between her physical passion for paralysed veteran Jon Voight and her loyalty to hawkish Marine Corps husband Bruce Dern. No shots are fired but the war is always there on the screen. Quieter than *The Deer Hunter* but no less effective. A mosaic of songs by The Beatles, Mick Jagger, Bob Dylan and others helps recreate the atmosphere of the period (68).

Box-office rental	$13,389,000
Average rental (78)	$39,443,850
Oscars (3)	Best Actor (Voight); Actress (Fonda); Screenplay
Oscar nominations (5)	Best Film; Direction; Supporting Actor (Dern); Supporting Actress (Milford); Editing

1978. Directed by Hal Ashby.
Starring Jane Fonda, Jon Voight, Bruce Dern, Robert Carradine, Penelope Milford, Robert Ginty, Chalres Cyphers. Colour.
128 minutes.

Intervision

Confessions Of A Window Cleaner

Eager young window cleaner Robin Askwith finds that many of his lady clients expect rather more for their money than just a few washed panes of glass. Sexploitation comedy with the usual crude lavatory humour so beloved of English audiences. A depressing piece of video; the observations of the working class hero's home life, with Dandy Nichols as ma and Bill Maynard as pa, are its only redeeming features.

1974. Directed by Val Guest.

Starring Robin Askwith, Anthony Booth, Sheila White, Dandy Nichols, Bill Maynard, Linda Hayden, John Le Mesurier, Joan Hickson. Colour. 90 minutes.

RCA/Columbia International Video

Convoy

There's this independent trucker known as "Rubber Duck". And he's always having run-ins with the local sheriff. Through citizens' band radio he becomes a folk hero to his fellow truckers who form a mile-long convoy of lorries as a symbol of protest ... Doesn't sound very exciting, does it? And it's not, despite the fact that it is directed by Sam Peckinpah. Those who enjoy watching cars being smashed, cops being injured and trucks overturned might find it has some appeal. The movie was based, rather unusually, on a song. And that was good.

| Box-office rental | $9,525,000 |
| Average rental (78) | $39,443,850 |

1978. Directed by Sam Peckinpah.
Starring Kris Kristofferson, Ali MacGraw, Ernest Borgnine, Burt Young, Madge Sinclair. Colour.
110 minutes.

Thorn EMI Video

Cool Hand Luke

Paul Newman in one of his best screen roles as an indomitable outsider who refuses to conform and becomes a hero to his fellow convicts – thus providing them with a new strength of purpose and restoring their dignity as human beings. Among the most impressive of contemporary prison movies, although not one that bears too much repeated viewing. Plenty of sadism from the guards; an Oscar-winning portrayal by George Kennedy as fellow prisoner Dragline.

| Box-office rental | $7,200,000 |

Average rental (67) $13,081,250
Oscars (1)   Best Supporting Actor (Kennedy)
Oscar nominations (3)   Best Actor (Newman); Screenplay; Music

1967. Directed by Stuart Rosenberg.
Starring Paul Newman, George Kennedy, Jo Van Fleet, J. D. Cannon, Lou
Antonio, Strother Martin. Colour.
126 minutes.

Warner Home Video

Cornered

One of those well-crafted thrillers that RKO used to churn out so efficiently
in the post-World War II era. This one revolves around an embittered
and vengeful Canadian flier (Dick Powell) who travels to South America
to track down and kill the Vichy official responsible for the murder of his
wife. Great stuff from Powell as the vengeful hero, equally impressive
silky menace from Walter Slezak as the heavy. And although the time,
place and subject now seem light years away, the film itself holds up
remarkably well and is excellent video value. Sharing the same tape: *The
Woman On Pier 13*.

1945. Directed by Edward Dmytryk.
Starring Dick Powell, Walter Slezak, Micheline Cheirel, Nina Vale, Morris
Carnovsky. Black and White.
102 minutes.

Kingston Video

Corridors Of Blood

Surgeon Boris Karloff on the side of right for once but falling victim to his
own drugs as he experiments with anaesthetics for his patients in Victorian London. Body snatchers Christopher Lee (Resurrection Joe) and
Francis De Wolff (Black Ben) help him sink even lower as they supply
his hospital with corpses for dissection. Passable costume horror fare; set
in the 1840s.

1958. Directed by Robert Day.
Starring Boris Karloff, Betta St. John, Francis Matthews, Francis De Wolff, Adrienne Corri, Finlay Currie, Christopher Lee. Black and White. 85 minutes.

Iver Films

Cotter

Don Murray – unusually cast as a Sioux Indian who works as a rodeo clown – causes the death of a rodeo rider because he is too drunk to rescue him. After that things go from bad to worse, especially when he tries to re-establish himself in his home town and finds himself up against a lynching party. Powerful modern Western drama with convincing small town atmosphere. Supported by *Island Of Lost Women* on a double feature video tape.

1973. Directed by Paul Stanley.
Starring Don Murray, Carol Lynley, Rip Torn, Sherry Jackson. Colour. 94 minutes.

Kingston Video

Countess Dracula

As a cure for advancing old age this is not to be recommended. Ingrid Pitt, a newly-widowed countess, learns that bathing in the blood of young girls can restore youth. So what better way to test the theory than by murdering her chambermaid and taking a bath. Eureka, it works! But only for so long. Then a new victim and new blood has to be found . . . Sounds rubbishy and of course it is. But every now and then there are moments which lift this movie onto a higher plane than that reached by most Hammer offerings. And they are due mostly to director Peter Sasdy. Not bad. Deserves a two-and-a-half star rating rather than two!

1971. Directed by Peter Sasdy.

Starring Ingrid Pitt, Nigel Green, Sandor Eles, Maurice Denham, Patience Collier, Peter Jeffrey, Lesley-Anne Down. Colour.
93 minutes.

Rank Video

The Count Of Monte Cristo ★★

This one was made for showing on TV in the States but is included here because it received a theatrical release in Britain. Richard Chamberlain stars as ship's officer Edmond Dantes who is wrongly jailed in the notorious island prison, the Chateau d'If, and then escapes to wreak vengeance on the three villains who sent him there. Tony Curtis, Louis Jourdan and Donald Pleasence are the unfortunate trio who get their come-uppance. Very one-dimensional, but it moves briskly and the younger members of the family will almost certainly enjoy it. Handsome colourwork by Aldo Tonti.

1975. Directed by David Greene.
Starring Richard Chamberlain, Tony Curtis, Trevor Howard, Louis Jourdan, Donald Pleasence, Kate Nelligan. Colour.
104 minutes.

Precision Video

Crack-Up ★★★

Neat little thriller with Pat O'Brien as an art expert who experiences a blackout on a train and finds himself framed by a gang of forgers bent on snatching a collection of art masterpieces from a museum. Murder is also part of their plans. Nicely put together and, with Val Lewton's miniature horror classic *I Walked With A Zombie* on the same tape, very good value for money.

1946. Directed by Irving Reis.

Starring Pat O'Brien, Claire Trevor, Herbert Marshall, Ray Collins, Wallace Ford. Black and White.
93 minutes.

Kingston Video

The Creeping Flesh

Bring back a giant prehistoric skeleton from New Guinea and let the English rain get at it and you're in big trouble. Or at least poor old Peter Cushing is, for he discovers that water brings the evil old skeleton back to life. And that's not to be wished on anyone. Barmy nonsense, but well-made barmy nonsense and as an exercise in imaginative horror not to be despised. Christopher Lee is also around in charge of the local asylum, which is more than appropriate. Set in late Victorian London; 2½ rating.

1972. Directed by Freddie Francis.
Starring Christopher Lee, Peter Cushing, Lorna Heilbron, George Benson, Kenneth J. Warren, Duncan Lamont. Colour.
91 minutes.

Vampix
(*Distributed by Videomedia*)

Crossfire

Historically important movie in that it was the first to raise the problem of anti-Semitism in the States in the post-war years. Couched in terms of a straightforward thriller it follows the efforts of cop Robert Young to track down murdering soldier Robert Ryan, a bigotted G.I. who has killed a man simply because of his race. Controversial stuff even now and a movie that holds up much better than the other 1947 film that dealt with the same theme, *Gentleman's Agreement*. Taught, gripping video entertainment; based on the novel *The Brick Foxhole* by Richard Brooks.

Oscars   Nil

Oscar nominations (5)	Best Film; Supporting Actor (Ryan); Supporting Actress (Grahame); Direction; Screenplay

1947. Directed by Edward Dmytryk.
Starring Robert Young, Robert Mitchum, Robert Ryan, Gloria Grahame, Paul Kelly, Richard Benedict, Sam Levene. Black and White.
86 minutes.

Thorn EMI Video

Cross Of Iron

Surprisingly, Sam Peckinpah's only war movie and his canvas is not the jungles of Vietnam but the Russian front in 1943, where the German officers are as much concerned with personal ambition as they are in battling against the enemy. Professional soldier James Coburn and Prussian officer Maximilian Schell, whose aim is to win the Iron Cross no matter what the cost in human life, are the main protagonists. The film is devastatingly effective in its war sequences but whether you will want to sit through this harrowing war epic more than once must be open to question.

1977. Directed by Sam Peckinpah.
Starring James Coburn, Maximilian Schell, James Mason, David Warner, Klaus Lowitsch, Roger Fritz. Colour.
133 minutes.

Thorn EMI Video

The Cruel Sea

"A story of the Battle of the Atlantic, of two ships and a handful of men". Thus states the foreword to this film version of Nicholas Monsarrat's best-selling novel of World War II. And that just about sums it up. What the foreword fails to do, however, is to give you an idea of the honesty of feeling of this picture, for it is the quintessential British war movie of the 50s; quiet, understated and admirably played, especially by Jack

Hawkins as the skipper of the corvette "Compass Rose". A realistic portrait of what it was like to fight on the high seas against the German navy, it stands the test of time well and is well served by the video process. One of the top box-office successes in Britain in 1953.

Oscars	Nil
Oscar nominations (1)	Best Screenplay

1953. Directed by Charles Frend.
Starring Jack Hawkins, Donald Sinden, Stanley Baker, John Stratton, Denholm Elliott, Jack Warner, Bruce Seton, Virginia McKenna, Moira Lister. Black and White.
126 minutes.

Thorn EMI Video

Cruising

New York cop Al Pacino goes underground and poses as a gay in order to track down the bloody killer of homosexuals. A quite loathsome piece of celluloid, not particularly well made (considering it comes from William Friedkin) and based on a real-life series of murders that occurred in New York in the 70s. Strictly after midnight video fare and not to be watched if in a depressed mood. The one star is for Pacino's performance, nothing else.

Box-office rental	$6,990,890
Average rental (80)	$30,086,027

1980. Directed by William Friedkin.
Starring Al Pacino, Paul Sorvino, Karen Allen, Richard Cox, Don Scardino, Joe Spinell. Colour.
100 minutes.

MGM/CBS Home Video

Cry Danger

The pity is they don't make thrillers like this any more, for it's taut, sardonic, unpretentious and highly entertaining. It all revolves around ex-con Dick Powell, who is alibied out of jail by a man who wants to get his hands on the $100,000 haul Powell is supposed to have stashed away. Director Robert Parrish (whose first film as a director this was) offers a crisp pace; lovely redhead Rhonda Fleming offers crisp sex. Top ratings all the way. As double-feature video tapes go, this one takes a lot of beating. On the same bill is Samuel Fuller's offbeat Western *Run Of The Arrow*.

1951. Directed by Robert Parrish.
Starring Dick Powell, Rhonda Fleming, Richard Erdman, William Conrad, Regis Toomey, Jean Porter. Black and White.
79 minutes.

Kingston Video

A Cry In The Night

Homicidal psychopath Raymond Burr kidnaps a policeman's daughter in a moment of panic and, not surprisingly, finds himself on the receiving end of a massive manhunt. Natalie Wood features as the girl. *Devil's Canyon* is the movie that shares this double feature tape.

1956. Directed by Frank Tuttle.
Starring Edmond O'Brien, Brian Donlevy, Natalie Wood, Raymond Burr, Richard Anderson. Black and White.
75 minutes.

Kingston Video

Crypt Of The Living Dead

The beautiful 700-year-old bride of crusader Louis VII is brought alive when an archaeologist's son opens up her tomb. And that means a blood-sucking rampage around her island, for she has vampire as well as vengeful tendencies. Familiar "vampire-on-the-loose" programmer with lots of blood and gore and silly nonsense, none of it very well done.

1972. Directed by Ray Danton.
Starring Andrew Prine, Mark Damon, Patty Sheppard, Teresa Gimpera. Colour.
93 minutes.

Intervision

Cul-De-Sac

A "what's it all about?" movie and arguably a good video purchase, in that you have to watch it again and again in order to unravel its true meaning. If then! Suffice it to say that it starts when a couple of gangsters hole up in a Holy Island castle occupied by a neurotic businessman-turned-artist and his bored, attractive young wife who is a bit on the promiscuous side. Once the gangsters intrude on their lives, their already edgy relationship begins to crumble. As you will have gathered, a rather ghoulish comedy which gets ever more absurd with each succeeding reel. Still, it *is* rather striking to look at, it *is* funny at times in a mad kind of way and it *is* directed by Roman Polanski, which means it's supposed to be good . . .

1966. Directed by Roman Polanski.
Starring Donald Pleasence, Francoise Dorleac, Lionel Stander, Jack Mac-Gowran, Iain Quarrier, Renee Houston, Geoffrey Sumner. Black and White.
111 minutes.

Zodiac Video
(*distributed by Videomedia*)

The Curse Of Simba

Bryant Halliday (the hypnotist in the other film on this double-feature video tape) is once again in trouble, although this time he's on the receiving end as a big game hunter who ventures into forbidden Simbasi territory, kills a lion, and gets saddled with a nasty curse for his trouble. Not exactly an earth-shattering experience but it makes up a not unattractive double-bill with *Devil Doll*.

1965. Directed by Lindsay Shonteff.
Starring Bryant Halliday, Dennis Price, Lisa Daniely, Mary Kerridge, Ronald Leigh Hunt, Jean Lodge. Black and White.
79 minutes.

Kingston Video

Curse Of The Crimson Altar

The only real interest in this movie lies in the fact that it marked one of the last screen appearances of horror master Boris Karloff. Otherwise it's the usual witchcraft-in-a-small-village-type horror flick, with Christopher Lee out to revenge himself on the descendants of those who sent one of his ancestors – black witch Barbara Steele – up in flames. Karloff is on the side of right as the professor who sorts it all out.

1968. Directed by Vernon Sewell.
Starring Boris Karloff, Christopher Lee, Mark Eden, Virginia Wetherell, Barbara Steele, Rupert Davies, Michael Gough. Colour.
89 minutes.

Vampix
(*distributed by Videomedia*)

Cyclone On Horseback

Tim Holt actioner with the bad guys involved in a swindle over a horse deal and the good guys bringing the first telephone line to their state. RKO B-Western that supports *Son Of Sinbad* on a double-feature tape.

1941. Directed by Edward Killy.
Starring Tim Holt, Marjorie Reynolds, Ray Whitley. Black and White.
60 minutes.

Kingston Video

D

The Dam Busters

Very careful and often very dull account of how brainy boffin Dr. Barnes
Wallis built a bouncing bomb that destroyed the Mohne and Eder dams
in Germany during World War II. Michael Redgrave plays Wallis, Richard
Todd the stiff-upper-lipped commander Guy Gibson who delivered the
weapon so effectively. The first half, as Redgrave struggles to convince
the authorities that the bomb might actually work, is interesting; the
second, which deals with the raid itself, is rather routine and equates with
something like average video viewing. Famous music score, fine performance by Redgrave and the top British box-office attraction of its year.

Oscars   Nil
Oscar nominations (1)   Best Special Effects

1955. Directed by Michael Anderson.
Starring Michael Redgrave, Richard Todd, Basil Sydney, Derek Farr,
Patrick Barr, Ernest Clark, Raymond Huntley, Ursula Jeans. Black and
White.
125 minutes.

Thorn EMI Video

Damien: Omen II

The further adventures of anti-Christ Damien Thorn, first seen in *The
Omen* and now a teenager enrolled in a military Academy in America.
Uncle William Holden is now in charge, but he fares no better than Greg
Peck who expired at the end of movie number one. Neither does Lew
Ayres, who drowns beneath a frozen lake (a brilliant scene); Sylvia Sidney, who dies of a heart attack after getting the eye from a raven; nor
reporter Elizabeth Shepherd who falls victim to the same bird on a lonely
country road. It all sounds very gory and indeed it is, but the continual
linking of evil with the military and big business makes this a cleverly
constructed piece of horror with some disturbing undertones. It's also
that cinematic rarity – a sequel that's as good as its predecessor!

| Box-office rental | $13,630,000 |
| Average rental (78) | $39,443,850 |

1978. Directed by Don Taylor.
Starring William Holden, Lee Grant, Jonathan Scott-Taylor, Robert Foxworth, Nicholas Pryor, Lew Ayres, Sylvia Sidney, Elizabeth Shepherd. Colour.
107 minutes.

Twentieth Century-Fox Video

The Damned

Two-and-a-half hours in the company of a wealthy German family – politically divided – but whose steel profits help finance Hitler's rise to power. Or, put another way, two-and-a-half hours of decadence, madness, rape, murder, suicide, even a drag rendering by Helmut Berger of "I Need A Real Man" from *The Blue Angel*. Some brilliant passages and a serious theme, but put across in grand opera style by Luchino Visconti. The result; exaggerated video and a film of missed opportunities. 2½ rating.

| Oscars | Nil |
| Oscar nominations (1) | Best Story & Screenplay |

1969. Directed by Luchino Visconti.
Starring Dirk Bogarde, Ingrid Thulin, Helmut Griem, Helmut Berger, Renaud Verley, Umberto Orsini. Colour.
153 minutes.

Warner Home Video

A Damsel In Distress

Fred Astaire; Burns and Allen; songs by George and Ira Gershwin; story by P. G. Wodehouse; direction by George Stevens. In the words of the song, "Who Could Ask For Anything More?" Well, you could, I suppose, ask for Ginger Rogers. But when this film was made she was taking a short break from her long partnership with Astaire and being replaced by the demure Joan Fontaine, who plays a rich English miss who lives in a castle and is ultimately rescued by Fred's dapper dancing man. Delightful entertainment, enriched by such songs as "A Foggy Day In London Town"; "Put Me To The Test" and "Nice Work If You Can Get It". On the same video tape: *Old Man Rhythm*.

Oscars (1)   Best Dance Direction
Oscar nominations (1)   Best Art Direction

1937. Directed by George Stevens.
Starring Fred Astaire, George Burns, Gracie Allen, Joan Fontaine, Reginald Gardiner, Constance Collier. Black and White.
101 minutes.

Kingston Video

The Dark Mirror

One of those "Which is the good twin, which is the bad twin?" movies that were so popular in Hollywood in the 40s and 50s. In this case there are two Olivia de Havillands – one as sweet as pie, the other as nutty as a fruitcake and a murderess into the bargain. Psychologist Lew Ayres has to figure out which is which. So do you. OK of its type but badly dated in parts. Thomas Mitchell is on hand as a cop.

Oscars   Nil
Oscar nominations (1)   Best Original Story

1946. Directed by Robert Siodmak.
Starring Olivia de Havilland, Lew Ayres, Thomas Mitchell, Richard Long, Charles Evans, Garry Owen. Black and White.
85 minutes.

Intervision

Dark Star

Cult movie that brought the name of director John Carpenter to prominence. The *Dark Star* of the title is a four-man scoutship that prowls the Universe blowing up unstable planets with a series of talking bombs. When one of the bombs gets caught in the bay and refuses to drop, it's curtains for everyone. An orange spacehopper alien and a sexy-voiced female computer help Carpenter send up the *genre* quite nicely although the movie is a long way from the 'great' category.

1974. Directed by John Carpenter.
Starring Brian Narelle, Andreijah Pahich, Carl Kuniholm, Dan O'Bannion, Joe Sanders. Colour.
83 minutes.

Iver Films

Davy Crockett, King Of The Wild Frontier ★★

Something of a cult film at the time of its release, not because of what it showed on screen but because of its theme song "The Ballad of Davy Crockett", and because everyone wanted to wear a coonskin cap like that worn by Fess Parker in the movie. The film follows Crockett's adventures from Washington to the Alamo and was made up of material from three segments on the Disneyland TV Show. Acceptable video for the kids.

1955. Directed by Norman Foster.
Starring Fess Parker, Buddy Ebsen, Basil Ruysdael, Hans Conried, William Bakewell, Kenneth Tobey. Colour.
93 minutes.

Walt Disney Home Video

The Day Of The Dolphin

Marine biologist George C. Scott researches the behaviour of dolphins off the Florida coast and discovers they are being used in a right-wing political plot to blow up the presidential yacht. Unusual to say the least, and for its first hour a quite ingenious and inventive thriller. After that, unfortunately, it becomes just another race-against-time adventure. Still, it is curiously affecting at times and the dolphins are marvellous to watch and almost worth the price of the cassette alone. There's one superb sequence in which Scott performs an underwater ballet with one of his prize specimens. Lovely colourwork. 2½ rating.

Oscars   Nil
Oscar nominations (2)   Best Sound; Music Score

1973. Directed by Mike Nichols.
Starring George C. Scott, Trish Van Devere, Paul Sorvino, Fritz Weaver, Jon Korkes. Colour.
104 minutes.

Twentieth Century-Fox Video

Day Of The Wolves

It's *High Noon* time all over again, although on this occasion, instead of Gary Cooper facing the outlaws alone it's ex-police chief Richard Egan who, with shotgun at the ready, prepares to do battle with a gang of trained killers planning to ransack his entire town. Routine. A minor gangster vehicle, *Gang Busters*, shares the same video tape.

1973. Directed by Ferde Grofe Jr.
Starring Richard Egan, Martha Hyer, Rick Jason, Jan Murray. Colour.
95 minutes.

Kingston Video

The Day The Earth Stood Still

Quite a subtle movie this one, warning of the dangers of international aggression and putting its message across within one of the most popular movie entertainment forms of the early 50s – the science-fiction *genre*. The reason the Earth stands still is because visitor from Outer Space Michael Rennie *makes* it stand still. And he does so to demonstrate the enormous power at his command and to warn Earth that unless it abolishes war the more advanced planets of the Universe will combine and destroy it. Thirty years on and the message is still pertinent, alas. Good if unambitious effects and a convincing robot called Gort who protects Rennie by beaming deadly rays through the visor of his helmet.

1951. Directed by Robert Wise.
Starring Michael Rennie, Patricia Neal, Hugh Marlow, Sam Jaffe, Billy Gray. Black and White.
92 minutes.

Twentieth Century-Fox Video

Deadline At Dawn

Familiar movie situation: a young sailor on leave in wartime New York finds himself involved in murder and then cleared at the last moment. But above-average handling and *denouement*, thanks to the screenplay of noted playwright Clifford Odets and nicely judged performances from Susan Hayward as a dance hall gal, Paul Lukas as a cab driver, and a host of supporting Hollywood notables including Joe Sawyer, Jerome Cowan and Joseph Calleia. Supports *Stagecoach* on a double-feature video tape.

1946. Directed by Harold Clurman.
Starring Susan Hayward, Paul Lukas, Bill Williams, Joseph Calleia, Osa Massen, Lola Lane, Jerome Cowan, Joe Sawyer. Black and White.
83 minutes.

Kingston Video

Dead Of Night

Horror tale centring on a small-town American family who discover that their son has been killed on army service. When he turns up on their doorstep they are naturally overjoyed. But then things begin to happen that make them realize that their son is no longer what he was, in fact he's a walking corpse. Above-average, disturbing little piece of ghoulish video directed by Bob Clark, who subsequently went on to direct the Sherlock Holmes thriller *Murder By Decree*. 2½ rating.

1972. Directed by Bob Clark.
Starring John Marley, Lynn Carlin, Henderson Forsythe, Richard Backus, Anya Ormsby. Colour.
89 minutes.

Intervision

Death Hunt

Run-of-the-mill actioner with tough Canadian mountie Lee Marvin pursuing framed trapper Charles Bronson across the Yukon in the 1930s. More of a stolid plod than a vigorous adventure; Angie Dickinson comes in at number seven on the cast list as an appealing widow but the main attractions are the lovely mountain snowscapes. Based on a true case but that doesn't make things any livelier.

1981. Directed by Peter Hunt.
Starring Charles Bronson, Lee Marvin, Andrew Stevens, Carl Weathers, Ed Lauter, Scott Hylands, Angie Dickinson. Colour.
97 minutes.

Twentieth Century-Fox Video

Death In Venice

The physical and spiritual disintegration of a celebrated German composer who finds himself trapped in Venice during a cholera epidemic and fatally infatuated by the charms of a 14-year-old boy staying at his hotel. Not exactly a film to bring a smile to one's face but a very faithful rendering of Thomas Mann's 1913 novella and one that captures both the beauty and sultry decadence of its settings with remarkable accuracy. Dirk Bogarde is the dying composer, Luchino Visconti the director. The music of Mahler adds considerably to the overall pessimism of the piece. Fine cinema but you have to be in the mood.

Oscars	Nil
Oscar nominations (1)	Best Costume Design

1971. Directed by Luchino Visconti.
Starring Dirk Bogarde, Bjorn Andresen, Silvano Mangano, Marisa Berenson, Mark Burns. Colour.
128 minutes.

Warner Home Video

Death On The Nile

Peter Ustinov takes over from Albert Finney as Hercule Poirot (see *Murder On The Orient Express*) and the action transfers to the decks and cabins of a luxury riverboat travelling up the Nile. And this time there is not one murder but several. But once again it's "guess the killer" time, and lining up for your perusal are Angela Lansbury, George Kennedy, Mia Farrow, Olivia Hussey, Bette Davis and Maggie Smith, who not only plays Davis' lady companion but also has some of the best lines to deliver: "If there are two things in this world I can't abide, it's heat and heathens". Ustinov eventually triumphs of course, but not before trusty David Niven has despatched a cobra with his swordstick and Jack Cardiff photographed the whole thing in a rich warm Technicolor. Too long for its own good. But not bad.

Box-office rental	$8,800,000
Average rental (78)	$39,443,850
Oscars (1)	Best Costume Design
Oscar nominations	Nil

1978. Directed by John Guillermin.
Starring Peter Ustinov, Jane Birkin, Lois Chiles, Bette Davis, Mia Farrow,

Jon Finch, Olivia Hussey, I. S. Johar, George Kennedy, Angela Lansbury, Simon MacCorkindale, David Niven, Maggie Smith, Jack Warden. Colour. 140 minutes.

Thorn EMI Video

Death Race 2000

Tongue-in-cheek movie about the futuristic society of the United Provinces of America where a no-holds-barred auto race is the top sporting event and the winner the driver with the fastest time *and* the highest number of road victims. Sylvester Stallone as a loud-mouthed hoodlum called Machine Gun Joe Viterbo and David Carradine as a masked driver named Frankenstein are the main protagonists. Comes from the Roger Corman stable; bears a close resemblance to *Rollerball*.

Box-office rental	$5,250,000
Average rental (75)	$27,300,250

1975. Directed by Paul Bartel.
Starring David Carradine, Simone Griffeth, Sylvester Stallone, Mary Woronov, Roberta Collins. Colour.
79 minutes.

Brent Walker Video
(distributed by Videospace)

Deathsport

Another garbage package from the Roger Corman stable about an annual gladiatorial contest called Deathsport in which some superhuman survivors of the Great Neutron Wars take on some lethal motorcyclists. It's set a thousand years from now. A pity they couldn't have delayed making the movie until then.

1979. Directed by Henry Suso & Allan Arkush.

Starring David Carradine, Claudia Jennings, Richard Lynch, William Smithers, Will Walker. Colour.
83 minutes.

Warner Home Video

Death Wish

Cunningly slanted tale of a mild-mannered businessman (Charles Bronson) who turns vigilante and stalks the streets of New York to kill muggers after his wife has been murdered and his daughter raped by a gang of hoodlums. A dangerous movie, in that it manipulates its audience into accepting Bronson going it alone and enjoying with him his bloodbath of killing. Despite claims to the contrary, the picture was no great record breaker, so luckily many people were put off by its gratuitous violence. They may also have wised up to the fact that as a movie it's not very good. After-midnight viewing – if at all!

Box-office rental	$8,800,000
Average rental (74)	$18,456,150

1974. Directed by Michael Winner.
Starring Charles Bronson, Hope Lange, Vincent Gardenia, Steven Keats, William Redfield. Colour.
93 minutes.

CIC Video

The Deep

Novelist Peter Benchley's follow-up to *Jaws*, with the underwater monster this time being a giant moray eel lurking in the blue waters off the coast of Bermuda. On this occasion, however, the monster has only a minor part to play, most of the action centring on the search for a huge consignment of morphine sunk in a munitions ship during World War II. Jacqueline Bisset looks splendid in diving gear and director Peter Yates manages to include his statutory car chase, but despite a tough hero, dope-running villains and a touch of voodoo, the end result is very ordinary. And very dull. A misfire.

Box-office rental	$31,300,000
Average rental (77)	$36,913,348
Oscars	Nil
Oscar nominations (1)	Best Sound

1977. Directed by Peter Yates.
Starring Jacqueline Bisset, Nick Nolte, Robert Shaw, Dick Anthony Williams, Earl Maynard, Bob Minor, Louis Gossett, Eli Wallach. Colour. 124 minutes.

RCA/Columbia International Video

The Deer Hunter

The moving story of three young Pennsylvanian steelworkers whose lives are drastically changed by their experiences in the Vietnam War. One commits suicide after losing his reason, one is maimed for life, the other survives. A huge, sprawling film with echoes of the Hemingway ethos that only the strong survive in this world and, although not perhaps the masterpiece many claim it to be, still with enough inspired sequences to put it among the very best American movies of the 70s. The hideous torture scenes involving Russian Roulette will have you turning your head away; the long sequence of a wedding in a Russian Orthodox church will have you marvelling at the beauty of it all. Robert De Niro, Christopher Walken and John Savage are faultless as the three heroes, but there are near-perfect performances all round.

Box-office rental	$30,425,000
Average rental (78)	$39,443,850
Oscars (5)	Best Film; Supporting Actor (Walken); Direction; Editing; Sound
Oscar nominations (4)	Best Actor (De Niro); Supporting Actress (Streep); Photography; Screenplay

1978. Directed by Michael Cimino.

Starring Robert De Niro, John Cazale, John Savage, Christopher Walken, Meryl Streep, George Dzundza, Chuck Aspegren. Colour.
182 minutes.

Thorn EMI Video

Deliverance

One of the most disturbing movies of recent times. A terrifying tale of four Atlanta businessmen, who decide to take a weekend off away from it all by canoeing down the rapids of an uncharted river in the Appalachian mountains. "Away from it all" means more than they bargained for and the further they go down river and leave the trappings of civilization, the more they are reduced to behaving like animals, with cripplement and death as the end result. Not everyone's cup of tea by any means, but if you would like to imagine how *you* would react under similar circumstances, try it. But take care, this film's brutal as well as brilliant and certainly not for the squeamish. Arguably director John Boorman's best film. Certainly the best of Burt Reynolds as the strong-man leader of the expedition.

Box-office rental	$22,500,000
Average rental (72)	$17,543,950
Oscars	Nil
Oscar Nominations (3)	Best Film; Direction; Editing

1972. Directed by John Boorman.
Starring Burt Reynolds, Jon Voight, Ned Beatty, Ronny Cox, James Dickey. Colour.
109 minutes.

Warner Home Video

The Detective

Remarkably successful attempt to film Roderick Thorpe's controversial novel about corruption in New York city government and in the city's police force. Frank Sinatra plays a police detective who investigates the murder of a young homosexual, railroads an innocent man to the electric chair for the crime, and only later, when he has been promoted for his efforts, comes to realise that he's sent the wrong man to his death. Made by Gordon Douglas, who was usually responsible for potboilers, this film has a sharp, controversial edge that one associates with directors of a higher pedigree. Tough, authentic and hard-hitting, it gets its message across without ever being offensive to the ear or the eye. Recommended adult video fare.

Box-office rental	$6,500,000
Average rental (68)	$14,411,950

1968. Directed by Gordon Douglas.
Starring Frank Sinatra, Lee Remick, Jacqueline Bisset, Ralph Meeker, Jack Klugman, Horace McMahon, William Windom, Robert Duvall. Colour.
114 minutes.

Twentieth Century-Fox Video

Devil Doll

Not to be confused with the Tod Browning film of 1936, but no less bizarre in its story of a hypnotist (Bryant Halliday) who has a penchant for transferring human souls into the frameworks of ventriloquists' dummies. The soul of his former partner has already suffered such a fate; that of the fiancée of American reporter William Sylvester is next in line. Atmospheric, not a little macabre and reasonable entertainment value. On the same tape: *The Curse Of Simba*, also starring Bryant Halliday.

1964. Directed by Lindsay Shonteff.
Starring William Sylvester, Bryant Halliday, Yvonne Romain, Sandra Dorne, Karel Stepanek. Black and White.
80 minutes.

Kingston Video

Devil's Canyon

Western prison drama with ex-marshal Dale Robertson holed up in a notorious Arizona jail where escape plots are hatched, prison riots take place and stagecoach bandit Virginia Mayo is the only woman prisoner among the 500 male inmates! Lucky her. Not so lucky for video viewers though, for this one's straight off the RKO conveyor belt and it shows in every reel. Originally made for release in 3-D, it shares a video tape with *A Cry In The Night*.

1953. Directed by Alfred L. Werker.
Starring Virginia Mayo, Dale Robertson, Stephen McNally, Arthur Hunnicutt, Robert Keith, Jay C. Flippen. Colour.
92 minutes.

Kingston Video

Devils Of Darkness

No reflection when staring in a lake! That can only mean one thing. A vampire! In this case a certain Count Sinistre, who was executed in the 16th century but pops up again to mess up a trio's holiday in Brittany. William Sylvester stems the blood flow and makes sure things don't get out of control.

1965. Directed by Lance Comfort.
Starring William Sylvester, Hubert Noel, Tracy Reed, Carole Gray, Diana Decker, Rona Anderson, Peter Illing. Colour.
88 minutes.

Derann Video

The Diamond Mercenaries

Run-of-the-mill adventure tale made when Telly Savalas was at the height of his *Kojak* popularity on TV. In this one he's a ruthless security officer out to track down a gang stealing diamonds from a South African mine. Heading the mercenary cut-throats up against him: Peter Fonda, O. J.

Simpson, Maud Adams and Christopher Lee as a disillusioned (and pathological) British army officer. Good performance by Savalas. Competent adventure fare but nothing more.

1975. Directed by Val Guest.
Starring Telly Savalas, Peter Fonda, O. J. Simpson, Maud Adams, Christopher Lee. Colour.
101 minutes.

VIPCO

The Diary Of Anne Frank ★★★

Deeply moving tale of a young Jewish girl who hid with her family and four others in an Amsterdam attic in a futile attempt to escape the Nazi holocaust of World War II. A bit too long, but director George Stevens makes sure his cameras pry into every corner of his gigantic one-house set and extracts some quite remarkable moments of tension from the proceedings. Alfred Newman's music score is an asset. So is Stevens' fearsome use of the soundtrack. Top performance? Not Millie Perkins, who looks right but sounds all wrong as Anne, but Joseph Schildkraut as her father – the lone survivor of the eight hideaways.

Oscars (3)	Best Supporting Actress (Winters); Photography; Art Direction
Oscar nominations (5)	Best Film; Supporting Actor (Wynn); Direction; Costume Design; Music Score

1959. Directed by George Stevens.
Starring Millie Perkins, Joseph Schildkraut, Shelley Winters, Richard Beymer, Lou Jacobi, Diane Baker, Ed Wynn. Black and White.
180 minutes (reduced to 144 on video)

Twentieth Century-Fox Video

The Dirty Dozen

Twelve GI prisoners – murderers, rapists, thieves – all awaiting execution or serving life sentences, are offered the chance of a pardon if they agree to form a commando unit that must embark on a suicide mission into France during World War II. They agree, and in no time at all become an efficient fighting force and a remarkably nice group of fellows, considering the unpleasant nature of their crimes. Still, Major Lee Marvin is at the helm and that counts for much. The moral questions raised about war creating its own standards in murder and brutality are rather scantily put across. Not so the action sequences, which carry this 2½-hour movie along at such a rapid rate that you never once get bored. An all-star cast performs efficiently and if you think you know the film backwards by now, try and remember the three who survive at the end.

Box-office rental	$20,300,000
Average rental (67)	$13,081,250
Oscars (1)	Best Sound Effects
Oscar nominations (3)	Best Supporting Actor (Cassavetes); Sound; Editing

1967. Directed by Robert Aldrich.
Starring Lee Marvin, Ernest Borgnine, Charles Bronson, John Cassavetes, Richard Jaeckel, Robert Ryan, Telly Savalas, Donald Sutherland, George Kennedy, Jim Brown, Trini Lopez, Ralph Meeker, Clint Walker, Robert Webber. Colour,
150 minutes.

MGB/CBS Video

Dirty Harry

The first, and by far and away the best of Clint Eastwood's Harry Callahan thrillers, with Eastwood breaking all the rules as a rogue cop who goes after a psychopathic rooftop killer terrorizing San Francisco. A provocative "do the ends justify the means?" screenplay allows Eastwood to perform at his persuasive best and helps the film remain the most compulsively watchable cops and robbers thriller currently available on video. But it's tough stuff. And if you still haven't caught the mood, here's a sample of Eastwood's dialogue to a would-be victim: "I know what you're thinking. Did he fire six shots or only five? Well, to tell you the truth, in all this excitement I've kinda lost track myself. But being this is a .44 magnum, the most powerful handgun in the world, and would blow your head clean off – you've got to ask yourself one question: do I feel lucky? Well, do ya, punk?"

Box-office rental	$17,900,000
Average rental (71)	$13,465,850

1971. Directed by Don Siegel.
Starring Clint Eastwood, Harry Guardino, Reni Santoni, John Vernon, John Larch, Andy Robinson. Colour.
102 minutes.

Warner Home Video

Dirty Mary, Crazy Larry

Racing driver Peter Fonda and mechanic Adam Roarke rob a supermarket of 150,000 dollars, pick up groupie Susan George and then spend the rest of the movie at high speed racing by car from the law. For *devotees* of car skids, car crashes, car jumps, car stunts and so on. Anyone looking for more substantial entertainment should look elsewhere.

Box-office rental	$15,200,000
Average rental (74)	$18,456,150

1974. Directed by John Hough.
Starring Peter Fonda, Susan George, Adam Roarke, Vic Morrow, Kenneth Tobey, Roddy McDowall. Colour.
92 minutes.

Twentieth Century-Fox Video

The Disappearance

International 'hit man' Donald Sutherland wants to quit his bloodthirsty career but finds himself unable to break free from the job he has come to despise. The disappearance of his wife leads to further complications and a trail that takes him from Montreal to London. Confusing thriller with a last page solution, Christopher Plummer is one part of the jigsaw, John Hurt another, David Hemmings yet another. A good cast and excellent location work, but not quite as good as it should have been.

1977. Directed by Stuart Cooper.
Starring Donald Sutherland, Francine Racette, David Hemmings, John Hurt, David Warner, Peter Bowles, Virginia McKenna, Christopher Plummer. Colour.
102 minutes.

Cinema Features
(distributed by VCL)

Divine Madness

A recording of one dynamic Bette Midler concert filmed over a four-day period at the Pasadena Civil Auditorium. Which should give you some idea of what to expect – shrieking pop, wisecracks, raunchy songs, handstands on stage, impressions of Sophie Tucker and Mae West. Vulgar, brash, vigorous. Depends on if you're a Bette Midler fan whether you go for it or not. The twenty numbers include "Big Noise From Winnetka", "The Boogie Woogie Bugle Boy" and "The Rose".

1980. Directed by Michael Ritchie.
Starring Bette Midler, Jocelyn Brown, Ula Hedwig and Diva Gray. Colour.
93 minutes

Warner Home Video

Doctor At Sea

Second in the long-running "Doctor" series, with Dirk Bogarde (the lone survivor of the student quartet in the first movie) cast once again as Simon Sparrow, but now fully qualified and opting for life as ship's doctor on a steamer bound for the tropics. James Robertson Justice makes things as unbearable as he can as the ship's ferocious captain but gets his come-uppance when Bogarde removes his appendix. Predictable jokes and mild entertainment for the most part, although there's a fascinating pre-Vadim glimpse of the young Brigitte Bardot, all prim and proper and well-behaved as Dirk's girlfriend.

1955. Directed by Ralph Thomas.
Starring Dirk Bogarde, Brenda de Banzie, Brigitte Bardot, James Robertson Justice, Maurice Denham, Michael Medwin, Hubert Gregg. Colour.
93 minutes

Rank Video

Doctor Dolittle

Rex Harrison is Dr. Dolittle of Puddleby-on-the-marsh. He can talk 500 animal dialects taught to him by his parrot Polynesia and he determines to set off adventuring in search of the Great Pink Sea Snail. Sounds just the thing for the kids. 'Fraid not. It's flat and wearying video that hardly ever comes to life and simply plods its way throught some of Hugh Lofting's most charming stories. A couple of the songs ("Talk To The Animals" and "I've Never Seen Anything Like It"), a well-filmed shipwreck and a boisterous cameo from Richard Attenborough as a circus owner are some of its attributes. But it's a long hard slog and you need a lot of stamina to see it through. Just below average.

Box-office rental	$6,215,000
Average rental (67)	$13,081,250
Oscars (2)	Best Special Visual Effects; Song ("Talk To The Animals")
Oscar nominations (7)	Best Film; Photography; Art Direction; Sound; Editing; Original Music Score; Scoring Of A Muscial

1967. Directed by Richard Fleischer.
Starring Rex Harrison, Samantha Eggar, Anthony Newley, Richard Attenborough, Peter Bull, Muriel Landers. Colour.
152 minutes.

Twentieth Century-Fox Video

Doctor In Distress

The "Doctor" series was well on the downward slide when this emerged in 1963, some nine years after the appearance of the record-breaking *Doctor In The House*. This one has Sir Lancelot Spratt, usually ill-tempered and terrifying, becoming as meek as a lamb when he falls in love with physiotherapist Barbara Murray. The result: sluggish entertainment. Dirk Bogarde goes through his range of expressions of surprise and raises one eyebrow now and then.

1963. Directed by Ralph Thomas.
Starring Dirk Bogarde, Samantha Eggar, James Robertson Justice, Mylene Demongeot, Donald Houston, Barbara Murray, Dennis Price. Colour.
112 minutes.

Rank Video

Doctor In The House

The antics of four medical students during their five-year training at the London hospital of St. Swithin's. The story has since become familiar through the long-running TV series, but this now rather quaint little British picture still has its moments of charm and James Robertson Justice's blustering surgeon is sheer delight. The film was the biggest British box-office success of its year although, when it was due for release, the Rank Organization was so frightened of the public appeal of a doctor film that they ordered all advertising to show Messrs. Bogarde, More, Sinden and co. in sports coats and not white hospital jackets!

1954. Directed by Ralph Thomas.
Starring Dirk Bogarde, Kenneth More, Donald Sinden, Donald Houston, Kay Kendall, Muriel Pavlow, James Robertson Justice. Colour.
91 minutes.

Rank Video

Dog Day Afternoon

A gay bank robber and his partner find themselves cornered in a Brooklyn bank when their planned heist goes awry. Forced to take hostages to protect themselves, they find their incompetent little escapade is blown up into a city-wide incident and that they become hot news. And all they wanted was some cash to finance a sex-change operation. Eh? Yeah, bizarre but true, for the events in this film actually happened in a Chase Manhattan bank back in 1972. Not that that makes them worth retelling on the screen. This one's highly overrated; much ado about nothing sums it up best.

Box-office rental	$22,500,000
Average rental (75)	$27,300,250
Oscars (1)	Best Original Screenplay
Oscar nominations (5)	Best Film; Actor (Pacino); Supporting Actor (Sarandon); Direction; Editing

1975. Directed by Sidney Lumet.
Starring Al Pacino, John Cazale, Charles Durning, James Broderick, Chris Sarandon, Carol Kane. Colour.
130 minutes.

Warner Home Video

Dogpound Shuffle

Cynical old Irish vaudevillian Ron Moody and footloose ex-boxer David Soul team up as a song and dance duo and search for the former's terrier dog Spot, which was impounded when Moody spent a night in jail. Sentimental potboiler. Good performance from Moody, a passable one from the dog and a lousy one from David Soul.

1974. Directed by Jeffrey Bloom.
Starring Ron Moody, David Soul, Pamela McMyler, Ray Stricklyn, Raymond Sutton. Colour.
88 minutes.

Precision Video

Dominique

Anyone who remembers Clouzot's masterly *The Fiends* or even *Gaslight* will find certain similarities in this story of a wife (Jean Simmons) who is driven close to madness by her husband (Cliff Robertson) and then mysteriously reappears "live" after being found dead hanging from a beam in the conservatory. But there any similarity ends, for whilst the afore-mentioned films both had class, this one is distinctly lacking in that commodity and comes over as a leaden thriller that misses out on most of its opportunities. Jenny Agutter and Simon Ward head the astonishingly strong supporting cast but don't help much.

1979. Directed by Michael Anderson.
Starring Cliff Robertson, Jean Simmons, Jenny Agutter, Simon Ward, Ron Moody, Judy Geeson, Michael Jayston, Flora Robson, David Tomlinson, Jack Warner. Colour.
100 minutes.

Guild Home Video

The Domino Killings

Gene Hackman, serving a 20-year prison sentence for murder, has escape offered to him on a plate by the head of a mysterious organization. But there is a price to pay. Once out, he must assassinate a leading American national figure and that's something he would rather not do. A mish-mash best described as a "Who's doing what to whom and why?" thriller, a question incidentally that one asks oneself many times during the film's running time. Tedious.

1977. Directed by Stanley Kramer.
Starring Gene Hackman, Candice Bergen, Richard Widmark, Mickey Rooney, Edward Albert, Eli Wallach. Colour.
100 minutes.

Precision Video

Don't Look Now

And don't unless you want to fall into the trap of believing that this is a good movie. For despite its impressive credentials, it falls firmly into the "most overrated films of the 70s" category. The slight story concerns a young married couple who visit Venice shortly after the death of their small daughter and discover that they may be able to contact her through a spiritualist. A grotesque, red-coated dwarf darts around the canal zones and Julie Christie and Donald Sutherland enjoy a steamy love scene to try to prevent you from dozing off. Flashy editing techniques tend to make you think you are watching something significant, whereas in fact you are watching nothing more than an empty cinematic puzzle. Many night scenes.

1973. Directed by Nicolas Roeg.
Starring Julie Christie, Donald Sutherland, Hilary Mason, Celia Matania, Massimo Serato. Colour.
110 minutes.

Thorn EMI Video

Doomwatch

The inhabitants of a small island off the Cornish coast fall victim to acromegaly – a disease that hideously distorts physical features. Scientist Ian Bannen investigates the matter and discovers that the disease is being caused by chemicals being illegally dumped in the sea. A serious theme then, but hardly given the serious treatment by the makers of this film, which emerges more as a horror flick than an attempt to focus on an important issue. The BBC TV series on which the film was based had much more going for it.

1972. Directed by Peter Sasdy.
Starring Ian Bannen, Judy Geeson, John Paul, Simon Oates, George Sanders, Percy Herbert, Geoffrey Keen. Colour.
92 minutes.

Guild Home Video

Double Dynamite

Frank Sinatra plus Jane Russell plus Groucho Marx should have added up to something a bit special, but this picture was made when Sinatra's early career as a crooning idol was coming to an end and it amounts to nothing more than a run-of-the-mill Hollywood comedy about the love life of a couple of banktellers – Sinatra and Russell, would you believe! Sinatra sings just two songs "Kisses And Tears" and "It's Only Money" and the film shares a tape with the John Ford western *Wagonmaster*.

1951. Directed by Irving Cummings.
Starring Frank Sinatra, Jane Russell, Groucho Marx, Don McGuire, Howard Freeman. Black and White.
80 minutes.

Kingston Video

A Double Life

The picture that finally won Ronald Colman a well-deserved Oscar; an unusual tale of a schizophrenic actor who finds himself becoming so identified with the role of Othello he is playing on the Broadway stage that he begins to live the part in real life. Even to the point where he commits murder. A sultry and slim-line Shelley Winters is his waitress victim. Nicely observed theatrical backgrounds, but it goes on a bit too long towards the end with too much Othello and not enough inventive action to sustain the interest.

| Oscars (2) | Best Actor (Colman); Music Score |
| Oscar nominations (2) | Best Direction; Original Screenplay |

1947. Directed by George Cukor.
Starring Ronald Colman, Signe Hasso, Edmond O'Brien, Shelley Winters, Ray Collins, Millard Mitchell, Joe Sawyer. Black and White.
104 minutes.

Intervision

The Dove

16-year-old yachtsman Robin Lee Graham embarks on a five-year voyage around the world and finds time for a nice romance with a Californian gal whom he seems to meet at every other port. Despite storms off Madagascar, a journey round the African coast and the perils of the Atlantic, this one emerges as an incredibly limp piece of video and makes one pleased that the switch-off knob is close to hand. Beautifully photographed of course (the cameraman is Sven Nykvist) but a bit of a no-no! And much too long.

1974. Directed by Charles Jarrott.
Starring Joseph Bottoms, Deborah Raffin, John McLiam, Dabney Coleman.
Colour.
104 minutes.

Thorn EMI Video

Dracula

You know the story, it's only the faces and fangs that change. But, that having been said, this 1979 version of Bram Stoker's vampire tale (based more on the stage play by Hamilton Deane and John L. Balderstone than Stoker's original novel) is more stylish than most and certainly more sexy. This time Frank Langella stars as the count, who finds himself washed ashore in his coffin during a violent storm off the Yorkshire coast and then proceeds to make the very devil of a nuisance of himself around the otherwise tranquil countryside. The film misses its way into unintentional comedy now and then, but basically it's powerful stuff and no less potent on the small screen than on the large. Some imaginative colourwork and gruesomely effective scenes in a mental institution add to the realism of the piece.

Box-office rental	$12,400,000
Average rental (79)	$31,964,775

1979. Directed by John Badham.

Starring Frank Langella, Laurence Olivier, Donald Pleasence, Kate Nelligan, Trevor Eve. Colour.
112 minutes.

CIC Video

Dressed To Kill

The last in the long series of Sherlock Holmes films starring Basil Rathbone and Nigel Bruce, with Holmes up against deadly female adversary Patricia Morison. The movie advertisements described her in these terms: "A price on her lovely head! A dare on her luscious lips! Danger in her icy heart!" But it makes no difference. Holmes wins!

1946. Directed by Roy William Neill.
Starring Basil Rathbone, Nigel Bruce, Patricia Morison, Edmond Breon, Frederic Worlock. Black and White.
72 minutes.

Mountain Video

The Driver

The only way to praise this dreary exercise in modern film technique is to recommend it to lovers of screen car chases, for there's a great deal of screeching of tyres around the neon-lit streets of Los Angeles. But that's about all there is. The rest of the movie is no more than a battle of wits between a strange cop and a getaway driver for a bank robbery gang. There's a great deal of talk, but one's no wiser at the end of the film than one was at the beginning. Mediocre and definitely a case of "will you or won't you stop the tape?" before boredom sets in.

1978. Directed by Walter Hill.
Starring Ryan O'Neal, Bruce Dern, Isabelle Adjani, Ronee Blakely. Colour.
90 minutes.

Thorn EMI Video

Dr. Jekyll And Mr. Hyde

The only straight version of this Robert Louis Stevenson tale available on video is this silent movie with John Barrymore as the doctor who drinks down an experimental potion and finds, to his delight and despair, that he has two sides to his personality, one good, one evil. Despite its age this one has some genuinely scary moments – the changeover scenes, Barrymore's apparition appearance as a giant spider, a savage murder – and a startling amount of cleavage from Nita Naldi.

1920. Directed by John S. Robertson.
Starring John Barrymore, Millicent Carewe, Brandon Hurst, Nita Naldi, Charles Lane. Black and White.
63 minutes.

Spectrum
(*distributed by Polygram*)

The Drum

A. E. W. Mason (*The Four Feathers*) tale, this time with the action switched from the Sudan to the Northwest Frontier of India, where a tyrant seizes power and plans to massacre a British regiment. Prince Sabu saves the day by sounding the alarm on a drum and finishes up in his rightful place on the throne. Good adventure yarn with lovely colour photography and spectacular mountain scenery. Raymond Massey is the Indian villain. Produced by Alex and directed by Zoltan Korda.

1938. Directed by Zoltan Korda.
Starring Sabu, Roger Livesey, Raymond Massey, Valerie Hobson, Desmond Tester, David Tree, Francis L. Sullivan. Colour.
96 minutes.

Spectrum
(*distributed by Polygram*)

Drum Beat

Indian fighter Alan Ladd is asked by President Grant to make peace with the warring Modoc Indians on the California-Oregon border during the late 1860s. Making his task that much more difficult: Charles Bronson as the renegade Modoc warrior Captain Jack, who rides the border with a ruthless band of warriors and refuses to give in. Quite a serious western, made in 1954 by Delmer Daves, who at the time was a bit of a dab hand at this kind of thing – *Broken Arrow, Jubal, 3.10 To Yuma*. Based on fact and supported on a double-feature tape by the musical *To Beat The Band*.

1954. Directed by Delmer Daves.
Starring Alan Ladd, Audrey Dalton, Marisa Pavan, Robert Keith, Charles Bronson. Colour.
111 minutes.

Kingston Video

Drummer Of Vengeance

Sergio Leone-type Western, with Ty Hardin as the inevitable "stranger" out to kill the Confederates responsible for the death of his Indian wife and son. Familiar theme; the only difference from the usual films of this kind being that the hero actually pays for the coffins for his victims, then disguises himself as a hellfire gravedigger and buries 'em. Bizarre? Yes. And brutal and banal.

1974. Directed by Robert Paget.
Starring Ty Hardin, Rossano Brazzi, Craig Hill, Gordon Mitchell, Edda Di Benedetta. Colour.
89 minutes.

Derann Video

The Duchess And
The Dirtwater Fox

Dim comedy western with bungling poker player George Segal and dance hall gal Goldie Hawn sharing adventures in the Old West, circa 1880. Director Melvin Frank can usually be relied upon to come up with the goods in the comedy stakes. Not on this occasion. This one's numbingly uninteresting. There's even a song called "Please Don't Touch My Plums!" The one star is for the always delightful Goldie Hawn. What a pity film-makers have never really given her the roles she deserves.

Box-office rental	$4,977,000
Average rental (76)	$22,752,350

1976. Directed by Melvin Frank.
Starring George Segal, Goldie Hawn, Conrad Janis, Thayer David, Roy Jenson. Colour.
104 minutes.

Twentieth Century-Fox Video

Duel In The Sun

"Lust In The Dust" is what they called this extravagant Western back in 1946. And they called it that because half-breed gal Jennifer Jones dies in the arms of bad 'un Greg Peck after shooting him to bits under the sweltering Arizona sun. Ridiculous? You bet! Entertaining? Enormously! For this is one of the most rewarding Westerns to be found on video, with producer David O. Selznick in full flow, staging everything on a massive scale and never once letting up on the spectacle. Tilly Losch's opening saloon dance is a *tour-de-force* by any standards; and the race to the picket fence by hundreds of mounted men quite breathtaking. The story – about two feuding brothers lusting after Miss Jones on a Texas ranch in the 1880s – is of little consequence. It's the spectacle that counts!

Box-office rental	$11,300,000
Average rental (46)	$5,720,000
Oscars	Nil

| Oscar nominations (2) | Best Actress (Jones); Supporting Actress (Gish) |

1946. Directed by King Vidor.
Starring Jennifer Jones, Gregory Peck, Joseph Cotten, Lionel Barrymore, Lillian Gish, Herbert Marshall, Walter Huston, Butterfly McQueen, Charles Bickford. Colour.
138 minutes.

Guild Home Video

The Duellists

Some novellas work when blown up into a full-scale movie (i.e. *Breakfast At Tiffanys*). Others *look* as though they have been expanded. Conrad's *The Duellists* falls into the latter category for it is no more than a series of elaborately staged duels between two Napoleonic army officers who carry on as a point of honour a ludicrous duel over a period of sixteen years. The film casts a cynical eye on the code of honour but that is hardly enough to keep one's interest from flagging. Keith Carradine and Harvey Keitel play the two officers. Beautiful to look at, but boring.

1978. Directed by Ridley Scott.
Starring Keith Carradine, Harvey Keitel, Albert Finney, Edward Fox, Cristina Raines, Robert Stephens, Diana Quick. Colour.
101 minutes.

CIC Video

E

The Eagle Has Landed

The idea behind this picture is a marvellous one: a group of German paratroopers drop into England during World War II and try to kidnap Churchill during his visit to a remote Norfolk village. But the handling is so pedestrian and the casting (Michael Caine as a German commander!) so unbelievable that the picture loses credibility long before the halfway mark. The opening plot-hatching scenes are convincingly handled and Donald Pleasence does his best to chill the blood as Himmler; after that it's just another "shoot-'em-up" exercise. Based on the novel by Jack Higgins.

Box-office rental	$4,500,000
Average rental (77)	$36,913,348

1977. Directed by John Sturges.
Starring Michael Caine, Donald Sutherland, Robert Duvall, Jenny Agutter, Donald Pleasence, Anthony Quayle, Jean Marsh, John Standing, Judy Geeson. Colour.
135 minutes.

Precision Video

Eagle's Wing

"The West The Way It Really Was . . . Before The Myths Were Born" read the advertisements for this movie when it was first released, and indeed the film does make a genuine effort to capture the primitive "feel" of the West before the outlaws and the army came. The colourwork too is remarkable. The trouble is that the film also gives off the impression of being deliberately arty and this, plus the thin plot and slow pace, finally equates with dullsville. The plot concerns a white trapper (Martin Sheen) and a redskin chief (Sam Waterston) who battle for the ownership of a magnificent white stallion. Highly regarded in some quarters.

1979. Directed by Anthony Harvey.
Starring Martin Sheen, Sam Waterston, Harvey Keitel, Stephane Audran, Caroline Langrishe, John Castle, Jorge Luke. Colour.
111 minutes.

Rank Video

East Of Eden

A twentieth century allegory of the Cain and Abel story, with James Dean and Richard Davalos as the two contrasted sons competing for the love of young Julie Harris and patriarchal father Raymond Massey. Highly regarded when it first appeared, the movie still has many fine things going for it, notably Dean's tortured performance and the period settings of 1917 California. The trouble is that it tends to drag in the later sequences and as a result becomes rather heavy going. Director Kazan's fine use of CinemaScope, notably the opening sequence in a seashore town, is also somewhat negated by the small video screen. The journey *is* worthwhile but you need perseverance. Based in part on the novel by John Steinbeck.

Box-office rental	$5,000,000
Average rental (55)	$7,239,750
Oscars (1)	Best Supporting Actress (Van Fleet)
Oscar nominations (3)	Best Actor (Dean); Direction; Screenplay

1955. Directed by Elia Kazan.
Starring James Dean, Julie Harris, Raymond Massey, Jo Van Fleet, Burl Ives, Richard Davalos, Albert Dekker. Colour.
115 minutes.

Warner Home Video

East Of Elephant Rock

Close to a reworking of Somerset Maugham's *The Letter*, with the setting transferred in time and place – to a British colony in South-East Asia circa 1948 – but with the basic theme remaining the same: wife of British plantation owner falls for a womanizing Embassy official then murders him when she discovers he's unfaithful. Poor script and rather weak entertainment; Jeremy Kemp as a bull-headed, native-hating plantation manager emerges as the best thing in an undistinguished film. No reference is made to *The Letter* in the credits.

1977. Directed by Don Boyd.

Starring John Hurt, Jeremy Kemp, Judi Bowker, Christopher Cazenove, Anton Rodgers. Colour.
92 minutes.

Precision Video

Easy Living

This one is based on a story by Irwin Shaw about an American football star (Victor Mature) who is advised to retire early when a doctor discovers he has a heart condition. The trouble is, he's saddled with luxury-loving wife Lizabeth Scott and she's expensive to keep. So, it's carry on playing. Still, there's always Lucille Ball on the sidelines to make sympathetic noises. Not bad and certainly easy watching. Supports the Astaire/Rogers musical *Carefree*.

1949. Directed by Jacques Tourneur.
Starring Victor Mature, Lizabeth Scott, Lucille Ball, Sonny Tufts, Lloyd Nolan, Paul Stewart. Black and White.
77 minutes.

Kingston Video

Easy Rider

Watershed movie that brought the "do-it-yourself" and "make-it-up-as-you-go-along" look to movies and started the downward slide from which American cinema has been trying to recover ever since. The movie is about the motor cycle odyssey of two young hippies who journey across America and discover what is right but mostly wrong with their country. The points it makes are valid, but despite the hippie trimmings not very new. Jack Nicholson features as an alcoholic small-town lawyer; Peter Fonda and Dennis Hopper are the two easy riders.

Box-office rental	$19,100,000
Average rental (69)	$13,660,950
Oscars	Nil

| Oscar nominations (2) | Best Supporting Actor (Nicholson); Story & Screenplay |

1969. Directed by Dennis Hopper.
Starring Peter Fonda, Dennis Hopper, Antonio Mendoza, Phil Spector, Mac Mashourian, Warren Finnerty, Tita Colorado, Luke Askew, Robert Walker, Jack Nicholson. Colour.
95 minutes.

RCA/Columbia International Video

El Cid

Select just one epic from those that emerged during the early 60s and you could do worse than settle for this one, a 184-minute account of the adventures of a half-legendary Castilian warrior who united the Moors and Christians under one king in 11th century Spain. There's a violently realistic hand-to-hand combat with sword and shield, plenty of spectacular battle sequences and some of the finest colourwork to be found on video, not least when the dead El Cid, dressed in armour and strapped to his white horse, rides along the misty seashore and is lit by the early morning sun. A poetic film then, and one that might just have touched greatness if, say, William Wyler and not Anthony Mann had been at the helm. But good enough as it is. Reduced to 150 minutes on video.

Box-office rental	$12,000,000
Average rental (61)	$8,103,100
Oscars	Nil
Oscar nominations (3)	Best Art Direction; Music Score; Song ("Theme from *El Cid*")

1961. Directed by Anthony Mann.
Starring Charlton Heston, Sophia Loren, Raf Vallone, Genevieve Page, John Fraser, Gary Raymond, Hurd Hatfield, Herbert Lom. Colour.
150 minutes.

Intervision

The Electric Horseman

Redford and Fonda together! Sounds like fireworks. Unfortunately they only fizzle in this lightweight little fable about a broken-down cowboy (Redford) who steals a 12-million dollar thoroughbred horse from his sponsors and makes off with it into the desert where he releases it into its natural habitat. Fonda? She's the TV reporter who tags along for the ride – and a story. Pleasant enough and with a few interesting things to say about modern man and his environment. But with Redford and Fonda together and Sydney Pollack at the helm, one expects more. And one doesn't get it.

Box-office rental	$30,917,000
Average rental (79)	$31,964,775
Oscars	Nil
Oscar nominations (1)	Best Sound

1979. Directed by Sydney Pollack.
Starring Robert Redford, Jane Fonda, Valerie Perrine, Willie Nelson, John Saxon. Colour.
120 minutes.

CIC Video

Elephant Boy

Version of Rudyard Kipling's *Toomai Of The Elephants*, about a native boy who claims to know where the elephants congregate in the jungle. Robert Flaherty's observations of elephant and other wildlife in India stand the film in good stead, but the rest of the picture dates badly. Some early Technicolor would have helped things along. As it is the film is in black and white. Mediocre.

1937. Directed by Robert Flaherty and Zoltan Korda.
Starring Sabu, Walter Hudd, Allan Jeayes, W. E. Holloway, Bruce Gordon, D. J. Williams, Wilfrid Hyde-White. Black and White.
80 minutes.

Spectrum
(distributed by Polygram)

The Elephant Man

Not a horror movie but a sympathetic, often poetic retelling of the story of John Merrick, a hideously deformed freak with a bulbous head and distorted limbs who is saved from his life as a sideshow exhibit by a young surgeon at the London Hospital. John Hurt's make-up as Merrick renders him totally unrecognizable, which makes his performance (basically acting with his eyes and mouth) all the more remarkable. David Lynch's images of fiery furnaces and industrial machinery, combined with a deafening soundtrack, conjure up a frightening portrait of life in late Victorian London. Recommended. 3½ video rating.

Box-office rental	$12,010,000
Average rental (80)	$30,086,027
Oscars	Nil
Oscar nominations (8)	Best Film; Actor (Hurt); Direction; Screenplay; Editing; Art Direction; Costume Design; Original Music Score

1980. Directed by David Lynch.
Starring Anthony Hopkins, John Hurt, Anne Bancroft, John Gielgud, Wendy Hiller, Freddie Jones, Michael Elphick, Hannah Gordon, John Standing. Black and White.
124 minutes.

Thorn EMI Video

Elvis – The Movie

The Elvis Presley story, from his youth in Mississippi to his comeback in concert in Las Vegas in 1969. Straight-down-the-line musical biography that takes in Elvis' girlfriends, his promotion by Colonel Parker, his break into films, his years in the army and so on, but does very little to suggest the distress suffered by the singer in later life. Still, the movie gained a bigger audience than *Gone With The Wind* when shown on telly in America and if you're a Presley addict you'll probably find it worthwhile. Kurt Russell is Elvis, Shelley Winters Elvis' mom, and country singer Ronnie McDowell does the vocal impersonations. Made-For-TV but shown theatrically in Britain. Television length: 160 minutes.

1979. Directed by John Carpenter.

Starring Kurt Russell, Shelley Winters, Bing Russell, Robert Gray, Season
Hubley, Pat Hingle. Colour.
119 minutes.

Picture Time Video
(*distributed by VCL*)

Embassy

State Department official Richard Roundtree is given the unenviable task
of smuggling Russian defector Max von Sydow out of Beirut. Unenviable
because KGB assassin Chuck Connors (posing as an American colonel)
is waiting for his first wrong move. Veterans Broderick Crawford and Ray
Milland lend a touch of authority to the events; the script by William
Fairchild deserves close attention and the pace is brisk. Unambitious but
effective spy thriller. Watch out for an intriguing sequence in which
Roundtree tracks Connors through a deserted embassy. 2½ video rating.

1972. Directed by Gordon Hessler.
Starring Richard Roundtree, Chuck Connors, Marie-Jose Nat, Ray Milland,
Broderick Crawford, Max von Sydow, David Bauer. Colour.
90 minutes.

Cinema Features
(*distributed by VCL*)

Emmanuelle

The rather limp sexual adventures of a young French bride when she
joins her Embassy official husband in Bangkok. The "adventures" include
dabbling in lesbianism, being instructed by an ageing sexologist, enjoying
the night life of Bangkok and being put through a series of humiliating
sexual encounters. Directed by former fashion photographer Just Jaeckin.
Sylvia Kristel looks attractive but that's about all.

Box-office rental $4,000,000

Average rental (74) $18,456,150

1974. Directed by Just Jaeckin.
Starring Sylvia Kristel, Marika Green, Daniel Sarky, Alain Cuny, Jeanne
Colletin. Colour.
92 minutes.

Brent Walker Video
(*distributed by Videospace*)

Enchanted Island

This adaptation of Herman Melville's *Typee* doesn't figure very promi-
nently in movie history books and it's easy to understand why, for its
cheap celluloid images are far removed from the majesty of Melville's
prose. It's all about a couple of sailors who desert an American whaling
ship during the 1840s and settle on a South Seas island. The main attraction
is pretty native girl Jane Powell; the major drawback is that the island is
infested with cannibals. Advice: forget the tape and read the book. Also
available on the same video double bill: *Westward Passage*.

1958. Directed by Allan Dwan.
Starring Dana Andrews, Jane Powell, Don Dubbins, Arthur Shields, Ted
de Corsia. Colour.
94 minutes.

Kingston Video

End Of The World

This one offers two Christopher Lees for the price of one. And even then
you're being overcharged. Lee plays both a priest and his sinister double
who between them are mixed up with the destruction of planet Earth by
invaders from a Utopian planet. Sounds crummy. And it is! There's one
interesting pre-credit sequence of telekinetic power.

1977. Directed by John Hayes.

Starring Christopher Lee, Sue Lyon, Kirk Scott, Lew Ayres, Macdonald Carey, Dean Jagger. Colour.
87 minutes.

Intervision

The Enforcer

Third time out for Clint Eastwood as Dirty Harry Callahan and a distinctly third-rate outing it is too. This story has Clint demoted because of his methods (about time!) and assigned a female cop as a partner. Together they set about rescuing a kidnapped mayor from the clutches of a terrorist gang operating in San Francisco. Cardboard characterizations; a plot that seems to have been concocted by a cinematic computer and the usual gratuitous violence. You pays your money you takes your choice! (See also *Dirty Harry* and *Magnum Force*)

Box-office rental	$24,000,000
Average rental (76)	$22,752,350

1976. Directed by James Fargo.
Starring Clint Eastwood, Tyne Daly, Harry Guardino, Bradford Dillman, John Mitchum. Colour.
96 minutes.

Warner Home Video

England Made Me

Not the best known adaptation of a Graham Greene work but certainly one of the most interesting, set in prewar Germany and following the experiences of a feckless young Englishman when he becomes involved with a German financier whose corruption is personified by the Europe crumbling around him. Thoughtful, intelligent video. Peter Finch is superb as the financier, Michael York impressive as the Englishman. And lending more than adequate support: Michael Hordern as a down-at-heel reporter and Joss Ackland as his assassin. Recommended!

1973. Directed by Peter Duffell.
Starring Peter Finch, Michael York, Hildegard Neil, Michael Hordern, Joss Ackland, Tessa Wyatt. Colour.
100 minutes.

Cinema Features
(distributed by VCL)

Enter The Dragon

The last movie to star Bruce Lee, the martial arts cult figure of the 70s, and really nothing more than an oriental 007 escapade with plenty of grunts and groans and kicks above and below the belt. Lee plays a master of martial arts who is enlisted by British Intelligence to put an end to the drug running and prostitution activities of a black gloved master criminal. Noisy rubbish if you don't like karate chops.

| Box-office rental | $11,000,000 |
| Average rental (73) | $22,271,150 |

1973. Directed by Robert Clouse.
Starring Bruce Lee, John Saxon, Shih Kien, Jim Kelly, Bob Wall, Yang Sze. Colour.
98 minutes.

Warner Home Video

Escapade In Japan

The real stars of this likeable little movie are the Japanese backgrounds, which are consistently pleasing to the eye and provide a fascinating backdrop to the story of a 7-year-old American boy, whose plane is forced down and who joins forces with a Japanese lad while his parents, the police and what seems like the entire US Air Force search for him. Unpretentious and made in the mid-50s when the RKO studio was about to close up shop. On the same tape: *A Gift For Heidi*.

1957. Directed by Arthur Lubin.

Starring Teresa Wright, Cameron Mitchell, Jon Provost, Philip Ober.
Colour.
92 minutes.

Kingston Video

Escape From Alcatraz

The true story of how three men broke out of America's maximum security prison in San Francisco bay in 1962. Not exactly a Clint Eastwood action movie, in fact the very opposite – an interior "chamber" picture, in which most of the drama is confined to within the walls of the prison. An abundance of night scenes slows down the action considerably and you'll probably have to pinch yourself to keep awake. Patrick McGoohan's over-the-top performance as a sadistic prison governor livens things up a bit.

Box-office rental	$21,500,000
Average rental (79)	$31,964,775

1979. Directed by Donald Siegel.
Starring Clint Eastwood, Patrick McGoohan, Robert Blossom, Jack Thibeau, Fred Ward. Colour.
112 minutes.

CIC Video

Escape To Athena

The cast is strong – Roger Moore (as a German major!), Telly Savalas, David Niven, Stefanie Powers, Elliott Gould, but that unfortunately does not ensure a good picture. Unless of course you have a good story to go with it. Which this one hasn't. The setting is a Greek island during World War II. The plot involves some POWs digging for art treasures and the Resistance battling against the SS. The usual Lew Grade misfire.

1979. Directed by George P. Cosmatos.
Starring Roger Moore, Telly Savalas, David Niven, Claudia Cardinale,

Stefanie Powers, Richard Roundtree, Elliott Gould, Anthony Valentine.
Colour.
117 minutes.

Precision Video

The Europeans ★★★

Elegant James Ivory version of Henry James' novel about two Europeans
– a baroness and her French-educated brother – who visit their wealthy
cousins in Boston in the hope of improving their fortunes. The most
delicate and richly toned of all Ivory's recent films and one that subtly
reflects the differences between European sophistication and high-
minded American innocence during the 1850s. Video entertainment of
the most rewarding kind. Lee Remick plays the baroness, Tim Woodward
her brother.

Oscars	Nil
Oscar nominations (1)	Best Costume Design

1979. Directed by James Ivory.
Starring Lee Remick, Robin Ellis, Tim Woodward, Wesley Addy, Lisa
Eichhorn, Nancy New, Tim Choate. Colour.
83 minutes.

Home Video Productions

Everything You Always Wanted To Know About Sex But Were Afraid To Ask ★★★

Multi-story Woody Allen comedy that investigates a series of sexual
hangups. Lynn Redgrave is a medieval queen trapped in a chastity belt;
doctor Gene Wilder falls in love with his sheep Daisy; Woody Allen
appears as a jester with a line in throwaway *Hamlet*-type jokes ("TB or
not TB, that is the congestion") and, in a climax that is as tasteless as it
is hilarious, as a sperm inside the male body worried about the speed

with which he will reach his destination. And also where he is going! Seven episodes in all with Allen appearing in four and directing the lot. Burt Reynolds guest stars.

Box-office rental $8,110,000
Average rental (72) $17,543,950

1972. Directed by Woody Allen.
Starring Woody Allen, John Carradine, Lou Jacobi, Louise Lasser, Anthony Quayle, Tony Randall, Lynn Redgrave, Burt Reynolds, Gene Wilder. Colour.
87 minutes.

Intervision

Every Which Way But Loose   ★

There are moments when Clint Eastwood (both as an actor and a director) seems a little bit special. There are others when he seems nothing more than a third-rate performer in search of suitable material. This film finds him very definitely in the latter category, for it's a no-no from the first reel. Clint's a trucker who enjoys a few fist fights on the side. Along the way he meets a double-crossing country and western singer, a lady hitch-hiker and an orangutan. And the result? Nearly 52 million at the box-office. Hmmm . . . One star for the monkey!

Box-office rental $51,800,000
Average rental (78) $39,443,850

1978. Directed by James Fargo.
Starring Clint Eastwood, Sondra Locke, Geoffrey Lewis, Beverly D'Angelo, Ruth Gordon. Colour.
119 minutes.

Warner Home Video

The Exorcist

Many consider this the most harrowing horror film of the lot. And with good reason. It's about the 12-year-old daughter of an American film actress who suddenly finds herself possessed by the Devil and unable to do anything about it. Only exorcism it seems will help. And that's duly provided by Jesuit archaeologist and priest Max von Sydow, who's been expecting such an occurrence since coming across a medallion and strange figurine in Iraq. The movie loses little of its enormous power on video other than in its soundtrack, which was used to brilliant and deafening effect in the cinema. So turn up the volume when watching this one. Mind you, it's one to watch well after the kids have gone to bed, for it's full of headturnings, green bile and things scratching away in the attic. And the language isn't too pretty either. Best sequence? The underrated prologue in Iraq, a scene full of menace and eerie expectation.

Box-office rental	$88,500,000
Average rental (73)	$22,271,150
Oscars (2)	Best Screenplay; Sound
Oscar nominations (8)	Best Film; Actress (Burstyn); Supporting Actor (Miller); Supporting Actress (Blair); Direction; Photograpy; Art Direction; Editing

1973. Directed by William Friedkin.
Starring Ellen Burstyn, Max von Sydow, Lee J. Cobb, Kitty Winn, Jack MacGowran, Jason Miller, Linda Blair. Colour.
122 minutes.

Warner Home Video

Exorcist II: The Heretic

The inevitable follow-up with the inevitable inferior results. This time it's Richard Burton who dons the cloth, as he sets about investigating the case of Max von Sydow, who died whilst exorcising the demon in Part 1 and apparently didn't make a very good job of it, for much of the Devil still lurks in the now adolescent Linda Blair. This one's a disaster on every level (even the special effects are mediocre with the Devil guesting as a locust) and it's hard to credit that it was made by the same man who filmed *Deliverance*. In America they call this type of movie a bomb. And they're right. As video fare it just doesn't rate.

Box-office rental $13,900,000
Average rental (77) $36,913,348

1977. Directed by John Boorman.
Starring Linda Blair, Richard Burton, Louise Fletcher, Max von Sydow,
Kitty Winn, Paul Henreid, James Earl Jones. Colour.
102 minutes.

Warner Home Video

The Exterminator

A perfect example of the depths to which modern moviemaking has
sunk. Christopher George has the lead as a Vietnam war veteran whose
black pal is made a paraplegic after the pair have tried to prevent a
robbery at a waterfront warehouse. Vengeance, vigilante-style, becomes
the order of the day and what follows are hoods being eaten alive by
vermin, a Mafia boss "getting his" in a giant mincing machine, threats
with a blow torch, and so on. Get the idea. Just make your hero a
battle-scarred veteran of Vietnam and you have the excuse to show every
kind of sadism and violence imaginable. And, modern day morality being
what it is, our hero is still alive at the final reel. Repulsive.

Box-office rental $4,000,000
Average rental (80) $30,086,027

1980. Directed by James Glickenhaus.
Starring Christopher George, Samantha Eggar, Robert Ginty, Steve James,
Tony Di Benedetto. Colour.
101 minutes.

Intervision

Eyes Of Laura Mars

High fashion photographer Faye Dunaway starts getting the creeps when
she begins experiencing premonitions of grisly murders just a few hours
before they actually occur. By the climax she "sees" the killer approaching

her own apartment. But who is he? Or she? Contrived little thriller that needed a director of Hitchcock's stature to surmount the plot's improbabilities. Part scripted by John Carpenter. New York locations. Tommy Lee Jones is the detective investigating the case.

Box-office rental	$8,600,000
Average rental (78)	$39,443,850

1978. Directed by Irvin Kershner.
Starring Faye Dunaway, Tommy Lee Jones, Brad Dourif, Rene Auberjonois, Raul Julia, Frank Adonis, Lisa Taylor. Colour.
103 minutes.

RCA/Columbia International Video

Eyewitness

A reworking of the classic RKO thriller *The Window* about a boy who cries "wolf" once too often and finds that no-one will believe him when he witnesses an assassination. Other than the killers that is. They put him at the top of their hit list. Set in Malta with 11-year-old Mark Lester as the boy, Susan George as his teenage sister and Lionel Jeffries as his grandad, a retired colonel who always makes sure he dresses for dinner. Always pleasant, never outstanding. Reasonable middle-of-the-road video fare.

1970. Directed by John Hough.
Starring Mark Lester, Lionel Jeffries, Susan George, Tony Bonner, Jeremy Kemp, Peter Vaughan, Peter Bowles. Colour.
91 minutes.

Precision Video

F

The Face Of Fu Manchu

Diabolical arch villain Dr. Fu Manchu was first brought to life by novelist
Sax Rohmer in 1913. Here he is again, this time portrayed by Christopher
Lee and determined to make another bid for world domination with the
aid of a new highly lethal gas distilled from a Tibetan poppy seed. Gad
sir! Can Scotland Yard, in the form of redoubtable Nayland Smith, save
Western civilization in time . . .? Par for the course I suppose, with assas-
sinations, kidnappings, beautiful slave girls and so on. Set in London in
the 20s.

1965. Directed by Don Sharp.
Starring Christopher Lee, Nigel Green, James Robertson Justice, Howard
Marion Crawford, Walter Rilla. Colour.
94 minutes.

Thorn EMI Video

The Fallen Idol

Graham Greene tale about an ambassador's small son who idolizes the
Embassy butler but almost involves him in a murder charge when the
butler's wife meets an accidental death. A poignant study of a child trying
painfully to bridge the gap between dreams and reality; made after *Odd
Man Out* and before *The Third Man* and making up a classic trio of Carol
Reed films, all of which are available on video. Set in a Foreign Embassy
in London and beautifully crafted. Adapted from Greene's short story *The
Basement Room*. Ralph Richardson gives one of his most distinguished
performances as the butler.

Oscars   Nil
Oscar nominations (2)   Best Direction; Screenplay

1948. Directed by Carol Reed.

Starring Ralph Richardson, Michele Morgan, Bobby Henrey, Sonia Dresdel, Jack Hawkins. Black and White.
94 minutes.

Thorn EMI Video

The Fall Of The Roman Empire

The actual fall takes 165 minutes and it's an uneven and uncertain journey downwards as Christopher Plummer (Commodus) schemes, cheats and murders his way to the Roman throne. Emperor Alec Guinness (Marcus Aurelius) had wanted it for his adopted son. No such luck. In the end the throne is empty and Roman senators are bidding with their wealth to occupy it. Hollywood spectacular of the mid-60s, more intelligent to listen to than usual but rather short on action, which means the journey is often ponderous as well as uneven. Fine sets. James Mason is the Greek philosopher Timonides. 2½ video rating.

Oscars	Nil
Oscar nominations (1)	Best Music Score

1964. Directed by Anthony Mann.
Starring Sophia Loren, Stephen Boyd, Alec Guinness, James Mason, Christopher Plummer, Anthony Quayle, John Ireland, Mel Ferrer, Omar Sharif, Eric Porter. Colour.
165 minutes.

Intervision

Fame

The lives of a disparate group of teenagers as they work their way through four years at Manhattan's High School For The Performing Arts. Singing, dancing, acting – it's all here in a noisy and affectionate tribute to the kids who dedicate themselves completely to their art even though they know that, at the end of the course, the "fame" of the title is very far from being guaranteed. But fame is the spur and that's what this one's all about. Very well done at times, but also uneven and a bit crude and its brash vigour takes a bit of a knock on the small video screen.

Box-office rental	$7,000,000
Average rental (80)	$30,086,027
Oscars (2)	Best Song ("Fame"); Original Music Score
Oscar nominations (4)	Best Screenplay; Editing; Sound; Song ("Out Here On My Own")

1980. Directed by Alan Parker.
Starring Irene Cara, Lee Curreri, Laura Dean, Antonia Franceschi, Paul McCrane, Barry Miller, Gene Anthony Ray, Maureen Teefy. Colour.
133 minutes.

MGM/CBS Home Video

Family Life

A 19-year-old girl suffers a mental collapse following an abortion, finds that she cannot adjust to her suffocating suburban life with her parents and has to undergo psychiatric treatment in a London hospital. Harrowing, forceful, depressing but oh-so-real video. Ken Loach examines the girl's environment, the methods of her psychiatric treatment and her overall family life quite relentlessly. From the 1967 play *In Two Minds* by David Mercer. Non-professional cast.

1971. Directed by Ken Loach.
Starring Sandy Ratcliff, Bill Dean, Grace Cave, Malcolm Tierney, Hilary Martyn, Michael Riddall, Alan MacNaughtan. Colour.
108 minutes.

Thorn EMI Video

Fantastic Voyage

A crew of five (Stephen Boyd, Raquel Welch, Arthur Kennedy, Donald Pleasence, William Redfield) are miniaturized and popped into a mini-submarine which is injected into the bloodstream of a dying scientist. Crazy? Depends on your political view. The scientist is a Czech with many secrets to hand over to the USA. An operation to save his life can only be performed from the inside but naturally there's a spy in the camp or, in this case, the blood. Neat idea, not worked out as well as it might have been but the effects are interesting.

Box-office rental	$5,500,000
Average rental (66)	$8,826,100
Oscars (2)	Best Art Direction; Visual Effects
Oscar nominations (3)	Best Photography; Editing; Sound Effects

1966. Directed by Richard Fleischer.
Starring Stephen Boyd, Raquel Welch, Edmond O'Brien, Donald Pleasence, Arthur O'Connell, Arthur Kennedy, William Redfield. Colour.
100 minutes.

Twentieth Century-Fox Video

Farewell My Lovely

Robert Mitchum, as laconic private eye Philip Marlowe, wanders wearily through this remake of Raymond Chandler's famous mystery tale of a double search – for a stolen jade necklace and the missing girlfriend of an ex-con. It's not a patch on the 1944 Dick Powell version, but an erotic Charlotte Rampling slinks effectively and causes a drowsy Mitchum to come awake with the remark: "She gave me a smile I could feel in my hip pocket." Such dialogue keeps the film afloat for much of its length.

Oscars	Nil
Oscar nominations (1)	Best Supporting Actress (Miles)

1975. Directed by Dick Richards.
Starring Robert Mitchum, Charlotte Rampling, John Ireland, Sylvia Miles, Anthony Zerbe, Harry Dean Stanton, Jack O'Halloran. Colour.
95 minutes.

Precision Video

Far From The Madding Crowd

Thomas Hardy's beloved Wessex brought vividly to life by John Schlesinger in one of the most neglected classic adaptations of the post-war years. Julie Christie is the passionate young Bathsheba Everdene, who enslaves three men when she inherits a farm from her uncle; shepherd Alan Bates, army officer Terence Stamp and wealthy landowner Peter Finch are her victims. In the acting stakes it's Finch's film from first to last but Schlesinger's handling and Nicolas Roeg's colourwork eventually overshadow all. Stimulating video entertainment and at times quite inspired.

Oscars	Nil
Oscar nominations (1)	Best Music Score

1967. Directed by John Schlesinger.
Starring Julie Christie, Terence Stamp, Peter Finch, Alan Bates, Fiona Walker, Prunella Ransome, Alison Leggatt, Paul Dawkins. Colour.
168 minutes.

Thorn EMI Video

The Farmer's Daughter

Old-fashioned but nonetheless entertaining Selznick movie about a headstrong Swedish farm girl (Loretta Young) from Minnesota who finds herself fighting for – and winning – a seat in Congress. Congressman Joseph Cotten is her romantic involvement, Ethel Barrymore a political matriarch. A bit naive but likeable and amusing and with classy production values. Not seen much on TV so worth a look on video.

Oscars (1)	Best Actress (Young)
Oscar nominations (1)	Best Supporting Actor (Bickford)

1947. Directed by H. C. Potter.
Starring Loretta Young, Joseph Cotten, Ethel Barrymore, Charles Bickford, Rose Hobart, Harry Davenport, Lex Barker. Black and White.
97 minutes.

Guild Home Video

The Fast Lady

The "Fast Lady" of the title is a car, a vintage Bentley, purchased by cycle-riding civil servant Stanley Baxter in order to impress the girl of his dreams – Julie Christie, attractive daughter of bombastic James Robertson Justice. An old-fashioned movie obviously but an entertaining one and, as the English social scene it depicts has long since disappeared, of some nostalgic appeal as well. Eric Barker enters into the spirit of things with a brilliant cameo of a jittery driving examiner whose job has turned him into a nervous wreck. Two-star rating but deserves 2½!

1962. Directed by Ken Annakin.
Starring Leslie Phillips, Stanley Baxter, Kathleen Harrison, James Robertson Justice, Julie Christie, Eric Barker. Colour.
95 minutes.

Rank Video

Fiddler On The Roof

Ukranian milkman Topol talks to God, attempts to find husbands for his five daughters and battles constantly against the oppression of Russian officialdom. Not perhaps everyone's idea of relaxing musical entertainment but Oswald Morris' locations are striking and many of the musical numbers – "Matchmaker, Matchmaker", "Sunrise, Sunset" and (especially) the rousing "Tradition" – are splendidly staged. The main problem is one of length. Three hours is a wee bit too long for the small screen, especially for a musical with such a desolate feel to it. Based on Sholom Aleichem's stories of village life in the Ukraine. Isaac Stern performs the rooftop violin solo.

Box-office rental	$40,498,669
Average rental (71)	$13,465,850
Oscars (3)	Best Photography; Sound; Scoring Of A Musical
Oscar nominations (5)	Best Film; Actor (Topol); Supporting Actor (Frey); Direction; Art Direction

1971. Directed by Norman Jewison.

Starring Topol, Norma Crane, Leonard Frey, Molly Picon, Paul Mann, Rosalind Harris, Michele Marsh, Neva Small, Michael Glaser. Colour. 180 minutes.

Intervision

The Fiend

Some rather nasty goings-on amongst an eccentric religious sect in a London suburban house. Patrick Magee is the sect's sinister boss; Ann Todd has a nutty son who goes round killing prostitutes because he believes he is ensuring their salvation. And there are three songs including one called "Wash Me In His Blood". An ugly little film.

1972. Directed by Robert Hartford-Davis.
Starring Ann Todd, Patrick Magee, Tony Beckley, Madeline Hinde, Percy Herbert, Suzanna Leigh, David Lodge. Colour.
87 minutes.

Derann Video

The Fiendish Plot Of Dr. Fu Manchu

A very recent movie that died the death in the cinemas and will probably suffer a similar fate on video. Peter Sellers features in a dual role – as the 168-year-old Chinese master criminal Fu Manchu and his old British adversary Nayland Smith. The plot has something to do with Sellers seeking a rejuvenation cure that somehow leads him to England that somehow leads him to steal diamonds from the Tower of London . . . Oh, well! Sadly, this was Sellers' last movie. It's a pity he couldn't have gone out with a bit more style, for just two words describe this mish-mash: feeble and witless.

Box-office rental $5,175,000

Average rental (80) $30,086,027

1980. Directed by Piers Haggard.
Starring Peter Sellers, Helen Mirren, David Tomlinson, Sid Caesar. Colour.
108 minutes

Warner Home Video

Fiend Without A Face

An isolated airforce base in Canada. A scientist conjures up thought
monsters from his own *id* and unleashes them all over the place so that
they latch onto the backs of their victims and feed off their brains for
food. Sounds a bit nasty and it is, but the effects aren't bad and the film
comprises an acceptable horror double-bill with the Boris Karloff thriller
Grip Of The Strangler.

1957. Directed by Arthur Crabtree.
Starring Marshall Thompson, Kim Parker, Kynaston Reeves, Stanely
Maxted, Terry Kilburn. Black and White.
73 minutes.

Kingston Video

55 Days At Peking

Or, the siege by the Chinese Boxers of eleven foreign embassies in the
legation compound of Peking in the year 1900. Unfortunately, the 55 days
seem like 55 days despite some sterling second-unit work by Andrew
Marton and the dynamic music themes of Dimitri Tiomkin. And video
shrinks the canvas considerably, which makes the events seem even
more pedestrian. Ever-reliable Charlton Heston as a two-dimensional
American marine; Ava Gardner as a two-dimensional Russian baroness;
and David Niven as a two-dimensional British ambassador lead the defence against the rebellious one-dimensional Chinese.

Box-office rental $5,000,000
Average rental (63) $8,360,900

Oscars   Nil
Oscar nominations (2)   Best Music Score; Song ("So Little Time")

1963. Directed by Nicholas Ray.
Starring Charlton Heston, David Niven, Ava Gardner, Robert Helpmann, Flora Robson, Leo Genn, John Ireland, Paul Lukas. Colour.
154 minutes.

Intervision

Firepower

Sophia Loren seeks revenge for the murder of her research chemist husband and hires her ex-lover James Coburn to track down the killer. Of the kind you have seen many times on television and a made-for-the-money exercise if ever there was one. Even the climactic chase by helicopter is badly handled. Only redeeming feature: the Caribbean locations, where most of the action is set.

1979. Directed by Michael Winner.
Starring Sophia Loren, James Coburn, O. J. Simpson, Eli Wallach, Anthony Franciosa, George Grizzard, Vincent Gardenia. Colour.
104 minutes.

Precision Video

Flash Gordon

30s science-fiction hero Flash Gordon gets the glossy, wide-screen treatment in this 1980 extravaganza, dealing with his battles against the despotic Emperor Ming, who dwells on his planet Mongo and gleefully anticipates the destruction of the planet Earth. Like all largish productions this one is cut down to size on video but, thanks to some gentle spoofing and camp jokes by screenwriter Lorenzo Semple, Jr, an array of glittering costumes and a great deal of attractive female anatomy, it just about gets by on the small screen. Good for kids, although be warned, the effects are nothing special!

| Box-office rental | $16,100,000 |
| Average rental (80) | $30,086,027 |

1980. Directed by Michael Hodges.
Starring Sam J. Jones, Melody Anderson, Topol, Max von Sydow,
Ornella Muti, Timothy Dalton, Brian Blessed. Colour.
115 minutes.

Thorn EMI Video

The Flesh And Blood Show

Old-fashioned horror thriller about a group of actors who accept an
invitation from a mysterious employer to appear in a play at "Eastcliffe-
on-Sea". The venue is a derelict theatre and (yes, you've guessed it) one
by one the corpses begin to mount until the villain of the piece – a man
with a pathological hatred of actors – is unmasked. Clichés all the way;
meagre video entertainment.

1972. Directed by Peter Walker.
Starring Jenny Hanley, Ray Brooks, Luan Peters, Judy Matheson, Candace
Glendenning, Robin Askwith, Tristan Rogers, Patrick Barr. Colour.
96 minutes.

Vampix
(*distributed by Videomedia*)

Flying Leathernecks

Hollywood rumour has it that Howard Hughes paid John Wayne a record
310,000 dollars to appear in this picture back in 1951. You might say that
Hughes was "done". Big John is no more than routine in an average tale
of a tough Marine Corps commander who is resented by his men, who
would have preferred more humane Robert Ryan to lead them into battle
in the South Pacific. Good colour and spectacular newsreel battle footage
are plus factors. Shares a video tape with *Beyond A Reasonable Doubt*.

1951. Directed by Nicholas Ray.

Starring John Wayne, Robert Ryan, Don Taylor, Janis Carter, Jay C. Flippen, William Harrigan. Colour.
102 minutes.

Kingston Video

The Fog

Director John Carpenter up to his nasty tricks once more with a tale of some ghostly mariners who return from their watery grave to take revenge on the inhabitants of a small Californian coastal town. Why? Because 100 years earlier their clipper ship carrying gold was deliberately wrecked and 100 years is about as long as they want to wait before getting their own back. Plenty of mist, not much horror but with a few eerie moments. Janet Leigh and John Houseman (not quite one's idea of an old sea salt) bring a certain dignity to the proceedings.

Box-office rental	$11,000,000
Average rental (80)	$30,086,027

1980. Directed by John Carpenter.
Starring Adrienne Barbeau, Hal Holbrook, Janet Leigh, Jamie Lee Curtis, John Houseman, Tom Atkins, Nancy Loomis. Colour.
89 minutes.

Twentieth Century-Fox Video

Follow Me Quietly

One of those efficient low-grade American thrillers that gave directors such as Richard Fleischer the opportunity to learn the fundamentals of film-making. It charts the hunting down by detectives of a psychopathic strangler who calls himself a judge and becomes obsessed with murder whenever it rains. A bit far-fetched perhaps, but not at all bad in its limited way. On a double-feature tape this one offers terror and suspense; its companion piece, *The Fugitive,* offers a drama of faith and betrayal.

1949. Directed by Richard Fleischer.

Starring William Lundigan, Dorothy Patrick, Jeff Corey. Black and White.
59 minutes.

Kingston Video

Footlight Varieties

A series of vintage variety acts interwoven with old RKO movie clips.
Leon Errol helps provide the tomfoolery and a young Liberace plays
Liszt's "Hungarian Rhapsody" – plus his own Boogie Woogie. Jack Paar
introduces it all. The supporting feature to *Without Reservations*.

1951. Directed by Hal Yates.
Starring Red Buttons, Jack Paar, Grace Romanos, Frankie Carle, Leon
Errol. Black and White.
61 minutes.

Kingston Video

Forbidden Planet

A quite ingenious sci-fi reworking of Shakespeare's *The Tempest* with
Walter Pidgeon (in the Prospero role) as a philologist working on a
distant planet and studying the advanced civilization left intact by the
planet's extinct peoples. When an expedition from Earth arrives and
begins meddling in his affairs he conjures up a monster from his psyche
and lets loose a terrifying invisible force that destroys people at will.
Highly inventive science fiction, set in the year 2200 and co-starring a
likeable little robot called Robby who isn't much to look at – he's shaped
like an old pot-bellied stove – but can speak 187 languages along with
their various dialects and sub-tongues!

Oscars	Nil
Oscar nominations (1)	Best Special Effects

1956. Directed by Fred M. Wilcox.
Starring Walter Pidgeon, Anne Francis, Leslie Nielsen, Warren Stevens,
Jack Kelly, Richard Anderson, Earl Holliman. Colour.

98 minutes.

MGM/CBS Home Video

The Formula

Roly-poly oil magnate Marlon Brando pretends he's Sydney Greenstreet; grim-faced George C. Scott pretends he's a hard-boiled cop. You too can pretend that you're watching a good movie, providing of course you can forget the oh-so-tedious pace and understand the complicated body-strewn plot, which has something to do with how the Germans discovered a formula for turning coal into petrol at the end of World War II. Watch out for the credits. There are four editors involved. That's always a tell-tale sign. If four of them couldn't do anything with this film what must it have been like in the first place?

Oscars   Nil
Oscar nominations (1)   Best Photography

1980. Directed by John V. Avildsen.
Starring George C. Scott, Marlon Brando, Marthe Keller, John Gielgud, G. D. Spradlin, Beatrice Straight. Colour.
117 minutes.

MGM/CBS Home Video

Fort Apache

The first in what has since become known as John Ford's cavalry trilogy, and really no more than a reworking of the General Custer story. The only surprise lies in the somewhat offbeat casting of Henry Fonda as a martinet army colonel whose military stupidity results in the death of his men. Not such a surprise is that good old John Wayne is in there too, as a second-in-command whose wise advice goes unheeded. Some good passages but not John Ford at his best and much, much too long.

1948. Directed by John Ford.

Starring John Wayne, Henry Fonda, Shirley Temple, Pedro Armendariz, John Agar, Anna Lee, Victor McLaglen, Ward Bond. Black and White. 127 minutes.

Thorn EMI Video

The Four Feathers

Old warhorse of a movie about young Harry Faversham (John Clements) who is branded a coward by his fiancée and fellow officers and sets out for Egypt where he perfoms fantastic feats of endurance in order to prove his courage. The outstanding location photography (Sudan, 1939) partly compensates for A. E. W. Mason's creaky "glorification of war" plot and there is one outstanding sequence when Ralph Richardson goes blind through sunstroke and finds himself alone in the desert with only his dead comrades and vultures for company. Remade as *Storm Over The Nile* (see page 404)

1939. Directed by Zoltan Korda.
Starring John Clements, Ralph Richardson, Sir C. Aubrey Smith, June Duprez, Allan Jeayes, Jack Allen, Donald Gray. Colour.
107 minutes.

Spectrum
(distributed by Polygram)

Frankenstein

An obsessed scientist believes he can assemble a living human from the organs of dead bodies. He can! But, like all good monsters, the creature quickly runs amok and makes the scientist rue the day he ever thought up the idea. This is the one in which Karloff played the monster for the first time and as it's now more than fifty years old it more than looks its age. And with a running time of only 71 minutes you might think twice about purchasing it on video. Still, there are plenty of effective moments remaining and the monster's coming alive during a raging thunderstorm is a *tour-de-force*.

1931. Directed by James Whale.
Starring Colin Clive, Mae Clarke, Boris Karloff, John Boles, Edward Van Sloan, Frederick Kerr, Dwight Frye. Black and White.
71 minutes.

CIC Video

Freaky Friday

13-year-old Jodie Foster and nagging mom Barbara Harris, forever getting on each other's nerves, wish that just for a moment they could change places. This being a Disney movie their wish is granted, with some amusing if occasionally predictable results. The film's initial comedy scenes as the two characters try to come to terms with their new roles come off the best; the later sequences dip into the inevitable chase and slapstick. Could have been better but quite endearing (the kooky Barbara Harris is a delight) and 12-year-old girls will love it, if only for vengeful reasons!

| Box-office rental | $11,500,000 |
| Average rental (76) | $22,752,350 |

1976. Directed by Gary Nelson.
Starring Barbara Harris, Jodie Foster, John Astin, Patsy Kelly, Dick Van Patten. Colour.
100 minutes.

Walt Disney Home Video

The French Connection

Enjoy a sample of police life in modern-day New York from the comfort of your armchair as Gene Hackman of the Narcotics Squad goes after the mastermind smuggling vast quantities of heroin into the USA. The chase with Hackman demoniacally pursuing by car a train commandeered by a killer is justifiably famous. The rest of the film wears less well and is full of beatings up, foul language, murky camerawork and other things that go to make present-day viewing such a pleasurable experience. Only Fernando Rey adds a touch of elegance and he's the villain of the piece!

Box-office rental	$26,315,000
Average rental (71)	$13,465,850
Oscars (5)	Best Film; Actor (Hackman); Direction; Screenplay; Editing
Oscar nominations (3)	Best Supporting Actor (Scheider); Sound; Photography

1971. Directed by William Friedkin.
Starring Gene Hackman, Fernando Rey, Roy Scheider, Tony Lo Bianco, Marcel Bozzuffi. Colour.
104 minutes.

Twentieth Century-Fox Video

The French Connection II

The inevitable sequel with Gene Hackman now in Marseilles and attempting to track down the narcotics mastermind who escaped scot free at the end of movie number 1. He succeeds but not before he has been pumped full of heroin to turn him into an addict. The drug scenes are grim and overlong (also unnecessary) and the colour has that washed out murky look of so many of today's movies. But the final chase, this time on foot through Marseilles harbour, is well staged. OK for a sequel.

Box-office rental	$5,618,000
Average rental (75)	$27,300,250

1975. Directed by John Frankenheimer.
Starring Gene Hackman, Fernando Rey, Bernard Fresson, Jean-Pierre Castaldi, Charles Milot, Cathleen Nesbitt. Colour.
119 minutes.

Twentieth Century-Fox Video

The French Line

Howard Hughes tried to promote this originally three-dimensional picture by selling Jane Russell's bust rather than the movie – "Jane Russell in 3-D. It'll knock *both* your eyes out!" And one can understand why. The picture is a dud. Miss Russell's bosom is not. The story concerns a millionairess who poses as a model and falls in love with a dashing playboy whilst journeying to Paris on a French liner. Miss Russell's revealing bump and grind shimmy "Lookin' For Trouble" brings things to life in a vulgar sort of way. On the same tape: three shorts – *Texas Tough Guy* with Leon Errol, *Murder In A Flat* with Skitch Henderson and *Dick Stabile Orchestra With The Sportsmen.*

1953. Directed by Lloyd Bacon.
Starring Jane Russell, Gilbert Roland, Arthur Hunnicutt, Mary McCarty, Joyce MacKenzie, Paula Corday. Colour.
102 minutes.

Kingston Video

From The Earth To The Moon

Quite what Joseph Cotten and George Sanders are doing in this piece of nonsense beggars the imagination but in it they are, right up to their elegant necks and saddled with dialogue that is not even good enough for extras to deliver. Derived from a story by Jules Verne, it's set in America just after the Civil War and centres on a scientist who discovers a new source of energy and determines to make it to the moon, via a rocket of course. Poor stuff. Abbott and Costello in *Jack And The Beanstalk* feature on the same tape.

1958. Directed by Byron Haskin.
Starring Joseph Cotten, George Sanders, Henry Daniell, Carl Esmond, Melville Cooper. Colour.
100 minutes.

Kingston Video

The Fugitive

Director John Ford called this adaptation of Graham Greene's *The Power And The Glory* one of his favourite pictures, and with its striking black and white camerawork it certainly has its poetic qualities. But the struggle between strength and weakness in a man's soul makes for better reading than it does watching and, despite all the care and attention, the end result is slow and laborious going. The movie is set in a South American police state and chronicles the plight of a tormented priest who refuses to support the anti-cleric government and is eventually betrayed by the man who once sheltered him. Henry Fonda plays the priest whose fate is paralleled with that of a wanted criminal. Supporting the movie on a double tape: the rather more lively *Follow Me Quietly*.

1947. Directed by John Ford.
Starring Henry Fonda, Dolores Del Rio, Pedro Armendariz, J. Carrol Naish, Leo Carrillo. Black and White.
104 minutes.

Kingston Video

Fun In Acapulco

"The Bullfighter Was A Lady"; "Bossa Nova Baby" and "You Can't Say No In Acapulco" plus eight other songs of similar ilk are what you get for your money in this Elvis Presley vehicle about a former trapeze artist who heads for Mexico in order to forget a tragic accident to his partner on the high wire. Consoling him in Acapulco are beautiful American socialite Ursula Andress and glamorous lady bullfighter Elsa Cardenas. Sounds corny and it is but Presley fans won't mind. As always with Hal Wallis' Presley vehicles, the Technicolor locations are stunning.

1963. Directed by Richard Thorpe.
Starring Elvis Presley, Ursula Andress, Paul Lukas, Alejandro Rey, Elsa Cardenas. Colour.
97 minutes.

Twentieth Century-Fox Video

The Fury

Director Brian De Palma goes right over the top with a daft story about a teenage boy with psychokinetic powers, who is kidnapped by a corrupt government official who intends using him for unlawful purposes. Kirk Douglas as the boy's father employs a girl with similar powers to discover their whereabouts. John Cassavetes is the bad guy who in the last reel is literally blown apart. Ludicrous and with absurd effects. No content, not much form either. 1½ rating.

Box-office rental	$12,174,000
Average rental (78)	$39,443,850

1978. Directed by Brian De Palma.
Starring Kirk Douglas, John Cassavetes, Carrie Snodgress, Charles Durning, Amy Irving, Fiona Lewis, Andrew Stevens. Colour.
118 minutes.

Twentieth Century-Fox Video

G

Gang Busters

Run-of-the-mill escape-from-prison yarn focussing on the breakout of gangster John Pinson, who at one time made it to number four in the FBI's Public Enemy charts. No more than B-picture fare and very inferior fare at that. Supports *Day Of The Wolves* on a double-feature video tape.

1955. Directed by Bill Karn.
Starring Myron Healey, Don C. Harvey, Sam Edwards, Frank Richards, Allan Ray. Black and White.
78 minutes.

Kingston Video

The Garden Of Allah

Marlene Dietrich seeks peace in the Algerian desert but finds instead Trappist monk Charles Boyer who has broken his vows. The result: tragic romance. Interesting to movie buffs for its early Technicolor (it was made just a year after the first 3-colour feature *Becky Sharp* was released) and for the stunning beauty of Dietrich, dressed in white but adorned with colour scarves to really show off her slimline figure. One critic described her as "a monosyllabic clothes horse." See for yourself.

Oscars (1)	Special Award for Colour Photography
Oscar nominations (2)	Best Music Score; Assistant Director

1936. Directed by Richard Boleslawski.
Starring Marlene Dietrich, Charles Boyer, Basil Rathbone, C. Aubrey Smith, Tilly Losch, Joseph Schildkraut, John Carradine. Colour.
85 minutes.

Guild Home Video

The Gauntlet

Drunken, disreputable cop Clint Eastwood (he's not Dirty Harry in this one) is given an assignment to pick up hooker Sondra Locke in Las Vegas and escort her to Phoenix where she will figure as an important trial witness. The trouble is that corrupt police officials are out to get her before she reaches her destination. And that means plenty of action, noise and demolition work as a car and a house are totally destroyed and an armoured bus makes it to safety through a hail of police bullets. All of which makes for a movie that is about par for the usual violent Eastwood course. Vigorous!

Box-office rental	$17,600,000
Average rental (77)	$36,913,348

1977. Directed by Clint Eastwood.
Starring Clint Eastwood, Sondra Locke, Pat Hingle, William Prince, Bill McKinney. Colour.
109 minutes.

Warner Home Video

The General

Buster Keaton at his peak as a Southern engine driver who, together with his beloved locomotive, finds himself chasing and being chased by Yankees along miles of railway track during the Civil War. The funniest train film ever made? Almost certainly, and incorporating some of the most brilliant stunt work and impeccably timed gags to be found on the silent screen. "The General", by the way, has nothing to do with the war. It's the name of Buster's train.

1927. Directed by Buster Keaton and Clyde Bruckman.
Starring Buster Keaton, Glen Cavender, Jim Farley, Frederick Vroom, Marion Mack. Black and White (colour tints).
76 minutes.

Spectrum
(distributed by Polygram)

Genevieve

Two vintage motor car enthusiasts make their annual excursion to Brighton during the "old crocks" race and experience as much trouble from their female travelling companions as they do from their vehicles. The word "vintage" applies not only to the cars but also the film itself, for it's now nearly 30 years old. But that matters not one jot. Other words that serve equally well include delightful, charming and entertaining. In short, lovely video entertainment for all the family and made at a time when all seemed right with the world. Stands up to many viewings; famous harmonica score by Larry Adler.

Oscars	Nil·
Oscar nominations (2)	Best Story & Screenplay; Original Music Score

1953. Directed by Henry Cornelius.
Starring Dinah Sheridan, John Gregson, Kay Kendall, Kenneth More, Geoffrey Keen, Reginald Beckwith, Arthur Wontner, Joyce Grenfell. Colour.
86 minutes.

Rank Video

Gentlemen Prefer Blondes

Marilyn Monroe and Jane Russell together are more than enough to
ensure that this tape is value for money, even though the story – two
gold-diggers shipbound for Paris – is so thin it can almost be blown away.
No matter, the musical numbers are dynamite, especially "Two Little Girls
From Little Rock", during which the pair shake about everything they
have in sight (and a few other things besides) and "Diamonds Are A
Girl's Best Friend" in which MM comes close to melting the screen. Miss
Russell also shows that she has a good line in wisecracks. Based on the
musical comedy by Joseph Fields and Anita Loos.

Box-office rental $5,100,000
Average rental (53) $6,098,850

1953. Directed by Howard Hawks.
Starring Jane Russell, Marilyn Monroe, Charles Coburn, Tommy Noonan,
George Winslow. Colour.
91 minutes.

Twentieth Century-Fox Video

George And Mildred

Spin-off from the long-running TV series about the misadventures of dull
working-class hubby Brian Murphy and his sex-starved wife Yootha
Joyce. The film revolves around the pair becoming involved with two
rival gangs of crooks when they embark on a weekend package holiday
at a London hotel. Stratford Johns features as a gangland boss. Dismal.

1980. Directed by Peter Frazer Jones.
Starring Yootha Joyce, Brian Murphy, Stratford Johns, Norman Eshley,
Sheila Fearn, Kenneth Cope. Colour.
93 minutes.

Precision Video

The Ghost Ship

Not a movie that springs instantly to mind when producer Val Lewton's name is mentioned in conversation but nonetheless among his most impressive films. Richard Dix is an authoritarian sea captain who is also a psychopathic murderer and who has killed off several of his shipmates. Russell Wade is the luckless young seaman who discovers the captain's nasty secret. Small-scale but macabre and menacing and not a little spooky. Makes up an admirable double feature tape with *Mr. Kingstreet's War*. 2½ rating.

1943. Directed by Mark Robson.
Starring Richard Dix, Russell Wade, Edith Barrett, Ben Bard, Lawrence Tierney. Black and White.
69 minutes.

Kingston Video

The Ghoul

Peter Cushing giving another of his tormented souls portrayals: this time as a former clergyman who has lost his faith witnessing heathen practices in India and who lives in a house of horror with a ghoulish creature that feeds off human flesh. Veronica Carlson, Ian McCulloch, John Hurt and co. are among the actors who discover the deadly secret and finish up as monster grub. Set in the 20s and a bit like a cut-price flapper version of *Psycho* at times. And there's fog everywhere.

1975. Directed by Freddie Francis.
Starring Peter Cushing, John Hurt, Alexandra Bastedo, Gwen Watford, Veronica Carlson, Ian McCulloch. Colour.
87 minutes.

Rank Video

GI Blues

The movie in which Elvis Presley made his comeback after a well-publicized two years in the U.S. Army in Germany. Appropriately enough, the setting is West Germany where Elvis and a couple of army buddies form a musical combo and our hero sets about wooing zippy cabaret singer Juliet Prowse. Strictly routine stuff but Elvis as a singing GI was a hit with movie audiences, who put this film second to *Blue Hawaii* as the most popular Presley movie of all time.

Box-office rental	$4,300,000
Average rental (60)	$6,787,500

1960. Directed by Norman Taurog.
Starring Elvis Presley, Juliet Prowse, Robert Ivers, Leticia Roman, Arch Johnson. Colour.
104 minutes.

Twentieth Century-Fox Video

A Gift For Heidi

Or the further adventures of the little Swiss mountain girl created by Johanna Spyri. Simple and charming might be words used to describe the girl's adventures. Mawkish and dull might be two others. Shares a double bill with *Escapade In Japan*.

1959. Directed by William Cruikshank.
Starring Sandy Descher, Douglas Fowley. Colour.
75 minutes.

Kingston Video

A Girl In Every Port

Lovers of Groucho Marx's zany humour will be disappointed with this little opus, which attempts to extract the maximum amount of humour (and that's minimal) from a situation in which two sailors – Groucho and William Bendix – are tricked into buying a useless racehorse and forced to conceal it aboard their ship. The result, unfortunately, is horsemeat. Supported on a double-feature video tape by the Western *Return Of The Badmen.*

1952. Directed by Chester Erskine.
Starring Groucho Marx, William Bendix, Marie Wilson, Don DeFore, Gene Lockhart. Black and White.
86 minutes.

Kingston Video

The Girl Most Likely

Pleasant little musical about a pretty young miss (Jane Powell) who has trouble in deciding which of three men she will marry. A musical version of the Ginger Rogers comedy *Tom, Dick And Harry*, the film was the last to be shot on the RKO lot before the studio closed down. Excellent choreography by the late Gower Champion; on the same tape, *Stage Struck*, a remake of Katharine Hepburn's Oscar-winning *Morning Glory*.

1957. Directed by Mitchell Leisen.
Starring Jane Powell, Cliff Robertson, Keith Andes, Tommy Noonan, Una Merkel. Colour.
98 minutes.

Kingston Video

Girls! Girls! Girls!

The one in which Elvis Presley sings "Return to Sender", co-stars with delicious Stella Stevens and works as a nightclub singer in order to earn enough money to buy the sailboat he helped build with his father. Filmed on location in Hawaii and about par for the course, which means 13 songs, among them "Girls! Girls! Girls!", "Because Of Love" and "We'll Be To-gether" which, in turn, means value for money if you're a Presley fan . . . and purgatory if you're not!

1962. Directed by Norman Taurog.
Starring Elvis Presley, Stella Stevens, Laurel Goodwin, Jeremy Slate.
Colour.
106 minutes.

Twentieth Century-Fox Video

The Go-Between

One of those rare occasions when the mood of a novel (in this case by
L. P. Hartley) has been perfectly transposed to the screen. Director Joseph
Losey allows his Technicolor cameras to range lovingly over a languid
Edwardian countryside and observe the lives of an aristocratic family
during one eventful summer. The "go-between" of the title is a 12-year-
old boy, who is invited to stay with the family and acts as a messenger
for the beautiful daughter and the neighbouring lower-class farmer whom
she loves. The result is a tragedy of classic proportions and an elegaic
film that probes into the moral corruption of a society fraying at the edges
and destined for oblivion. Bears much reviewing; superb on video.

Oscars	Nil
Oscar nominations (1)	Best Supporting Actress (Leighton)

1971. Directed by Joseph Losey.
Starring Julie Christie, Alan Bates, Dominic Guard, Margaret Leighton,
Michael Redgrave, Michael Gough, Edward Fox. Colour.
116 minutes.

Thorn EMI Video

The Godfather

There aren't too many masterpieces to be found in this book but this is
one of them, an epic crime story about the violent career of the Don
Corleone family who reign supreme over rival Mafia outfits, first under
ageing chief Marlon Brando, then under heir apparent Al Pacino. The
actual story is no more than pulp fiction but the way Francis Ford Coppola
transcends his material by sheer film technique leaves one open-mouthed

in amazement. It *is* violent, make no mistake about it, and the bloodletting, such as the murder at a tollgate and the climactic rubbing out of all the rival gangster leaders is quite ferocious at times but this is a remarkable achievement in every way. You can argue all night long about the film's moral virtues (or lack of them) but as a piece of movie-making it is superb. Video does it full justice.

Box-office rental	$86,275,000
Average rental (72)	$17,543,950
Oscars (3)	Best Film; Actor (Brando); Screenplay
Oscar nominations (7)	Best Supporting Actor (Caan); Supporting Actor (Duvall); Supporting Actor (Pacino); Direction; Costume Design; Sound; Editing

1972. Directed by Francis Ford Coppola.
Starring Marlon Brando, Al Pacino, James Caan, Richard Castellano, Robert Duvall, Sterling Hayden, John Marley, Richard Conte, Diane Keaton. Colour.
176 minutes.

CIC Video

Gold

Inept adventure yarn about a plot to boost prices on the world market by destroying a South African gold mine. Big names but rotten film. Roger Moore is the tough mine *manager* working underground; Bradford Dillman the scheming mine *boss* working up above; and Ray Milland is the tycoon mine *owner* working on nothing but answering the telephone and looking worried. The lovely Susannah York provides a few compensations. Filmed on location in South Africa. 1½ rating.

1974. Directed by Peter Hunt.
Starring Roger Moore, Susannah York, Ray Milland, Bradford Dillman, John Gielgud, Tony Beckley. Colour.
124 minutes.

Picture Time Video
(distributed by VCL)

The Gold Rush

Charlie Chaplin trying his luck as a prospector in turn-of-the-century Alaska but reduced to cooking one of his shoes because of hunger. Pathos, humour, tragedy all rolled into one masterly movie that ranks as the finest achievement of Chaplin's silent career. One hilarious scene has Charlie battling with Mack Swain in a small cabin teetering backwards and forwards on the edge of a precipice. Four-star rating, providing you can accept silent movies as good value for money. Some can't. Supported by the Chaplin two-reeler *Pay Day*.

1925. Directed by Charles Chaplin.
Starring Charles Chaplin, Mack Swain, Georgia Hale, Tom Murray, Henry Bergman, Malcolm Waite, Betty Morrissey. Black and White.
82 minutes.

Spectrum
(distributed by Polygram)

The Good, The Bad
And The Ugly

The usual Sergio Leone exercise in Western sadism with three men – killer Lee Van Cleef and confidence tricksters Clint Eastwood and Eli Wallach – all after a Confederate treasure chest during the American Civil War. The chest is worth 200,000 dollars and is hidden in a cemetery. But in which grave? It takes all of 148 minutes to find out, which, considering the two-dimensional nature of the characters, seems like an eternity. Huge close-ups of gunmen staring at each other forever before they fire often make for hilarious cinema. Bad, Bad and Ugly!

Box-office rental	$6,030,000
Average rental (67)	$13,081,250

1967. Directed by Sergio Leone.
Starring Clint Eastwood, Eli Wallach, Lee Van Cleef, Aldo Giuffre, Mario Brega. Colour.
148 minutes.

Intervision

Goodbye, Norma Jean

The career of Marilyn Monroe from 1941 to the moment she stood on the threshold of stardom. Not exactly the most complimentary portrait of a Hollywood actress ever put on screen, in fact often downright cheap and nasty. Misty Rowe manages to look like Marilyn Monroe on occasion; the script takes in rape, assault, blue movies, attempted suicide, nude modelling and so forth. Very seamy, "This is the way it was", concludes the prologue title. Doubtful.

1975. Directed by Larry Buchanan.
Starring Misty Rowe, Terrence Locke, Patch Mackenzie, Preston Hanson, Marty Zagon. Colour.
95 minutes.

Intervision

The Good Die Young

British attempt to produce an American-styled heist movie with three Yank stars – Richard Basehart, Gloria Grahame and John Ireland – imported to add to the authenticity. The setting is London in the early 50s. Four men are involved in the hold-up of a GPO mail van. Things go wrong and the men finish up destroying each other. Realistic but routine. A young Joan Collins adds a touch of sexual promise.

1954. Directed by Lewis Gilbert.
Starring Laurence Harvey, Gloria Grahame, Richard Basehart, Joan Collins, John Ireland, Rene Ray, Stanley Baker, Margaret Leighton, Robert Morley. Black and White.
100 minutes.

Twentieth Century-Fox Video

Grease

Will innocent college gal Olivia Newton-John succeed in snaring school tough guy John Travolta at Rydell High? It's touch and go for most of this film's noisy 110 minutes but in the end she manages it, although not until she's donned shimmering black leather. This one survives better than Travolta's companion hit *Saturday Night Fever* mainly because its songs (of which there are many) are not so reliant on the big screen and amplified sound. Stockard Channing as an "I know all about sex" college girl gives the standout performance and also has the best song, the skittish "Look At Me, I'm Sandra Dee". The highest grossing musical of all time.

Box-office rental	$96,300,000
Average rental (78)	$39,443,850
Oscars	Nil
Oscar nominations (1)	Best Song ("Hopelessly Devoted To You")

1978. Directed by Randal Kleiser.
Starring John Travolta, Olivia Newton-John, Stockard Channing, Jeff Conway, Didi Conn, Eve Arden, Sid Caesar. Colour.
110 minutes.

CIC Video

Great Day In The Morning

Slightly off-beat Western set in Colorado gold-mine country and centring on a Southerner who becomes involved in financial and political rivalries prior to and during the Civil War. Goodish cast; shares a double feature tape with *Second Chance*.

1956. Directed by Jacques Tourneur.
Starring Virginia Mayo, Robert Stack, Ruth Roman, Alex Nicol, Raymond Burr, Regis Toomey. Colour.
92 minutes.

Kingston Video

The Great Dictator

Two Chaplins for the price of one – he's a timid Jewish barber and the
dictator of a mythical European country – in a cry of anger against the
perils of Fascism. Chaplin does a ballet dance with the globe of the
world; Jack Oakie appears as a Mussolini-style tyrant Napaloni; and
Paulette Goddard is an impoverished girl from the ghetto. The final
moralising is a bit hard to take. Not so the mixture of satire and slapstick
that precedes it. Chaplin's first sound movie.

Oscars   Nil
Oscar nominations (5)   Best Film; Actor (Chaplin); Supporting Actor
                            (Oakie); Original Screenplay; Music Score

1940. Directed by Charles Chaplin.
Starring Charles Chaplin, Jack Oakie, Paulette Goddard, Reginald Gardiner, Henry Daniell, Billy Gilbert, Grace Hayle. Black and White.
128 minutes.

Spectrum
(*distributed by Polygram*)

Great Expectations

Still the finest Dickens movie ever made, charting the experiences of a
young country blacksmith who becomes a gentleman in London society
through the generosity of an unknown benefactor. As a rule of thumb for
filming Dickens, the more you prune down the lesser characters the
better the end result. And it's certainly the case with this David Lean
masterwork, which is a remarkable achievement on every level. John
Mills is the adult Pip, Valerie Hobson is Estella, Finlay Currie is Magwitch,
Francis L. Sullivan features as the lawyer Jaggers and Martita Hunt is Miss
Havisham. The standout sequence occurs in the opening minutes when
the boy Pip encounters the escaped convict in the churchyard.

Oscars (2)   Best Photography; Art Direction
Oscar nominations (3)   Best Film; Direction; Screenplay

1947. Directed by David Lean.
Starring John Mills, Valerie Hobson, Alec Guinness, Bernard Miles,

Francis L. Sullivan, Finlay Currie, Anthony Wager, Jean Simmons, Martita Hunt. Black and White.
118 minutes.

Rank Video

Great Expectations

Well, yes, they had to remake it, didn't they, and this 1975 version was originally going to have songs to accompany the action. But the idea was dropped and the decision made to tell the story straight. A pity because musical numbers would at least have livened things up a bit. This is an uninspired piece of work, cluttered with two-dimensional characters and totally lacking any Dickensian atmosphere. Meagre video. Michael York is Pip, Sarah Miles Estella, James Mason Magwitch and Margaret Leighton Miss Havisham.

1975. Directed by Joseph Hardy.
Starring Michael York, Sarah Miles, James Mason, Margaret Leighton, Robert Morley, Anthony Quayle, Joss Ackland, Rachel Roberts, Heather Sears. Colour.
124 minutes.

Precision Video

The Great Muppet Caper

More Muppet adventures, this time in London, as investigating reporters Kermit and Fozzie Bear fly to England to track down the villains behind a large-scale jewel robbery. And much better entertainment value this time out, with the musical numbers on a more ambitious satirical level and even including an Esther Williams-type water ballet by Miss Piggy. The human guest stars don't count for much but they're not really what you're paying for. 2½ rating. (See also *The Muppet Movie*).

Box-office rental	$16,000,000
Average rental (81)	$32,180,110
Oscars	Nil

Oscar Nominations (1) Best Song ("The First Time it Happens")

1981. Directed by Jim Henson.
Starring Diana Rigg, Charles Grodin, John Cleese, Robert Morley, Peter Ustinov, Jack Warden. Colour.
97 minutes.

Precision Video

The Great Race

If you're a fan of *Those Magnificent Men In Their Flying Machines*, *Around The World In Eighty Days* and so forth, you'll probably enjoy this one, for it's in similar vein, a long journey full of comic incident and what seems like hundreds of sight gags. The year is 1908; the race is in automobiles between New York and Paris; the participants are shining, clean-cut hero Tony Curtis, black-hearted villain Jack Lemmon and lady reporter Natalie Wood. It's all pleasant enough and if length is anything to go by (150 minutes), reasonable value for money. But it works only occasionally and I'm afraid it's another case of "it all seemed so much more effective on the big screen". 2½ rating.

Box-office rental	$11,000,000
Average rental (65)	$13,881,050
Oscars (1)	Best Sound Effects
Oscar Nominations (4)	Best Photography; Sound; Editing; Song ("The Sweetheart Tree")

1965. Directed by Blake Edwards.
Starring Tony Curtis, Natalie Wood, Jack Lemmon, Peter Falk, Keenan Wynn, Larry Storch, Dorothy Provine, Arthur O'Connell. Colour.
150 minutes.

Warner Home Video

The Green Berets

"Out here due process is a bullet", says American colonel John Wayne to reporter David Janssen. "Out here" is Vietnam, although for all the thought that went into this crude fiasco it might just as well have been the Wild West, for the philosophy is the same – the only good Indian (Vietnamese) is a dead one. The film, about the participation of American Special Forces troops in Vietnam, incorporates every movie cliché imaginable including the one in which Wayne puts the beret of a dead soldier on the head of a Vietnamese boy and walks off with him into the sunset. Ugh!

Box-office rental $9,750,000
Average rental (68) $14,411,950

1968. Directed by John Wayne and Ray Kellogg.
Starring John Wayne, David Janssen, Jim Hutton, Aldo Ray, Raymond St. Jacques, Jack Soo, Bruce Cabot. Colour.
141 minutes.

Warner Home Video

Green Ice

Electronics wizard Ryan O'Neal finds himself involved with lovely Anne Archer and Italian exile Omar Sharif who keeps his emerald millions (the green ice of the title) locked away in an impregnable fortress in Colombia. O'Neal eventually goes after the emeralds with the aid of hot air balloons but by the time he gets round to things it's doubtful whether you'll care one way or the other. Mundane; like a Made-For-TV Movie. A non-starter.

1981. Directed by Ernest Day.
Starring Ryan O'Neal, Anne Archer, Omar Sharif, Domingo Ambriz, John Larroquette, Philip Stone. Colour.
116 minutes.

Precision Video

Gregory's Girl

A 16-year-old schoolboy is given a bit of a jolt, physically and emotionally, when he loses his place as striker in his school soccer team and sees it given to a girl. Naturally enough he falls in love with her. Slight, disarming comedy by Bill Forsyth that looks with humour and some insight into the traumas of being a teenager in the 80s. Likeable; set in a Scottish new town. 2½ rating.

1981. Directed by Bill Forsyth.
Starring Gordon John Sinclair, Dee Hepburn, Jake D'Arcy, Clare Grogan, Robert Buchanan. Colour.
91 minutes.

Hokushin

Grip Of The Strangler

Nice old criminologist Boris Karloff decides to investigate a 20-year-old murder case in which he is sure a miscarriage of justice has taken place. He's right, for nice old Boris turns into nasty old Boris during a series of blackouts and discovers that he himself is the murderer. Daft as they come of course, but the period atmosphere (London, 1860) isn't bad and the movie's not without a few genuine thrills. Shares a horror double-bill with *Fiend Without A Face*.

1958. Directed by Robert Day.
Starring Boris Karloff, Elizabeth Allan, Jean Kent, Vera Day, Anthony Dawson. Black and White.
78 minutes.

Kingston Video

The Grissom Gang

James Hadley Chase's *No Orchids For Miss Blandish* given a second outing (it was first filmed in Britain in 1948) by director Robert Aldrich, who piles on the action and gore for all it's worth but still only comes up with a mediocre movie of Depression America. Kim Darby plays a young heiress who is kidnapped by some crooks and then finds herself attracted to one of the psychotic killers holding her to ransom. Plenty of Freudian overtones and plenty of crudity, violence and sadism as well. In short, not Mr Aldrich at his best and definitely one to be selected with care. Thoroughly deserves its X-certificate.

1971. Directed by Robert Aldrich.
Starring Kim Darby, Scott Wilson, Tony Musante, Robert Lansing, Connie Stevens, Irene Dailey. Colour.
128 minutes.

Guild Home Video

Guns Don't Argue

Gangster movie telling of the FBI's battle against the most dangerous mobsters of the Depression: Pretty Boy Floyd, Ma Barker, Alvin Karpis, etc. Small-budget video fare; shares a double bill with the sci-fi opus *The Projected Man*.

1955. Directed by Bill Karn & Richard C. Kahn.
Starring Myron Healy, Jean Harvey. Black and White.
87 minutes.

Kingston Video

The Guns Of Navarone

Archetypal adventure yarn about a band of Allied commandos who destroy two huge guns on a Nazi-held Greek island during World War II. Over-exposure on TV has meant that the film has become rather too familiar, but if you haven't yet seen it and admire the work of Alistair MacLean (on whose novel the movie is based) then it will keep you on the go. The personalities of Peck, Niven, Quinn, and others tend to make you forget the inferior colourwork. Shot on the island of Rhodes.

Box-office rental $13,000,000

Average rental (61)	$8,103,100
Oscars (1)	Best Special Effects
Oscar nominations (6)	Best Film; Direction; Screenplay; Sound; Editing; Music Score

1961. Directed by J. Lee Thompson.
Starring Gregory Peck, David Niven, Anthony Quinn, Stanley Baker, Anthony Quayle, Irene Papas, Gia Scala, James Darren, James Robertson Justice, Richard Harris, Bryan Forbes. Colour.
157 minutes.

RCA/Columbia International Video

Guns Of The Timberland

Not by any means the best Alan Ladd movie to be found on video, in fact no more than a routine lumberjacks-versus-ranchers story of the American West of the late '90s. The lumberjacks, under orders from the government, want to cut down some trees; the local ranchers want 'em to stay up. It's as simple and routine as that. Jeanne Crain adds a touch of beauty but Ladd was near the end of his career when he made this one and it shows. *Bengazi* is the other movie on this double-feature video tape.

1960. Directed by Robert D. Webb.
Starring Alan Ladd, Jeanne Crain, Gilbert Roland, Frankie Avalon, Lyle Bettger. Colour.
91 minutes.

Kingston Video

H

Hair

Quite why film-makers decided to leave it so long to make a movie of this 1967 stage hit remains something of a mystery. Had it been made at the time of its theatrical success it would probably have been a smash. As it is, both its story – Oklahoma cowboy falls in with a gang of New York hippies in Central Park – and its Flower Power characters seem more than a little dated. Still, the anti-war message comes across powerfully and some of the musical numbers ("Aquarius", "Let The Sunshine In") are very inventive. A brave try but too late.

Box-office rental $6,800,000
Average rental (79) $31,964,775

1979. Directed by Milos Forman.
Starring John Savage, Treat Williams, Beverly D'Angelo, Annie Golden, Dorsey Wright, Don Dacus. Colour.
121 minutes.

Intervision

The Half Breed

A prairie gambler and an Indian half breed try to put an end to the machinations of an unscrupulous white man stirring up the Apaches because he's after gold on their territory. A so-so video purchase although *Walk Softly Stranger*, its companion piece on a double feature video tape, is in a much higher class.

1952. Directed by Lewis D. Collins.
Starring Robert Young, Janis Carter, Jack Buetel, Barton MacLane, Porter Hall. Colour.
81 minutes.

Kingston Video

Halloween

John Carpenter switches *genres* – sci-fi in *Dark Star*, thriller in *Assault On Precinct 13* – to concentrate on an old-fashioned horror flick about a psychopath who escapes from a mental institution determined to kill off a few unsuspecting victims. Really no more than one scary scene after another and practically eschewing plot but still succeeding in making you jump out of your skin every five minutes or so. Lots of creepy scenes; Donald Pleasence heads the cast list but he's not the killer – just the psychiatrist!

Box-office rental	$18,500,000
Average rental (78)	$39,443,850

1978. Directed by John Carpenter.
Starring Donald Pleasence, Jamie Lee Curtis, Nancy Loomis, P. J. Soles, Charles Cyphers, Kyle Richards, Brian Andrews. Colour.
91 minutes.

Media Video
(*distributed by Video Programme Distributors*)

Hamlet

Shakespeare's tragic play reduced from 4½ hours to 2½, but despite the text omissions still a good enough picture to become the first British production to win the Hollywood Oscar as best film of the year. Endless tracking and dolly shots around the bleak interiors of Elsinore Castle slow things up quite a bit, but there's still much to admire, not least Olivier's interpretation of the doomed Danish prince who vows to avenge the murder of his father. 18-year-old Jean Simmons features as Ophelia. Overall, it doesn't hold up as well as Olivier's *Henry V* but it's still well above average video for students of filmed Shakespeare.

Oscars (4)	Best Film; Actor (Olivier); Art Direction; Costume Design
Oscar nominations (3)	Best Supporting Actress (Simmons); Direction; Music Score

1948. Directed by Laurence Olivier.
Starring Laurence Olivier, Eileen Herlie, Basil Sydney, Jean Simmons, Norman Wooland, Felix Aylmer. Black and White.
155 minutes.

Rank Video

Hands Of The Ripper

Quite clever variation of the Jack The Ripper theme with the daughter of Jack (having seen him stab her mother to death) inheriting her father's murderous tendencies and seeking help from Freudian psychiatrist Eric Porter. He does his best but to no avail, and after a homicidal rampage around Victorian London she perishes in St. Paul's Cathedral. The film has all the good and bad points of the Hammer horror movies – authentic atmosphere, good performances, poor script, but the balance comes down on the side of the good points rather than the bad and makes it one of the more impressive Hammer offerings on video. Peter Sasdy's direction is at its best in the opening sequences.

1971. Directed by Peter Sasdy.
Starring Eric Porter, Angharad Rees, Jane Merrow, Keith Bell, Derek Godfrey, Dora Bryan, Marjorie Rhodes, Lynda Baron. Colour.
85 minutes.

Rank Video

Hannie Caulder

Raquel Welch vows vengeance on the three gunslingers who have raped her and killed her husband. The three she's after are Ernest Borgnine, Jack Elam and Strother Martin. And she gets 'em all. Quite a girl! She's quite a girl to look at as well and the best thing in this otherwise routine revenge Western is the sight of her padding across the desert clad in only a blanket. "She wants to be a man. She'll never make it", quotes someone in the movie. True!

1971. Directed by Burt Kennedy.
Starring Raquel Welch, Robert Culp, Ernest Borgnine, Strother Martin, Jack Elam, Christopher Lee, Diana Dors. Colour.
85 minutes.

Hokushin

Harlequin

A mysterious faith healer, disguised as a children's party entertainer, worms his way into the household of a political senator and has an unusual effect on those around him. He cures the senator's dying son, wins the admiration of the mother and finishes up dead as he plunges into the sea from a clifftop. Or does he? The ending leaves room for doubt. Routine horror flick, made in Australia.

1980. Directed by Simon Wincer.
Starring Robert Powell, David Hemmings, Carmen Duncan, Broderick Crawford, Gus Mercurio, Alan Cassell. Colour.
93 minutes.

Picture Time Video
(*distributed by VCL*)

The Haunted House Of Horror

More haunted house nonsense about a group of swinging youngsters who visit an elegant old country house just outside London to see if they can discover its ghost – that of a lunatic who once hacked six of his relatives to death. When one of their number finishes up a corpse they realize there's a psychopath in their midst. Conveyor belt stuff that hardly raises a scream. Forgettable.

1969. Directed by Michael Armstrong.
Starring Frankie Avalon, Jill Haworth, Dennis Price, Mark Wynter, Julian Barnes, Richard O'Sullivan, Gina Warwick. Colour.
92 minutes.

Vampix
(*distributed by Videomedia*)

Hawk The Slayer

Medieval sword and sorcery adventure about two brothers, one good (John Terry), the other bad (Jack Palance), who are left a magical flying sword by their dying pa. Made on a shoe-string budget (the lack of cash shows through in every set design), this one is laughably inadequate on just about every level, not least in its screenplay. During the course of the movie someone actually says: "My blood is forever on the move."

1980. Directed by Terry Marcel.
Starring Jack Palance, John Terry, Bernard Bresslaw, Ray Charleson, Peter O'Farrell, Morgan Sheppard. Colour.
94 minutes.

Precision Video

The Heartbreak Kid

Neil Simon comedy about a New York salesman who finds himself falling out of love with his young wife just a few days into his honeymoon and becoming infatuated by the beautiful blonde he meets on the beach whilst his wife is in bed suffering from sunburn. Tragi-comedy that works well on both levels with Jeannie Berlin contributing several poignant moments as the discarded wife. Charles Grodin does well with the *Room At The Top*-ish hero, Cybill Shepherd is the blonde. Directed by Elaine May (Jeannie Berlin's ma); 2½ rating.

Box-office rental	$5,530,460
Average rental (72)	$17,543,950
Oscars	Nil
Oscar nominations (2)	Supporting Actor (Albert); Supporting Actress (Berlin)

1972. Directed by Elaine May.
Starring Charles Grodin, Cybill Shepherd, Jeannie Berlin, Eddie Albert, Audra Lindley, William Prince. Colour.
106 minutes.

Twentieth Century-Fox Video

Heaven Can Wait

Los Angeles footballer Warren Beatty finds himself dead and on the way up to heaven before his time and demands that he be returned to Earth immediately. He is put into the body of another man, a millionaire who is about to be bumped off by his wife and male secretary. This romantic fantasy was very much admired in the United States, less so elsewhere, but the framework of its intimate story makes it ideal video viewing and an engaging way of spending a couple of hours. James Mason as Beatty's cynical guardian angel is an additional plus factor.

Box-office rental	$49,400,000
Average rental (78)	$39,443,850
Oscars (1)	Best Art Direction
Oscar nominations (8)	Best Film; Actor (Beatty); Supporting Actor (Warden); Supporting Actress (Cannon); Direction; Photography; Music Score; Screenplay

1978. Directed by Warren Beatty and Buck Henry.
Starring Warren Beatty, Julie Christie, Jack Warden, Dyan Cannon, Charles Grodin, James Mason. Colour.
100 minutes.

CIC Video

Heavens Above!

The last of the Boulting Brothers' satires of the late 50s and early 60s. The Church of England and the clergy are the targets this time, although the attacks are relatively mild and even Peter Sellers is in somewhat subdued form. He plays a prison chaplain who is appointed vicar of a country parish by mistake and causes panic amongst rich and poor alike by taking the gospels a bit too literally. Rather tepid, although a host of British character actors help pass the time.

1963. Directed by John Boulting.
Starring Peter Sellers, Cecil Parker, Isabel Jeans, Eric Sykes, Bernard

Miles, Brock Peters, Ian Carmichael, Irene Handl, Miriam Karlin, Eric Barker. Black and White.
118 minutes.

Thorn EMI Video

Hell In The Pacific

A variation of the "Robinson Crusoe" theme, set during the latter days of World War II and centring on just two characters – an American pilot and a Japanese naval officer – who find themselves stranded on a tiny Pacific island and forced to live with each other despite the fact that neither speaks the other's language. A bit of a slow starter, but once it gets going this movie's totally involving and makes you wonder how you would react in similar circumstances (as also does the same director's *Deliverance*). Amusing, moving and an above-average video purchase. Deserves a 2½ star rating!

1968. Directed by John Boorman.
Starring Lee Marvin, Toshiro Mifune. Colour.
103 minutes.

Guild Home Video

Hello, Dolly!

Barbra Streisand as matchmaker *extraordinaire* Dolly Levi working her wiles to great effect in 1890s New York. Walter Matthau as the Yonkers grain merchant on whom she sets her sights, energetic Michael Crawford and even Louis Armstrong do their best to compete but all to no avail. This is Streisand's film from first to last and she dominates throughout, even though she is at least 25 years too young for the part. The colour is variable and the spectacular production numbers "Put On Your Sunday Clothes" and "The Parade Passes By" lose much by being reduced to video size. Still, this *was* the last of Hollywood's musical biggies and as such it deserves a look.

Box-office rental $15,200,000

Average rental (69)	$13,660,950
Oscars (3)	Best Art Direction; Sound; Scoring Of A Musical
Oscar nominations (4)	Best Film; Photography; Costume Design; Editing

1969. Directed by Gene Kelly.
Starring Barbra Streisand, Walter Matthau, Michael Crawford, Marianne McAndrew, E. J. Peaker, Louis Armstrong. Colour.
148 minutes.

Twentieth Century-Fox Video

Hell On Frisco Bay

In the left corner: Alan Ladd as an embittered ex-cop who has just served five years in prison after being framed for manslaughter. In the right corner: ruthless cigar-chewing waterfront boss Edward G. Robinson, the man who sent Ladd up in the first place. Result of the contest: a knockout by Ladd when he disposes of Edward G. during a climactic battle in a speedboat hurtling across the San Francisco bay. Very watchable and two or three cuts above the average screen gangster fare. The other film on this double-feature tape is the slightly more humorous *The Mad Miss Manton*. 2½ rating.

1955. Directed by Frank Tuttle.
Starring Alan Ladd, Edward G. Robinson, Joanne Dru, William Demarest, Fay Wray, Paul Stewart. Colour.
98 minutes.

Kingston Video

Hell's Highway

1932 chain gang movie with Richard Dix as the one behind bars. Brutal chain gang fights, violent prison guards, plenty of tough action; supports the classic *film noir Out Of The Past* on a double-feature tape.

1932. Directed by Rowland Brown.
Starring Richard Dix, Tom Brown, Louis Carter, Rochelle Hudson. Black and White.
59 minutes.

Kingston Video

Henry V

The most imaginative of Olivier's four Shakespearean films, starting on stage during the first London performance at the Globe Theatre and then flashing back to a realistic 15th century, before returning to the theatre and finishing as it began as a photographed play. Fine colourwork by Robert Krasker and stirring music by William Walton; the Battle Of Agincourt, when the English bowmen defy the might of the French cavalry, remains a *tour-de-force* and one of the most exhilarating scenes in British movies of the 40s. Olivier appears as the heroic young king, Robert Newton as Ancient Pistol, Leslie Banks as the Chorus. Rousing stuff and superior video whichever way you look at it.

Oscars	Nil
Oscar nominations (4)	Best Film; Actor (Olivier); Art Direction; Music Score

1945. Directed by Laurence Olivier.
Starring Laurence Olivier, Robert Newton, Leslie Banks, Renee Asherson, Esmond Knight, Leo Genn, Ralph Truman. Colour.
137 minutes.

Rank Video

Note: Laurence Olivier received a special Academy Award "for his outstanding achievement as actor, producer and director in bringing *Henry V* to the screen".

Henry VIII And His Six Wives ★★

A reworking of the BBC TV series *The Six Wives Of Henry VIII* although, as the title indicates, the emphasis is here on old Henry rather than the wives, who each finish up with roughly 15 minutes of screentime. The net result unfortunately makes for rather dull viewing, although the costumes are stunning and Keith Michell's portrait of Henry (surely the most detailed and realistic yet given of this flamboyant monarch) just about makes it worth giving it a go.

1972. Directed by Waris Hussein.
Starring Keith Michell, Frances Cuka, Charlotte Rampling, Jane Asher, Jenny Bos, Lynne Frederick, Barbara Leigh-Hunt, Donald Pleasence. Colour.
125 minutes.

Thorn EMI Video

High Anxiety

Mel Brooks in top form with a spoof of just about every famous Hitchcock film you can remember. He's a psychiatrist who's appointed as head of the Institute For The Very, Very Nervous (which includes himself as he has a fear of heights) and discovers that the staff of the asylum are running a profitable racket. *Psycho*, *Spellbound*, *The Birds*, *Vertigo*, all get the Brooks send-up treatment. In fact, if you're a buff it's just as much fun trying to spot the Hitchcock references as it is to enjoy Brooks' zany humour. Cloris Leachman takes the acting honours with her portrait of a sadistic head nurse.

Box-office rental	$19,163,000
Average rental (77)	$36,913,348

1977. Directed by Mel Brooks.
Starring Mel Brooks, Madeline Kahn, Cloris Leachman, Harvey Korman, Ron Carey, Howard Morris, Dick Van Patten. Colour.
94 minutes.

Twentieth Century-Fox Video

Higher And Higher

Frank Sinatra was 23 years old and an idol of swooning "bobby-soxers" when he made his acting debut in this movie – a version of a Broadway musical about a bankrupt socialite who tries to rescue his finances by marrying his pretty kitchen maid to the richest man around. Sinatra is the young guy next door and sings "I Couldn't Sleep A Wink Last Night" and "A Lovely Way To Spend An Evening". Supported on the same tape by *Strictly Dynamite*.

Oscars	Nil
Oscar nominations (2)	Best Song ("I Couldn't Sleep A Wink Last Night"); Scoring Of A Musical

1943. Directed by Tim Whelan.
Starring Michele Morgan, Jack Haley, Frank Sinatra, Leon Errol, Marcy McGuire, Victor Borge, Mary Wickes. Black and White.
90 minutes.

Kingston Video

High Plains Drifter

This Western starts out like a violent reworking of *High Noon* and ends up as *Dante's Inferno*. It's not a spaghetti Western, although it often seems like one as Clint Eastwood helps defend some townsfolk from three killers just released from jail, stays on with a dwarf as deputy and quite literally paints the town red as he renames it Hell! Bizarre? You bet, and very sadistic into the bargain with whippings as a prominent feature. A moody, self-conscious effort; the only thing that makes it different from hundreds of others of its kind is the supernatural element.

Box-office rental	$7,694,000
Average rental (73)	$22,271,150

1973. Directed by Clint Eastwood.
Starring Clint Eastwood, Verna Bloom, Mariana Hill, Mitchell Ryan, Jack Ging, Stefan Gierasch, Bill Curtis. Colour.
102 minutes.

CIC Video

History Of The World Part I ★★

Mel Brooks comedy that presents a potted history of the world from The Stone Age to the French Revolution. Brooks misses the targets more often than he hits them in this one, although his portrait of Moses descending the mountain with 15 commandments, dropping a tablet and reducing them at a stroke to 10 is marvellous. So too is his cameo as a waiter at the Last Supper who carefully sums up the assembled group and enquires: "Are you all together or is it separate checks?"

Box-office rental	$13,852,000
Average rental (81)	$32,180,110

1981. Directed by Mel Brooks.
Starring Mel Brooks, Dom DeLuise, Madeline Kahn, Harvey Korman, Cloris Leachman, Ron Carey, Gregory Hines, Pamela Stephenson, Sid Caesar. Colour.
92 minutes.

Twentieth Century-Fox Video

Hobson's Choice ★★★

Charles Laughton in full flow as a tyrannical Lancashire bootmaker who finds himself being bested by his plain, sharp-tongued daughter when she marries his humble bootmaker and turns him into a successful businessman. Minor David Lean but with a strong sense of period (Salford in the 1890s) and made at a time when English films were directed by real craftsmen. Skilful *and* enjoyable. Brenda de Banzie plays the daughter; John Mills the boothand.

1954. Directed by David Lean.
Starring Charles Laughton, John Mills, Brenda de Banzie, Daphne Anderson, Prunella Scales, Richard Wattis. Black and White.
107 minutes.

Thorn EMI Video

Hombre

Very close to being a remake of John Ford's *Stagecoach;* the main difference being that instead of John Wayne we have Paul Newman (as a white man brought up by the Apaches) reluctantly coming to the aid of a group of stagecoach travellers in their fight against Richard Boone and his gang of bandits. Screenwriters Irving Ravetch and Harriet Frank, Jr make the journey sound interesting although it's a long, hot and very torrid one at times. And the shootout in an abandoned mining shack on the edge of the desert is a long time a coming! Western enthusiasts and Paul Newman fans will enjoy it; others will probably find it slow going. Top performance? Fredric March as a dishonest Indian agent.

Box-office rental   / $5,610,000
Average rental (67) $13,081,250

1967. Directed by Martin Ritt.
Starring Paul Newman, Fredric March, Richard Boone, Diane Cilento, Martin Balsam, Barbara Rush, Cameron Mitchell. Colour.
111 minutes.

Twentieth Century-Fox Video

Hooper

There have been plenty of films about "the making of the movies" but very few about the work of stunt men. This one makes amends, with Burt Reynolds as an ageing stunt man always on the look out for some new and dangerous stunt to perform but, at the same time, frequently glancing over his shoulder to size up the competition from the younger men coming into the business. Motor cycle stunts, a chariot race, a car jump, a rescue dash through flames – they're all here and it's fascinating to watch how it's all done. Over 60 stuntmen and women took part in the action sequences; unusual and amiable entertainment.

Box-office rental $34,900,00
Average rental (78) $39,443,850
Oscars   Nil

Oscar nominations (1)   Best Sound

1978. Directed by Hal Needham.
Starring Burt Reynolds, Jan-Michael Vincent, Sally Field, Brian Keith, John Marley, Robert Klein. Colour.
99 minutes.

Warner Home Video

Horror Hospital

Crippled doctor Michael Gough operates on teenagers, controls their brains and turns 'em into zombie bike boys with scars on their foreheads. The hero is a young pop singer who visits Mr. Gough's health hotel. Gough's supposed to be mad. But when one takes into account the sound of current pop music he may be saner than he looks. Entertaining horror flick, amusing (deliberately so) on occasion.

1979. Directed by Antony Balch.
Starring Michael Gough, Robin Askwith, Vanessa Shaw, Ellen Pollock, Skip Martin, Dennis Price. Colour.
91 minutes.

Iver Films

The Hot Rock

Heist movies have become two-a-penny through over-exposure but this engaging addition to the *genre* stands out from the rest in that it is as amusing as it is absorbing. And the fun starts *after* the robbery, when ex-con Robert Redford and his cronies, having stolen a priceless diamond from a Brooklyn museum, bungle things so badly that they are never quite sure where the diamond is. Their ineptness has to be seen to be believed. So does a thrilling helicopter ride across the skyscrapers of New York. Great fun. Known also as *How To Steal A Diamond In Four Uneasy Lessons.*

Oscars   Nil

Oscar nominations (1)   Best Editing

1972. Directed by Peter Yates.
Starring Robert Redford, George Segal, Zero Mostel, Ron Leibman, Paul
Sand, Moses Gunn, William Radfield. Colour.
101 minutes.

Twentieth Century-Fox Video

House Of The Living Dead

What's prowling about in the attic laboratory in a large manor house in
the African veldt? Could it be the son of the house? It is, it is! And he
passes his time by popping out now and then to commit the odd murder
or two and then popping back in to keep an eye on the "souls" of the
baboons, dogs, horses, etc. he keeps pickled in large jars. The alternative
title of this mish-mash is *Doctor Maniac* which probably says it all!

1973. Directed by Ray Austin.
Starring Mark Burns, Shirley Anne Field, David Oxley, Margaret Inglis,
Dia Sydow. Colour.
83 minutes.

Intervision

House Of Wax

There's not too much of Vincent Price around on video but this one more
than makes amends, for it's the movie that started him off on his long
horror career back in 1953. He plays a dedicated wax sculptor who is
badly disfigured when his beloved museum burns to the ground. Thereafter it's a case of profit first and art second as he goes around stealing
corpses from the morgue and covering them with boiling hot wax. The
methods are a bit ghoulish but the results are extraordinarily effective.
Originally made in 3-D (as certain scenes betray) this is one of the few
horror films to retain its power even though nearly thirty years have
passed since it was first released. And when heroine Phyllis Kirk strikes

out at Price's face watch out for some startling results. Excellent value for students of the macabre.

Box-office rental	$4,650,000
Average rental (53)	$6,098,850

1953. Directed by Andre de Toth.
Starring Vincent Price, Frank Lovejoy, Phyllis Kirk, Carolyn Jones, Paul Cavanagh, Charles Buchinski (Bronson). Colour.
88 minutes.

Warner Home Video

How Do I Love Thee

A sentimental comedy, bedroom farce and small-town satire all rolled into one unappetizing chunk of video entertainment as philosophy professor Rick Lenz boards a plane for Lourdes to visit his sick father Jackie Gleason and recalls in flashback some of the traumas he suffered with his parents during childhood. A good cast can do little with second-rate material, although Shelley Winters as a voluptuous lady artist gives things a lift now and then!

1970. Directed by Michael Gordon. Starring Jackie Gleason, Maureen O'Hara, Shelley Winters, Rosemary Forsyth, Rick Lenz. Colour.
109 minutes.

Rank Video

Hue And Cry

Schoolboy Harry Fowler discovers that members of a gang of fur thieves are sending coded messages to one another through the serial of his weekly comic. After that, there's no stopping him and with the aid of what seems like hundreds of boys he brings the thieves to book. A bit like an Ealing version of *Emil And The Detectives* and now very much a period piece but nonetheless enjoyable and in its scenes of a post-war, bomb-devastated London, historically interesting. Alastair Sim adds to the fun as an eccentric author of bloodcurdling stories; Jack *(Dixon Of Dock Green)* Warner is, believe it or not, the top crook! 2½ rating.

1947. Directed by Charles Crichton.
Starring Alastair Sim, Jack Warner, Valerie White, Harry Fowler, Frederick Piper. Black and White.
82 minutes.

Thorn EMI Video

The Human Factor

Arguably Graham Greene's finest novel of recent years reduced to a movie travesty by Otto Preminger who, admittedly, had a great deal of financial trouble making it, although of course that is no help to the video viewer. The Philby-type story involves a Foreign Office official who has been leaking information to the Russians and finds that the authorities are at last on his tail. A faithful script by Tom Stoppard and some impressive cameos from Robert Morley as an odious Secret Service doctor and Derek Jacobi as an innocent victim can't disguise the fact that the film is almost a total failure.

1979. Directed by Otto Preminger.
Starring Nicol Williamson, Richard Attenborough, Joop Doderer, John Gielgud, Derek Jacobi, Robert Morley, Ann Todd. Colour.
114 minutes.

Rank Video

The 'Human' Factor

Same title, different story but equally rotten film with electronics expert George Kennedy using a computer to track down the killers of his family and then disposing of them in the bloodiest way possible. Run-of-the-mill vigilante-type movie with *Death Wish* overtones. Crude and unpalatable. Set in Naples.

1976. Directed by Edward Dmytryk.

Starring George Kennedy, John Mills, Raf Vallone, Arthur Franz, Rita Tushingham, Barry Sullivan. Colour.
96 minutes.

Guild Home Video

The Hunchback Of Notre Dame

A four-pound hump of rubber foam; a false eye set in the middle of a cheekbone; a body covered entirely in thick rubber. And what have you got? Charles Laughton's bellringer Quasimodo in the 1939 version of *The Hunchback Of Notre Dame,* Victor Hugo's tragedy about a hunchback's unrequited love for a gypsy girl in 15th century Paris. Much of this once-impressive movie now looks a little pedestrian and Cedric Hard-wicke's villainous Frollo is a deadweight from the first reel. But, despite its aged look, there are still compensations and they count for much: Van Nest Polglase's gigantic sets of Paris; Maureen O'Hara's lovely Esmeralda and, of course, Laughton who was here at the peak of his powers. Summing up: an uneven film but retaining some great moments.

Oscars	Nil
Oscar nominations (2)	Best Music Score; Sound Recording

1939. Directed by William Dieterle.
Starring Charles Laughton, Cedric Hardwicke, Maureen O'Hara, Edmond O'Brien, Thomas Mitchell, Harry Davenport. Black and White.
117 minutes.

Thorn EMI Video

The Hunchback Of Notre Dame

The silent version without sound but with the "man of a thousand faces", Lon Chaney, as the deformed bellringer and Patsy Ruth Miller as the object of his hopeless love. A one-and-a-half million dollar super production with colour tints. Chaney's make-up included a matted wig, fanged false teeth, and a leather harness that prevented him from standing upright during shooting. Unique video fare. You won't see this very often on the telly.

1923. Directed by Wallace Worsley.
Starring Lon Chaney, Patsy Ruth Miller, Ernest Torrence, Norman Kerry, Raymond Hatton, Tully Marshall, Brandon Hurst, Nigel de Brulier. Black and White.
93 minutes.

Spectrum
(distributed by Polygram)

The Hunter

The true story of Ralph "Papa" Thorson (Steve McQueen), a cynical modern-day bounty hunter who earns a dubious living bringing in criminals who have skipped bail. The movie follows McQueen on his various escapades and emerges as a slightly above-average thriller, with a chase on an elevated train and by car as a spectacular high spot. McQueen's last film. OK but nothing special.

Box-office rental	$8,314,000
Average rental (80)	$30,086,027

1980. Directed by Buzz Kulik.
Starring Steve McQueen, Eli Wallach, Kathryn Harrold, LeVar Burton, Ben Johnson. Colour.
97 minutes.

CIC Video

Hussy

Calculated exploitation movie about a prostitute/hostess whose affair with a footloose American leads to her involvement in a drug-running plot and murder. The only real attraction is Helen Mirren in a state of nudity. It's up to you to decide whether that's worth the price of a tape.

1980. Directed by Matthew Chapman.
Starring Helen Mirren, John Shea, Daniel Chasin, Murray Salem, Paul Angelis, Jenny Runacre, Patti Boulaye. Colour.
94 minutes.

VIPCO

The Hustler

Robert Rossen movie about arrogant young pool shark Paul Newman who cons a living in cheap poolrooms as he prepares for a rematch with Jackie Gleason, the world champ, who has already taken him once to the cleaners. Crippled girl friend Piper Laurie offers him sex and sympathy; ruthless gambler George C. Scott turns him from a loser into a winner. Perfect dingy pool-room atmosphere; an inspired opening sequence; American movie-making at its finest. Depressing though, and downbeat nearly all the way.

Oscars (2)	Best Photography; Art Direction
Oscar nominations (7)	Best Film; Actor (Newman); Actress (Laurie); Supporting Actor (Gleason); Supporting Actor (Scott); Direction; Screenplay

1961. Directed by Robert Rossen.
Starring Paul Newman, Piper Laurie, George C. Scott, Jackie Gleason, Myron McCormick, Murray Hamilton. Black and White.
135 minutes.

Twentieth Century-Fox Video

I

I Am A Camera

The straight version of the adventures of Sally Bowles in prewar Berlin. Very tame and uninspired compared with Liza Minnelli's subsequent encounters in the musical *Cabaret*. Julie Harris is Sally, Laurence Harvey features as Christopher Isherwood. Hardly worth the effort other than from a curiosity angle. Based on the stage play by John Van Druten which, in turn, was adapted from Isherwood's stories "Goodbye To Berlin".

1955. Directed by Henry Cornelius.
Starring Julie Harris, Laurence Harvey, Shelley Winters, Ron Randell, Lea Seidl, Anton Diffring. Black and White.
99 minutes.

Twentieth Century-Fox Video

Ice Cold In Alex

Oh no, not another of those countless British war movies churned out with such regularity in the 50s. Well no, not quite, for despite the presence of such stalwarts as John Mills, Anthony Quayle and Harry Andrews, this one is more an exercise in tension than false heroics. The setting is the Libyan desert. The year, 1942. The objective of a small medical team: to get their ambulance across minefields, through sand storms and past every other kind of hazard that stands between them and Alexandria, 1000 miles away. Goodish, certainly above average. The title by the way refers to the drinks the group are planning to enjoy when they reach Alexandria.

1958. Directed by J. Lee-Thompson.
Starring John Mills, Sylvia Syms, Anthony Quayle, Harry Andrews. Black and White.
129 minutes.

Thorn EMI Video

An Ideal Husband

A British under-secretary has a brilliant career ahead of him but his future and domestic happiness are suddenly imperiled by the reappearance of an old flame who threatens him with blackmail. Terribly stilted and static version of Oscar Wilde's drawing room comedy although the author's wit still shines through and the late 19th century designs of Cecil Beaton just about make things worthwhile. Paulette Goddard is the best of the acting fraternity as the unscrupulous Mrs. Cheveley.

1947. Directed by Alexander Korda.
Starring Paulette Goddard, Michael Wilding, Diana Wynyard, Hugh Williams, Sir. C. Aubrey Smith, Glynis Johns, Constance Collier. Colour.
96 minutes.

Spectrum
(distributed by Polygram)

I'll Be Seeing You

Uneven, sentimental soap opera with woman prisoner Ginger Rogers getting a furlough and falling in love with a soldier undergoing psychiatric treatment. Sounds unlikely but this was made at the height of World War II and it didn't seem so unlikely then. And William Dieterle's handling is as assured as always. Some good moments and rarely seen. Ginger Rogers and Joseph Cotten hold the centre stage; parents Spring Byington and Tom Tully and sis Shirley Temple lend support.

1944. Directed by William Dieterle.
Starring Ginger Rogers, Joseph Cotten, Shirley Temple, Spring Byington, Tom Tully, Chill Wills. Black and White.
85 minutes.

Guild Home Video

I'm All Right Jack

A movie that took a few hefty swipes at British trade unions was quite an event in 1959 and it is to this film's credit (and perhaps the country's detriment) that it still holds up today. The bosses come in for the same treatment (although in their case the satire is less barbed) as the film follows the misadventures of upper-class young idiot Ian Carmichael, who decides to make a career as an industry executive but succeeds only in bringing the workers out on strike. Still funny; anti-left rather than anti-right and with some brilliant stuff from Peter Sellers as a trade union official. Terry-Thomas also chips in with an underrated cameo as a harassed personnel officer.

1959. Directed by John Boulting.
Starring Ian Carmichael, Terry-Thomas, Peter Sellers, Richard Attenborough, Dennis Price, Irene Handl, Miles Malleson, Victor Maddern, Liz Fraser, John Le Mesurier. Black and White.
105 minutes.

Thorn EMI Video

Indiscretion Of An American Wife

Curiosity of a movie about two lovers – Italian college professor Montgomery Clift and Philadelphia housewife Jennifer Jones – parting at a large railway station during the agonizing hour before the woman's train is due to leave. Nothing very much happens and some of the dialogue (despite being penned by Cesare Zavattini and Truman Capote) resembles that of a low-grade novelette but the tape does offer the chance to see Clift in one of his lesser-known screen roles. Students of film technique will also find De Sica's frequent use of close-ups (rarely used these days) or interest.

Oscars	Nil
Oscar nominations (1)	Best Costume Design

1954. Directed by Vittorio De Sica.

Starring Jennifer Jones, Montgomery Clift, Gino Cervi, Richard Beymer, Paolo Stoppa. Black and White.
75 minutes.

Guild Home Video

The In-Laws

Conventional dentist Alan Arkin and CIA agent Peter Falk meet in New York when the daughter of one wants to marry the son of the other. But things get out of hand. The wedding plans lead to them becoming involved with the dictator of a South American banana republic and finishing up in front of a firing squad. A bit like a Made-For-TV movie at times. Fast moving and zany but its humour is more American than British and it didn't exactly set the world alight on release in this country. Admirers of Peter (*Columbo*) Falk will probably find it has some appeal.

Box-office rental	$18,900,000
Average rental (79)	$31,964,775

1979. Directed by Arthur Hiller.
Starring Peter Falk, Alan Arkin, Richard Libertini, Nancy Dussault, Penny Peyser. Colour.
103 minutes.

Warner Home Video

Innocent Bystanders

Example of the thick-ear espionage thriller so popular in the 60s and 70s. Stanley Baker is the British agent assigned to bring back a Russian scientist who has escaped from Siberia. Donald Pleasence and Dana Andrews are his double-crossing superiors who want him out of the way. But Baker turns the tables despite the odds. A bit heavy on the sadism and violence and not very original, but it doesn't bore. And the cast performs well. Scripted by James Mitchell who authored *Callan*.

1972. Directed by Peter Collinson.

Starring Stanley Baker, Geraldine Chaplin, Dana Andrews, Donald Pleasence, Sue Lloyd, Vladek Sheybal, Derren Nesbitt, Warren Mitchell. Colour.
111 minutes.

Home Video Productions

Inseminoid

A distant planet. A hysterical Judy Geeson finds she is pregnant and suffers nightmares about a horrific rape. Then she goes berserk and feeds off the bodies of a couple of spacemen. Then she gives birth to a couple of monsters ... low budget rubbish that caters for the lowest of all possible tastes!

1981. Directed by Norman J. Warren.
Starring Robin Clarke, Jennifer Ashley, Stephanie Beacham, Steven Grives, Barry Houghton, Rosalind Lloyd, Judy Geeson. Colour.
92 minutes.

Brent Walker Video
(distributed by Videospace)

The Inspector General

Danny Kaye is now out of fashion but this version of a Gogol story ranks with his most amusing efforts, and also marks one of the few occasions he stepped into costume. He's an illiterate vagrant who is mistaken by the corrupt town council for the dreaded Inspector General and lavishly feted by its members until they discover he's an imposter. There are some vintage moments of Kaye humour, especially during a long ceremonial dinner scene and a strong Hollywood supporting cast has a good time trying to be Russians.

1949. Directed by Henry Koster.

Starring Danny Kaye, Walter Slezak, Barbara Bates, Elsa Lanchester, Gene Lockhart, Alan Hale, Walter Catlett. Colour.
102 minutes.

Mountain Video

The Intelligence Men

Something of a disastrous attempt by TV's Morecambe and Wise to break into the world of the cinema. Little more than an innocuous spy spoof, it has Eric and Ernie being hired by MI5 to safeguard a visiting Russian ballerina who is a target for some international killers. The pair's humour just doesn't translate from small screen to large (and back again!), which is a pity because the British cinema could have done with a new injection of comedy at the time this was made. Not a success, although the duo did try again (see *That Riviera Touch* and *The Magnificent Two*).

1965. Directed by Robert Asher.
Starring Eric Morecambe, Ernie Wise, William Franklyn, April Olrich, Gloria Paul, Richard Vernon. Colour.
104 minutes.

Rank Video

Intermezzo

World-famous Swedish violinist Leslie Howard falls in love with young pianist Ingrid Bergman and finds his marriage is in jeopardy. An old, old story that still brings tears to female eyes. Male viewers may well find it a bit of a drag even though the tearful events are covered in just 70 minutes, one of the shortest ever running times for a major feature. The film, produced by Selznick, introduced Ingrid Bergman to American audiences and was a remake of a 1936 Swedish production in which Bergman also appeared. World-famous music score.

Oscars   Nil

Oscar nominations (1)   Best Music Scoring

1939. Directed by Gregory Ratoff.
Starring Leslie Howard, Ingrid Bergman, Edna Best, Cecil Kellaway, John Halliday. Black and White.
70 minutes.

Guild Home Video

Intolerance

Arguably still the greatest epic of them all, telling, in parallel action, four stories in different periods of history, all dealing with the theme of "Love's struggle and intolerance through the ages". The four stories – a modern tale of the slums, the persecution and execution of Christ, the massacre of the Huguenots and the sacking of Babylon by Cyrus – were all shot without a script. The last story contained some of the biggest sets ever constructed for a Hollywood film, the full-scale replica of Belshazzar's Empire City covering 254 acres and standing 200 feet tall. Over sixty years old but still mind-boggling.

1916. Directed by D. W. Griffith.
Starring Mae Marsh, Fred Turner, Robert Harron, Sam de Grasse (modern story); Howard Gaye, Lillian Langdon, Olga Grey, Bessie Love (Judean story); Margery Wilson, Eugene Pallette, Spottiswoode Aiken, Ruth Handforth (Medieval French story); Constance Talmadge, Elmer Clifton, Alfred Paget, Seena Owen (Babylonian story) Black and White.
113 minutes (video length).

Spectrum
(*distributed by Polygram*)

Invaders From Mars

This one got a bit lost amongst all the sci-fi thrillers of the early 50s. Actually, despite its limited budget and rather cheap look, it's not at all bad thanks to the direction of William Cameron Menzies. The story may be as familiar as sliced bread – 12-year-old American boy witnesses the midnight arrival of a flying saucer and is powerless to prevent the aliens taking over the residents of his town – but the handling is really imaginative and so too is the camerawork of John Seitz, who also photographed George Pal's *When Worlds Collide*. Recommended.

1953. Directed by William Cameron Menzies.
Starring Helena Carter, Arthur Franz, Jimmy Hunt, Leif Erickson, Hillary Brooke. Colour.
78 minutes.

Intervision

The Ipcress File

Cockney agent Harry Palmer, blackmailed into intelligence work because of his crooked army record, is assigned to track down a British scientist snatched by Russian agents. Michael Caine, staring blankly through thick-lensed glasses, duly solves the case but not before he has undergone a particularly nasty form of torture and Canadian director Sidney Furie has made some imaginative use of London locations. An assassination in a car at some traffic lights is a standout sequence. Good spy stuff with hardly anyone in the cast putting a foot wrong, although it would only be half the film without John Barry's moody, atmospheric music.

1965. Directed by Sidney J. Furie.
Starring Michael Caine, Nigel Green, Guy Doleman, Sue Lloyd, Gordon Jackson, Aubrey Reynolds. Colour.
109 minutes.

Rank Video

The Island

Another thriller derived from the somewhat lurid pen of Peter (*Jaws*) Benchley; a sub-standard movie about a magazine journalist (Michael Caine) who investigates a spate of mysterious disappearances in Caribbean waters and then finds himself captured, along with his 12-year-old son, by a band of inbred pirates who have operated on a lost island since the 17th century. Not exactly *Peter Pan*. In fact, rather unsavoury and with plenty of graphic massacres and sadism to fill its 114 minutes. And very little else!

Box-office rental	$9,600,000
Average rental (80)	$30,086,027

1980. Directed by Michael Ritchie.
Starring Michael Caine, David Warner, Angela Punch McGregor, Frank Middlemass, Don Henderson. Colour.
114 minutes.

CIC Video

The Island At The Top Of The World ★★

Disney hokum about a hazardous airship expedition made in the early 1900s to the North Pole where a lost Viking civilisation has remained undisturbed for over a thousand years. Once redoubtable English explorer Donald Sinden and his pals arrive however, all tranquillity comes to an end. Only to be expected perhaps when Sinden calls a high priest "a bloodthirsty bounder!" OK of its type, with killer whales, the airship ablaze and a journey into the crater of a volcano as some of its highlights. Undemanding video; male youngsters of the household will probably go for it rather than the gals.

Box-office rental	$10,200,000
Average rental (74)	$18,456,150
Oscars	Nil
Oscar nominations (1)	Best Art Direction

1974. Directed by Robert Stevenson.
Starring Donald Sinden, David Hartman, Jacques Marin, Mako, David Gwillim. Colour.
94 minutes.

Walt Disney Home Video

Island Of Lost Women

An atomic scientist isolates his lovely daughters on a jungle isle. A reporter and a pilot crashland in a plane and the gals find that certain aspects of the outside world aren't so bad after all. Comic book rubbish. Shares a double-feature tape with *Cotter*.

1959. Directed by Frank Tuttle.
Starring Jeff Richards, Venetia Stevenson, John Smith, Diane Jergens, Alan Napier, June Blair. Black and White.
71 minutes.

Kingston Video

Island Of Terror

Tortoise-like monsters roam about a small island off the coast of Ireland. They seem to be indestructible. Worse, they divide and multiply every six hours. The island is in mortal danger. But with Dr. Peter Cushing in charge it's only a matter of time before they meet their fate and are destroyed by radio-active poisoning. Directed by Hammer horror man Terence Fisher.

1967. Directed by Terence Fisher.
Starring Peter Cushing, Edward Judd, Carole Gray, Eddie Byrne, Sam Kydd, Niall MacGinnis. Colour.
90 minutes.

Derann Video

Isle Of The Dead

A cataleptic woman, buried alive, escapes from a coffin completely insane. Bad enough perhaps, but when you're stuck on a Balkan island stricken with plague, doubly so. Good Val Lewton horror stuff, set in the year 1912 and with Boris Karloff as a Greek general. On the same tape: *Berlin Express*. A good mix.

1945. Directed by Mark Robson.
Starring Boris Karloff, Ellen Drew, Marc Cramer, Katherine Emery, Alan Napier. Black and White.
72 minutes.

Kingston Video

It Shouldn't Happen To A Vet ★★

Sequel to *All Creatures Great And Small*, or more adventures of country vet James Herriot in Yorkshire just prior to the outbreak of World War II. This time Herriot has to decide whether to stay with bluff partner Siegfried Farnon or move to a more profitable town practice. John Alderton takes over from Simon Ward as the curer of all animal ills; cats, dogs, chicks, cattle and a goat (which has a pair of men's underdrawers removed from its throat) are among the animals receiving his attention. Pleasant if unexceptional.

1976. Directed by Eric Till.
Starring John Alderton, Colin Blakely, Lisa Harrow, Bill Maynard, Richard Pearson, Paul Shelley. Colour.
93 minutes.

Thorn EMI Video

I Walked With A Zombie ★★★

One of Val Lewton's earliest horror pics for RKO, a revamping of the *Jane Eyre* theme about a young nurse who is hired by a wealthy West Indies planter to care for his sick wife. The trouble is she's no ordinary patient. She's under the spell of voodoo and one of the walking dead. Most of it's terribly old-fashioned of course (the year of production was 1943) but even now there are still a few sequences that grip the imagination. Certainly a collector's item and comprising an intriguing double-bill with the thriller *Crack-Up*.

1943. Directed by Jacques Tourneur.

Starring Frances Dee, Tom Conway, James Ellison. Black and White.
69 minutes.

Kingston Video

J

Jack And The Beanstalk

Abbott & Costello, 1952 vintage. Lou (the tubby one) dreams himself into
the world of the fairy story – magic beans, huge beanstalk, talking harp
– and duels *à la* Errol Flynn around a castle with giant Buddy Baer.
Strictly for the kids. Starts off in black and white then turns into colour in
the dream segment. On the same video double-bill: *From The Earth To
The Moon*.

1952. Directed by Jean Yarbrough.
Starring Bud Abbott, Lou Costello, Dorothy Ford, Barbara Brown, Buddy
Baer. Colour.
87 minutes.

Kingston Video

Jaguar Lives

The supporting cast of this movie might lead you to believe that you're
in for something special. You're not. This is a wretchedly unconvincing
tale of a secret agent cum karate champion out to break down a huge
drug network operating all over the world. John Huston is a shipping
magnate, Donald Pleasence a South American dictator, Christopher Lee
a drug pedlar, and so on. Forget it!

1979. Directed by Ernest Pintoff.
Starring Joe Lewis, Christopher Lee, Donald Pleasence, Barbara Bach,
Joseph Wiseman, Woody Strode, John Huston. Colour.
90 minutes.

Rank Video

Jailhouse Rock

Elvis Presley's third movie; the one in which he's sent to jail for man-slaughter, makes amends by learning to play the guitar and then inflicts himself once again on the unsuspecting public by becoming a rather unlovable rock star. The title song, of course, became one of Elvis' biggest hits; the others include "Young And Beautiful", "Treat Me Nice", "I Wanna Be Free", "Don't Leave Me Now" and "Baby, I Don't Care". For those who care about things other than rock 'n roll, there are always the talents of character actor Mickey Shaughnessy (as Elvis' cellmate) to enjoy. Perhaps the most surprising thing about this movie is that it failed to make the four million dollar mark.

1957. Directed by Richard Thorpe.
Starring Elvis Presley, Judy Tyler, Mickey Shaughnessy, Vaughn Taylor, Dean Jones. Black and White.
96 minutes.

MGM/CBS Home Video

Jane Austen In Manhattan

The rivalries between two groups of actors, each of whom wants to perform a version of a play-fragment by the 12-year-old Jane Austen when it is purchased at a New York auction. An *avant-garde* group led by Robert Powell sees the play as a Punch And Judy affair; the rival group headed by Anne Baxter views it as a Mozartian opera. Elusive little James Ivory film based on the real-life sale of a Jane Austen manuscript at Sotheby's in London.

1980. Directed by James Ivory.
Starring Anne Baxter, Robert Powell, Michael Wager, Tim Choate, John Guerrasio, Katrina Hodiak. Colour.
111 minutes.

Home Video Productions

Jaws

There was a time when the subject of a giant shark chewing up people off the beaches of an American holiday resort would have been reserved for B-picture status. But times have changed. Audiences have become more "sophisticated" and this cleverly assembled adventure-thriller struck just the right nerve when it was released in 1975. Does it hold up on video? Yes, surprisingly well, although one does lose that claustrophobic effect when "you" are the shark and travelling underwater to bite your next victim. The famous horror jump effects remain effective however and Roy Scheider, Richard Dreyfuss and Robert Shaw are more than efficient as the three men in the boat who set out to do the monster in!

Box-office rental	$133,435,000
Average rental (75)	$27,300,250
Oscars (3)	Best Sound; Editing; Music Score
Oscar nominations (1)	Best Film

1975. Directed by Steven Spielberg.
Starring Roy Scheider, Robert Shaw, Richard Dreyfuss, Lorraine Gary, Murray Hamilton. Colour.
124 minutes.

CIC Video

Jaws II

It's four years later and another great white shark has surfaced in the waters around the peaceful town of Amity. Police chief Roy Scheider is once more involved, and so too are the same silly townsfolk who once again refuse to believe that a new shark is on the loose. A superficial sequel that covers much of the same water as its predecessor and not nearly as efficiently. But it took an awful lot of money very quickly before audiences discovered that the shark looked mechanical, which it didn't (apart from one scene) in the first movie. One effective horror scene to look out for: Scheider investigating some suspicious driftwood and finding it's attached to a half-devoured corpse.

Box-office rental	$55,608,000

Average rental (78) $39,443,850

1978. Directed by Jeannot Szwarc.
Starring Roy Scheider, Lorraine Gary, Murray Hamilton, Joseph Mascolo,
Jeffrey Kramer. Colour.
117 minutes.

CIC Video

The Jazz Singer

A cantor's son refuses to follow his father into a New York synagogue
and opts for a life in show-biz instead. This one was old-fashioned even
in 1927 when it became the first talkie with Al Jolson. Fifty years on and
things haven't changed much, apart from the fact that Jolson has become
Neil Diamond and the songs changed to "America", "Hello Again", "Summer Love" and "Love On The Rocks". Laurence Olivier as Diamond's pa
is presumably supposed to add a touch of class but instead adds only to
the schmaltz. Verdict: the LP is better.

Box-office rental $13,000,000
Average rental (80) $30,086,027

1980. Directed by Richard Fleischer.
Starring Neil Diamond, Laurence Olivier, Lucie Arnaz, Catlin Adams,
Franklyn Ajaye, Paul Nicholas. Colour.
116 minutes.

Thorn EMI Video

Jenny

Anti-Vietnam protest mixed in with a little soap opera in a story about a
young New York film-maker who marries a pregnant girl so that he can
avoid being drafted. A rather self-conscious little movie, well-meaning at
times, but not of any great interest other than to those who want to catch
a glimpse of Alan Alda in his pre-*M.A.S.H.* days.

1970. Directed by George Bloomfield.
Starring Marlo Thomas, Alan Alda, Marian Hailey, Elizabeth Wilson, Vincent Gardenia. Colour.
89 minutes.

Rank Video

Jessie's Girls

A young Mormon wife turns outlaw to avenge the death of her husband and her own rape by a gang of outlaws. Three women – a female gunslinger, a prostitute and an Indian squaw – help her in her task. Disagreeable rubbish, badly made.

1975. Directed by Al Adamson.
Starring Sondra Currie, Geoffrey Land, Ben Frank, Regina Carroll, Jennifer Bishop, Ellen Stern. Colour.
84 minutes.

Intervision

Jesus Christ Superstar

Legendary rock opera about a group of young tourists who arrive in Israel, deck themselves out in the costumes of apostles, priests, soldiers, etc. and act out the last days of Christ's life. Even in 1973 this one translated rather uneasily from stage to screen and today, despite the continuing success of composers Tim Rice and Andrew Lloyd Webber, it seems almost a period piece. Far from convincing video entertainment that perhaps should have remained on the stage where it truly belongs.

Box-office rental	$13,291,000
Average rental (73)	$22,271,150
Oscars	Nil
Oscar nominations (1)	Best Music Scoring

1973. Directed by Norman Jewison.

Starring Ted Neeley, Carl Anderson, Yvonne Elliman, Barry Dennen, Joshua Mostel. Colour.
107 minutes.

CIC Video

Jour De Fete

Surely one of the funniest movies to be found on video, with Jacques Tati (in his first feature and before his Monsieur Hulot days) as a village postman who is influenced by an advertising film at a visiting fair and decides that he can deliver the mail just as fast as the streamlined New York Postal Service. The result, as you might expect, is chaos. For those who find Tati's humour and mime less than hilarious this tape is probably not worth the expense; for those who find his work to be close to genius it is a "must buy", a minor French masterpiece that is rarely seen nowadays. The atmosphere of French village life on a lazy summer's day is beautifully evoked.

1949. Directed by Jacques Tati.
Starring Jacques Tati, Guy Decombe, Paul Frankeur, Santa Relli, Maine Vallee. Black and White.
87 minutes.

Zodiac Video
(distributed by Videomedia)

Journey To The Centre Of Time ★

Three scientists – two men and a girl – hurtle backwards and forwards in time when one of their experiments goes wrong. One minute they're in the year 6968 AD and finding that Earth has been destroyed by a laser beam war. The next, they're back in the year one million B.C. with prehistoric monsters for company. One scientist tries to have it both ways and is killed when he meets himself travelling in the opposite direction. Honest!

1967. Directed by David L. Hewitt.

Starring Scott Brady, Anthony Eisley, Gigi Perreau, Abraham Sofaer, Austin Green, Poupee Gamin. Colour.
82 minutes.

Derann Video

Julia

Adaptation of Lillian Hellman's *Pentimento* about the author's unusual relationship with her childhood friend Julia, who brings about her political awareness when she involves her in the fight against Fascism in Europe during the 1930s. A technical *tour-de-force*, told in a variety of flashbacks, and made with a style and polish only rarely seen in modern-day cinema. A hazardous train journey in which Hellman smuggles $50,000 through the customs and into Nazi Berlin is worthy of Hitchcock at his best. Fine performances from Jane Fonda (Hellman) and Vanessa Redgrave (Julia); two telling cameos from Jason Robards as novelist Dashiell Hammett and Maximilian Schell as a resistance worker. A class movie.

Box-office rental	$13,055,000
Average rental (77)	$36,913,348
Oscars (3)	Best Supporting Actor (Robards); Best Supporting Actress (Redgrave); Screenplay
Oscar nominations (8)	Best Film; Actress (Fonda); Supporting Actor (Schell); Direction; Photography; Costume Design; Editing; Original Music Score

1977. Directed by Fred Zinnemann.
Starring Jane Fonda, Vanessa Redgrave, Jason Robards, Maximilian Schell, Hal Holbrook, Rosemary Murphy, Meryl Streep. Colour.
117 minutes.

Twentieth Century-Fox Video

Junior Bonner

Arguably Sam Peckinpah's finest film (certainly his most likeable), with Steve McQueen as a rodeo star who knows that he's slipping from the number one spot and tries to come to terms with the fact that he's no longer the best. The film spreads over a couple of days when McQueen returns to his home town for the Fourth of July rodeo celebrations and pushes home the chilling message that the modern world no longer has any time for individualism. The definitive McQueen movie? Whatever, it's good video all along the line, with great support from Robert Preston and Ida Lupino as McQueen's parents and Joe Don Baker as his younger brother.

1972. Directed by Sam Peckinpah.
Starring Steve McQueen, Robert Preston, Ida Lupino, Joe Don Baker, Barbara Leigh, Mary Murphy, Ben Johnson. Colour.
103 minutes.

Rank Video

Just A Gigolo

David Bowie as a young Prussian officer who is deprived of fame and fortune in World War I and drifts along in the Germany of the 20s and 30s where he finishes up as a gigolo. Hardly worth all the expense (at 12 million Deutschmarks it is reputedly one of the most expensive movies to come out of Germany) and in the end a rather minor film, despite the lavishness of the period sets. Marlene Dietrich appears as an ageing baroness who commands an army of gigolos; Sydne Rome and Kim Novak provide some of the female allure. But if you're a Bowie fan you would do better to turn your attention to his other film on video, *The Man Who Fell To Earth*.

1978. Directed by David Hemmings.
Starring David Bowie, Sydne Rome, Kim Novak, David Hemmings, Maria Schell, Curt Juergens, Marlene Dietrich. Colour.
105 minutes.

Cinema Features
(distributed by VCL)

K

The Kid

Chaplin's little tramp adopts an abandoned baby boy and rears him as
his own son before returning him eventually to his mother. A combination
of slapstick and sentiment, the film launched five-year-old Jackie Coogan
on a remarkable screen career and showed Chaplin in a more serious
vein than ever before. Supported on a double-feature tape by the 1921
Chaplin two-reeler *The Idle Class* in which Charlie features in a dual role
– as the tramp and as a rich, alcoholic fop.

1921. Directed by Charles Chaplin.
Starring Charles Chaplin, Jackie Coogan, Carl Miller, Edna Purviance,
Chuck Riesner, Tom Wilson. Black and White.
60 minutes.

Spectrum
(distributed by Polygram)

Kidnapped

Robert Louis Stevenson's famous tale has been filmed many times without
ever achieving real distinction on the screen. This most recent of adaptations is pleasing because of Michael Caine's surprisingly effective portrait of the Jacobite outlaw Alan Breck, who helps the young David Balfour
gain his rightful inheritance. Donald Pleasence is the miserly Uncle Ebe-
nezer, Jack Hawkins a villainous ship's captain, Trevor Howard the Lord
Advocate. Pleasant locations; good value for the kids. 2½ rating.

1971. Directed by Delbert Mann.
Starring Michael Caine, Trevor Howard, Jack Hawkins, Donald Pleasence,
Gordon Jackson, Vivien Heilbron, Lawrence Douglas, Freddie Jones.
Colour.
107 minutes.

Rank Video

The Kidnapping Of The President

Race-against-time kidnap thriller of the old school but given an up-to-date twist by casting the kidnapper as a terrorist and the victim as the President Of The United States. The ransom for Mr. Pres. is one hundred million dollars in diamonds but with William Shatner of *Star Trek* fame as a Secret Service chief, there's little doubt that the president will get to see the White House again. Miguel Fernandes plays the kidnapper, Hal Holbrook the President and former MGM star Van Johnson a conniving Vice-President. Passable, nothing more.

1980. Directed by George Mendeluk.
Starring William Shatner, Hal Holbrook, Van Johnson, Ava Gardner, Miguel Fernandes. Colour.
113 minutes.

Guild Home Video

Killer Fish

Once dear old Bruce (the shark in *Jaws)* began snapping his giant molars across human limbs, Hollywood quickly began searching for other underwater monsters to eat up their leading actors. And what better than piranha fish that can strip flesh from a human body in just a few seconds! Here they guard some stolen diamonds dumped in a dammed reservoir by a gang of crooks. The crooks (Lee Majors, James Franciscus, etc.) are then left with the problem of grabbing the loot before the fish grab them. Indifferent fishboiler, filmed in Brazil.

1979. Directed by Anthony M. Dawson.
Starring Lee Majors, Karen Black, Margaux Hemingway, Marisa Berenson, James Franciscus. Colour.
99 minutes.

Precision Video

The Killing Of Sister George ★★★

This movie made the headlines because it deals in part with lesbianism. But that's only part of its storyline. The rest is a study of loneliness and despair as ageing, drink-sodden actress Beryl Reid finds that the character she plays on a long-running TV serial – that of the lovable district nurse "George" – is to be killed off and that her career is about to take an almighty dive. Susannah York is Reid's flat mate; Coral Browne the BBC producer who intrudes on their relationship. The performances might occasionally seem over-pitched but you don't stop watching. Late-night adult viewing, often disturbing.

1968. Directed by Robert Aldrich.
Starring Beryl Reid, Susannah York, Coral Browne, Ronald Fraser, Patricia Medina, Hugh Paddick. Colour.
135 minutes.

Rank Video

Kind Hearts And Coronets ★★★★

Vengeful young draper's assistant Dennis Price kills off, one by one, the eight relatives standing between him and a dukedom – all of them played by Alec Guinness, who pops up then quickly pops off again as a clergyman, an amateur photographer, a general, a suffragette and so on. Impeccably designed and directed and, along with *The Lavender Hill Mob,* one of the high water marks of the post-war Ealing canon. *Devotees* of British character acting will relish Miles Malleson's cameo as an eager hangman; admirers of Valerie Hobson's beauty and Joan Greenwood's husky tones will also be rewarded. Black comedy at its best. Superior video.

1949. Directed by Robert Hamer.
Starring Dennis Price, Valerie Hobson, Joan Greenwood, Alec Guinness, Audrey Fildes, Miles Malleson, Clive Morton. Black and White.
106 minutes.

Thorn EMI Video

A Kind Of Loving

Working class life in Britain's industrial North examined with telling effect
in a film that relates a story as old as the Northern hills themselves – a
young draftsman makes a girl from the typing pool pregnant and then
has to make the best of the resulting loveless marriage. Gloomy stuff
then, but Alan Bates and June Ritchie are more than convincing as the
unfortunate pair and John Schlesinger's shrewd observations of the working class environment stand the film in good stead. Another plus factor
is Thora Hird, an absolute powerhouse as the shrewish mother-in-law
whose only interests in life are her clean carpet and watching endless
panel games on the telly. Strikingly photographed industrial landscapes;
adapts well to video.

1962. Directed by John Schlesinger.
Starring Alan Bates, June Ritchie, Thora Hird, Bert Palmer, Pat Keen, James
Bolam, Jack Smethurst. Black and White.
112 minutes.

Thorn EMI Video

The King And I

English governess Deborah Kerr falls foul of then falls for tyrannical king
Yul Brynner when she travels to old Siam to care for his children in the
royal household. You know the rest. Popular now for over 25 years and
likely to remain so for another 25 if for no other reason than every one
of its numbers is a hit. Yul Brynner sings all his own songs; Miss Kerr is
dubbed by Marni Nixon; Lyle Wheeler and John DeCuir are responsible
for the sumptious sets. Standout sequence: the "Shall We Dance" number.
One major carp: the colour quality leaves much to be desired, probably
because the DeLuxe process of the mid-50s was then only in its infancy.

Box-office rental	$8,500,000
Average rental (56)	$8,814,900
Oscars (5)	Best Actor (Brynner); Art Direction; Costume Design; Sound Recording; Scoring Of A Musical

Oscar nominations (4)   Best Film; Actress (Kerr); Direction;
                         Photography

1956. Directed by Walter Lang.
Starring Yul Brynner, Deborah Kerr, Rita Moreno, Martin Benson, Terry
Saunders, Rex Thompson, Alan Mowbray. Colour.
133 minutes.

Twentieth Century-Fox Video

King Creole

If you have to name a best Elvis Presley vehicle – best in terms of
construction, direction and acting – it would almost certainly be this one,
a realistic adaptation of Harold Robbins' novel *A Stone For Danny Fisher*,
about a mixed-up, ex-high school kid who becomes involved with some
murderous gangsters in New Orleans. Director Michael Curtiz, actor
Walter Matthau (as a heavy) and Elvis might seem an odd combination
but for the most part this one works dramatically as well as muscially.
"Hard-Headed Woman", "As Long As I Have You", "Dixieland Rock",
"Don't Ask Me Why" and "King Creole" are among the musical numbers.

1958. Directed by Michael Curtiz.
Starring Elvis Presley, Carolyn Jones, Dean Jagger, Walter Matthau, Dolores Hart, Paul Stewart. Black and White.
116 minutes.

Twentieth Century-Fox Video

Kingdom Of The Spiders

A tarantula army versus the inhabitants of a small town in Arizona. And
who wins? You might be surprised for, despite its title, this is a not
unimaginative little movie that has plenty of creepy moments and even
a few comedy scenes, including the one in which the entomologist heroine picks up a spider that has been stalking her in the shower and
exclaims: "Well, hello there. My goodness, what are *you* doing here?"
Worth a look, unless of course you can't abide spiders!

1977. Directed by John "Bud" Cardos.
Starring William Shatner, Tiffany Bolling, Woody Strode, Lieux Dressler,
David McLean. Colour.
94 minutes.

Intervision

King Kong

A 40-foot ape is captured on an unexplored island off the coast of Africa
and taken to New York, where he runs amok in the city streets before
plunging to his death from the Empire State Building. The spectacle in
the last thirty minutes is tremendous; heroine Fay Wray screams like mad
but, according to many contemporary critics, secretly enjoys wriggling
sensuously in the furry palm of Kong's giant paw. Too sensuously for the
censor of the day, who excised several such scenes including some in
which Kong nibbled at a few human heads. What remains, however, is
great cinema – and great video. Certainly one for the collection.

1933. Directed by Merian C. Cooper & Ernest B. Schoedsack.
Starring Fay Wray, Robert Armstrong, Bruce Cabot, Frank Reicher, Sam
Hardy, Noble Johnson. Black and White.
100 minutes.

Thorn EMI Video

King Solomon's Treasure

Dreadful bowdlerization of Rider Haggard's novel *Alan Quartermain,* with
David McCallum and Patrick Macnee as the adventurers involved in the
inevitable safari and Britt Ekland as the white queen they find at the end
of their journey. The safari takes in leopard men, prehistoric monsters,
hidden treasure and a volcanic eruption, all of which are photographed
in the most appalling colour. Even kids will fall about in unintentional
laughter at this one.

1978. Directed by Alvin Rakoff.

Starring David McCallum, John Colicos, Patrick Macnee, Britt Ekland, Yvon Dufour, Ken Gampu, Wilfrid Hyde-White. Colour.
88 minutes.

Intervision

Klondike Fever

Tepid account of novelist Jack London's youthful experiences in the gold-rush Yukon. The discovery of gold, the crossing of some rapids and a dog race are among the things you get for your money. You also get some rather uninspired performances from Rod Steiger as the all-powerful, town-owning baddie, Lorne Greene as a mountie and Jeff East as the young London. Forgettable on just about every count. Not for the discerning.

1980. Directed by Peter Carter.
Starring Rod Steiger, Angie Dickinson, Lorne Greene, Jeff East, Barry Morse. Colour.
106 minutes.

Intervision

Klute

"Men have paid 200 dollars for me, and here you are turning down a freebie. You could get a perfectly good dishwasher for that." So says luscious New York call-girl Jane Fonda to Donald Sutherland early on in this movie. Well, it's not all like that, for this one turns into the blackest of black thrillers by the halfway mark as Fonda finds herself the prey of a psychopath just waiting for the chance to put her away for good. Sutherland is quietly effective as a private eye searching for a husband last seen in New York City, but this is Fonda's movie from first to last and it chills to the very marrow. A nightmare but a highly effective one.

Box-office rental	$8,000,000
Average rental (71)	$13,465,850
Oscars (1)	Best Actress (Fonda)

Oscar nominations (1)   Best Story & Screenplay

1971. Directed by Alan J. Pakula.
Starring Jane Fonda, Donald Sutherland, Charles Cioffi, Roy Scheider, Dorothy Tristan, Rita Gam. Colour.
114 minutes.

Warner Home Video

Knight Without Armour

English journalist Robert Donat helps countess Marlene Dietrich flee across the border during the Russian Revolution. Much underrated Korda adventure romance with great chemistry between the two stars and plenty of last-minute escapes to keep things on the boil. Splendid sets, in fact quite splendid all round, with the husky Dietrich taking a couple of baths and showing her beautiful legs as an extra bonus. A rarity. From the novel by James Hilton.

1937. Directed by Jacques Feyder.
Starring Marlene Dietrich, Robert Donat, Irene Vanbrugh, Herbert Lomas, Austin Trevor, Basil Gill, John Clements. Black and White.
108 minutes.

Spectrum
(distributed by Polygram)

Kotch

Jack Lemmon proves he's as talented a film-maker as he is an actor with this, his first directorial effort, a sentimental little comedy about an eccentric old widower who finds himself constantly at odds with his family and experiencing some hazardous adventures with an abandoned young mother-to-be. If you don't enjoy this one there must be something wrong with you, for its qualities include two ingredients sadly missing from most of today's movies – warmth and humanity. Matthau's timing as the 72-year-old Kotch is nigh on perfect.

Oscars	Nil
Oscar nominations (4)	Best Actor (Matthau); Sound; Editing; Song ("Life Is What You Make It")

1971. Directed by Jack Lemmon.
Starring Walter Matthau, Deborah Winters, Felicia Farr, Charles Aidman, Ellen Geer, Donald and Dean Kowalski. Colour.
114 minutes.

Guild Home Video

L

Lady Caroline Lamb

Even a distinguished "Who's Who" of British performers – John Mills, Margaret Leighton, Laurence Olivier, Ralph Richardson – cannot prevent this movie about the reckless exhibitionism of Lady Caroline Lamb from tumbling over into the absurd. Sarah Miles is the neurotic wildcat of the title; Jon Finch her luckless hubbie; and Richard Chamberlain Lord Byron with whom she embarks on a disastrous affair that scandalizes British society during the early 1800s. To say the least, a rather lamentable portrait of life in Regency England.

1972. Directed by Robert Bolt.
Starring Sarah Miles, Jon Finch, Richard Chamberlain, Margaret Leighton, John Mills, Ralph Richardson, Laurence Olivier. Colour.
123 minutes.

Thorn EMI Video

The Ladykillers

Alec Guinness of *Lavender Hill Mob* fame up to his robbery tricks once more, this time as a mad criminal genius who brings together a bizarre gang of crooks, disguises them as a musical string quartet and pulls off a £60,000 wages snatch near King's Cross Station. Where he comes unstuck is renting accommodation at the house of little old lady Katie Johnson who, quite inadvertently, brings about the gang's demise, one by one. Much darker in tone than *The Lavender Hill Mob*, this one retains its freshness, despite its age and some rather harsh colour which makes one wish it had been in black and white. Still, you can always turn the colour down. Cecil Parker (phoney major), Herbert Lom (Soho gangster), Peter Sellers (teddy boy) and Danny Green (moronic muscle man) make up the string quartet!

Oscars   Nil
Oscar nominations (1)   Best Original Screenplay

1955. Directed by Alexander Mackendrick.
Starring Alec Guinness, Cecil Parker, Peter Sellers, Herbert Lom, Danny Green, Katie Johnson. Colour.
97 minutes.

Thorn EMI Video

The Lady Vanishes

Arguably the best train movie of them all, with young Michael Redgrave and pretty Margaret Lockwood becoming more and more perplexed as they investigate the disappearance of a charming old lady from a train travelling across the Balkans. Plenty of suspects on board – Paul Lukas, Cecil Parker, Googie Withers – plus the cricket-loving duo of Basil Radford and Naunton Wayne. Hitchcock's most accomplished prewar thriller. Only one train coach was used during the making of the film, all the other train shots being transparencies or miniatures.

1938. Directed by Alfred Hitchcock.
Starring Margaret Lockwood, Michael Redgrave, Paul Lukas, Dame May Whitty, Googie Withers, Cecil Parker, Linden Travers, Naunton Wayne, Basil Radford. Black and White.
97 minutes.

Rank Video

The Lady Vanishes

The 1979 remake, with Elliott Gould and the alluring Cybill Shepherd less than adequate replacements for Redgrave and Lockwood, sloppy direction from Anthony Page and a mediocre supporting cast. Only Arthur Lowe and Ian Carmichael give a good account of themselves as the cricket lovers. For all the technical improvements and the excellent colour work it's not a patch on the original.

1979. Directed by Anthony Page.
Starring Elliott Gould, Cybill Shepherd, Angela Lansbury, Herbert Lom, Arthur Lowe, Ian Carmichael, Gerald Harper. Colour.
97 minutes.

Rank Video

Laserblast

A teenager drives into the desert in the American South-West, finds a laser gun left over by an alien and then goes on the rampage when he is taken over by the alien's persona ... Yep folks, this one's rubbish all the way despite the fact that character actors Roddy McDowall and Keenan Wynn can be found in the cast. Zero rating.

1978. Directed by Michael Rae.
Starring Kim Milford, Cheryl Smith, Gianni Russo, Roddy McDowall, Ron Masock, Keenan Wynn. Colour.
90 minutes.

Intervision

The Last Days Of Pompeii

The climactic scenes of a city being torn apart by an earthquake and volcanic eruption make this creaky old movie worth a look, although hardly worth purchasing unless you're in the multi-millionaire class. Like many films made in the 30s, it shows its age and at times looks almost as old as Pompeii itself. Preston Foster features as a humble blacksmith who fights his way to wealth and power by becoming a champion gladiator. The Tim Holt western *The Mysterious Desperado* hardly improves the value of this inferior double feature tape.

1935. Directed by Merian C. Cooper and Ernest Schoedsack.
Starring Preston Foster, Basil Rathbone, Alan Hale, Dorothy Wilson, Louis Calhern. Black and White.
96 minutes.

Kingston Video

Last Tango In Paris

Time has its own way of eroding the inflated opinions of intellectual critics, so if you thought this was nothing but a load of pretentious rubbish when you first saw it back in 1973 then you're in good company. There are those, of course, who still regard it as a masterpiece. The "plot" concerns a middle-aged American (Marlon Brando) who makes love to a young French girl (Maria Schneider) while apartment hunting in Paris. Explicit sex scenes of course but it takes rather more than that to make a good movie. Or does it these days? Mediocre late night viewing.

Box-office rental	$16,095,000
Average rental (73)	$22,271,150
Oscars	Nil
Oscar nominations (2)	Best Actor (Brando); Direction

1973. Directed by Bernardo Bertolucci.
Starring Marlon Brando, Maria Schneider, Jean-Pierre Leaud, Darling Legitimus, Catherine Sola, Mauro Marchetti. Colour.
129 minutes.

Intervision

Last Train From Gun Hill

Kirk Douglas is a marshal who sets out to get the men responsible for the death of his wife. One of them happens to be the son of old friend, cattle

baron Anthony Quinn. Douglas must cast friendship aside and take the
killer in. Quinn, not unnaturally, says no. The whole thing is settled in a
gunfight on the station platform of the town of Gun Hill. Adult, plausible
Western; interesting to listen to as well as look at. 2½ rating.

1959. Directed by John Sturges.
Starring Kirk Douglas, Anthony Quinn, Carolyn Jones, Earl Holliman, Brad
Dexter, Brian Hutton. Colour.
94 minutes.

Twentieth Century-Fox Video

The Last Valley

A rarity, a thinking man's "intimate epic" about a conflict of minds –
ruthless captain Michael Caine and liberal scholar Omar Sharif – when
they stumble across a peaceful valley in the Alps that has remained
untouched by the pillage and plunder of the Thirty Years War. The
performances of Caine and Sharif are of a remarkable standard for a film
of this kind, probably because both actors have something interesting
and intelligent to say – thanks to the script of James Clavell. Something
of a forgotten movie but well worth seeking out on video. Elegant camerawork by John Wilcox.

1971. Directed by James Clavell.
Starring Michael Caine, Omar Sharif, Florinda Bolkan, Nigel Davenport,
Per Oscarsson, Arthur O'Connell. Colour.
129 minutes.

Rank Video

Laura

A beautiful advertising girl is murdered with a shotgun and the detective
investigating the case falls in love with her portrait. Then comes the twist.
The supposedly dead girl walks in through her apartment door. So who's
the corpse? And who shot her? A classic thriller with a fine cast –
Andrews, Tierney, Price, and especially Clifton Webb as an acid-tongued

gossip columnist whose egotism borders on paranoia and who delights in listening to himself speak: "In my case, self-absorption is completely justified. I have never discovered any other subject quite so worthy of my attention." David Raksin's lush music score is another attribute.

Oscars (1)	Best Photography
Oscar nominations (4)	Best Supporting Actor (Webb); Direction; Screenplay; Art Direction

1944. Directed by Otto Preminger.
Starring Gene Tierney, Dana Andrews, Clifton Webb, Vincent Price, Judith Anderson. Black and White.
88 minutes.

Twentieth Century-Fox Video

The Lavender Hill Mob ★★★★

Meek little bowler-hatted bank clerk Alec Guinness leads the mob. His plan? To rob the bank at which he has worked for many years of a million pounds worth of gold bars, melt them down into souvenir models of the Eiffel Tower and retire on the proceeds to South America. Sharing his enthusiasm for an early retirement: jovial sculptor Stanley Holloway and small-time crooks Alfie Bass and Sidney James. A delightful little movie that, despite its short running time – just 78 minutes – is better value for money than many a longer video offering and proves that crime can pay, almost! Watch out for a brief appearance of a young Audrey Hepburn in the last scene.

Oscars (1)	Best Story & Screenplay
Oscar nominations (1)	Best Actor (Guinness)

1951. Directed by Charles Crichton.
Starring Alec Guinness, Stanley Holloway, Sidney James, Alfie Bass, Marjorie Fielding, John Gregson, Clive Morton. Black and White.
78 minutes.

Thorn EMI Video

Law Of The Underworld

B-movie about an innocent young couple who find themselves arrested for a robbery they did not commit and then saved by the benevolent gangster who has taken them under his wing. Strictly cut-rate routine stuff off the Hollywood treadmill. Supports *The Outlaw* on a double feature video tape.

1938. Directed by Lew Landers.
Starring Chester Morris, Anne Shirley, Eduardo Ciannelli, Walter Abel, Lee Patrick. Black and White.
58 minutes.

Kingston Video

The League Of Gentlemen ★★★

Ingenious British heist movie with Jack Hawkins heading a robbery team of eight ex-army officers, who put their military training to good effect by relieving a London bank of one million pounds. The way they get their come-uppance is unconvincing. Not so the rest of the film, which boasts hardly a violent scene but still manages to be exciting. A good example in fact for modern movie-makers hung up on the theory that sex and violence do a good movie make. Great cast; good video.

1960. Directed by Basil Dearden.
Starring Jack Hawkins, Nigel Patrick, Roger Livesey, Richard Attenborough, Bryan Forbes, Kieron Moore, Robert Coote, Terence Alexander, Melissa Stribling. Black and White.
113 minutes.

Rank Video

The Legacy

Americans Katharine Ross and Sam Elliott arrive in Britain and wish they'd stayed at home, for they find themselves as guests in a spooky old mansion – and you know what happens when you stay at old houses in the movies. In this case death by choking, impalement and fire are just a few of the things on offer. There's also witchcraft, a touch of telekinesis and reincarnation. Routine horror stuff; many unpleasant scenes.

Box-office rental	$5,207,000
Average rental (78)	$39,443,850

1978. Directed by Richard Marquand.
Starring Katharine Ross, Sam Elliott, John Standing, Ian Hogg, Margaret Tyzack, Charles Gray, Lee Montague, Hildegard Neil. Colour.
102 minutes.

VIPCO

The Legend Of Frenchie King ★

Notorious train robber Brigitte Bardot and her four half-sisters ride the range down New Mexico way, settle down on a ranch and fall foul of equally ruthless Claudia Cardinale, who discovers that oil lies below the surface of the land. Not much lies below the surface of this crude little movie which is so apallingly dubbed it offends the ear. Even admirers of Miss Bardot will be hard put to cheer.

1971. Directed by Christian-Jaque.
Starring Brigitte Bardot, Claudia Cardinale, Michael J. Pollard, Micheline Presle, Georges Beller, Emma Cohen. Colour.
96 minutes.

Picture Time Video
(distributed by VCL)

The Legend Of The Lone Ranger ★

Yet another attempt to revamp the glories of the past. This time it is the creations of George Trendle and Fran Striker that come in for the treatment, as director William Fraker tries to bring a new lease of life to the Lone Ranger tale. He fails. The first half of the film deals with how the avenger got his mask; the second with his battles with a would-be dictator who kidnaps President Grant. Lamentable stuff. Frequently makes you pose the question: "Why did they bother?"

Box-office rental	$6,900,000
Average rental (81)	$32,180,110

1981. Directed by William A. Fraker.
Starring Klinton Spilsbury, Michael Horse, Christopher Lloyd, Matt Clark, Juanin Clay, John Bennett Perry. Colour.
97 minutes.

Precision Video

Legend Of The Werewolf

So-called horror movie about a young zoo attendant who gets all hairy at full moon time and goes about committing murder in 19th century Paris. Even Peter Cushing (as a police pathologist) can't save this lamentable exercise from becoming laughably inept. The wonder is that the fragile sets managed to stay up until they'd finished shooting. One star for trying and for Cushing's presence.

1975. Directed by Freddie Francis.
Starring Peter Cushing, Ron Moody, Hugh Griffith, Roy Castle, David Rintoul. Colour.
90 minutes.

Rank Video

Lenny

Your reaction to this film will depend largely on your opinion of American nightclub comedian Lenny Bruce, whose irreverent and obscene humour made him such a controversial figure in the 50s and 60s. If you regard him as a brilliant humourist who broke down some of the hypocrisies of American society you will probably enjoy this Bob Fosse film. If you regard him as nothing more than a sleazy and dangerous opportunist with an eye for the half chance and the quick buck you will probably find it repugnant. The language is foul, the acting exceptional, the direction imaginative. The entertainment value? Debatable.

Box-office rental	$11,600,000
Average rental (74)	£18,456,150
Oscars	Nil
Oscar nominations (6)	Best Film; Actor (Hoffman); Actress (Perrine); Direction; Screenplay; Photography

1974. Directed by Bob Fosse.
Starring Dustin Hoffman, Valerie Perrine, Jan Miner, Stanley Beck, Gary Morton, Rashel Novikoff. Black and White.
111 minutes.

Intervision

Leopard In The Snow

Soggy little romantic trifle about a once-famous racing driver (now living as a recluse because of the death of his brother in a crash) and a young woman he saves from a blizzard in the Cumberland Fells. The leopard of the title belongs to the racing driver; Jeremy Kemp (manservant), Kenneth More (girl's titled father) and Billie Whitelaw (girl's step mother) make events seem a great deal more believable than they deserve to be. But lame. And limp.

1978. Directed by Gerry O'Hara.
Starring Susan Penhaligon, Keir Dullea, Jeremy Kemp, Billie Whitelaw, Kenneth More. Colour.
94 minutes.

Derann Video

Let George Do It

Northern music hall comedian George Formby is supposed to go to Blackpool for a concert party but finishes up instead in Norway where he gets mistaken by the Nazis for a British spy. Believe that and you'll believe anything! The first of the Ealing comedies to deal directly with the war against Germany but no more than standard comic fare. Formby sings "Grandad's Flannelette Nightshirt".

1940. Directed by Marcel Vanel.
Starring George Formby, Phyllis Calvert, Garry Marsh, Romney Brent, Bernard Lee, Coral Browne. Black and White.
82 minutes.

Thorn EMI Video

Letter From An Unknown Woman

Max Ophuls' best American film; a sad, characteristic little story of the brief love affair between a 16-year-old girl (Joan Fontaine) and a philandering concert pianist (Louis Jourdan) in turn-of-the-century Vienna. The story is told in flashback and remembered years later by the dying woman as she writes a last letter to the pianist who has long since forgotten her. Slight but beautifully rendered; exquisite photography by German-born cameraman Franz Planer. A video "must" for all cineastes.

1948. Directed by Max Ophuls.
Starring Joan Fontaine, Louis Jourdan, Mady Christians, Marcel Journet, Art Smith, Howard Freeman. Black and White.
90 minutes.

Intervision

Licensed To Kill

Tom Adams as a British agent assigned by the Foreign Office to protect the life of a Swedish scientist who has invented an anti-gravity machine. The Brits want to buy it, the Ruskies want the scientist dead. Routine thrills, some comedy. British character actors Peter Bull and Francis De Wolff help keep things moving. Known as *The Second Best Secret Agent In The Whole Wide World* in the USA.

1965. Directed by Lindsay Shonteff.
Starring Tom Adams, Karel Stepanek, Veronica Hurst, Peter Bull, John Arnatt, Francis De Wolff, Felix Felton. Colour.
96 minutes.

Derann Video

The Lifetaker ★

The bored young wife of a wealthy city businessman picks up and seduces a youth whilst out driving in the country. The husband, a former mercenary with a fetish for guns and swords, discovers the seduction but decides to play cat and mouse with the pair before taking revenge. Extremely unpleasant.

1975. Directed by Michael Papas.
Starring Terence Morgan, Lea Dregorn, Peter Duncan. Colour.
98 minutes.

Intervision

The Likely Lads ★★

The all-too-real experiences of Geordie pals Bob and Terry made for one of the very best TV series, so one had high hopes for this movie spin-off. They are quickly dashed. The unique appeal of the ideally contrasted characters quickly evaporates and one is left with just another second-rate British farce in which the two heroes take wife and girlfriend on a touring caravan holiday. Disappointing. Brigit Forsyth adds a bit of sparkle as the socially ambitious Thelma.

1976. Directed by Michael Tuchner.
Starring Rodney Bewes, James Bolam, Brigit Forsyth, Mary Tamm, Sheila Fern, Zena Walker. Colour.
90 minutes.

Thorn EMI Video

Limelight

Charlie Chaplin as an ageing music hall comedian whose career has long since faded but who finds new meaning in life when he makes a successful ballerina out of the young dancer he saves from suicide and nurses back to health. Old-fashioned even when it was made back in 1952, but its pathos and Chaplin's deep insight into human nature give it a strangely lasting quality. The film reaches the heights in the last 15 minutes when Chaplin and Buster Keaton (together for the only time on screen) combine in a brilliant knockabout duet.

Oscars (1)   Best Music Score
Oscar nominations   Nil

1952. Directed by Charles Chaplin.
Starring Charles Chaplin, Claire Bloom, Sydney Chaplin, Nigel Bruce, Norman Lloyd, Buster Keaton. Black and White.
143 minutes.

Spectrum
(distributed by Polygram)

Note: The Oscar was awarded in 1972, twenty years after the film was first released, because the picture had not played in Los Angeles (as the rules require) until that date.

The Lion In Winter

Or, a rather hectic Christmas at Chinon Castle where Henry II (Peter O'Toole) and his estranged wife Eleanor Of Aquitaine (Katherine Hepburn) set about choosing a successor to the throne of England. He favours John, she wants Richard and it's quarrel, quarrel, nag, nag, all the way with much shouting and cursing and spitting of venom. Not exactly the most enjoyable way of spending an evening, although the acting is of a high standard and in the case of Hepburn, frequently brilliant. But it's a movie that just seems to go on and on without getting anywhere and that tends to make it something of a wearisome experience on video. Set in the year 1183; based on the play by James Goldman.

Box-office rental $9,053,000
Average rental (68) $14,411,950
Oscars (3)   Best Actress (Hepburn); Screenplay; Music

| Oscar nominations (4) | Best Film; Actor (O'Toole); Direction; Costume Design |

1968. Directed by Anthony Harvey.
Starring Peter O'Toole, Katharine Hepburn, Jane Merrow, John Castle, Timothy Dalton, Anthony Hopkins, Nigel Terry. Colour.
134 minutes.

Twentieth Century-Fox Video

Little Orvie

Routine Hollywood B-picture with Johnny Sheffield as a 7-year-old who is not allowed to have a pet then tries to hide one from his parents. When that fails he runs away from home. Supports *Mighty Joe Young* on a double-feature video tape.

1940. Directed by Ray McCarey.
Starring Johnny Sheffield, Ann Todd, Ernest Truex, Dorothy Tree. Black and White.
63 minutes.

Kingston Video

Logan's Run

One of the sci-fi flops of the 70s, a story of society in 2274 (long after the devastation of a nuclear war) in which people live an idyllic life in a huge domed city. Or at least they live an idyllic life until they're thirty. Then it's "renewal" time. And when looked at closely that means death. Logan is the guy who wants out and makes a run for it to the outside world. Poor special effects (its Oscar created a bit of a rumpus) hampered the film in its cinema release. They are even less impressive on video. Watch out for Farrah Fawcett-Majors on the way up the ladder in a supporting role.

Box-office rental	$9,500,000
Average rental (76)	$22,752,350
Oscars (1)	Best Visual Effects

Oscar nominations (2)   Best Photography; Art Direction

1976. Directed by Michael Anderson.
Starring Michael York, Richard Jordan, Jenny Agutter, Roscoe Lee Browne, Farrah Fawcett-Majors, Peter Ustinov. Colour.
118 minutes.

MGM/CBS Home Video

The Longest Day

The events of D Day, 6th Of June, 1944 (courtesy of Darryl F. Zanuck) unfolding for three dramatic, spectacular and ear-splitting hours. It's all here – the preparations, the sea crossing, the beach attacks, the parachute jumps, even the German activity in occupied France. A star name in every major role ensured huge box-office success in 1962; on video their faces help tell you who is where and why! Some great moments (notably a swooping aerial shot of the beach landings) and some mundane ones, but all told a rewarding experience and quite the most detailed recon-struction of a wartime event ever put on celluloid.

Box-office rental	$17,600,000
Average rental (62)	$7,477,500
Oscars (2)	Best Photography; Special Effects
Oscar nominations (3)	Best Film; Art Direction; Editing

1962. Directed by Ken Annakin, Andrew Marton and Bernhard Wicki.
Starring John Wayne, Robert Mitchum, Robert Ryan, Rod Steiger, Peter Lawford, Henry Fonda, Red Buttons, Mel Ferrer, Richard Burton and all star cast. Black and White.
180 minutes.

Twentieth Century-Fox Video

The Long Good Friday

Highly regarded British crime movie about an East End ganglord who finds himself being persecuted whilst trying to pull off a deal with the

American Mafia. A double-crossing second-in-command and the IRA are among those putting the boot (and the knives and bombs) in. Bob Hoskins is the gangleader, Helen Mirren his high class girlfriend and Dave King a bent cop. Efficient, tough and well-made but, despite its reputation, nothing exceptional.

1980. Directed by John MacKenzie.
Starring Bob Hoskins, Helen Mirren, Dave King, Bryan Marshall, Derek Thompson, Eddie Constantine. Colour.
114 minutes.

Thorn EMI Video

Long Weekend

A young couple on the brink of divorce set out by car for a holiday weekend and find that animals and nature have a few unpleasant surprises in store for them when they reach a secluded beach. Routine "man destroys nature/nature destroys man" thriller. A few eerie moments but not the best example of Australian cinema to be found on video.

1977. Directed by Colin Eggleston.
Starring John Hargreaves, Briony Behets, Mike McEwen, Michael Aitkins, Roy Day. Colour.
97 minutes.

Home Video Productions

Looking For Mr. Goodbar

You need a strong stomach for this one. It starts as a probing study into the life of a young woman who teaches deaf children by day and wanders the singles bars in search of sex by night; it ends as a nightmare with the girl's horrific rape and slaying at the hands of one of her pick-ups. Referred to in some quarters as a parable of fate. Sordid, although Keaton is exceptionally good in the lead.

Box-office rental $16,900,000

Average rental (77)	$36,913,348
Oscars	Nil
Oscar nominations (2)	Best Supporting Actress (Weld); Photography

1977. Directed by Richard Brooks.
Starring Diane Keaton, Tuesday Weld, William Atherton, Richard Kiley, Richard Gere, Tom Berenger. Colour.
136 minutes.

CIC Video

Loophole

Heist thrillers have become two-a-penny and need an original twist to make them attractive entertainment. This one has no twist at all and is simply a routine tale of some crooks who get together to try and crack the supposedly impregnable vault of a large London holding bank. The way in is through the sewers infested with rats. Albert Finney, Martin Sheen, Susannah York and company do what they can with the yawn-yawn material but they're on a loser from the word go. Dull.

1981. Directed by John Quested.
Starring Albert Finney, Martin Sheen, Susannah York, Colin Blakely, Jonathan Pryce, Robert Morley, Alfred Lynch. Colour.
105 minutes.

Brent Walker Video
(distributed by Videospace)

The Lost Moment

Eerie, set-bound rendering of Henry James' *The Aspern Papers*, with Robert Cummings as an American publisher trying to track down the lost love letters of a famous poet and concentrating his search on the poet's 105-year-old ex-fiancée. Artificial, not a little strange and set mostly within the confines of an old Venetian house. Agnes Moorehead (then forty years of age) being transformed by the wizardry of Hollywood make-up into a woman of a hundred plus remains the most impressive feature of an antiquated film.

1947. Directed by Martin Gabel.
Starring Robert Cummings, Susan Hayward, Agnes Moorehead, Joan Lorring, Eduardo Ciannelli. Black and White.
88 minutes.

Intervision

Love And Bullets

For Charles Bronson fans only. He's a Phoenix cop who is assigned to go to Switzerland and bring back gangster's moll Jill Ireland who might come up with some useful information for a Senate investigating committee. Naturally, gangleader Rod Steiger wants to stop him. Naturally Bronson falls in love with the moll . . . and so on until many bodies later the whole tame exercise comes to a bloody and explosive conclusion. Rod Steiger's outrageous overplaying as the mobster earns the film its one star; but that writer Wendell Mayes and director Stuart Rosenberg should be associated with anything so inadequate as this is beyond belief.

1979. Directed by Stuart Rosenberg.
Starring Charles Bronson, Jill Ireland, Rod Steiger, Henry Silva, Strother Martin, Bradford Dillman, Michael V. Gazzo. Colour.
101 minutes.

Precision Video

Love At First Bite

Any movie that begins with Count Dracula snapping at some howling wolves, "Children of the night – shut up!" can't be all bad. And indeed, this one's rather good with George Hamilton as a suave and sexy modern vampire count who finds himself forced to emigrate from Transylvania and opt instead for New York. The main attraction there: model girl Susan Saint James whom he eventually gets between the sheets and who elicits from him the response, "Oh, that's so kinky! Are *you* biting *me*?"

Box-office rental $20,600,000

Average rental (79) $31,964,775

1979. Directed by Stan Dragoti.
Starring George Hamilton, Susan Saint James, Richard Benjamin, Dick Shawn, Arte Johnson, Sherman Hemsley. Colour.
96 minutes.

Guild Home Video

The Love Bug

A magical Volkswagen with a mind and heart of its own helps its owner – unsuccessful racing driver Dean Jones – become a winner on the track and defeat villainous rival David Tomlinson. Ideal video for undemanding youngsters who found the mixture of slapstick and mechanical humour just about perfect back in 1969, when they dragged parents into the cinemas and turned the movie into one of Disney's most successful sleepers of all time. Set in San Francisco. Buddy Hackett comes second only to the car as the film's chief laughtermaker.

Box-office rental $23,150,000

Average rental (69) $13,660,950

1969. Directed by Robert Stevenson.
Starring Dean Jones, Michele Lee, David Tomlinson, Buddy Hackett, Joe Flynn, Benson Fong, Joe E. Ross, Barry Kelley. Colour.
107 minutes.

Walt Disney Home Video

Note: the box-office figure of 23 million is made up of the original release rentals plus those of reissues.

Lovers And Other Strangers ★★★

A young couple decide to take the plunge and get married after living together for eighteen months then find at the wedding reception that their guests and friends have plenty of marital problems of their own. Witty and amusing sex comedy played to the hilt by a remarkably talented cast with Gig Young superb as the oh so happy father of the bride. Inclined to be buried away on the video lists but well worth digging out.

Box-office rental	$6,750,000
Average rental (70)	$16,881,800
Oscars (1)	Best Song ("For All We Know")
Oscar nominations (2)	Best Supporting Actor (Castellano); Screenplay

1970. Directed by Cy Howard.
Starring Gig Young, Bea Arthur, Bonnie Bedelia, Anne Jackson, Harry Guardino, Michael Brandon, Richard Castellano, Cloris Leachman, Diane Keaton. Colour.
106 minutes.

Rank Video

Love Story

"Love means never having to say you're sorry." The tears flowed like wine in 1970 when this movie, surely the dampest of recent times, oozed into the cinemas and allowed moviegoers to weep buckets, as rich college boy Ryan O'Neal loves and loses in death poor college girl Ali MacGraw. And they'll flow again today for this one is real schmaltz from beginning to end. But it's schmaltz that's exceptionally well put together and suits the video screen far more than some of the larger extravaganzas of the 70s. Handsome colour; well photographed New England backgrounds.

Box-office rental	$50,000,000
Average rental (70)	$16,881,800
Oscars (1)	Best Original Music Score
Oscar nominations (6)	Best Film; Actor (O'Neal); Actress (MacGraw); Supporting Actor (Marley); Direction; Story And Screenplay

1970. Directed by Arthur Hiller.

Starring Ali MacGraw, Ryan O'Neal, Ray Milland, John Marley. Colour.
100 minutes.

CIC Video

Lucky Jim

Accident-prone young history professor Ian Carmichael tries to make a
name for himself at a provincial British university but finds the only way
to get ahead is by crawling to the boss of his department. Unfortunately,
a weekend at his professor's home turns out to be a disaster of the first
magnitude and not the much hoped-for step forward in his career. A
breezy little comedy that presents Britain when it was a country of old
cars, coffee bars and "digs", and although it only occasionally hits the
targets of Kingsley Amis' best-selling novel – pomposity, pretentiousness
and hypocrisy – it's still a very pleasant way to spend an hour and a half.
And there's a marvellous cameo from Terry-Thomas as the professor's
son who has literary aspirations but who can't get past the title!

1957. Directed by John Boulting.
Starring Ian Carmichael, Terry-Thomas, Hugh Griffith, Sharon Acker, Jean
Anderson, Maureen Connell. Black and White.
95 minutes.

Thorn EMI Video

The Lusty Men

Rodeo movie about rancher Arthur Kennedy who has ambitions to become a top rider and enlists broken-down rodeo king Bob Mitchum to
help him reach his goal. Lovely Susan Hayward is the gal in the middle
of all the wrangling, dazzling horsemanship and bull talk. A Nicholas Ray
film, which means it's deserving of some respect. Holds up well on video
despite its age and boasts some interesting glimpses of life behind the
scenes on the rodeo circuits. Not seen too often on TV. 2½ rating.

1952. Directed by Nicholas Ray.

Starring Susan Hayward, Robert Mitchum, Arthur Kennedy, Arthur Hunnicutt, Frank Faylen, Walter Coy, Carol Nugent. Black and White.
113 minutes.

21st Century Video
(distributed by VCL)

M

Macbeth

Orson Welles' first attempt at filmed Shakespeare, a trifle bizarre to say the least, very stylized and with some striking images in the early sequences. And, considering the film was made in 23 days on old Western sets for £75,000, not too bad an effort. But value for money as video entertainment? Hmm! Jeanette Nolan is a disastrous Lady Macbeth; Dan O'Herlihy as Macduff, Roddy McDowall as Malcolm and Edgar Barrier as Banquo fare rather better. A curiosity. For film buffs only.

1948. Directed by Orson Welles.
Starring Orson Welles, Jeanette Nolan, Dan O'Herlihy, Edgar Barrier, Roddy McDowall, Robert Coote. Black and White.
89 minutes.

Intervision

Macho Callahan

Oh-so-familiar Western yarn about a soldier who escapes from a Confederate Army prison and sets out to revenge himself on the man who put him there. Once at large however, he finds that he himself has become the hunted and that his pursuer is the young widow of a man he killed in a gunfight. A depressingly bad European-type Western (shot in Mexico), poorly photographed. That excellent actor Lee J. Cobb somehow got mixed up in it all and finishes up hanging from a flagpole. Squalid.

1970. Directed by Bernard Kowalski.

Starring David Janssen, Jean Seberg, Lee J. Cobb, James Booth, Pedro Armendariz, Jr, David Carradine, Anne Revere. Colour.
100 minutes.

Twentieth Century-Fox Video

Madame Sin

Just about the only thing missing from this Bond-type spoof is 007 himself. In his place we have Robert Wagner as a former Intelligence man who is kidnapped by an oriental villainess (a stand-in for Dr. No), who wants to get her greedy little hands on a Polaris submarine. Bette Davis revels in the title role, Denholm Elliott steals the movie from her as a nervous villain, the Scottish locations outdo them both. Routine.

1972. Directed by David Greene.
Starring Bette Davis, Robert Wagner, Denholm Elliott, Gordon Jackson, Dudley Sutton, Catherine Schell. Colour.
90 minutes.

Precision Video

The Mad Miss Manton

Screwball society girl Barbara Stanwyck and her hairbrained friends discover a dead body and call the police, only to find that it has disappeared when they arrive. "Oh yeah" say the cops, suspecting a prank. "Yeah", snaps Miss Stanwyck, determined to stand her ground and prove she's not as unreliable as the police and newspaper columnist Henry Fonda believe. It's all a bit wacky but it's also fun and makes up an excellent video double bill with the 1950s crime thriller *Hell On Frisco Bay*. 2½ rating.

1938. Directed by Leigh Jason.
Starring Barbara Stanwyck, Henry Fonda, Sam Levene, Frances Mercer, Stanley Ridges. Black and White.
80 minutes.

Kingston Video

The Mafu Cage

Another of those nasty cinematic forays into the goings-on in an old mansion. The house in this one is set on the West Coast of California and has as its chief occupant a deranged young girl, who enjoys killing monkeys and chaining up people in a cage and then watching them starve to death. Her sister-guardian Lee Grant is one of her victims. So is her sister's boyfriend James Olson. Rather repellent and certainly not of any great quality.

1978. Directed by Karen Arthur.
Starring Lee Grant, Carol Kane, Will Geer, James Olson, Will Sherwood. Colour.
101 minutes.

Home Video Productions

The Maggie

American millionaire businessman Paul Douglas has plans to settle in the Hebrides, but quickly has second thoughts (and nearly a dozen heart attacks) when he finds that his valuable cargo is being carried around the Scottish islands by a rickety little puffer boat that is just about ready for the scrapyard. Not the best known of Ealing comedies and released in 1954 when the series was coming to an end, but one that stands the test of time better than most. Filmed in the waterways, harbours and islands of Scotland. Pleasant.

1954. Directed by Alexander Mackendrick.
Starring Paul Douglas, Alex Mackenzie, James Copeland, Abe Barker, Dorothy Alison, Hubert Gregg, Geoffrey Keen. Black and White.
93 minutes.

Thorn EMI Video

The Magnificent Matador

Ageing matador Anthony Quinn gets the cold sweats because he fears death in the ring; rich American Maureen O'Hara dishes out a bit of romance; and Quinn, together with his young protégé, returns in triumph. Run-of-the-ring bullfighting story with Mexican locations.

1955. Directed by Budd Boetticher.
Starring Anthony Quinn, Maureen O'Hara, Manuel Rojas, Thomas Gomez, Richard Denning, Lola Albright. Colour.
94 minutes.

Intervision

The Magnificent Seven Deadly Sins

The French once made a portmanteau movie about the seven deadly sins and it was a rather more imaginative affair than this hapless British ragbag of stories about avarice, envy, gluttony, lust and so on. Spike Milligan adds a few zany moments in the "sloth" sequence; the rest do what they can with the material which isn't much. Uninspired.

1971. Directed by Graham Stark.
Starring Bruce Forsyth, Joan Sims, Roy Hudd, Harry Secombe, Leslie Phillips, Julie Ege, Harry H. Corbett, Ian Carmichael, Alfie Bass, Spike Milligan, Ronald Fraser. Colour.
107 minutes.

Guild Home Video

The Magnificent Two

Morecambe and Wise's last despairing crack at screen humour, with the accident-prone duo as a pair of travelling salesmen caught up in a South American revolution. Eric becomes president; Margit Saad provides the glamour; four scriptwriters try to make the screenplay seem funny. Poor value. After this third attempt at trying to make it in the movies the pair went back to the telly.

1967. Directed by Cliff Owen.
Starring Eric Morecambe, Ernie Wise, Margit Saad, Virgilio Teixeira, Cecil Parker, Isobel Black. Colour.
100 minutes.

Rank Video

Magnum Force

Clint Eastwood back at work as "Dirty Harry" Callahan in a movie that's even more violent than its predecessor but far less effective as a piece of film-making. In fact, the plot – about Eastwood's hunt for a gang of sharpshooting motor cycle cops who form a kind of mini-execution squad rubbing out the scum of society – seems to have been constructed simply for the purpose of allowing Eastwood to indulge in even more graphic forms of brutality. In short, a mediocre movie that employs violence for violence's sake.

Box-office rental	$20,100,000
Average rental (73)	$22,271,150

1973. Directed by Ted Post.
Starring Clint Eastwood, Hal Holbrook, Mitchell Ryan, David Soul, Felton Perry. Colour.
124 minutes.

Warner Home Video

The Main Event

So-so comedy that was meant to bring a late 70s look to those screwball Hollywood movies of the 30s and 40s. It doesn't. Ryan O'Neal is a retired prize fighter and fast-talking Barbra Streisand his new manager, a perfume manufacturer who needs O'Neal to win in the ring in order to stay financially solvent. The film has its moments and adapts well enough down to video size, but if you've money to spare it might be best to try elsewhere. Streisand belts out an unmemorable theme song by Paul Jabara and Bruce Roberts.

Box-office rental	$26,300,000
Average rental (79)	$31,964,775

1979. Directed by Howard Zieff.
Starring Barbra Streisand, Ryan O'Neal, Paul Sand, Whitman Mayo, Patti D'Arbanville. Colour.
109 minutes.

Warner Home Video

Malpertuis

Orson Welles (a long way from the splendours of *Citizen Kane*) gasping his last in a mysterious house full of weird and wonderful rooms and containing a deadly secret about some Greek Gods reborn. The relations that hover around Welles' bedside are told they will each receive a fortune but only if they never leave the house. Susan Hampshire does a triple-act as three alluring sisters and is eventually revealed as a gorgon. Rather curious video entertainment; could well send you to sleep before all is revealed in the final reels.

1971. Directed by Harry Kumel.
Starring Orson Welles, Susan Hampshire, Michel Bouquet, Mathieu Carriere, Jean-Pierre Cassel, Sylvie Vartan, Daniel Pilon. Colour.
96 minutes.

Intervision

A Man, A Woman And A Bank

Really no more than just another caper movie, the main difference from the others in the *genre* being that the target (in Vancouver) is a fully automated bank and that a lot of messing about with computers is needed before the crooks can crack the joint. Their prize is four million dollars. Your prize for paying out your hard-earned cash? Affable entertainment, nothing more. Bored civil engineer Donald Sutherland is the mastermind behind it all.

1979. Directed by Noel Black.
Starring Donald Sutherland, Brooke Adams, Paul Mazursky, Allan Magicovsky, Leigh Hamilton, Nick Rice. Colour.
101 minutes.

Twentieth Century-Fox Video

The Man In The White Suit ★★★

Cambridge graduate Alec Guinness runs into trouble with both management and labour when he tries to put his invention – a fabric that won't get dirty and won't wear out – on the market. The management see the fabric as a threat to their profits; the workers see it as a threat to their jobs. In the end it matters little. The fabric simply disintegrates. The most satirical of Ealing's comedies, set in a Northern textile town and, in its final scenes, almost Chaplinesque in its combination of humour and pathos. Cecil Parker, Ernest Thesiger and Michael Gough make up a formidable trio of capitalists; Vida Hope is a vigorous trade unionist. Unusual video entertainment.

Oscars   Nil
Oscar nominations (1)   Best Screenplay

1951. Directed by Alexander Mackendrick.
Starring Alec Guinness, Joan Greenwood, Cecil Parker, Michael Gough, Ernest Thesiger, Vida Hope, Miles Malleson. Black and White.
85 minutes.

Thorn EMI Video

The Manitou

A 400-year-old witch doctor decides to reincarnate himself through a foetus growing on Susan Strasberg's neck! And once he's out it's rampage time in San Francisco. The silly moments far outweigh the effective ones in this horror movie, but the physical appearance of the evil and rather nicely-named Misquamacus causes a few shudders. The Frisco settings help take one's mind off the horrors and Tony Curtis gets in on the act as a professional fortune teller.

1978. Directed by William Girdler.
Starring Tony Curtis, Michael Ansara, Susan Strasberg, Stella Stevens, Jon Cedar, Ann Sothern, Burgess Meredith. Colour.
105 minutes.

Twentieth Century-Fox Video

The Man Who Fell To Earth ★★★

Alien David Bowie descends to Earth from a drought-ridden planet to secure a permanent water supply for the dying family he has left behind. In order to achieve his ends, he amasses vast wealth and power, but naively reckons without the cunning of the human race which double-crosses him, medically strips him of his clairvoyant powers and condemns him to an everlasting life on Earth. A thinking man's piece of science-fiction that manages to be both intellectually stimulating and deeply depressing at the same time. Its slow pace and lack of galactic hardware caused it to miss out with movie audiences in 1976, but all sci-fi buffs should try to make amends by catching it on video. Highly original.

1976. Directed by Nicolas Roeg.
Starring David Bowie, Rip Torn, Candy Clark, Buck Henry, Bernie Casey, Jackson D. Kane. Colour.
138 minutes.

Thorn EMI Video

The Man With The Golden Arm

A controversial movie of the mid-50s filmed by Otto Preminger, who made something of a habit of getting into trouble with film censors of the period. This one caused a rumpus because it dealt with drug addiction. Frank Sinatra stars as an addicted poker dealer struggling to kick "the monkey on his back" and come to terms with his crippled wife. Elmer Bernstein's strident jazz score remains effective, although Sinatra's last-minute rehabilitation is a bit hard to take!

Box-office rental	$4,100,000
Average rental (55)	$7,239,750
Oscars	Nil
Oscar nominations (3)	Best Actor (Sinatra); Art Direction; Music Score

1955. Directed by Otto Preminger.
Starring Frank Sinatra, Eleanor Parker, Kim Novak, Arnold Stang, Darren McGavin, Robert Strauss. Black and White.
119 minutes.

Twentieth Century-Fox Video

March Or Die

Gene Hackman as a tough major in a Foreign Legion adventure set in Morocco in 1918. Hackman's adversary is Ian Holm, an Arab chieftain who goes by the somewhat goonish name of El Krim; the inevitable archaeologist who keeps getting in both their ways as he digs for buried treasure in a desert tomb is Max von Sydow. Director Dick Richards tries hard to make this *Boy's Own Paper* yarn work but it desperately needs the guiding hand of an old pro like Henry Hathaway or Henry King. And that's decidedly what it hasn't got. The presence of the beautiful Catherine Deneuve pushes the movie into the average category.

1977. Directed by Dick Richards.

Starring Gene Hackman, Terence Hill, Catherine Deneuve, Max von Sydow, Ian Holm, Jack O'Halloran. Colour
107 minutes.

Precision Video

M.A.S.H.

This is the original anarchic black farce about a group of army surgeons operating on the wounded in the Korean War and trying to keep their sanity amid all the blood and gore by acting in as zany a manner as possible. It's still amusing, but no matter how hard you try you can't get the subsequent TV series with Alan Alda, Harry Morgan, and co. out of your mind. And the reason? The TV series is better, which must be something of a record "first". Donald Sutherland is Hawkeye Pierce, Elliott Gould his buddy, Sally Kellerman is Hot Lips. Variable colour. M.A.S.H. incidentally, stands for Mobile Army Surgical Hospital.

Box-office rental	$36,720,000
Average Rental (70)	$16,881,800
Oscars (1)	Best Screenplay
Oscar nominations (4)	Best Film; Supporting Actress (Kellerman); Direction; Editing

1970. Directed by Robert Altman.
Starring Donald Sutherland, Elliott Gould, Tom Skerritt, Sally Kellerman, Robert Duvall, Jo Ann Pflug. Colour.
113 minutes.

Twentieth Century-Fox Video

Massacre At Fort Holman

A cut-price, Italian-made, American Civil War reworking (are you still with me?) of *The Dirty Dozen* with Yankee James Coburn offering seven men, all condemned to death, a chance of salvation if they can take a fort held by sinister Confederate Telly Savalas. Colourless video fare of the kind you have seen many times before. The question you must ask yourself is: "Do I want to see it all again?" especially when Savalas utters such lines as "Napoleon said there's a time to fight and a time to wait. We're gonna wait."

1974. Directed by Tonino Valerii.
Starring James Coburn, Telly Savalas, Bud Spencer, Robert Burton. Colour.
92 minutes.

Guild Home Video

Matilda

A boxing kangaroo takes on all challengers and finishes up fighting the champ in a title bout in Reno. Yes, you *did* read that line correctly and this *is* a film about a boxing kangaroo and a right old mess it is as well. Somehow or other Robert Mitchum (as a boxing writer) got himself involved in it all. So too did Elliott Gould plus a host of talented supporting players. Also, an uncredited actor who plays "Matilda" in a kangaroo suit! Hardly surprising that the rating is poor.

1978. Directed by Daniel Mann.
Starring Elliott Gould, Robert Mitchum, Harry Guardino, Clive Revill, Lionel Stander, Karen Carlson, Roy Clark. Colour.
91 minutes.

Rank Video

McQ

The only notable thing about this movie is that it was the first in which John Wayne played a cop or detective. Otherwise, it's a Western on wheels with Wayne resigning from the force and uncovering corruption as he sets about investigating the murder of his buddy. Nothing new then, with an ageing Wayne using a car instead of a horse to track down the bad guys. Filmed in Seattle; low-grade video fare. Wayne should have plumped for *Dirty Harry* which he was offered before Clint Eastwood took the role.

| Box-office rental | $4,100,000 |
| Average rental (74) | $18,456,150 |

1974. Directed by John Sturges.
Starring John Wayne, Eddie Albert, Diane Muldaur, Colleen Dewhurst, Clu Gulager. Colour.
111 minutes.

Warner Home Video

The Mean Machine

Former football pro Burt Reynolds gets more than he bargained for when he's sentenced to one year in jail. No quiet time for him. Instead, the job of bringing together a squad of convicts and turning them into a football team to play against a semi-pro group handpicked by the warden. Or, if you like, the bad guys versus the good guys. And who's who? Director Robert Aldrich leaves you in no doubt. Not unlike a reworking of the same film-maker's *Dirty Dozen*. Very good. Known also as *The Longest Yard*.

Box-office rental	$23,017,000
Average rental (74)	$18,456,150
Oscars	Nil
Oscar nominations (1)	Best Editing

1974. Directed by Robert Aldrich.
Starring Burt Reynolds, Eddie Albert, Ed Lauter, Michael Conrad, Jim Hampton, Bernadette Peters. Colour.
123 minutes.

CIC Video

The Mean Machine

Mild little British disco musical in which Gerry Sundquist and Patti Boulaye take their first steps to stardom when they win a dancing contest at the

Mean Machine Disco. Sounds like a British rip-off of *Saturday Night Fever*.
And it is. Mediocre music, mediocre value for money.

1979. Directed by Ian Sharp.
Starring Gerry Sundquist, Patti Boulaye, David Easter, Michael Feast,
Ferdy Mayne. Colour.
90 minutes.

Alpha Video
(distributed by Intervision)

The Medusa Touch

Telekinetic novelist Richard Burton has been willing people to death ever
since he was a lad and it's a habit he finds hard to break. When he starts
becoming more ambitious in his choice of targets – the passengers of a
jumbo jet, the astronauts of a space mission, those working at the atomic
plant at Windscale – it's obvious he must be stopped. But how? The guy
simply won't die! Psychiatrist Lee Remick tries to come up with a solution
but to no avail. Still, she's certainly the kind of shrink worth going nuts
for. As for the film, well some thrills but mostly unconvincing.

1978. Directed by Jack Gold.
Starring Richard Burton, Lino Ventura, Lee Remick, Harry Andrews, Alan
Badel, Marie-Christine Barrault, Jeremy Brett, Michael Hordern. Colour.
109 minutes.

Precision Video

Meet Me In St. Louis

Nostalgic, warm-hearted portrait of an American family living in St. Louis
during the World Fair of 1903. There's ma (Mary Astor), there's pa (Leon
Ames), there's grandpa (Harry Davenport) and there are three sisters –
Lucille Bremer, Margaret O'Brien and, above all, Judy Garland who gets
to sing "The Trolley Song", "The Boy Next Door" and "Have Yourself A
Merry Little Christmas". Beautifully done; based on a series of recollec-
tions published by Sally Benson in *The New Yorker*.

Box-office rental	$5,200,000
Oscars	Nil
Oscar nominations (4)	Best Screenplay; Song ("The Trolley Song"); Photography; Scoring Of A Musical

1944. Directed by Vincente Minnelli.
Starring Judy Garland, Margaret O'Brien, Tom Drake, Leon Ames, Mary Astor, Lucille Bremer, June Lockhart, Marjorie Main, Harry Davenport. Colour.
113 minutes.

MGM/CBS Home Video

Men In War

"War is hell" type movie of the mid-50s; grim, realistic and anti-heroic, but routine for much of its length despite its humanist attitudes and the honesty of its intentions. Good performances from Aldo Ray and Robert Ryan as a couple of those belonging to an American platoon cut off from headquarters. Set in Korea in 1950. Tough script by Philip Yordan; early music score by Elmer Bernstein.

1957. Directed byAnthony Mann.
Starring Robert Ryan, Aldo Ray, Robert Keith, Vic Morrow, James Edwards, Scott Marlowe. Black and White.
104 minutes.

Video Unlimited

Mexican Spitfire At Sea

Lupe Velez, the Mexican spitfire of the 40s, involved with Charles "Buddy" Rogers on a Honolulu-bound pleasure boat. She thinks it's a second honeymoon. He wants to clinch a big business deal with a couple of social climbers. Leon Errol adds to the madness. Supports *Mr. Blandings Builds His Dream House* on a double-feature video tape.

1942. Directed by Leslie Goodwins.

Starring Lupe Velez, Leon Errol, Charles 'Buddy' Rogers, Zasu Pitts, Florence Bates. Black and White.
72 minutes.

Kingston Video

Midnight Express

Not for the squeamish this one, a true story of a young American college student (Brad Davis) who was caught smuggling hashish out of Turkey in 1970 and imprisoned in the notorious Sagamilcar jail, where he suffered from just about every kind of bestial act imaginable. Very tough stuff indeed and so sustained an account of graphic brutality that it hardly qualifies as entertainment. John Hurt adds top notch support as a dissipated English prisoner. But be prepared.

Box-office rental	$15,305,000
Average rental (78)	$39,443,850
Oscars (2)	Best Screenplay; Original Music Score
Oscar nominations (4)	Best Film; Supporting Actor (Hurt); Direction; Editing

1978. Directed by Alan Parker.
Starring Brad Davis, Randy Quaid, John Hurt, Irene Miracle, Bo Hopkins, Paolo Bonacelli, Paul Smith. Colour.
121 minutes.

RCA/Columbia International Video

The Mighty Gorga

Independent circus owner Anthony Eisley flies to Africa to search for a monster gorilla that might help his financially ailing circus. Villainous Scott Brady and some prehistoric monsters stand in his way. Cut-price fantasy made on a shoestring. The cast tries hard not to laugh at their lines. There are, however, no such restrictions on you.

1971. Directed by David L. Hewitt.

Starring Anthony Eisley, Megan Timothy, Kent Taylor, Scott Brady, Lee Parrish. Colour.
83 minutes.

Derann Video

Mighty Joe Young

It's *King Kong* time all over again folks! Well, not quite, for mighty monkey Mr. Joseph Young Of Africa is nowhere near as large, although he does suffer the same fate. He is taken to America (Hollywood this time) where he performs in a night club with girlfriend Terry Moore, who plays "Beautiful Dreamer" to him on the piano ... Aw, come on, not even Hollywood could dream this one up. Wrong, they did, and it's on video to prove it. The special effects work of Willis O'Brien is admirable, however, and makes the movie well worth searching around for. *Little Orvie* supports it on a double-feature video bill.

Oscars (1)   Best Special Effects.
Oscar nominations   Nil

1949. Directed by Ernest B. Schoedsack.
Starring Terry Moore, Ben Johnson, Robert Armstrong, Frank McHugh, Douglas Fowley. Black and White.
94 minutes.

Kingston Video

Million Dollar Duck

A dim-witted duck, brought home as a pet by young science professor Dean Jones, starts causing a bit of a stir when it starts laying eggs with solid gold yolks. The Treasury Department and the underworld soon become interested. Sounds like Disney and it is, but only average-to-middling Disney with most of the fun devoted to slapstick, chases and so on. However, one engaging scene does have the scatty wife of the household trying to deposit one of the eggs in her bank account!

Box-office rental $5,250,000
Average rental (71) $13,465,850

1971. Directed by Vincent McEveety.
Starring Dean Jones, Sandy Duncan, Joe Flynn, Tony Roberts, James Gregory, Jack Kruschen. Colour.
92 minutes.

Walt Disney Home Video

The Mirror Crack'd

It's amazing how much more cosy murder seems in the hands of Agatha Christie than it does in the hands of the Mafia, for instance. And when a couple of poisonings take place in a small Kentish village during the early 50s, it seems no more than part of the usual run of things, especially when amateur sleuth Miss Marple is in close proximity. The murders occur when an American film crew arrives in the village to make a movie of *Mary, Queen Of Scots.* And with Miss Marple on hand there's no chance of anyone getting away with anything. An all-star cast can do little with this old-fashioned thriller (made in 1980), although it does come over rather better on video than it did in the cinema. Edward Fox is the terribly polite Scotland Yard Inspector who elicits such responses from his suspects as: "All right Inspector, let's stop playing games . . ."

Box-office rental $5,500,000
Average rental (80) $30,086,027

1980. Directed by Guy Hamilton.
Starring Angela Lansbury, Geraldine Chaplin, Tony Curtis, Edward Fox, Rock Hudson, Kim Novak, Elizabeth Taylor. Colour.
105 minutes.

Thorn EMI Video

Mission Galactica: The Cylon Attack ★

Second of the "Galactica" TV spin-offs, with poor old Battlestar commander Lorne Greene still up there in outer space and doing his best to combat the evil plans of a megalomaniac count who wants to destroy the human race with his army of chrome-covered Cylons. Poor stuff, even for kids, with the age limit of the script set somewhere around 6½. Hackneyed effects.

1980. Directed by Vince Edwards, Christian 1, Nyby 11.
Starring Richard Hatch, Dirk Benedict, Lorne Greene, Lloyd Bridges, John Colicos. Colour.
107 minutes.

CIC Video

Mr. Blandings Builds His Dream House ★★★

94 minutes of sheer delight as advertising man Cary Grant – fed up with living with wife Myrna Loy and two precocious daughters in a cramped New York apartment – opts for the country life in Connecticut with dire and expensive results. The movie's well over thirty years old but it's still funny, probably because the basic situation of naive city guy trying to come to grips with a natural environment is just as pertinent today. Melvyn Douglas co-stars as Grant's pipe-smoking best friend and has some of the wittiest lines to deliver, including some good advice to Grant: "The next time you decide to do anything or say anything or buy anything – think it over very carefully then, when you're sure you're right, forget the whole thing!" Supported on a double bill by *Mexican Spitfire At Sea*.

1948. Directed by H. C. Potter.
Starring Cary Grant, Myrna Loy, Melvyn Douglas, Reginald Denny. Black and White.
94 minutes.

Kingston Video

Mister Jericho

Amusing little romp concerning the escapades of international con-man Patrick MacNee, who steals a precious diamond from unscrupulous gangster Herbert Lom then sells it back to him as its twin. Then Connie Stevens becomes involved and she has her own plans for the stone. Pleasant to look at (European locations); also rather pleasant to listen to on occasion.

1969. Directed by Sidney Hayers.
Starring Patrick MacNee, Connie Stevens, Herbert Lom, Marty Allen.
Colour.
85 minutes.

Precision Video

Mr. Kingstreet's War

The opposing armies of World War II find themselves in desperate need of water supply in North Africa. The main source can be found in a wildlife centre run by John Saxon and Tippi Hedren. But, as the armies start to move in, Saxon, with the aid of an old "Tiger Moth" plane and not a little ingenuity, begins a life and death struggle to protect his territory. Rather neatly done and just one of two very good films on a double video tape. The other? Val Lewton's *The Ghost Ship*. 2½ rating.

1973. Directed by Percival Rubens.
Starring John Saxon, Tippi Hedren, Rossano Brazzi, Brian O'Shaughnessy.
Colour.
92 minutes.

Kingston Video

Mister Roberts

Henry Fonda (the "Mister Roberts" of the title) is desperate to get into action but finds himself stuck on a cargo ship during the latter days of World War II; James Cagney, whose only concern is for his potted plant, is the eccentric ship's captain who stands in his way. A big hit on the Broadway stage, but something of an acquired taste and often rather slow going. Only so-so technically with the Warner Color nothing very special. Jack Lemmon won his first Oscar for his performance as the young Ensign Pulver.

Box-office rental	$8,500,000
Average rental (55)	$7,239,750
Oscars (1)	Best Supporting Actor (Lemmon)
Oscar nominations (2)	Best Film; Sound Recording

1955. Directed by John Ford and Mervyn LeRoy.
Starring Henry Fonda, James Cagney, William Powell, Jack Lemmon, Betsy Palmer, Ward Bond. Colour.
123 minutes.

Warner Home Video

Moby Dick

Remarkable adaptation of Herman Melville's great novel about the vengeful Captain Ahab, who embarks on one last journey to seek out and kill the great White Whale that has maimed him. Somewhat talky and slow-moving early on, but director Huston is after the atmosphere of New Bedford, Massachusetts in the 1840s and he gets it, as he does excitement in the electrifying climax when Ahab does battle with the huge beast that has so obsessed him. A climax, incidentally, that puts the final few reels of *Jaws* to shame. Intelligently adapted by Ray Bradbury, this one does full justice to Melville's prose although be warned, it does need concentration from the viewer. Gregory Peck, cast against type, is Ahab; Richard Basehart, Leo Genn and Harry Andrews among his crew.

Box-office rental	$4,800,000
Average rental (56)	$8,814,900

1956. Directed by John Huston.
Starring Gregory Peck, Richard Basehart, Friedrich Ledebur, Leo Genn, Orson Welles, James Robertson Justice, Harry Andrews, Bernard Miles. Colour.
116 minutes.

Thorn EMI Video

Modern Times

Sociological satire on the perils of the machine age, with Charlie Chaplin as a factory worker tightening bolts on a moving belt and running amok when his job unbalances his mind. Also involved: co-worker Chester Conklin and orphan girlfriend Paulette Goddard. The last scene in which Chaplin and Goddard walk hand in hand towards the horizon was the very last in which the little tramp appeared on the screen. Chaplin's last silent movie.

1936. Directed by Charles Chaplin.
Starring Charles Chaplin, Paulette Goddard, Henry Bergman, Chester Conklin, Stanley Sanford, Hank Mann, Allan Garcia. Black and White.
85 minutes.

Spectrum
(distributed by Polygram)

Mohawk

Boston artist Scott Brady settles down to frontier life with Boston gal Lori Nelson after becoming involved in a war between Indians and settlers in the Mohawk Valley. The period is pre-Revolutionary America; the Indian cause is helped by fierce warrior Neville Brand; and you get nothing but mediocrity for your money!

1956. Directed by Kurt Neumann.
Starring Scott Brady, Rita Gam, Neville Brand, Lori Nelson, Allison Hayes. Colour.
79 minutes.

Intervision

Mon Oncle

Jacques Tati's easy-going Monsieur Hulot tries to cope with the electronic mysteries of his sister's mechanised house and a factory that makes plastic hosepipes. He loses, but the audience wins especially when he tries his hand at operating an ultra-modern garage, experiments with bouncing glasswear, tinkers with an ornamental fountain, etc. Overlong, and many of the gags are a bit too elaborately worked out but with a lot of charm and when it's funny it's *very* funny.

| Oscars (1) | Best Foreign Language Film |
| Oscar nominations | Nil |

1958. Directed by Jacques Tati.
Starring Jacques Tati, Jean-Pierre Zola, Alain Becourt, Lucien Fregis, Dominique Marie, Betty Schneider. Colour.
116 minutes.

Zodiac Video
(*distributed by Videomedia*)

The Monster Club

An attempt to try and revive the multi-storied horror movies that Amicus used to do quite well in the 70s. But despite Vincent Price (as a vampire) and John Carradine (as a horror writer) this omnibus is way below par. There are three stories, one about a lethal whistle, one about a vampire and one about a humgoo. A what? A humgoo! That's the offspring of a human and a ghoul. A very loud pop score tries to hide the fact that the stories are all pretty crummy.

1981. Directed by Roy Ward Baker.
Starring Vincent Price, John Carradine, Anthony Steel, Barbara Kellerman, Simon Ward, Donald Pleasence, Richard Johnson, Britt Ekland, Anthony Valentine. Colour.
97 minutes.

Precision Video

Monty Python And The Holy Grail ★★

The lunatic Monty Python team as members of the Round Table in search of the Holy Grail. Which means you should know what to expect – a series of outrageous sketches linked by something approaching a story-line. A seemingly never-ending credit sequence nearly prevents the story from getting under way at all but when it does Graham Chapman leads the group as King Arthur, John Cleese pops up in four roles, Eric Idle in another four. Something of a hit-and-miss affair, filmed amongst the lochs, castles and moors of Scotland.

| Box-office rental | $5,170,000 |
| Average rental (75) | $27,300,250 |

1975. Directed by Terry Gilliam & Terry Jones.
Starring Graham Chapman, John Cleese, Terry Gilliam, Eric Idle, Terry Jones, Michael Palin. Colour.
90 minutes.

Brent Walker Video
(*distributed by Videospace*)

Monty Python's Life Of Brian ★★

The picture with something to offend everyone, at least if you take it that seriously. It's the Monty Python gang hitting out at religion in a story of a blundering New Testament prophet called Brian whose life closely parallels that of the Saviour. A difficult movie to recommend or criticize, it is either funny or tasteless depending on your point of view, although there's no denying that crudity frequently intrudes on the satire and that the final impression is of a talented team of comedians trying rather desperately to "have a go at the Gospels!" Still, it did well at the box-office, so a great many people found it to their taste. But if you are of a religious persuasion, be careful.

| Box-office rental | $10,100,000 |
| Average rental (79) | $31,964,775 |

1979. Directed by Terry Jones.

Starring Terry Jones, Graham Chapman, Michael Palin, John Cleese, Eric Idle, Terry Gilliam, Ken Colley, Gwen Taylor. Colour.
93 minutes.

Thorn EMI Video

The Moon Is Blue

Hard to believe that this harmless little comedy caused such a furore back in 1953. The trouble occurred because the screenplay included such previously forbidden words as "virgin", "seduction" and "mistress". And that simply wasn't done back in the days of rigid censorship. But director Otto Preminger went ahead and did it anyway. And got away with it! Today, of course, its story – a young girl's experiences with a couple of New York wolves – looks as racey as *Rebecca Of Sunnybrook Farm*. But it's pleasant enough as entertainment. Based on the 1951 Broadway play by F. Hugh Herbert.

Box-office rental	$4,000,000
Average rental (53)	$6,098,850
Oscars	Nil
Oscar nominations (3)	Best Actress (McNamara); Editing; Song ("The Moon Is Blue")

1953. Directed by Otto Preminger.
Starring William Holden, David Niven, Maggie McNamara, Tom Tully, Dawn Addams, Gregory Ratoff. Black and White.
99 minutes.

Twentieth Century-Fox Video

Morgan: A Suitable Case For Treatment

Young working-class anarchist David Warner spends most of his time living in a dream world inhabited by gorillas. When he comes out of it he makes ingenious attempts to win back his divorced wife (Vanessa Redgrave), including abducting her *King Kong* style from her wedding reception. A bit of a mixture to say the least and definitely a "make-of-it-what-you-will" movie, although black farce, compassion for the outsider and near madness are all essential ingredients. Still funny, even though it's rather dated now. Set in the Swinging London of the 60s.

Oscars   Nil
Oscar nominations (2)   Best Actress (Redgrave); Costume Design

1966. Directed by Karel Reisz.
Starring Vanessa Redgrave, David Warner, Robert Stephens, Irene Handl, Bernard Bresslaw, Arthur Mullard. Black and White.
97 minutes.

Thorn EMI Video

Moulin Rouge

John Huston's attempt at producing an intelligent, in-depth biography of crippled French artist Toulouse-Lautrec doesn't really come off but there are compensations. Among them: the opening ten-minute dance sequence inside the Moulin Rouge, the imaginative camerawork of Oswald Morris and Colette Marchand's portrait of a hard-hearted whore heading straight for the gutter. Jose Ferrer makes a brave attempt at the deformed Lautrec by playing the entire role on his knees. Ravishing to look at, but a disappointment considering the obvious care and attention that went into its production.

Box-office rental $4,230,000
Average rental (52) $4,824,400
Oscars (2)   Best Art Direction; Costume Design
Oscar nominations (5)   Best Film; Actor (Ferrer); Supporting Actress
                            (Marchand); Direction; Editing

1952. Directed by John Huston.
Starring Jose Ferrer, Colette Marchand, Suzanne Flon, Zsa Zsa Gabor, Katherine Kath, Claude Nollier, Muriel Smith. Colour.
123 minutes.

Twentieth Century-Fox Video

Movie Movie

Affectionate parody of a 1930s double-feature cinema programme, comprising a black and white boxing saga called *Dynamite Hands* and a colourful Busby Berkeley-type musical *Baxter's Beauties Of 1933*. Slotted neatly between the two features is a trailer of a forthcoming attraction, a flying drama of World War I. George C. Scott appears in both movies, as do other members of the cast, although Scott deserves top billing as he features in the trailer also. A real treat for movie buffs and very well done; but of somewhat limited appeal to a younger video audience who might well find the proceedings not a little quaint. Introduced by George Burns. 2½ rating.

1978. Directed by Stanley Donen.
Starring George C. Scott, Trish Van Devere, Eli Wallach, Red Buttons, Barbara Harris, Art Carney. Colour.
106 minutes.

Precision Video

The Muppet Movie

A journey across America with Kermit, Fozzie, Miss Piggy and co., as they head for Hollywood and careers as big time entertainers. The journey should have been fun but despite the presence of innumerable guest stars it springs to life only occasionally, most notably when mad professor Mel Brooks tries to liquefy Kermit's brains! It's the kind of picture that you desperately want to succeed but which, after half-an-hour or so, you reluctantly give up as hopeless. Which is a pity, for within the confines of their tiny TV theatre the Muppets can be quite inspired.

Box-office rental	$32,000,000
Average rental (79)	$31,964,775
Oscars	Nil
Oscar nominations (2)	Best Song ("The Rainbow Connection"); Original Song Score

1979. Directed by James Frawley.
Starring Charles Durning, Edgar Bergen, Bob Hope, Milton Berle, Mel

Brooks, James Coburn, Dom DeLuise, Elliott Gould, Cloris Leachman,
Telly Savalas, Orson Welles. Colour.
97 minutes.

Precision Video

Murder By Death

Neil Simon spoof of the great detective thrillers of the past. The setting
is a spooky old mansion owned by eccentric electronics wizard Truman
Capote. Invited to share a weekend with him and solve a murder due to
take place at midnight are some of the world's greatest detectives. The
prize is one million dollars. Peter Falk as Sam Diamond, Peter Sellers as
Sidney Wang, Elsa Lanchester as Jessica Marbles, David Niven and Maggie Smith as Dick and Dora Charleston are among those involved. So too
is Alec Guinness as a blind butler. Good fun, with a laugh a minute in the
first half. Trails off a bit towards the end.

Box-office rental	$22,000,000
Average rental (76)	$22,752,350

1976. Directed by Robert Moore.
Starring Eileen Brennan, Truman Capote, James Coco, Peter Falk, Alec
Guinness, Elsa Lanchester, David Niven, Peter Sellers, Maggie Smith,
Nancy Walker, Estelle Winwood. Colour.
95 minutes.

RCA/Columbia International Video

Murder By Decree

Sherlock Holmes versus Jack The Ripper in London's murky Whitechapel
during the 1880s. No prizes for guessing who wins (after all, Holmes has
covered this ground before in *A Study In Terror*) but full marks to the
film-makers for creating just the right atmosphere of menace and, in the
Grand Guignol denouement, horror. Freemasons, royalty, mad physicians,
spiritualists and anarchists all have their part to play. Christopher Plummer is passable as Holmes, James Mason excellent as Watson.

1979. Directed by Bob Clark.
Starring Christopher Plummer, James Mason, David Hemmings, Susan Clark, Anthony Quayle, John Gielgud, Frank Finlay, Donald Sutherland, Genevieve Bujold. Colour.
112 minutes.

Twentieth Century-Fox Video

Murder On The Orient Express

Arguably the most successful screen adaptation of a Christie novel and considering the static nature of the story, remarkably cinematic. Richard Widmark is the American tycoon stabbed to death in his *wagon-lit* compartment as the Orient Express speeds through the night. On board are a dozen or so suspects, all of whom could have done the foul deed. Swedish missionary Ingrid Bergman for instance. Or Indian army colonel Sean Connery? Or American matron Lauren Bacall? Or John Gielgud, Vanessa Redgrave, Michael York, etc? It's a case of can you spot the killer before fussy little Belgian sleuth Hercule Poirot (Albert Finney)? Director Sidney Lumet keeps things on the move with flashbacks, snappy editing techniques, unusual camera angles and such like. Good fun, elegantly designed. Good value too.

Box-office rental	$19,124,000
Average rental (74)	$18,456,150
Oscars (1)	Best Supporting Actress (Bergman)
Oscar nominations (5)	Best Actor (Finney); Screenplay; Photography; Costume Design; Music Score

1974. Directed by Sidney Lumet.
Starring Albert Finney, Lauren Bacall, Martin Balsam, Ingrid Bergman, Jacqueline Bisset, Jean-Pierre Cassel, Sean Connery, John Gielgud, Wendy Hiller, Anthony Perkins, Vanessa Redgrave, Rachel Roberts, Richard Widmark, Michael York. Colour.
131 minutes.

Thorn EMI Video.

My Brilliant Career

Among the best of the interesting Australian films to reach Great Britain in recent years; the story of a young girl living on her father's farm in the Australian bush and who determines that she will do much more with her life than just marry and settle down. In the end she opts for a writing career and proves that you *can* do your own thing, even if you're a woman living in turn-of-the-century Australia. A minor gem, well worth a look on video. Judy Davis plays the girl.

Oscars	Nil
Oscar nominations (1)	Best Costume Design

1979. Directed by Gillian Armstrong.
Starring Judy Davis, Sam Neill, Wendy Hughes, Robert Grubb, Max Cullen, Pat Kennedy. Colour.
100 minutes.

Guild Home Video

My Fair Lady

There was some disappointment expressed at the time of this film's release that it wasn't more cinematic, more inventive. The answer to that, of course, is how *do* you improve on a stage musical that is close to being a perfect entity in itself. Well, you don't. You just let well alone and allow the story of how Professor Henry Higgins transforms a cockney flower girl into a well-spoken lady of society speak and sing for itself. And that's more than sufficient. Cecil Beaton's costumes dazzle the eye in a film that probably deserves the title of being the most elegant available on video.

Box-office rental	$12,000,000
Average rental (64)	$9,305,550
Oscars (8)	Best Film; Actor (Harrison); Direction; Photography; Art Direction; Costume Design; Sound; Scoring Of Music
Oscar nominations (3)	Supporting Actor (Holloway); Screenplay; Editing

1964. Directed by George Cukor.

Starring Rex Harrison, Audrey Hepburn, Stanley Holloway, Wilfrid Hyde-White, Gladys Cooper, Jeremy Brett, Theodore Bikel. Colour. 170 minutes.

MGM/CBS Home Video

My Learned Friend

The last of Will Hay's comedies and not really in the usual vein, for this one's nearer the black humour of *Kind Hearts And Coronets* than the usual Will Hay knockabout stuff. Mervyn Johns is a sinister ex-convict who proceeds to bump off everyone who sent him to jail including our Will, who plays an incompetent barrister and finishes up hanging in desperation from the hands of Big Ben. A mad black farce, directed by Robert Hamer who, in fact, went on to make *Kind Hearts*. And you can see the seeds being sown! 2½ rating.

1943. Directed by Robert Hamer.
Starring Will Hay, Claude Hulbert, Mervyn Johns, Ernest Thesiger, Charles Victor. Black and White.
76 minutes.

Thorn EMI Video

Myra Breckinridge

The story of a sex-change operation that transforms dedicated young film critic Rex Reed into man-eating Raquel Welch, who heads for Hollywood hellbent on destroying the American male. A Mack Gordon-Harry Revel song "You Got To Smile" sung by Shirley Temple is included on the soundtrack. But I'm afraid this is a time for crying not smiling, for if ever a studio made a mess of a good satirical novel (by Gore Vidal) it was Twentieth Century-Fox with this one. The one star is for the appearance of Mae West. John Huston appears as a veteran Western star; the movie belongs firmly in the dustbin.

Box-office rental $4,300,000

Average rental (70) $16,881,800

1970. Directed by Michael Sarne.
Starring Mae West, John Huston, Raquel Welch, Rex Reed, Farrah Fawcett, Roger C. Carmel. Colour.
91 minutes.

Twentieth Century-Fox Video

The Mysterians

Japanese sci-fi offering about some intellectual aliens whose planet has
been blown to bits by atomic warfare and who invade the Earth in order
to carry on their civilization. How to do it? Bring with them giant robots
and lethal death rays as persuaders and intermarry with the poor earth-
lings. Usual *War Of The Worlds* type stuff, although the effects are quite
elaborate at times and might well find favour with the younger members
of the household. On the same video tape: *Sons Of The Musketeers.*

1959. Directed by Inoshiro Honda.
Starring Kenji Sahara, Yumi Shirakawa, Momoko Kochi, Akihiko Hirata.
Colour.
85 minutes.

Kingston Video

The Mysterious Desperado

Tim Holt in action helping his saddle pal make a rightful claim to the
estate of his late uncle who died in mysterious circumstances. Usual B-
Western fare. Supports *The Last Days Of Pompeii* on a double-feature
video tape.

1949. Directed by Leslie Selander.
Starring Tim Holt, Richard Martin. Black and White.
61 minutes.

Kingston Video

N

The Naked And The Dead

A great book but a routine movie! How often has that cry of anguish been heard when a best-seller has been adapted to the screen? Norman Mailer's fine novel about the conflict between officers and men during the war in the Pacific suffers just such a fate and instead of becoming an exceptional movie, emerges as a very ordinary one. The major portion of the film deals with the exploits of a platoon of US infantrymen behind enemy lines. Supported by the Tim Holt B-Western *Target*.

1958. Directed by Raoul Walsh.
Starring Aldo Ray, Cliff Robertson, Raymond Massey, William Campbell, Richard Jaeckel, James Best. Colour.
131 minutes.

Kingston Video

The Naked Kiss

Don't expect anything very refined from this little opus. It's about a prostitute who decides to give it all up and make a new life for herself in a small town as a nurse of handicapped children. When she is forced into an act of murder the whole community turns against her. Constance Towers is strikingly effective as the prostitute; the picture itself is primitive, bizarre, brutal and lurid – and well made. Samuel Fuller is a cult director. This one may help you to find out why.

1964. Directed by Samuel Fuller.
Starring Constance Towers, Anthony Eisley, Virginia Grey, Betty Bronson, Patsy Kelly, Michael Dante. Black and White.
93 minutes.

Video Unlimited

National Lampoon's Animal House

Like all comedy this one depends very much on your own personal taste, and if you enjoy the *National Lampoon* type of humour (similar to that to be found in *Mad* magazine) you might well enjoy this movie about the zany adventures of a couple of disreputable freshmen at an American college in the early 60s. There are plenty of anti-establishment jokes, there is plenty of noise and plenty of slapstick. There is also plenty of vulgarity and downright rubbish. In this writer's assessment hardly worth a heavy financial outlay, although just look at those box-office figures – and the film cost under three million to make!

| Box-office rental | $74,000,000 |
| Average rental (78) | $39,443,850 |

1978. Directed by John Landis.
Starring John Belushi, Tim Matheson, John Vernon, Verna Bloom, Thomas Hulce, Cesare Danova. Colour.
109 minutes.

CIC Video

Neither The Sea Nor The Sand ★★

Susan Hampshire falls in love with a young airport controller while winter holidaying in Jersey but then finds to her dismay that he dies from a heart attack and then, to her horror, that he comes to life again as a zombie and begins caressing her as he disintegrates. Macabre; enough to put you off winter hols for good!

1972. Directed by Fred Burnley.
Starring Susan Hampshire, Michael Petrovitch, Frank Finlay, Michael Craze, Jack Lambert. Colour.
94 minutes.

Guild Home Video

Network

A washed-up and slightly barmy TV newscaster (Peter Finch) suddenly finds himself top of the ratings again when he threatens to commit suicide on the air. Ruthless programming executive Faye Dunaway sees the possibilities of being able to improve the ratings still further and also advance her own career. Thereafter Finch becomes a kind of "Religious Messiah" of the box. This wickedly perceptive Paddy Chayefsky satire is a bit too strident for its own good at times but it's certainly strong viewing. It's also very uncomfortable viewing, for it leaves one feeling angry at the media-dominated consumer society in which we live. Poor camerawork is a technical minus.

Box-office rental	$13,683,000
Average rental (76)	$22,752,350
Oscars (4)	Best Actor (Finch); Actress (Dunaway); Supporting Actress (Straight); Screenplay
Oscar nominations (6)	Best Film; Actor (Holden); Supporting Actor (Beatty); Direction; Photography; Editing

1976. Directed by Sidney Lumet.
Starring Faye Dunaway, William Holden, Peter Finch, Robert Duvall, Wesley Addy, Ned Beatty, Beatrice Straight. Colour.
121 minutes.

Intervision

Newsfront

The blending of fact with fiction and old newsreels with reconstructed events isn't exactly new but it's doubtful whether the technique has been used more effectively than in this film, which reconstructs the social and political history of Australia from 1948 to 1956. The movie pivots on the personal life of a newsreel cameraman and includes the election of Robert Menzies, the visit of Vice-President Nixon and the referendum to ban the Communist Party, the terrifying Maitland floods and the coming of Australian television. Interesting video.

1978. Directed by Phillip Noyce.

Starring Bill Hunter, Chris Haywood, John Dease, Wendy Hughes, Gerard Kennedy. Part Colour/Part Black and White.
111 minutes.

Home Video Productions

Nicholas Nickleby

The misfortunes of a Victorian schoolteacher who is deprived of his rightful inheritance by a wicked uncle. A great book (and one of Dickens' longest) but a stilted and uninspired film and very antiquated video fare. Alfred Drayton takes the acting honours as Wackford Squeers, the notorious headmaster of Dotheboys Hall up in darkest Yorkshire.

1947. Directed by Cavalcanti.
Starring Cedric Hardwicke, Stanley Holloway, Alfred Drayton, Cyril Fletcher, Bernard Miles, Derek Bond, Sally Ann Howes, Sybil Thorndike.
Black and White.
105 minutes.

Thorn EMI Video

Nickelodeon

This should have been good; young lawyer Ryan O'Neal and small-time performer Burt Reynolds stumble into the early days of film-making and discover to their cost that the business is fraught with danger and insecurity. But instead of being a riot, as director Peter Bogdanovich intended, the whole thing falls flat on its face and ends up as a lame "Can I stay with it to the finish?" exercise for the video viewer. Based in part on the experiences of veteran directors Raoul Walsh and Allan Dwan, the film comes alive only during its elaborate reconstruction of the premiere of D. W. Griffith's silent epic *Birth Of A Nation*.

| Box-office rental | $6,000,000 |
| Average rental (76) | $22,752,350 |

1976. Directed by Peter Bogdanovich.

Starring Ryan O'Neal, Burt Reynolds, Tatum O'Neal, Brian Keith, Stella Stevens, John Ritter. Colour.
122 minutes.

Thorn EMI Video

A Night At The Opera

Vintage Marx Brothers fare with Groucho, Chico and Harpo all involved (inevitably) with buxom Margaret Dumont, who in this one is a patron of opera and Sig Rumann who is the director of the New York Opera Company. Contains the famous scene in which scores of people pour into and then tumble out of a ship's cabin and an evening of insanity at a performance of Grand Opera. The Marx Brothers are an acquired taste but if you like 'em then this is one of the best.

1935. Directed by Sam Wood.
Starring Groucho, Chico and Harpo Marx, Kitty Carlisle, Allan Jones, Margaret Dumont, Sig Rumann. Black and White.
90 minutes.

MGM/CBS Home Video

The Night God Screamed

Lovely Jeanne Crain used to be one of Fox's classiest lady stars of the 40s and 50s. A pity she was reduced to appearing in such a mish-mash as this, in which she's alone in a house with four adolescent children, threatened by vengeful telephone calls and besieged by a gang led by a hooded monk! It all adds up to nothing more than a predictable "heroine-alone-in-an-old-house" movie. Scarcely value for money. Known also under the title, *Scream*.

1971. Directed by Lee Madden.
Starring Jeanne Crain, Alex Nicol, Daniel Spelling, Michael Sugich, Barbara Hancock, Dawn Cleary, Gary Morgan. Colour.
80 minutes.

Guild Home Video

Night Moves

One of those darkly obscure thrillers that has a hidden meaning in every scene and proves that you are somewhat lacking in brainpower if you don't sit around for hours on end discussing its relevance once it has come to a close. At least that's what the posh movie magazines say. The trouble is that the end seems a long, long time in coming and that this is a very complicated detective puzzle indeed, with private eye Gene Hackman running into no end of trouble when he tracks down a runaway teenager to the Florida Keys. A meandering thriller that starts off no place and gets nowhere and takes 99 minutes to do so.

1975. Directed by Arthur Penn.
Starring Gene Hackman, Jennifer Warren, Edward Binns, Harris Yulin, Kenneth Mars, Janet Ward. Colour.
99 minutes.

Warner Home Video

Night Of The Big Heat

A small island off the coast of Britain suddenly starts getting uncomfortably warm despite the fact that it's November. Some alien invaders need the hot temperatures to survive. Christopher Lee and Peter Cushing are among those battling against the odds. Both perish. They should have waited. A thunderstorm does the trick. Standard sci-fi, based on the novel by John Lymington.

1967. Directed by Terence Fisher.
Starring Christopher Lee, Peter Cushing, Patrick Allen, Sarah Lawson, Jane Merrow, William Lucas, Kenneth Cope. Colour.
94 minutes.

Derann Video

Night Of The Living Dead

The movie that helped establish the reputation of cult horror director George A. Romero, about some corpses which are revived by radiation and go on the rampage seeking out potential victims in rural America. A few survivors hole up in a deserted farmhouse and try to survive the zombie onslaught. Sounds a bit like a Saturday morning matinee for adults. And that's just about what it is, a grisly stomach-turning exploitation flick that hardly deserves all the attention it has received. Overrated.

1968. Directed by George A. Romero.
Starring Judith O'Dea, Russell Streiner, Duane Jones, Karl Hardman, Keith Wayne. Black and White.
90 minutes.

Alpha Video
(*distributed by Intervision*)

A Night To Remember

Probably the most authentic screen version of the sinking of the Titanic, told from the viewpoint of second officer Lightoller (Kenneth More) and carefully reconstructing not only the tragedy itself but also the sequence of events that led up to it. Handsome settings by art director Alex Vetchinsky; thoughtful and occasionally probing script by Eric Ambler. Looks a little bit ancient nowadays but the scenes of chaos and panic as the ship strikes the iceberg are all too convincing. 2½ rating.

1958. Directed by Roy Baker.
Starring Kenneth More, David McCallum, Jill Dixon, Laurence Naismith, Frank Lawton, John Cairney, Michael Goodliffe. Black and White.
123 minutes.

Rank Video

9 To 5

Three secretaries fantasizing about how they would like to get even with their chauvinistic boss and then getting the chance to put their dreams into practice *sounds* like a good idea. And for the first 30 minutes this one crackles along at a fair old pace. After that, however, invention rapidly deserts writer/director Colin Higgins and the film descends to the level of broad comedy and knockabout farce. Dolly Parton's theme tune is bright and breezy and there are some amusing observations of American secretarial life but at the final count, Jane Fonda, Lily Tomlin and the buxom Parton are simply defeated by their material. A pity. A caustic script by Billy Wilder for instance would have kept things bubbling along nicely. 2½ rating.

Box-office rental	$57,850,000
Average rental (80)	$30,086,027
Oscars	Nil
Oscar nominations (1)	Best Song ("9 To 5")

1980. Directed by Colin Higgins.
Starring Jane Fonda, Lily Tomlin, Dolly Parton, Dabney Coleman, Sterling Hayden, Elizabeth Wilson, Henry Jones. Colour.
109 minutes.

Twentieth Century-Fox Video

The Ninth Configuration

A group of Vietnam problem soldiers are housed in a military study centre in an old gothic mansion near Washington. A new psychiatrist arrives but because of a clerical error (!) he's not the right fella for the job. In fact, you might say he's the wrong chap altogether, a martial arts killer who suffers from nightmares . . . Rather a nasty little movie, written and directed by William Peter Blatty (of *Exorcist* fame) and also known as *Twinkle Twinkle Killer Kane*. Distinctly unpalatable.

1979. Directed by William Peter Blatty.
Starring Stacy Keach, Scott Wilson, Jason Miller, Ed Flanders, Neville Brand. Colour.
109 minutes.

Guild Home Video

Nobody Runs Forever

Detective sergeant Rod Taylor from the Australian outback arrives in London to arrest the Australian High Commissioner (Christopher Plummer) on a charge of murdering his first wife. But once in the capital, he finds that someone else wants Plummer out of the way and that his journey proves more eventful than he had imagined. Dreadful thriller that drags on aimlessly through 101 boring minutes without ever raising one's hopes that it's ever going to get any better. A waste of time and money.

1968. Directed by Ralph Thomas.
Starring Rod Taylor, Christopher Plummer, Lilli Palmer, Camilla Sparv, Daliah Lavi, Clive Revill. Colour.
101 minutes.

Rank Video

Norma Rae

Martin Ritt movie showing how the workers at a Southern textile mill achieve union status through the persistence of New York labour organizer Ron Leibman and the heroic fight of mill worker Sally Field. Not perhaps the most entertaining movie to be found on video but certainly one that makes you sit up and take notice. Standout sequence: when Field brings about a stoppage at the mill and the formerly apathetic workers turn off their machines in support. Definitely worth a look. Don't be put off by the political tag.

Box-office rental	$11,413,000
Average rental (79)	$31,964,775
Oscars (2)	Best Actress (Field); Song ("It Goes Like It Goes")
Oscar nominations (2)	Best Film; Screenplay

1979. Directed by Martin Ritt.
Starring Sally Field, Beau Bridges, Ron Leibman, Pat Hingle, Barbara Baxley, Gail Strickland. Colour.
114 minutes.

Twentieth Century-Fox Video

North Sea Hijack

A group of American and Japanese crooks pose as journalists and hijack a British oil rig in the North Sea. Anthony Perkins (in his usual role of psychopath) demands a ransom of 25 million pounds to be paid within one day. Bearded Roger Moore (named Rufus Excalibur Ffolkes) and his commandos are brought in to restore the status quo. Dopey stuff, not very well handled. James Mason has a few moments as Admiral Of The Fleet.

1980. Directed by Andrew V. McLaglen.
Starring Roger Moore, James Mason, Anthony Perkins, Michael Parks, David Hedison, Jack Watson, George Baker, Faith Brook. Colour.
100 minutes.

CIC Video

Northwest Frontier

On the face of it no more than routine adventure stuff about a trainload of assorted passengers who escort a five-year-old prince, the symbol of Hindu unity, to safety across the plains of turn-of-the-century India. But it's one of those movies that bears watching again and again simply because of the adventures that befall the group along the way – getting the train safely across a damaged bridge, mending a broken rail in a desperate race against time, fighting off a tribal attack. If it hadn't been so expertly put together, this would have been just another of those instantly forgettable movies that belong in the trash can. But it *is* well made and character actors Wilfrid Hyde White, Eugene Deckers and Herbert Lom as a murderous Moslem journalist do much to make the journey worthwhile.

1959. Directed by J. Lee-Thompson.
Starring Kenneth More, Lauren Bacall, Herbert Lom, Ursula Jeans, Wilfrid Hyde White, I. S. Johar, Eugene Deckers, Ian Hunter. Colour.
129 minutes.

Rank Video

Nothing But The Night

Call Christopher Lee of the Special Branch! And call pathologist Peter Cushing! Why all the urgency? Well, the trustees of an orphanage are dropping like flies, murdered by assailants unknown. Could the orphans themselves be responsible? And why does Diana Dors go up in smoke on Guy Fawkes Night? For answers to these and other questions watch this movie, a murder mystery with supernatural elements. And, if it's not much cop at times, take refuge in its unintentionally humorous moments, such as when Peter Cushing picks his way among the scant remains of an explosion victim and utters: "At least death was instantaneous!"

1972. Directed by Peter Sasdy.
Starring Christopher Lee, Peter Cushing, Diana Dors, Georgia Brown, Keith Barron, Gwyneth Strong, Fulton MacKay. Colour.
90 minutes.

Rank Video

Not Now Darling

Womanizing furrier Leslie Phillips hopes for great things when he tries to sell a fur coat to prospective mistress Julie Ege. But all he gets is trouble, first from current mistress Barbara Windsor and then from wife Moira Lister. What *you* get for your money is a predictable screen version of a West End farce with the usual misunderstandings, hurried exits and *double-entendres*. Not very good.

1973. Directed by Ray Cooney and David Croft.
Starring Leslie Phillips, Ray Cooney, Moira Lister, Julie Ege, Joan Sims, Barbara Windsor. Colour.
97 minutes.

Guild Home Video

Notorious

Ingrid Bergman, embittered and footloose because her German pa has been convicted of treason, is hired by FBI man Cary Grant to worm her way into a household of Nazis experimenting with uranium down South America way. After that it's basically a dramatic conflict between love and loyalty, although in all honesty it's hardly anything to get worked up about. Plus factors: the always magnificent Claude Rains, a fine tension sequence in a wine cellar and some dazzling black and white camerawork. On the debit side: a seriously off-form Mr. Grant. In view of its reputation, disappointing video fare.

Box-office rental	$4,800,000
Average rental (46)	$5,720,000
Oscars	Nil
Oscar nominations (2)	Best Supporting Actor (Rains); Original Screenplay

1946. Directed by Alfred Hitchcock.
Starring Cary Grant, Ingrid Bergman, Claude Rains, Louis Calhern. Black and White.
101 minutes.

Guild Home Video

O

Odd Man Out

The last hours in the life of a wounded Irish gunman (James Mason) as he makes a desperate flight from the police through Belfast in mid-winter. A kind of cinematic *danse-macabre*, performed in rain-swept streets, back alleys, air raid shelters, pubs and junk yards and spanning eight hours – from 4 pm when the chase begins until midnight when the gunman meets his death. Supporting the brilliant Mason: Robert Newton as a drunken artist obsessed with painting the death in the fugitive's eyes; F. J. McCormick as a disreputable old tramp; W. G. Fay as a priest. Stark but memorable cinema; equally memorable video.

Oscars   Nil
Oscar nominations (1)   Best Editing

1947. Directed by Carol Reed.
Starring James Mason, Robert Newton, Kathleen Ryan, Robert Beatty, W. G. Fay, Fay Compton, F. J. McCormick. Black and White.
115 minutes.

Rank Video

Oh, God!

The assistant manager (John Denver) of a California supermarket gets a visit from a benevolent old guy who tells him to help spread the word of God. Not only does the old man ask him to spread the word of God, He is God. He's also played by George Burns, which means that a great deal of this lightweight little piece is very funny indeed. The screenplay by Larry Gelbart also allows God the luxury of making a few mistakes, such as when he's reminiscing about the great days of the Creation: "One of my big mistakes ... Ostriches, funny looking things ... Avocados? ... pips too big, you try".

Box-office rental $31,440,000
Average rental (77) $36,913,348

| Oscars | Nil |
| Oscar nominations (1) | Best Screenplay |

1977. Directed by Carl Reiner.
Starring George Burns, John Denver, Teri Garr, Ralph Bellamy, Donald Pleasence, William Daniels, Paul Sorvino. Colour
104 minutes.

Warner Home Video

Oklahoma!

Fairly straight version of the historic Rodgers and Hammerstein show that changed the course of the American stage musical. Looks a bit quaint nowadays, but the songs (every one a hit) come up as fresh as ever, especially "Oh, What A Beautiful Morning", "All Or Nothin" and "Everything's Up-To-Date In Kansas City". The story concerns the on-off love affair between ranch-hand Gordon MacRae and farmer's daughter Shirley Jones in turn-of-the-century Oklahoma. Rod Steiger is the bad guy and even has his own number – "Poor Jud". Choreography by Agnes DeMille; overlong, generally pleasing.

Box-office rental	$7,100,000
Average rental (55)	$7,239,750
Oscars (2)	Best Scoring Of A Musical; Sound Recording
Oscar nominations (2)	Best Photography; Editing

1955. Directed by Fred Zinnemann.
Starring Gordon MacRae, Shirley Jones, Charlotte Greenwood, Rod Steiger, Gloria Grahame, Eddie Albert, James Whitmore, Gene Nelson. Colour.
145 minutes.

MGM/CBS Home Video

Old Man Rhythm

Minor RKO college musical, vintage 1935. The goings-on among the co-eds are of interest primarily because Hermes Pan was in charge of the choreography and because of the early appearances of Betty Grable (fifth on the cast list); songwriter Johnny Mercer, who features ninth as one of the students; and Lucille Ball who comes in at number 18 under the general heading of "college girl". Supports the Fred Astaire musical *A Damsel In Distress* which won Pan an Academy Award for dance direction.

1935. Directed by Edward Ludwig.
Starring Charles "Buddy" Rogers, George Barbier, Barbara Kent, Grace Bradley, Betty Grable, Eric Blore. Black and White.
74 minutes.

Kingston Video

Oliver Twist

David Lean's follow up to his brilliant *Great Expectations* and only marginally less effective. Alec Guinness is Fagin; Robert Newton Bill Sykes; Kay Walsh Nancy and Francis L. Sullivan a looming Mr. Bumble. Wan John Howard Davies is the orphan boy who suffers at their hands. Certain scenes i.e. the opening journey of Oliver's mother to the parish workhouse, the murder of Nancy, and a *tour-de-force* in The Three Cripples, rank with Lean's finest ever work, indeed with some of the finest scenes in all British cinema. If you haven't yet seen this make sure you make amends by watching it on video; if you have you will probably want to reserve it a permanent place on your library shelf. The black and white camerawork is of the highest quality.

1948. Directed by David Lean.
Starring Robert Newton, Alec Guinness, Kay Walsh, Francis L. Sullivan, Henry Stephenson, Mary Clare, John Howard Davies, Anthony Newley. Black and White.
116 minutes.

Rank Video

The Omen

At first sight the story doesn't sound much: American diplomat Gregory Peck adopts a baby in a Rome hospital only to discover that the boy is the anti-Christ reborn and out to make something of a name for himself on Earth. In fact, put in those terms, it sounds no more than a routine Hammer horror cheapie of the mid-60s. What lifts it into the "must-see" class is the clever handling of director Richard Donner, whose use of close-ups and imaginative editing techniques prove that even a Satanic blood and thunder exercise can be worthwhile. The movie ends with hardly anyone in the cast surviving (there's a corpse roughly every 15 minutes) and little Damien off to America, one step closer to the White House. Very watchable. See also *Damien: Omen 11* (page 121)

Box-office rental	$28,544,000
Average rental (76)	$22,752,350
Oscars (1)	Best Original Music Score
Oscar nominations (1)	Best Song ("Ave Satani")

1976. Directed by Richard Donner.
Starring Gregory Peck, Lee Remick, David Warner, Billie Whitelaw, Harvey Stephens, Leo McKern, Patrick Troughton. Colour.
111 minutes.

Twentieth Century-Fox Video

One Flew Over The Cuckoo's Nest

Cheerful prison farm misfit Jack Nicholson is transferred for observation to a mental asylum, where he immediately becomes the hero of the downtrodden inmates and instils in them a feeling that all is not lost and life is worth living after all. That, unfortunately, counts as rebellion. In the end, the authorities decide enough is enough and put a stop to Nicholson's activities in the most horrific way possible. Not many films make you cry one minute and laugh the next. This one does and hits you where it hurts – and often. Some extraordinary moments and at the final count, emotionally overwhelming. Tremendous performance by Nicholson.

Box-office rental	$59,166,036
Average rental (75)	$27,300,250
Oscars (5)	Best Film; Actor (Nicholson); Actress (Fletcher); Direction; Screenplay
Oscar nominations (4)	Supporting Actor (Dourif); Photography; Editing; Music Score

1975. Directed by Milos Forman.
Starring Jack Nicholson, Louise Fletcher, William Redfield, Michael Beryman, Brad Dourif, Will Sampson. Colour.
129 minutes.

Thorn EMI Video

100 Rifles

Negro American deputy Jim Brown, half breed Burt Reynolds and fiery Indian girl Raquel Welch team up as the Yaqui Indians rebel against the cruelty of their brutal Mexican oppressors. One of them perishes, the other two survive. Standard Western fare with the usual attributes of well-staged action sequences and well-photographed settings. Moves fast.

1969. Directed by Tom Gries.
Starring Jim Brown, Raquel Welch, Burt Reynolds, Fernando Lamas, Dan O'Herlihy. Colour.
109 minutes.

Twentieth Century-Fox Video

One Million Years B.C.

Prehistoric frolics with scantily-clad Raquel Welch, huge lizards, giant turtles, a pterodactyl, tribes of uncouth cavemen, etc. Great female anatomy, passable special effects, rotten (Ugh! Ugh! type) script.

1966. Directed by Don Chaffey.

Starring Raquel Welch, John Richardson, Percy Herbert, Robert Brown, Martine Beswick. Colour.
91 minutes.

Thorn EMI Video

One Touch Of Venus

A young man falls in love with a store window statue of Venus and finds to his delight that the statue turns into Ava Gardner. A pleasant enough adaptation of the 1943 Broadway success, although a little on the mild side and because of its age, only an average video purchase. The music score by Kurt Weill and Ogden Nash includes the song "Speak Low".

1948. Directed by William A. Seiter.
Starring Ava Gardner, Robert Walker, Dick Haymes, Eve Arden, Olga San Juan, Tom Conway. Black and White.
81 minutes.

Intervision

The Onion Field

Sobering story (a true one) about a young Los Angeles cop who cracks up after his partner has been murdered by a couple of hoods, and the subsequent seven-year court case from which the villains emerge with more honour than the cop, who almost commits suicide. A rather uncomfortable movie that shows how the law can be bent to protect the guilty and accuse the innocent. Hardly entertainment with a capital E but compelling for much of the time. A more talented director might have given it a bit more edge and a bit more pace. Adapted from his own novel by Joseph Wambaugh. 2½ rating.

| Box-office rental | $5,000,000 |
| Average rental (79) | $31,964,775 |

1979. Directed by Harold Becker.

Starring John Savage, James Woods, Franklyn Seales, Ted Danson, Ronny Cox. Colour.
126 minutes.

Twentieth Century-Fox Video

Only Two Can Play

Peter Sellers as a frustrated Welsh librarian who has reached the awkward age and finds himself restricted by his family life and eager for some fun and games on the side. Attractive councillor's wife Mai Zetterling seems a likely target. And things go well until the night of the seduction. After that it's disasterville all the way. A surprisingly durable movie that shows Sellers in one of his most successful roles and emerges as a more than adequate adaptation of the Kingsley Amis novel *That Uncertain Feeling*. Virginia Maskell co-stars as Sellers' long suffering wife; Kenneth Griffith nearly steals the film with his portrait of his henpecked librarian colleague. The whole thing is set within the confines of a small Welsh provincial town.

1962. Directed by Sidney Gilliat.
Starring Peter Sellers, Mai Zetterling, Virginia Maskell, Richard Attenborough, Kenneth Griffith. Black and White.
106 minutes.

Thorn EMI Video

On The Waterfront

Corruption on New York's waterfront exposed as ex-boxer Marlon Brando turns informer and denounces the criminal activities of scab-union boss Lee J. Cobb and his cronies. Fine acting from all concerned with the cab scene between Brando and Rod Steiger frequently held up as a model of how great screen acting can be. And deservedly so! The film has lost little of its power even though it is now over 25 years old. The opening murder sequence is riveting cinema; Brando's closing stumble back to work controversial in its political implications. Dynamic music score by Leonard Bernstein. A must!

Box-office rental	$4,200,000
Average rental (54)	$6,012,700
Oscars (8)	Best Film; Actor (Brando); Supporting Actress (Saint); Direction; Story & Screenplay; Photography; Art Direction; Editing
Oscar nominations (4)	Best Supporting Actor (Cobb); Supporting Actor (Malden); Supporting Actor (Steiger); Music Score

1954. Directed by Elia Kazan.
Starring Marlon Brando, Karl Malden, Lee J. Cobb, Rod Steiger, Pat Henning, Eva Marie Saint, Leif Erickson. Black and White.
108 minutes.

RCA/Columbia International Video

The Optimists Of Nine Elms ★★★

Peter Sellers in one of his most accomplished roles as an ex-music hall performer who earns a living busking in London's West End and has only a sick dog for company until he pals up with a couple of kids. More than just a children's movie. Much more, in fact, and at the final count a picture of some quality – melancholy, pessimistic and occasionally very moving. Lionel Bart's songs, which include "Sometimes", intrude on rather than help the mood of the picture which was shot on location on London's Thameside.

1973. Directed by Anthony Simmons.
Starring Peter Sellers, Donna Mullane, John Chaffey, David Daker, Marjorie Yates, Katyana Kass. Colour.
110 minutes.

Home Video Productions

Othello

Filmed record of the National Theatre production of Shakespeare's tragedy. Not to be confused with Olivier's cinematic adaptations of Shakespeare's plays, *Henry V* and *Hamlet*, but of interest historically for capturing for posterity the actor's performance as the noble Moor Of Venice. Frank Finlay schemes as Iago; Maggie Smith is the luckless Desdemona.

Oscars	Nil
Oscar nominations (4)	Best Actor (Olivier); Supporting Actor (Finlay); Supporting Actress (Smith); Supporting Actress (Redman)

1965. Directed by Stuart Burge.
Starring Laurence Olivier, Frank Finlay, Maggie Smith, Robert Lang, Anthony Nicholls, Roy Holder, Derek Jacobi, Joyce Redman. Colour.
166 minutes.

Rank Video

The Other Side Of Midnight ★★

Lush treatment of Sidney Sheldon's novel about a young Marseilles beauty who is seduced and abandoned by a Canadian flier in World War II Paris and who then sets out on a campaign of carefully planned revenge. Tosh of course and it plods a bit but thanks to its eroticism and the constantly changing scene – the fashion world, Hollywood, the Mediterranean – it keeps you interested. Very expensive looking and co-written by Daniel Taradash who once scripted *From Here To Eternity*. 2½ rating if you take it in the spirit in which it is offered.

Box-office rental	£18,408,000
Average rental (77)	$36,913,348
Oscars	Nil
Oscar nominations (1)	Best Costume Design

1977. Directed by Charles Jarrott.

Starring Marie-France Pisier, John Beck, Susan Sarandon, Raf Vallone, Clu Gulager, Christian Marquand, Michael Lerner. Colour.
166 minutes.

Twentieth Century-Fox Video

Our Man Flint

One of the innumerable Bond-type spoofs that flourished in the 60s with lanky secret agent James Coburn called in to try and stop the dastardly plans of the criminal organization Galaxy who plan to take over the world by controlling the weather! His only weapon? A cigarette lighter with 83 different functions! The organization *he* works for is named ZOWIE (Zonal Organization World Intelligence). Starts brightly then flags.

Box-office rental	$7,200,000
Average rental (66)	$8,826,100

1966. Directed by Daniel Mann.
Starring James Coburn, Lee J. Cobb, Gila Golan, Edward Mulhare, Benson Fong. Colour.
107 minutes.

Twentieth Century-Fox Video

The Outlaw

Former dental receptionist Jane Russell gives two added dimensions to the story of *Billy The Kid*. That's the flip way of describing this Howard Hughes movie, which was the first to introduce sex into the Western back in 1943. Actually, it's not nearly as erotic – nor as bad – as critics first made it out to be and at times is even rather impressive, thanks to character actors Thomas Mitchell as the vengeful Pat Garrett and Walter Huston as Doc Holliday. Originally advertised with the words "Sex has not been rationed", it grossed over five million dollars from its many releases. On the same video double-bill: the 1938 B-movie *Law Of The Underworld*.

1943. Directed by Howard Hughes.
Starring Jack Buetel, Jane Russell, Thomas Mitchell, Walter Huston, Joe Sawyer. Black and White.
117 minutes.

Kingston Video

The Outlaw Josey Wales ★★★★

From its title no more than a routine "man with no name" type Western but in reality much, much more – a moving saga of a peaceful farmer who joins a guerilla band after his wife and children are murdered during the Civil War then steadfastly refuses to give himself up at the War's close. As he is hunted down he collects a new "family" along the way – an old Cherokee, an Indian girl, a broken-down cowboy, etc – all of whom come to depend on him for their survival. Outstanding Western with more than a little point to its story and certainly Eastwood's finest film to date. Exciting and superior video.

Box-office rental	$13,500,000
Average rental (76)	$22,752,350
Oscars	Nil
Oscar nominations (1)	Best Original Music Score

1976. Directed by Clint Eastwood.
Starring Clint Eastwood, Chief Dan George, Sondra Locke, Bill McKinney, John Vernon, Paula Trueman, Sam Bottoms. Colour.
134 minutes.

Warner Home Video

Out Of The Past ★★★★

Retired private eye Robert Mitchum is hired by mobster Kirk Douglas to track down the gal who has taken a pot shot at him and made off with 40,000 dollars into the bargain. The search leads to Mexico where Mitch finds himself falling victim to the girl's treacherous charm and on a dark journey of no return. This is Mitch (complete with trenchcoat) at his laconic best, although it's Jane Greer as the erotic *femme fatale* (and is she erotic!) who gives the film its hard-grained edge. "She can't be all bad, no one is", says a woman to Mitchum during the film. "No, but she comes the closest" replies Mitchum. A beauty (both the film and Greer) and one to watch again and again. Supported on a double-feature tape by *Hells Highway*.

1947. Directed by Jacques Tourneur.
Starring Robert Mitchum, Jane Greer, Kirk Douglas, Rhonda Fleming, Richard Webb, Steve Brodie, Virginia Huston. Black and White.
97 minutes.

Kingston Video

Out Of Season

Moody, atmospheric little piece set in an English seaside hotel in winter and revolving around an American (Cliff Robertson) who returns to resume an affair with an English woman (Vanessa Redgrave) he had loved twenty years before. Not surprisingly, he finds her cool on the idea. He also finds she has a grown-up daughter (Susan George) who is rather more receptive to him than mum. Hints of incest and an intriguing, ambiguous ending when one of the women leaves on the train and the other waits naked in his bedroom. But which one? A puzzle movie but well performed and intelligently scripted.

1975. Directed by Alan Bridges.
Starring Vanessa Redgrave, Cliff Robertson, Susan George, Edward Evans, Frank Jarvis. Colour.
90 minutes.

Thorn EMI Video

Overlord

Unusual movie that mixes a fictional story with film from the Imperial War Museum Film Archives and brings alive one of the most important periods of World War II. The picture follows the experiences of an 18-year-old boy from the time he is called up in the early days of 1944, through his training and to his death during the Normandy landings. An imaginative piece of cinema that holds the attention throughout. Good value.

1975. Directed by Stuart Cooper.
Starring Brian Stirner, Davyd Harries, Nicholas Ball, Julie Neesam, Sam Sewell. Black and White.
83 minutes.

Thorn EMI Video

The Owl And The Pussycat ★★★

Bookstore assistant George Segal tries to convince himself that he's going to become a successful writer; street girl Barbra Streisand prefers to classify herself as a self-styled actress and model. After a few weeks together they do away with their pretensions and accept each other as they really are. Very funny for most of its length with Streisand suffering from insomnia and flashing her knickers beneath her mini-skirt. Her first words? "Hello, fink! Fink pansy! You rat! You fruitcake! Rat fink fruitcake! Creeps like yourself don't have dogs named Wolf. What creeps like you have are faggy, hairy bitty things with names like Pooky and Doodoo!" After that she never stops. Nor does the movie. Worthwhile.

Box-office rental	$11,645,000
Average rental (70)	$16,881,800

1970. Directed by Herbert Ross.
Starring Barbra Streisand, George Segal, Robert Klein, Allen Garfield, Roz Kelly. Colour.
96 minutes.

RCA/Columbia International Video

P

Pancho Villa

Given that Mexican revolutionary leader Pancho Villa led a reasonably exciting and eventful life, one would expect that any film, based however vaguely on his exploits, would be reasonably entertaining. Wrong! This one sinks well below the acceptable level and has Villa involved in buying arms from Americans across the border. Clint Walker does the gun-running; Chuck Connors is a military martinet; and Telly Savalas is Pancho! A train crash brings it all mercifully to a close.

1972. Directed by Gene Martin.
Starring Telly Savalas, Clint Walker, Anne Francis, Chuck Connors, Angel Del Pozo. Colour.
92 minutes.

Cinema Features
(distributed by VCL)

Panic City

A deranged assassin (disguised as a black man) begins a nightmarish bout of urban killing when he disposes of three nurses with a scalpel and leaves a message for the police that more are to follow. After that it becomes a "can-we-catch-him-in-time?" thriller, with a total of 13 murders chalked up before the cops nail the culprit. A tatty, brutal movie of the kind that is hardly worth taking out of the dust case.

1974. Directed by William Girdler.
Starring Austin Stoker, Hugh Smith, Jim Pickett, Charles Kissinger, Valery Rogers, Ruby Brown, Tom Brooks. Colour.
90 minutes.

Intervision

Panic In Needle Park

Grim saga of how a young New York girl is befriended by a small-time junkie and pulled down into his grimy world of drugs and thieves until she is even more hopelessly addicted than he is. Eventually she turns to prostitution to pay for her addiction. Unrelievedly grim with many explicit scenes of drug use. Fine acting, indeed you've got to act well to appear convincing in this sort of thing but who wants this sort of thing? Filmed in New York's Upper West Side.

1971. Directed by Jerry Schatzberg.
Starring Al Pacino, Kitty Winn, Alan Vint, Richard Bright, Kiel Martin. Colour.
110 minutes.

Twentieth Century-Fox Video

The Paradine Case

Lawyer Gregory Peck defends a beautiful woman (Valli) accused of murdering her blind husband, then finds himself falling in love with her. Sounds promising, especially with Alfred Hitchcock at the helm, but this was made when Hitch was going through his post-war "down-in-the-dumps" period. And you can't get much more "down-in-the-dumps" than this, for it's tedious in the extreme and its 115 minutes seem like 215. Charles Laughton as a lecherous judge with an acid turn of phrase ("I do not like to be interrupted in the middle of an insult") does his best to enliven the proceedings but this is Hitch at his dreariest.

Oscars	Nil
Oscar nominations (1)	Best Supporting Actress (Barrymore)

1947. Directed by Alfred Hitchcock.
Starring Gregory Peck, Alida Valli, Ann Todd, Louis Jourdan, Charles Laughton, Charles Coburn, Ethel Barrymore. Black and White.
115 minutes.

Guild Home Video

Paradise, Hawaiian Style

Among the last of Elvis Presley's 30-odd movies, made at a time when Hal Wallis, Presley's regular Paramount producer, was scratching his head to find new ways of coming up with the same old cornball stories. He shouldn't have bothered. This one's a misfire all along the line, as playboy airline pilot Elvis establishes a charter helicopter service to fly tourists around the islands. When he's on the ground he finds time for eleven unmemorable songs.

1966. Directed by Michael Moore.
Starring Elvis Presley, Suzanna Leigh, James Shigeta, Donna Butterworth. Colour.
91 minutes.

Twentieth Century-Fox Video

The Passage

Mundane World War II adventure about Basque shepherd-guide Anthony Quinn, who helps scientist James Mason and family escape from occupied France and over the mountains to the safety of Spain. Torturing his way in hot pursuit: sadistic SS captain Malcolm McDowell, whose pleasures include cutting off his victims' fingers and burning people alive. Distasteful as well as trivial. Massively overplayed by McDowell. Third rate video.

1978. Directed by J. Lee Thompson.
Starring Anthony Quinn, James Mason, Malcolm McDowell, Patricia Neal, Kay Lenz, Paul Clemens, Christopher Lee. Colour.
98 minutes.

Picture Time Video
(distributed by VCL)

Patton

By the time this film's reached the end of its 164 minutes you feel you know everything there *is* to know about old "Blood And Guts" Patton, one of the most controversial American generals of World War II. The movie traces his career through the North African, Sicilian and European campaigns, and highlights the famous incident when he slapped a soldier for cowardice and forfeited command of the Seventh Army in Italy. The battle scenes are strikingly photographed in a film that holds up admirably on video and is difficult to stop watching once its got you in its grip. Brought respectability to the previously despised Hollywood *genre*, the bio-pic. Co-scripted by Francis Ford Coppola.

Box-office rental	$28,100,000
Average rental (70)	$16,881,800
Oscars (7)	Best Film; Actor (Scott); Direction; Story & Screenplay; Art Direction; Sound; Editing
Oscar nominations (3)	Best Photography; Music Score; Special Visual Effects

1970. Directed by Franklin Schaffner.
Starring George C. Scott, Karl Malden, Michael Bates, Stephen Young, Michael Strong, Cary Loftin. Colour.
164 minutes.

Twentieth Century-Fox Video

The Pawnbroker

If it's great acting you're after, then you need look no further than this powerful movie which boasts arguably Rod Steiger's finest screen performance. He's Jewish pawnbroker Sol Nazerman, a man so embittered by his past experiences in a German concentration camp where his wife and children died, that he has been left devoid of human emotion. It takes yet another death – that of his young Puerto Rican assistant, shot while defending him during a robbery in his shop – to make him care once more about the world about him. A harrowing experience; not many films have explored the question of human responsibility as thoroughly as this one. Too strong for many people.

Oscars	Nil
Oscar nominations (1)	Best Actor (Steiger)

1965. Directed by Sidney Lumet.

Starring Rod Steiger, Geraldine Fitzgerald, Jamie Sanchez, Brock Peters, Thelma Oliver, Marketa Kimbrell, Juano Hernandez. Black and White.
116 minutes.

Spectrum
(distributed by Polygram)

Percy

When Alexander Mackendrick was making *The Man In The White Suit* and Charles Crichton was filming *The Lavender Hill Mob* at Ealing in 1951, it is doubtful whether audiences of the time would have expected that just twenty years later the British cinema would be offering as comedy entertainment the story of the transplant of a man's penis. But here it is folks, and about as numbingly bad and coarse as you might expect. Who thought up the idea? Who cares? Those responsible for its filming, however, were producer Betty Box and director Ralph Thomas who, 17 years earlier, had been responsible for the quaintly charming *Doctor In The House*. If you feel embarrassed, don't worry. You're in good company!

1971. Directed by Ralph Thomas.
Starring Hywel Bennett, Elke Sommer, Denholm Elliott, Britt Ekland, Cyd Hayman. Colour.
103 minutes.

Thorn EMI Video

Performance

The worlds of crime and pop music mix when nasty on-the-run gangster James Fox takes refuge in the home of nasty reclusive pop star Mick Jagger and gets the benefit of the star's first performance for years. Somewhat baffling in its message and quite frankly not very nice although many top critics found that it held intellectual pleasures when it was first released in the cinemas. One who did not was the critic of *The New Yorker* who summed it up thus: "a humourless, messy mixture of crime and decadence and drug-induced hallucination" Jagger sings "Memo

From Turner" if that's of any help to you in making up your mind. The film marked the directorial debut of Nicolas Roeg.

1970. Directed by Donald Cammell & Nicolas Roeg.
Starring James Fox, Mick Jagger, Anita Pallenberg, Michele Breton, Ann Sidney. Colour.
105 minutes.

Warner Home Video

Persecution

Lana Turner came out of retirement to make this one, although heaven knows why. She's a rich American with a past, crippled and slightly crazy and living in a grand old country house with a son who hates her. So what do you get for your money? The list starts here: a cat drowned in a bowl of milk; a nervous breakdown; a fatal breaking of a neck; insanity; a stabbing in the back; a skeleton on the bed; another drowning . . . ho, hum!

1974. Directed by Don Chaffey.
Starring Lana Turner, Ralph Bates, Olga Georges-Picot, Suzan Farmer, Mark Weavers, Patrick Allen, Trevor Howard. Colour.
96 minutes.

Rank Video

Pete's Dragon

One of those Disney combined animation/live-action adventures that doesn't come off, mainly because the pace is too slow and the actual joining together of cartoon characters and human figures is unconvincingly handled, a strange "beef" about Disney, but in this case unfortunately valid. Pete of the title is a 9-year-old orphan boy living in Maine at the turn of the century; the dragon is named Elliott and comes to the boy's aid whenever needed. Jim Dale, Helen Reddy, Mickey Rooney and co. try to give it a lift but to no avail. It's a disappointment all round. Even the songs are mediocre.

Box-office rental	$16,100,000
Average rental (77)	$36,913,348
Oscars	Nil
Oscar nominations (2)	Best Song ("Candle On The Water"); Original Song Score

1977. Directed by Don Chaffey.
Starring Sean Marshall, Charlie Callas, Helen Reddy, Jim Dale, Mickey Rooney, Red Buttons, Shelley Winters. Colour.
127 minutes.

Walt Disney Home Video

Phantasm ★

Contemporary horror movies often plumb the depths in their search for terror material. This one is no exception, as it follows the experiences of two teenage boys who become fascinated by some weird goings-on in a mortuary, including a grisly murder by a "Silver Sphere" which clamps down on its victim's head and drains away its blood. A global plot involving *homunculi* is at the bottom of it all. As if you hadn't guessed!

| Box-office rental | $6,000,000 |
| Average rental (79) | $31,964,775 |

1979. Directed by Don Coscarelli.
Starring Angus Scrimm, Michael Baldwin, Bill Thornbury, Reggie Bannister, Kathy Lester. Colour.
89 minutes.

*Picture Time Video
(distributed by VCL)*

The Phantom Of The Opera ★★★

Horror movie of the 20s with a masked Lon Chaney creating havoc as he haunts the underground caves of the Paris Opera House before perishing in the Seine. Despite its age, still a film with plenty of chilling moments, not least when Chaney is unmasked by Mary Philbin in reel five. Good value for film historians, who might be interested to know that Chaney's skull-like appearance was achieved by his wearing false teeth, pushing wires into his nose and eye sockets, fixing adhesive tape to expose the nostrils, and attaching celluloid discs inside the mouth to distort the cheek bones!

1925. Directed by Rupert Julian.
Starring Lon Chaney, Mary Philbin, Norman Kerry, Snitz Edwards, Gibson Gowland. Black and White. (2-colour Technicolor sequences).
74 minutes.

Spectrum
(distributed by Polygram)

Picnic At Hanging Rock

Why did two girls and a teacher disappear from sight, never to be seen again, when they accompanied a picnic party to Hanging Rock on St. Valentine's Day, 1900? This atmospheric, rather slow-moving Australian movie doesn't attempt to provide any answers. Instead, it recreates the incident in loving and intricate detail and in the first hour comes over as a genuinely spooky exercise. But then it gets bogged down in a plethora of themes about Victorian repressions, personal guilt and sexual hysteria at the girls' school and throws away all the gains it made in the first half. A pity, a good opportunity missed.

1975. Directed by Peter Weir.
Starring Rachel Roberts, Dominic Guard, Helen Morse, Jacki Weaver, Vivean Gray, Kirsty Child, Anne Lambert. Colour.
115 minutes.

Home Video Productions

The Pied Piper

Jacques Demy's version of the old fairy tale about a strolling minstrel who rids the town of Hamelin of a plague of rats by piping them tunefully into the river, and then spirits away the town's children when he fails to receive his agreed payment of one thousand guilders. Set in 14th century Germany and a bit too horrific at times to qualify as a fairy tale. Donovan (who composed his own songs) plays the lead and is backed up by a strong supporting cast: Donald Pleasence as the baron, Michael Hordern as the alchemist, Roy Kinnear as the Burgermeister. Uneven.

1972. Directed by Jacques Demy.
Starring Donovan, Donald Pleasence, Jack Wild, Michael Hordern, John Hurt, Cathryn Harrison, Roy Kinnear, Peter Vaughan, Diana Dors. Colour. 90 minutes.

Home Video Productions

The Pink Panther Strikes Again

Number four in the Peter Sellers canon of Pink Panther films, with Clouseau's now completely mad superior Herbert Lom escaping from his psychiatric hospital and forming a vast criminal network dedicated to the extermination of the accident-prone Inspector. The result? Manic disorder on all fronts. Not as inventive as *The Return Of The Pink Panther* but with enough engaging material to make you feel as though the 100-odd minutes have been well spent. Some highlights: Sellers tipping Lom three times into a lake and performing some dental work on his infuriated superior who has been reduced to helpless giggles because of a dose of laughing gas. Another set of inspired credit designs by Richard Williams. 2½ rating.

Box-office rental	$20,003,000
Average rental (76)	$22,752,350
Oscars	Nil
Oscar nominations (1)	Best Song ("Come To Me")

1976. Directed by Blake Edwards.
Starring Peter Sellers, Herbert Lom, Colin Blakely, Leonard Rossiter, Lesley-Anne Down, Burt Kwouk, Richard Vernon. Colour.
103 minutes.

Intervision

Pioneer Builders

1932 movie that charts some sixty years (from 1873) in the life of a pair of newlyweds who go west to Nebraska where they make their fortune and build a banking empire. Known as *The Conquerors* in the States, the film bears a strong resemblance to the 1931 epic *Cimarron* which also starred Richard Dix. It shares a double-feature tape with the Alan Ladd Western *The Big Land* and is something of a rarity in that it has not been shown on TV in this country.

1932. Directed by William A. Wellman.
Starring Richard Dix, Ann Harding, Edna May Oliver, Guy Kibbee, Donald Cook. Black and White.
88 minutes.

Kingston Video

Planet Of The Apes

Charlton Heston and fellow astronauts land on an arid planet after flying about in space for two thousand years. The atmosphere's OK. The trouble is the planet's ruled by intelligent English-speaking apes. And they haven't got much time for humans. And for good reason . . . From then on in it's best to see the movie which is based on Pierre Boulle's ingenious novel *Monkey Planet* and which still sends shivers down the spine in the very last sequence when Mr. Heston finds out where he really is. The enormous screen made that climax shattering in the cinema. On video it loses drastically, not quite fatally, but almost!

Box-office rental	$15,000,000
Average rental (68)	$14,411,950
Oscars	Nil
Oscar nominations (2)	Best Costume Design; Music Score

1968. Directed by Franklin J. Schaffner.
Starring Charlton Heston, Roddy McDowall, Kim Hunter, Maurice Evans, James Whitmore, James Daly, Linda Harrison. Colour.
112 minutes.

Twentieth Century-Fox Video

Please Sir!

Movie version of the ITV comedy series about a young teacher at Fenn Street Secondary School and his problems with his pupils in form 5c. The film hinges on the school's yearly visit to a country recreation camp and incorporates all the familiar teaching faces from the TV series. The result is not displeasing video with John Alderton's likeable personality compensating for much of the film's dated look. Probably the best of the TV spin-offs to be found on video.

1971. Directed by Mark Stuart.
Starring John Alderton, Deryck Guyler, Noel Howlett, Joan Sanderson, Richard Davies, Erik Chitty, Patsy Rowlands, Peter Cleall. Colour.
101 minutes.

Rank Video

Porridge

Rather like three episodes of the popular TV series strung together and hinging on a football match – inmates of Slade Prison versus a show-biz eleven – that acts as a front for an escape plan. The expansion to 90 minutes stretches the humour to breaking point, although all the familiar actors give good accounts of themselves, especially Ronnie Barker as the long serving "Fletch" and Fulton Mackay as his prison officer adversary. Slightly up on the standard of most TV spin-offs but still not good enough. And if you're a fan of the series you'll probably be disappointed.

1979. Directed by Dick Clement.
Starring Ronnie Barker, Richard Beckinsale, Fulton Mackay, Brian Wilde, Peter Vaughan, Julian Holloway, Geoffrey Bayldon. Colour.
93 minutes.

Precision Video

Portrait Of Jennie

One of the most underrated films of the 40s; a sensitive, tender little story about a struggling artist who becomes infatuated with a young girl he meets in Central Park only to find that she is a spirit and has been dead for many years. Worth every penny as video value, if only for the fact that there is no one making movies today who could recapture its delicacy of tone in a remake. Colour tints add to the haunting quality of the film which stays with you long after it has finished and makes you opt for an instant replay. Which, after all, is what buying video tapes is all about.

Oscars (1)   Best Special Effects
Oscar nominations (1)   Best Photography

1948. Directed by William Dieterle.
Starring Jennifer Jones, Joseph Cotten, Ethel Barrymore, Cecil Kellaway, Florence Bates, Esther Somers, David Wayne. Black and White.
86 minutes.

Guild Home Video

The Poseidon Adventure

117 minutes in the company of Gene Hackman, Ernest Borgnine, Shelley Winters and company as they reach the top (or rather the bottom) of a luxury liner that has capsized after being struck by a tidal wave. Daylight and freedom seem an awful long time a coming on the small screen even though the occasional heart attack, explosion, leaky steam valve and sacrificial act are thrown in to keep you from dozing off. The moment when the tidal wave strikes is spectacular enough but after that the film just plods and plods and plods . . .

Box-office rental $42,000,000
Average rental (72) $17,543,950
Oscars (2)   Best Song ("The Morning After"); Visual
                            Effects

Oscar nominations (7)	Best Supporting Actress (Winters); Photography; Art Direction; Costume Design; Sound; Editing; Music Score

1972. Directed by Ronald Neame.
Starring Gene Hackman, Ernest Borgnine, Red Buttons, Carol Lynley, Roddy McDowall, Stella Stevens, Shelley Winters, Jack Albertson, Arthur O'Connell. Colour.
117 minutes.

Twentieth Century-Fox Video

The Possession Of Joel Delaney

Manhattan divorcee/novelist Shirley MacLaine comes face to face with a rather unpleasant reality when she discovers that her brother has been taken over by the spirit of a dead Puerto Rican who used to enjoy cutting off people's heads in New York. A bit silly but also a bit chilling with voodoo, ritual exorcism and a rather scary scene when Miss MacLaine wakes to find a severed head on her kitchen shelf! Turns the old tum a bit at times but doesn't come off when it tries to mix horror with social comment. 2½ rating.

1972. Directed by Waris Hussein.
Starring Shirley MacLaine, Perry King, Michael Hordern, David Elliott, Lisa Kohane, Barbara Trentham. Colour.
108 minutes.

Precision Video

The Postman Always Rings Twice

Two young lovers bump off the woman's ageing cafe-owning hubby then find that life together ain't so hot after all. Not the 1946 version with malevolent Lana Turner dressed all in white and John Garfield prepared to go to any lengths to kill for her. Instead, the murky 1981 remake with a tousled Jessica Lange and a glazed-looking Jack Nicholson going through the motions. Closer to James Cain's novel in its recreation of the Depression 30s but not a patch on the MGM movie as far as entertainment goes. And although sexually explicit (lots of grunts and groans on the kitchen table) it ends up as sluggish video fare hampered by some inferior colourwork.

Box-office rental	$5,920,000
Average rental (81)	$32,180,100

1981. Directed by Bob Rafelson.
Starring Jack Nicholson, Jessica Lange, John Colicos, Michael Lerner, John P. Ryan, Anjelica Huston, William Traylor. Colour.
121 minutes.

Guild Home Video

Power Play

Liberal army colonel David Hemmings leads a military coup against the corrupt government of his country. But when the military overthrow is complete he finds that one of his aides – double-crossing tank commander Peter O'Toole – beats him to the top spot and becomes dictator supreme. And that's curtains for Hemmings. A cynical, violent, unpleasant movie that purports to accurately reflect today's headlines. Hardly entertainment.

1978. Directed by Martyn Burke.
Starring Peter O'Toole, David Hemmings, Donald Pleasence, Barry Morse, Jon Granik, Marcella Saint-Amant. Colour.
102 minutes.

Rank Video

Pretty Baby

A 1917 New Orleans brothel might not sound the perfect setting for subtle entertainment. But that's exactly what emerges in this remarkable and

341

decorative Louis Malle film about the marriage between a 12-year-old girl prostitute and the gentle stills photographer who frequents her abode. The plush world of the whorehouse is examined with loving care by Malle and cameraman Sven Nykvist, who between them indicate that not only do the clients enjoy the girls but that the girls actually enjoy their work. Too leisurely for some but this really is a beauty and deserves several viewings.

Box-office rental	$4,197,000
Average rental (78)	$39,443,850
Oscars	Nil
Oscar nominations (1)	Best Adaptation Music Score

1978. Directed by Louis Malle.
Starring Brooke Shields, Keith Carradine, Susan Sarandon, Frances Faye, Antonio Fargas, Matthew Anton. Colour.
110 minutes.

CIC Video

Prey

Daft combination of sex and science-fiction with an alien from a UFO killing a man, taking over his human form and intruding on the lesbian relationship between two less than likeable young women. He finishes up eating 'em both, and radioing to his planet that humans make good grub and that they're there for the taking! Rotten monster make-up; OK performances.

1978. Directed by Norman J. Warren.
Starring Glory Annen, Sally Faulkner, Barry Stokes, Sandy Chinney, Eddie Stacey, Jerry Crampton. Colour.
83 minutes.

Vampix
(*distributed by Videomedia*)

The Prisoner Of Second Avenue

If you like Neil Simon's comedies (*Barefoot In The Park*, *The Odd Couple*, etc.) you'll probably go for this one, although at times you won't know whether to laugh or cry, for the movie verges on that dangerous tightrope between comedy and tragedy. Jack Lemmon stars as a clerical worker who loses his job in a New York advertising office then heads quickly for a nervous breakdown as he tries to exist in his 14th storey apartment in which nothing ever works. The stress of New York life is the main subject of this movie which is enhanced by an excellent performance from Anne Bancroft as Lemmon's wife. Look out for Sylvester Stallone, 18th on the cast list as a would-be pickpocket!

1975. Directed by Melvin Frank.
Starring Jack Lemmon, Anne Bancroft, Gene Saks, Elizabeth Wilson. Colour.
98 minutes.

Warner Home Video

Private Benjamin

Comedy about a rich young widow (Goldie Hawn) who decides on a life in today's army and finds that the service holds more attractions for her than the men she encounters, all of whom turn out to be chauvinist pigs of one kind or another. Plenty of pro-feminist angles and the usual sight gags of Goldie having to tackle assault courses, make parachute jumps, etc. But of uneven quality. Eileen Brennan's repressed lesbian captain is a plus factor.

Box-office rental	$34,000,000
Average rental (80)	$30,086,027
Oscars	Nil
Oscar nominations (3)	Best Actress (Hawn); Supporting Actress (Brennan); Screenplay

1980. Directed by Howard Zieff.

Starring Goldie Hawn, Eileen Brennan, Armand Assante, Robert Webber, Sam Wanamaker, Barbara Barrie. Colour.
110 minutes.

Warner Home Video

The Producers

Bizarre comedy about a lecherous Broadway producer who finds himself on the skids but saved from financial disaster by a scheme thought up by his young accountant. The scheme? To make money not from a hit but from a flop – always providing that more money can be raised than is actually needed. "Springtime For Hitler", a gay romp with Adolf and Eva in Berchtesgaden, is selected for the disaster stakes. As double insurance a pop singing hippy is selected for the role of Hitler. But things go wrong. The musical is a hit! Zero Mostel (producer) and Gene Wilder (accountant) carry this early Mel Brooks comedy which is among the funniest, especially during the early sequences, to be found on video. Good value.

Oscars (1)	Best Story & Screenplay
Oscar nominations (1)	Best Supporting Actor (Wilder)

1968. Directed by Mel Brooks.
Starring Zero Mostel, Gene Wilder, Kenneth Mars, Estelle Winwood, Renee Taylor. Colour.
88 minutes.

Twentieth Century-Fox Video

The Projected Man

Scientist Bryant Halliday succeeds in disintegrating objects into energy and reassembling them elsewhere through laser power. The next step? Obviously to experiment on himself, but in the reassembly stage things go wrong and the result is a crazed, facially disfigured monster. Familiar theme and routine entertainment. Supported on a double-feature tape by the gangster movie *Guns Don't Argue*.

1966. Directed by Ian Curteis.
Starring Bryant Halliday, Mary Peach, Norman Wooland, Ronald Allen, Derek Farr. Colour.
90 minutes.

Kingston Video

Prom Night

Run-of-the-mill rip-off shocker about a crazed young murderer seeking revenge and turning a school prom celebration into a night of terror. Murders by axe, knife, and so on. Corpses everywhere. Lurid and lousy. Not for watching alone at night.

Box-office rental $6,000,000
Average rental (80) $30,086,027

1980. Directed by Paul Lynch.
Starring Leslie Nielsen, Jamie Lee Curtis, Casey Stevens, Eddie Benton, Antoinette Bower, Michael Tough. Colour.
93 minutes.

Twentieth Century-Fox Video

Prophecy

This is one of those "supposed to be horrific but unintentionally funny" movies that makes you squirm in your seat with embarrassment. It centres on an idealistic doctor and his wife who stumble across the fact that some mercury from a lumber mill is spilling into a river and causing all kinds of ecological freaks – a huge mutant bear, tadpoles the size of otters, hideously deformed infants, and so on. All of which have to be seen to be disbelieved. Hilarious. And yes, the name of the director *is* John Frankenheimer, the man who gave us *The Manchurian Candidate, Seconds* and *Seven Days In May*.

Box-office rental $10,499,000

Average rental (79) $31,964,775

1979. Directed by John Frankenheimer.
Starring Talia Shire, Robert Foxworth, Armand Assante, Richard Dysart, Victoria Racimo. Colour.
102 minutes.

CIC Video

Psycho

Sexy Janet Leigh of the white bra steals 40,000 dollars from her boss and heads off for the weekend to start a new life with lover John Gavin. During her getaway she stops overnight at a lonely motel. It's her first and last mistake, although if she'd have had any sense she would have skipped the joint as soon as nervous young motel owner Anthony Perkins confesses: "A boy's best friend is his mother". Result: a horrific death by stabbing in a shower, arguably Hitchcock's finest ever film and one that miraculously hasn't dated one iota since it was made over twenty years ago. As effective on video as it was on the large screen. Incidentally, the film was based on a novel that, in turn, was based on a newspaper article about a man who kept his mother's body in his house somewhere in Wisconsin!

Box-office rental	$11,200,000
Average rental (60)	$6,787,500
Oscars	Nil
Oscar Nominations (4)	Best Supporting Actress (Leigh); Direction; Photography; Art Direction

1960. Directed by Alfred Hitchcock.
Starring Anthony Perkins, Vera Miles, John Gavin, Janet Leigh, Martin Balsam. Black and White.
109 minutes.

CIC Video

Q

Quadrophenia

Reconstruction of the mid-60s youth movement that allows you to partici-
pate in the adventures of the film's hero – a teenager who gets his kicks
from the Mod life style, driving scooters, raiding chemists' shops for pills,
making love in back alleys, and invading Brighton seafront to enjoy a
pitched battle with the leather-clad Rockers. Turn you on? Well, then this
could be the tape for you. Turn you off? Well, then you will find it all
ugly, noisy, boring and pointless!

1979. Directed by Franc Roddam.
Starring Phil Daniels, Leslie Ash, Philip Davis, Mark Wingett, Raymond
Winstone. Colour.
120 minutes.

Spectrum
(distributed by Polygram)

Quartet

James Ivory chamber movie concerning four expatriates whose lives
intertwine in 1927 Paris: Polish "art dealer" Anthony Higgins who is imprisoned for trafficking; his aimless young wife Isabelle Adjani; and English couple Alan Bates and Maggie Smith, who take her in and both
cosset and take advantage of her whilst her husband is serving his
sentence. From the novel by Jean Rhys and quite splendid to look at with
lovely settings and costume designs. But complicated and talky; needs
concentration and close attention.

1981. Directed by James Ivory.
Starring Isabelle Adjani, Anthony Higgins, Maggie Smith, Alan Bates,
Pierre Clementi, Suzanne Flon. Colour.
101 minutes.

Twentieth Century-Fox Video

The Queen Of Spades

A penniless young Russian, obsessed with making his fortune at the game of faro, attempts to wrest the secret of the winning cards from an aged countess who years before had sold her soul for the same reason. The result, as you might expect, is madness. A curiosity of a film, hampered by inferior sets, a limited budget and some quite atrocious supporting acting, but occasionally, just occasionally, delivering some quite eerie shocks. Edith Evans' countess is a *tour-de-force*. From a story by Pushkin.

1949. Directed by Thorold Dickinson.
Starring Anton Walbrook, Edith Evans, Ronald Howard, Mary Jerrold, Yvonne Mitchell, Anthony Dawson. Black and White.
95 minutes.

Thorn EMI Video

The Quiller Memorandum

Screenplay by Harold Pinter. A cast that includes Alec Guinness, George Sanders and Max von Sydow. Sounds OK. Wrong! This spy thriller set in Germany and focussing on the activities of a neo-Nazi party is pedestrian from the opening reel and entertains only when the afore-mentioned performers are on screen, which isn't often. George Segal is our man in Berlin who survives the usual tortures and assassination attempts. It's difficult to put a finger on what exactly went wrong with this but something most certainly did. Totally lacking in excitement.

1966. Directed by Michael Anderson.
Starring George Segal, Alec Guinness, Max von Sydow, Senta Berger, George Sanders, Robert Helpmann, Robert Flemyng. Colour.
103 minutes.

Rank Video

R

Rabid

A girl becomes the victim of a motor cycle accident and is operated on at a nearby plastic surgery clinic. Unfortunately, during the skin grafts, she develops a form of human rabies and awakes with a thirst for blood. Infection is spread. Everyone runs amok. Panic ensues. For David Cronenberg fans only.

1977. Directed by David Cronenberg.
Starring Marilyn Chambers, Frank Moore, Joe Silver, Howard Ryshpan, Patricia Gage, Susan Roman. Colour.
91 minutes.

Alpha Video
(*distributed by Intervision*)

The Railway Children

"Charming" is not a word that one can use to describe many of today's films. But it definitely applies to this faithful version of E. Nesbit's novel about three Edwardian children who are taken off to Yorkshire by their mother when their father is arrested on a spy charge. Once there, they become known as "The Railway Children" because of their escapades on the railway embankment at the bottom of their garden. Delicious entertainment with just about everyone perfectly cast, although Bernard Cribbins just about takes the honours with his portrait of the enthusiastic railway porter, Perks. Could have been made for the video screen.

1971. Directed by Lionel Jeffries.
Starring Dinah Sheridan, Bernard Cribbins, William Mervyn, Iain Cuthbertson, Jenny Agutter, Sally Thomsett, Gary Warren. Colour.
108 minutes.

Thorn EMI Video

Raise The Titanic

At the moment there are two films available on video on the sinking of the Titanic (*A Night To Remember* and *S.O.S. Titanic*) so it's perhaps only fair that there should be one about bringing the old girl up again. Not through any noble motive, of course, but because of something called byzanium in its hold and byzanium is a rare mineral that can be used in a defence system. So up she comes and what a ponderous and uninspiring bore it all is. If you're looking for action or plot or spectacle try elsewhere. This picture is sadly lacking in all three commodities.

Box-office rental $6,800,000
Average rental (80) $30,086,027

1980. Directed by Jerry Jameson.
Starring Jason Robards, Richard Jordan, David Selby, Anne Archer, Alec Guinness, Norman Bartold. Colour.
114 minutes.

Precision Video

Rattle Of A Simple Man

Likeable little British comedy of the mid-60s with Harry H. Corbett falling in love with attractive prostitute Diane Cilento after he has agreed to spend the night with her to honour a bet. The whole thing takes place during a visit of Manchester football fans to London to see the Cup Final. Not great but not bad either and with a slight edge to the comedy. Worth looking out for.

1964. Directed by Muriel Box.
Starring Harry H. Corbett, Diane Cilento, Thora Hird, Michael Medwin, Charles Dyer. Black and White.
96 minutes.

Thorn EMI Video

Reach For The Sky

This honest and painstaking picture was the number one box-office attraction in 1956 when British audiences had never had it so good and were casting their minds back affectionately to the glories of World War II. Nowadays, "honest and painstaking" equates with routine. Kenneth More does his sincere best as Douglas Bader, the young pilot who lost his limbs in a plane crash and fought his way back on tin legs but the whole thing comes over as two-dimensional. And if ever a story needed to be three-dimensional it is this one.

1956. Directed by Lewis Gilbert.
Starring Kenneth More, Muriel Pavlow, Lyndon Brook, Lee Patterson, Alexander Knox, Dorothy Alison. Black and White.
135 minutes.

Rank Video

Rebecca

A shy young ladies companion marries the handsome master of the Cornish mansion of Manderley, only to find herself haunted by the evil presence of her husband's dead first wife – the Rebecca of the title. And if that isn't enough, there's a nasty sinister housekeeper with lesbian tendencies to add to her problems. If you like Daphne du Maurier's novel you will probably enjoy this, as it's a remarkably faithful rendition – thanks primarily to producer Selznick. And as video viewing it holds up well, not least because of Hitchcock's masterly gothic direction and the mostly British supporting cast.

Oscars (2)	Best Film; Photography
Oscar nominations (9)	Best Actor (Olivier); Actress (Fontaine); Supporting Actress (Anderson); Direction; Screenplay; Editing; Art Direction; Music Score; Special Effects

1940. Directed by Alfred Hitchcock.
Starring Laurence Olivier, Joan Fontaine, George Sanders, Judith Anderson, Nigel Bruce, Gladys Cooper. Black and White.
130 minutes.

Guild Home Video

Rebel Without A Cause

The film with which 50s cult hero James Dean is most identified and now something of a period piece, although back in 1955 it caused something of a stir by daring to suggest that juvenile delinquency existed not only in slum areas (where it had usually been portrayed on screen) but also in the more affluent, middle-class sections of society. Dean, Natalie Wood and Sal Mineo play the three teenagers whose lives the film examines; the perceptive direction is by Nicholas Ray, who spent eight months researching the subject with politicians, judges, youth leaders and juvenile welfare officers. The Warnercolor is inferior and the CinemaScope process hampers video viewing.

Box-office rental	$4,600,000
Average rental (55)	$7,239,750
Oscars	Nil
Oscar nominations (3)	Best Supporting Actor (Mineo); Supporting Actress (Wood); Story

1955. Directed by Nicholas Ray.
Starring James Dean, Natalie Wood, Sal Mineo, Jim Backus, Ann Doran, Dennis Hopper, Nick Adams. Colour.
111 minutes.

Warner Home Video

The Red Shoes

The film that introduced Moira Shearer to the screen as the young ballerina torn between her passion for dancing and her love for her composer husband. A trite story but ballet lovers will revel in it all, connoisseurs of great acting will appreciate the subtlety of Anton Walbrook's ruthless impresario, and those with an eye for technical detail will marvel at the rich Technicolor photography of Jack Cardiff. In short, a "must buy" on just about every count and an enduring British classic. Rich entertainment, flawlessly executed by Powell and Pressburger.

Box-office rental	$5,000,000
Average rental (48)	$3,956,250
Oscars (2)	Best Art Direction; Music Score
Oscar nominations (3)	Best Film; Motion Picture Story; Editing

1948. Directed by Michael Powell and Emeric Pressburger.
Starring Anton Walbrook, Marius Goring, Moira Shearer, Robert Helpmann, Leonide Massine, Albert Basserman, Ludmilla Tcherina, Esmond
Knight. Colour.
134 minutes.

Rank Video

Repulsion

The mental crack-up of a human being is hardly the subject for uplifting
entertainment. But this story of the descent into madness of a beautiful
young Belgian girl (Catherine Deneuve) living in a seedy flat in Earls
Court is such riveting cinema (and now video) that you can't keep your
eyes off the screen for a minute. Cracks in walls, eerie sounds, a reflection
of a man in a mirror, an imagined rape, are some of the ingredients. It
sounds like scores of other films in this book. But it isn't. This is a work
of art. The "repulsion" of the title comes from the girl's loathing of sex-
uality. Raw, intense; beware a dreadful murder sequence with a razor.

1965. Directed by Roman Polanski.
Starring Catherine Deneuve, Ian Hendry, John Fraser, Patrick Wymark,
Yvonne Furneaux, Renee Houston, Helen Fraser. Black and White.
105 minutes.

Zodiac Video
(*distributed by Videomedia*)

The Restless Breed

Western made when Twentieth Century-Fox didn't realise that Anne
Bancroft had any acting ability. She plays a half-breed Indian girl who
wins the love of Scott Brady, son of a secret service agent and out to get
his father's killer. Utter tosh! No wonder Miss Bancroft went back to
Broadway!

1957. Directed by Allan Dwan.

Starring Scott Brady, Anne Bancroft, Jim Davis, Scott Marlowe, Evelyn Rudie. Colour.
85 minutes.

Intervision

Return Of The Bad Men

Legendary lawman Randolph Scott versus a gang of notorious outlaws including The Youngers, The Daltons and Billy The Kid in Badman's Territory. Par for the course for a Randolph Scott 40s Western, which isn't saying much. On the same bill with the granite-faced Mr. Scott: *A Girl In Every Port*.

1948. Directed by Ray Enright.
Starring Randolph Scott, Robert Ryan, Anne Jeffreys, George "Gabby" Hayes, Jacqueline White, Steve Brodie. Black and White.
90 minutes.

Kingston Video

The Return Of The Pink Panther

The film that marked Peter Sellers' return as the accident-prone Inspector Clouseau; a delicious mixture of farce, slapstick and satire in which the clumsy French cop is once again on the trail of the Pink Panther diamond when it is stolen from a Lugash museum. And that means having a personal duel with a revolving door, donning numerous disguises, driving into a swimming pool twice, fighting a losing battle with a door bell and shouting "Follow that car" to a taxi driver who immediately sets off in pursuit – but on foot! Marvellous animated credit sequence by Richard Williams, admirable support from Herbert Lom as Sellers' gibbering superior, who finishes up in a straitjacket in a padded cell.

Box-office rental	$20,122,000
Average rental (75)	$27,300,250

1975. Directed by Blake Edwards.
Starring Peter Sellers, Christopher Plummer, Catherine Schell, Herbert Lom, Peter Arne, Peter Jeffrey, Gregoire Aslan. Colour.
113 minutes.

Precision Video

Revenge Is My Destiny ★

Thriller set in Miami where Vietnam war veteran Chris Robinson begins a search for his missing wife and finds himself up against a Nazi mastermind. An uninspiring 1971 movie that makes up a three-hour tape with the Western *Tension At Table Rock*.

1971. Directed by Joseph Adler.
Starring Chris Robinson, Sidney Blackmer, Elisa Ingram, Joe E. Ross. Colour.
86 minutes.

Kingston Video

Revenge Of The Pink Panther ★

There comes a moment in any series of films when it becomes apparent that everyone connected with it has run out of ideas. That point is reached in this excuse for a movie, in which a gangster band decide to eliminate Inspector Clouseau once and for all. Neither Peter Sellers, who dons a variety of crude disguises, nor director Blake Edwards can do anything to make this remotely interesting. There are, inevitably, a few laughs and one or two nice little scenes that pay homage to Laurel and Hardy, but generally this is a movie searching desperately for a story and never finding it. Herbert Lom's Dreyfus is reduced to a few guest appearances during which he passes out every time he spies Sellers. Poor!

Box-office rental	$25,000,000
Average rental (78)	$39,443,850

1978. Directed by Blake Edwards.

Starring Peter Sellers, Herbert Lom, Dyan Cannon, Robert Webber, Burt Kwouk, Paul Stewart. Colour.
100 minutes.

Intervision

The Riddle Of The Sands

A young Englishman enjoying a sailing holiday off the North Sea coast of Germany encounters a mysterious German yachtsman and his beautiful daughter and then finds an attempt is made on his life. What's afoot? Call Carruthers of the FO, that's what, for our hero smells spies and dirty work. A routine and rather mundane version of Erskine Childers' 1903 classic that lacks any real zip or excitement and, if truth be told, was made some thirty years too late. The 40s was the time for this kind of movie, not the 70s.

1979. Directed by Tony Maylam.
Starring Michael York, Jenny Agutter, Simon MacCorkindale, Alan Badel, Jurgen Andersen. Colour.
102 minutes.

Rank Video

Riding High

Just the thing for a quiet night in with roaring motor cycles, music by Dire Straits, Chic, Boomtown Rats, etc and a story of a young motor cycle messenger who challenges the status of a champion stunt rider by agreeing to jump at the infamous Devil's Leap. Stuntman Eddie Kidd has the lead; Irene Handl (Eddie's eccentric gran) is the best thing in an otherwise forgettable movie.

1981. Directed by Ross Cramer.
Starring Eddie Kidd, Irene Handl, Murray Salem, Marella Oppenheim, Bill Mitchell. Colour.
96 minutes.

Picture Time Video
(distributed by VCL)

Ring Of Bright Water

A London civil servant chucks his job and takes his pet otter to the Scottish Highlands so that the animal can enjoy more hospitable surroundings. This type of "entertainment" movie is usually frowned upon by serious critics but forget them and their kind. This is a very pleasant way of spending a couple of hours and is excellent video value for the family. Bill Travers and Virginia McKenna do their best to out-act the otter but they're on a hiding to nothing! Based on the autobiographical book by Gavin Maxwell.

1969. Directed by Jack Couffer.
Starring Bill Travers, Virginia McKenna, Peter Jeffrey, Roddy McMillan, Jameson Clark. Colour.
107 minutes.

Guild Home Video

Rio Bravo

Even though this one has been seen a countless number of times on TV it still bears watching, which makes it great video value. Director Howard Hawks brings together sheriff John Wayne, alcoholic deputy Dean Martin, crippled old-timer Walter Brennan and young gunslinger Ricky Nelson for the sole purpose of preventing a rancher and his gang from rescuing one of their number being held in jail. That's about it really, other than to say that it's set in a small, isolated Texas town and that long-legged Angie Dickinson is in there somewhere helping out on the side of law and order. It all takes 141 minutes, although it seems like half that length. A lovely old-fashioned Western, the like of which they don't make any more and probably never will again.

Box-office rental	$5,750,000
Average rental (59)	$8,360,350

1959. Directed by Howard Hawks.
Starring John Wayne, Dean Martin, Ricky Nelson, Angie Dickinson, Walter Brennan, Ward Bond, John Russell. Colour.
141 minutes.

Warner Home Video

Rio Lobo

Howard Hawks rings the changes yet again on his *Rio Bravo/El Dorado* theme with John Wayne (who else?) as a former Union colonel being joined by two young Confederates in his battle against wartime traitor Victor French. It all worked so beautifully in *Rio Bravo* and, to a lesser extent, in *El Dorado*, but third time round it seems a bit too familiar and also a bit stale. Assets are the Hawksian humour, a well-staged hijacking of a train and a cameo from Jack Elam as a half-crazy old rancher.

Box-office rental	$4,250,000
Average rental (70)	$16,881,800

1970. Directed by Howard Hawks.
Starring John Wayne, Jorge Rivero, Jennifer O'Neill, Jack Elam, Victor French, Chris Mitchum. Colour.
114 minutes.

MGM/CBS Home Video

Rise And Fall Of Idi Amin

Unmemorable piece of film-making about an unmemorable character that leaves you asking after 100 minutes: "Was it all worthwhile?" The answer is no. The only way you can present a true portrait of a character such as Amin so shortly after his rule is by documentary techniques. This one covers the events from 1971, when Amin took power, to when he was toppled by invading Tanzanian troops in 1978. Joseph Olita offers a physically believable portrayal of Amin. Other real life characters are also featured, including British academic Denis Hills, who plays himself.

1980. Directed by Sharad Patel.
Starring Joseph Olita, Geoffrey Keen, Denis Hills, Leonard Trolley, Andre Maranne, Diane Mercer, Tony Sibbald, Thomas Baptiste. Colour.
101 minutes.

VIPCO

The Rise And Rise Of Casanova ★

Or the sad decline of the career of Tony Curtis, who here not only has to appear as the legendary lover Giacomo Casanova, but also as his double and in one scene, in drag. Marisa Berenson, Marisa Mell, Sylvia Koscina and Britt Ekland are among his conquests and if you are enamoured with any one of these ladies, the expense of the tape might be worthwhile. But be warned. The screenplay includes such lines as: "This is the most fun I've had since my vibrator got stuck!"

1977. Directed by Francois Legrand.
Starring Tony Curtis, Marisa Berenson, Hugh Griffith, Marisa Mell, Britt Ekland, Jean Lefebvre, Andrea Ferreole, Sylvia Koscina. Colour.
101 minutes.

Precision Video

Rising Damp

The inevitable movie version of the TV series, with Leonard Rossiter recreating his role of Rigsby, landlord of a London boarding house, and Frances de la Tour doing likewise as the passionate but lofty tenant Miss Jones. A newcomer to the scene is the talented Denholm Elliott as an upper-class con man, but with second-rate material such as this even he can't lift the proceedings above the mundane.

1980. Directed by Joe McGrath.
Starring Leonard Rossiter, Frances de la Tour, Don Warrington, Christopher Strauli, Denholm Elliott. Colour.
98 minutes.

Precision Video

Roadblock

Insurance investigator Charles McGraw turns to a life of crime in order to keep his wife-to-be in the style to which she's accustomed. Disaster for McGraw, of course. Not so for the viewer, for this modest and fatalistic little thriller is infinitely more enjoyable than *Back To Bataan*, the movie it supports on a double-feature tape.

1951. Directed by Harold Daniels.
Starring Charles McGraw, Joan Dixon, Lowell Gilmore, Louis Jean Heydt, Milburn Stone. Black and White.
73 minutes.

Kingston Video

Robbery

A version of The Great Train Robbery, with Stanley Baker as the criminal mastermind who brings together a specialist gang of crooks to hijack a night train carrying three million pounds worth of banknotes from Glasgow to London. Directed by Peter Yates in 1967 when British movies were still efficient and well made, and boasting a supercharged car chase that is very nearly as exciting as the one Yates went on to film in San Francisco for *Bullitt*. 114 minutes in length, but it never flags. A U-certificate in the cinemas, so acceptable to all the family.

1967. Directed by Peter Yates.
Starring Stanley Baker, James Booth, Frank Finlay, Joanna Pettet, Barry Foster, William Marlowe, George Sewell. Colour.
114 minutes.

Twentieth Century-Fox Video

The Robe

Richard Burton as the centurion in charge of Christ's robe at the Crucifixion; Jean Simmons as the inevitable Christian girl who teaches him to mend his ways; Victor Mature as a devoted slave ... yes, it all takes a bit of believing, but it *was* the biggie in 1953 when TV forced the movies to widen their screens and opt for more spectacular entertainment. Now the wheel has come full circle and the film is available on video. And naturally the small screen has trouble getting it all in. Hollywood gave it a couple of Oscars, although it didn't really deserve them; Jay Robinson provides the laughs with an over-the-top performance as Caligula.

Box-office rental	$17,500,000
Average rental (53)	$6,098,850
Oscars (2)	Best Art Direction; Costume Design
Oscar nominations (3)	Best Picture; Actor (Burton); Photography

1953. Directed by Henry Koster.
Starring Richard Burton, Jean Simmons, Victor Mature, Michael Rennie, Richard Boone, Dawn Addams, Dean Jagger, Jay Robinson. Colour.
135 minutes.

Twentieth Century-Fox Video

Rocky

Can amiable, slightly dumb boxer Rocky Balboa (Sylvester Stallone) take on and beat sleek world heavyweight champion Apollo Creed when the leading contender is injured and Creed throws out the challenge as a gimmick? It takes 119 minutes to find out, but the two hours are well spent, for this is a Cinderella-type fairy story that gives vent to the theme that just occasionally, the small no-hoper can come through and topple the odds. John Avildsen directs with a commendable lack of flashy technique and the final punch-up is quite a battle. Talia Shire plays Rocky's shy girlfriend, veteran Burgess Meredith his trainer. Made in 28 days for under a million dollars.

Box-office rental	$55,892,428
Average rental (76)	$22,752,350
Oscars (3)	Best Film; Direction; Editing
Oscar nominations (7)	Best Actor (Stallone); Actress (Shire); Supporting Actor (Meredith); Supporting Actor (Young); Screenplay; Sound; Song ("Gonna Fly Now")

1976. Directed by John G. Avildsen.
Starring Sylvester Stallone, Talia Shire, Burt Young, Carl Weathers, Burgess Meredith, Thayer David. Colour.
119 minutes.

Intervision

Rocky II

Here we go again! Can Rocky Balboa take on and beat sleek world heavyweight champion Apollo Creed in a rematch? Believe it or not, it takes exactly the same number of minutes to find out, although this time the going is a bit harder, for the movie covers much the same ground as part one and ranks as more of a remake than a sequel. The same cast reappears, the same slugging boxing match (a more preposterous Round 15 would be hard to find) brings everything to a close. Several points lower than *Rocky* but if you liked the first movie you'll almost certainly like this one. Sylvester Stallone himself directs. 2½ rating.

Box-office rental $43,049,274
Average rental (79) $31,964,775

1979. Directed by Sylvester Stallone.
Starring Sylvester Stallone, Talia Shire, Burt Young, Carl Weathers, Burgess Meredith. Colour.
119 minutes.

Intervision

Rollerball

A view of society in the year 2018 when poverty, sickness and war have all been eliminated and the world is run by an international team of managerial executives. Rollerball, a violent spectator sport, is the one opportunity for the population to unleash its latent violence. Everything is as it should be, then one man defies the system ... Several million dollars went into the making of this film, although just where the money went is difficult to say. What finally emerges is a spurious movie that tries to be philosophical, finds it has nothing to say and then simply wallows in the violence of its horrific climax. Only redeeming feature: Ralph Richardson, who is allowed a few moments of humour as a dotty librarian.

Box-office rental $9,050,208
Average rental (75) $27,300,250

1975. Directed by Norman Jewison.

Starring James Caan, John Houseman, Maud Adams, John Beck, Moses Gunn, Pamela Hensley, Barbara Trentham, Ralph Richardson, Shane Rimmer. Colour.
125 minutes.

Intervision

The Romantic Englishwoman ★★

Comedy-drama centring on a triangular relationship between novelist Michael Caine, wife Glenda Jackson and young German gigolo Helmut Berger, with whom Miss Jackson has fallen in love and who arrives at her home as a house guest – at the invitation of hubby Caine! Stylish and quite watchable as it unreels, although a bit difficult to fathom once it's over. OK if you're in a thinking mood, a bit irritating if you're not. Based on the novel by Thomas Wiseman.

1975. Directed by Joseph Losey.
Starring Glenda Jackson, Michael Caine, Helmut Berger, Marcus Richardson, Kate Nelligan, Rene Kolldehof, Michael Lonsdale. Colour.
116 minutes.

Picture Time Video
(*distributed by VCL*)

Room At The Top

Or, how to make it in one bounce by laying a rich industrialist's daughter, making her pregnant and then landing a top job in father-in-law's firm once the wedding celebrations are out of the way. A watershed British movie of the late 50s, now terribly creaky and old-fashioned, although the craft with which it was made still holds it in good stead. The minor mood of Britain during the period. The film's one major flaw is Laurence Harvey's clumsy performance as the working class hero; its greatest asset is Simone Signoret as the aged and tragic mistress he discards on the way to the top. Shot in and around Bradford.

Oscars (2)	Best Actress (Signoret); Screenplay
Oscar nominations (4)	Best Film; Actor (Harvey); Supporting Actress (Baddeley); Direction

1959. Directed by Jack Clayton.
Starring Simone Signoret, Laurence Harvey, Heather Sears, Donald Wolfit, Donald Houston, Hermione Baddeley.
117 minutes.

Twentieth Century-Fox Video

The Rose

If you're a Bette Midler fan, a *devotee* of hard rock, or you like your screenplays littered liberally with four-letter words then this one might hold out some attractions. If not, stay away, for this story of the decline – through drink and drugs – of a 60s rock star hardly qualifies as ideal family entertainment. The film is modelled closely on the career of the late Janis Joplin. Fine acting from Midler but very, very downbeat. The deafening rock score makes it unsuitable for migraine sufferers.

Box-office rental	$22,620,000
Average rental (79)	$31,964,775
Oscars	Nil
Oscar nominations (4)	Best Actress (Midler); Supporting Actor (Forrest); Editing; Sound

1979. Directed by Mark Rydell.
Starring Bette Midler, Alan Bates, Frederic Forrest, Harry Dean Stanton, Barry Primus, David Keith, Sandra McCabe. Colour.
134 minutes.

Twentieth Century-Fox Video

Roseland

Three stories, each merging and each set against the background of a different dance at the world-famous dance hall in New York. Genteel widow Teresa Wright meets coarse widower Lou Jacobi during "The Waltz"; Geraldine Chaplin is caught up in a romantic triangle in "The Hustle"; and Lilia Skala rebels against the physical limitations of old age in "The Peabody". Multi-storied themes are never easy to weave into a satisfactory whole but James Ivory succeeds admirably with this unique movie. Leisurely, interesting video.

1977. Directed by James Ivory.
Starring Geraldine Chaplin, Joan Copeland, Don De Natele, Helen Gallagher, Lou Jacobi, Conrad Janis, Lilia Skala, David Thomas, Christopher Walken, Teresa Wright. Colour.
104 minutes.

Home Video Productions

Roustabout

Minor Elvis Presley vehicle with Elvis as an embittered orphan who earns his living as a singer-guitarist and helps Barbara Stanwyck's struggling carnival become a successful money-making operation. Somewhat limp and with not even a hit Presley number among the eleven songs to help it along. Pleasant colour although that's a minor attribute.

1964. Directed by John Rich.
Starring Elvis Presley, Barbara Stanwyck, Leif Erickson, Joan Freeman, Sue Ann Langdon. Colour.
101 minutes.

Twentieth Century-Fox Video

Ruby Gentry

A gal from the wrong side of the tracks causes problems for the inhabitants of a class-conscious North Carolina town. Torrid, small-town melodrama with Jennifer Jones in the title role and Charlton Heston and Karl Malden as the men she enslaves. It all finishes up rather muckily in a swamp. Highlight for male viewers: Miss Jones, clad in tight-fitting sweater and jeans, silhouetted in a lighted doorway. Good Heinz Roemheld music score.

1952. Directed by King Vidor.
Starring Jennifer Jones, Charlton Heston, Karl Malden, Tom Tully, Bernard Phillips. Black and White.
82 minutes.

Guild Home Video

The Runner Stumbles

Small town American priest Dick Van Dyke shows rather too much affection for a pretty young nun, becomes the target of gossipmongers and is eventually accused of the nun's murder. The offbeat casting of Van Dyke can't compensate for the fact that this is very slow going indeed and frequently dull video fare. Kathleen Quinlan adds a few bright *Sound Of Music*-type spots as the nun but I'm afraid it's not only the runner that stumbles; it's the movie itself. Set in the 20s; based on the Broadway play by Milan Stitt.

1979. Directed by Stanley Kramer.
Starring Dick Van Dyke, Kathleen Quinlan, Maureen Stapleton, Ray Bolger, Tammy Grimes, Beau Bridges. Colour.
110 minutes.

Guild Home Video

Run Of The Arrow

Very unusual (even now) Western by Sam Fuller about a Confederate soldier who, sickened by the violence of the Civil War, opts out of the white man's world and goes to live among the Sioux Indians. But when, eventually, the Sioux find themselves persecuted by the cavalry, he finds it difficult to decide where his loyalties truly lie. Compelling, thoughtful, interesting and very watchable and well ahead of its time. Shares a superior double-bill video tape with *Cry Danger*.

1957. Directed by Samuel Fuller.
Starring Rod Steiger, Brian Keith, Sarita Montiel, Ralph Meeker, Charles Bronson. Colour.
86 minutes.

Kingston Video

Ruthless

Can nasty financier Zachary Scott reach the top in his relentless pursuit of wealth and power? The answer is "yes", but not before he has destroyed the lives of most of those around him. Sydney Greenstreet as a Southern tycoon gets his own back by taking Scott with him during a death-by-drowning climax. Well-made, polished thriller.

1948. Directed by Edgar G. Ulmer.
Starring Zachary Scott, Louis Hayward, Diana Lynn, Sydney Greenstreet, Lucille Bremer, Martha Vickers, Raymond Burr. Black and White.
104 minutes.

Intervision

S

Sabotage

Disappointing Hitchcock thriller tracing the attempts of master saboteur Oscar Homolka and his gang of anarchist agitators to destroy London. But even if it's substandard Hitchcock, there are still the inevitable moments of suspense – notably a murder scene played in silence in which Sylvia Sidney kills her husband with a knife, and when a young boy unknowingly carries a time bomb across London. Adapted from Joseph Conrad's *The Secret Agent*.

1936. Directed by Alfred Hitchcock.

Starring Oscar Homolka, Sylvia Sidney, John Loder, Desmond Tester, Joyce Barbour, Matthew Boulton. Black and White.
76 minutes.

Rank Video

The Sailor Who Fell From Grace With The Sea ★★

Disturbing mixture of love, horror, passion and youthful evil in which the son of a young widow decides to put an end to the love affair between his mother and an American sailor. Lovely scenery and coastal locations, something of an acquired taste and quite erotic at times. The disquieting climax has the boy and his gang borrowing knives, ropes and surgical instruments and embarking on the ritual murder of the seaman. You don't see anything. The inference as to what is going on (filmed in long shot) is enough. From the Japanese novel by Yukio Mishima.

Box-office rental $7,000,000
Average rental (76) $22,752,350

1976. Directed by Lewis John Carlino.
Starring Sarah Miles, Kris Kristofferson, Jonathan Kahn, Margo Cunningham, Earl Rhodes, Paul Tropea. Colour.
105 minutes.

Twentieth Century-Fox Video

Saludos Amigos ★★

43-minute Walt Disney opus made during World War II as part of the United States' good neighbour policy towards South America. The movie pivots around the adventures of Donald Duck, who meets up with a then new Disney character, a parrot named Joe Carioca. Part travelogue, part cartoon, the film takes in the Carnival in Costa Rica and includes the songs "Brazil" and "Tico Tico". Goofy also makes an appearance.

| Oscars | Nil |
| Oscar nominations (3) | Best Sound Recording; Song ("Saludos Amigos"); Scoring Of A Musical |

1943. Production supervised by Norman Ferguson.
Colour.
43 minutes.

Walt Disney Home Video

The Sand Pebbles

An American gun boat patrols the Yangtse River during the mid-20s. Its mission? To protect American trade and missionary interests in China as the warring Nationalists and Communists battle for power and demand that all foreign powers retreat from Chinese soil. Steve McQueen plays a naval machinist who finds himself aboard the boat and caught up in the events. The parallels with the US involvement in Vietnam are hammered home fairly consistently, especially when someone comes up with the statement: "All these people want is to be left alone. How would you like it if the Chinese had a gun boat on the Mississippi?" Point taken. Very long (over three hours) in the cinema, reduced to under two for video. Spectacular camerawork and action scenes; absorbing for much of its running time. 2½ rating.

Box-office rental	$13,500,000
Average rental (66)	$8,826,100
Oscars	Nil
Oscar nominations (8)	Best Film; Actor (McQueen); Supporting Actor (Mako); Photography; Art Direction; Sound; Editing; Music Score

1966. Directed by Robert Wise.
Starring Steve McQueen, Richard Attenborough, Richard Crenna, Candice Bergen, Mako, Larry Gates. Colour.
110 minutes.

Twentieth Century-Fox Video

Santa Fe Trail

Western saga set in the 1850s, with Errol Flynn and Ronald Reagan (George Armstrong Custer) as two West Point cadets, both after the hand of dewy-eyed Olivia de Havilland and both up against fiery Abolitionist John Brown (Raymond Massey). Well-staged action sequences as one would expect in a Mike Curtiz movie, but the rest of the film looks distinctly naive and two-dimensional by today's standards. Not the best of the Warner studio's Westerns.

1940. Directed by Michael Curtiz.
Starring Errol Flynn, Olivia de Havilland, Raymond Massey, Ronald Reagan, Alan Hale, Van Heflin, Gene Reynolds. Black and White.
110 minutes.

Mountain Video

Satan's Slave

When her parents are killed in a car explosion at her uncle's country mansion, a young woman finds herself caught up in black magic, murder and necromancy, menaced by hooded figures and succumbing to dreams of being sacrificed on an altar. You know the kind of thing. Michael Gough is nasty Uncle Alex!

1976. Directed by Norman J. Warren.
Starring Michael Gough, Martin Potter, Candace Glendenning, Barbara Kellermann, Michael Craze. Colour.
86 minutes.

Intervision

Saturday Night Fever

A young Italian-American (John Travolta) comes alive only on Saturday nights when he is king of his local disco; a young rebel falls to his death while skylarking on a bridge; a teenage Brooklyn gang battles it out with a teenage Puerto Rican gang. In short, many of the stock elements from the teenage protest films of the 50s rolled into one very ordinary musical drama, which sparkles only in its disco scenes. On the big screen and in Dolby Sound these were visually and musically attractive. On video, unfortunately, they are reduced to the mundane and although the music of the Bee Gees is still pleasing to the ear, the end result is no more than average value for money.

Box-office rental	$74,100,000
Average rental (77)	$36,913,348
Oscars	Nil
Oscar nominations (1)	Best Actor (Travolta)

1977. Directed by John Badham.
Starring John Travolta, Karen Lynn Gorney, Barry Miller, Joseph Cali, Paul Pape, Donna Pescow, Bruce Ornstein. Colour.
119 minutes.

CIC Video

Saturn 3

This one might have emerged with honours if designer John Barry, who thought up the idea, had lived to make the film. Sadly, he did not and the result is a bit of a hodge-podge, although not nearly as bad as some critics have suggested. Kirk Douglas and Farrah Fawcett star as a scientist and his beautiful colleague working peacefully on a research station on one of the remote moons of Saturn. But when psychopath Harvey Keitel arrives and starts putting together a giant robot called Hector, their idyllic existence quickly comes to an end. Scary at times; keeps you on the go and the set designs are well thought out.

Box-office rental	$4,900,000
Average rental (80)	$30,086,027

1980. Directed by Stanley Donen.
Starring Farrah Fawcett, Kirk Douglas, Harvey Keitel. Colour.
86 minutes.

Precision Video

Savages

Surrealistic James Ivory movie about ... well, yes, what is it about? It's set in a deserted mansion in which a band of savages make camp, find the house exerting a civilizing influence on them and slowly turning them into twentieth century socialites. Then comes a drowning, orgiastic games, parties and such like before the savages revert back to their primitive selves. Make of it what you will. Luis Bunuel would certainly have made it more entertaining than it appears here!

1972. Directed by James Ivory.
Starring Louis Stadlen, Anne Francine, Thayer David, Susie Blakely, Russ Thacker, Salome Jens, Margaret Brewster. Colour.
106 minutes.

Home Video Productions

Scanners

David Cronenberg gets his name above the title of this movie, which concentrates on a group of people possessed of a rare and unique talent. They can mutilate and destroy at will other human beings. And they can do it by simply using the power of their minds. Not surprisingly, certain underground organizations decide they might be useful as weapons. Hardly cosy fun. A close-up of an exploding head is a highlight. If that's your cup of tea then this is the one for you.

Box-office rental	$6,000,000
Average rental (81)	$32,180,110

1981. Directed by David Cronenberg.
Starring Jennifer O'Neill, Stephen Lack, Patrick McGoohan, Lawrence Dane, Michael Ironside, Adam Ludwig. Colour.
103 minutes.

Guild Home Video

The Scarlet Pimpernel

Adaptation of Baroness Orczy's French Revolution tale about the adventures of The Scarlet Pimpernel (alias Englishman Sir Percy Blakeney) who snatches aristocrats from the shadow of the guillotine and whisks them away to safety. It's a bone of contention that this classic story has never been brought satisfactorily to the screen, but this Alexander Korda version of 1934 is probably the most accomplished. Certainly Leslie Howard is Blakeney to the life. And Raymond Massey also has his moments as the villainous Chauvelin.

1934. Directed by Harold Young.
Starring Leslie Howard, Merle Oberon, Raymond Massey, Nigel Bruce, Bramwell Fletcher, Anthony Bushell, Joan Gardner, Walter Rilla. Black and White.
98 minutes.

Spectrum
(distributed by Polygram)

Scott Of The Antarctic

The British upper lips are stiff long before they get frozen in this honourable, but oh-so-tedious account of Captain Scott's ill-fated 1912 expedition to the South Pole. A little imagination would have made all the difference. Plus factors for video viewing: the magnificent colour photography of the bleak Antarctic wastes and Ralph Vaughan Williams' dramatic music score. John Mills heads the team; Derek Bond plays the heroic Oates, who walked out of his tent and into a blizzard so as not to be a burden to his comrades.

1948. Directed by Charles Frend.
Starring John Mills, James Robertson Justice, Derek Bond, Harold Warrender, Reginald Beckwith, Kenneth More, James McKechnie, John Gregson. Colour.
111 minutes.

Thorn EMI Video

Scum ★

The experiences of three new arrivals at an English Borstal. The guards are sadistic thugs who revel in beating up the inmates; the inmates themselves simply enjoy beating up each other – to the delight of the guards. That's entertainment folks! Or perhaps not. The BBC thought it not really ideal armchair viewing and banned it. As one watches one violent close-up after another one can understand why.

1979. Directed by Alan Clarke.
Starring Ray Winstone, Mick Ford, Julian Firth, John Blundell, Phil Daniels, John Fowler. Colour.
97 minutes.

Picture Time Video
(distributed by VCL)

Sealed Cargo

An apparently abandoned Danish ship is found drifting in the coastal waters off Newfoundland and towed to safety by a well-meaning fisherman. But it's an error of judgment on the fisherman's part, for the ship has a hidden cargo of torpedoes, the captain is a Nazi and the crew are ready to take over the area at a moment's notice. Ingenious and atmospheric little movie, graced by the presence of Claude Rains in top form as the sophisticated Nazi captain. *Best Of The Badmen* makes up a video double-bill.

1951. Directed by Alfred L. Werker.
Starring Dana Andrews, Carla Balenda, Claude Rains, Philip Dorn. Black and White.
90 minutes.

Kingston Video

The Searchers

A John Ford Western that, if anything, seems to have improved with age. It concerns the five-year search by an embittered ex-Confederate soldier (John Wayne) and a half-breed Indian boy (Jeffrey Hunter) for a young white girl kidnapped by Comanche Indians. The film takes a couple of hours to unreel, but they are two of the most rewarding hours you will find on video. Wayne has never been better; the Ford regulars (Ward Bond plays a Texas Ranger who is also a preacher!) do their bit; and the distinctive rock formations of Monument Valley tower majestically over the proceedings. A piece of cinematic poetry.

Box-office rental	$4,900,000
Average rental (56)	$8,814,900

1956. Directed by John Ford.
Starring John Wayne, Natalie Wood, Jeffrey Hunter, Vera Miles, Ward Bond, John Qualen, Olive Carey, Henry Brandon. Colour.
119 minutes.

Warner Home Video

The Sea Wolves

Bring together a couple of stars from *The Guns Of Navarone*, add "James Bond", a handful of well-known British character actors and you should have the recipe for a commercial success. Wrong! You have a creaky old World War II vehicle about a group of army geriatrics who band together and relive past glories, as they knock off a German ship docked in a neutral harbour in Portuguese Goa. The reason the ship has to be knocked over is because its radio transmitter is sending out vital information about British ship movements. The reason the film was made in the first place is unclear, for the end result is distinctly second-rate adventure fare.

1980. Directed by Andrew V. McLaglen.
Starring Gregory Peck, Roger Moore, David Niven, Trevor Howard, Barbara Kellermann, Patrick MacNee, Patrick Allen, Bernard Archard, Martin Benson, Faith Brook, Allan Cuthbertson, Kenneth Griffith. Colour.
122 minutes.

Rank Video

Second Chance

Gambler's moll Linda Darnell, hunted across South America by a ruthless killer, is befriended by an ex-boxer and finds that being on the run has its compensations after all, especially when the friend-in-need is played by Bob Mitchum. The story is strictly routine but the scenery is splendid, and the film is of historic interest in that it was the first RKO movie to be shot in the short-lived 3-D process. On video, unfortunately, it unfolds flat although it's fun trying to imagine the expertly-filmed climax on a dangling cable car coming at you in three dimensions. Available on a double-feature tape with the Western *Great Day In The Morning*.

1953. Directed by Rudolph Mate.
Starring Robert Mitchum, Linda Darnell, Jack Palance, Reginald Sheffield, Roy Roberts. Colour.
81 minutes.

Kingston Video

Second Chorus

Fred Astaire enjoying himself with one of his lesser-known dancing partners, Paulette Goddard, in a tale of two young trumpeters (Astaire and Burgess Meredith) trying to keep their band together as they try for the same gal. Not Astaire's best, but easy going and with an appearance of the Artie Shaw band. Songs include "But I'll Dig It", "Love Of My Life", "I'm Yours" and Shaw's "Swing Concerto".

Oscars	Nil
Oscar nominations (2)	Best Song ("Love Of My Life"); Music Score

1940. Directed by H. C. Potter.
Starring Fred Astaire, Paulette Goddard, Charles Butterworth, Burgess Meredith, Artie Shaw And His Orchestra. Black and White.
83 minutes.

Vintage Classics
(distributed by VCL)

Secret Beyond The Door

Little-known Fritz Lang thriller about newly-married wife Joan Bennett, who discovers that hubby Michael Redgrave is obsessed with murder and has turned his house into a museum of famous homicides. There are some elements of Hitchcock's *Suspicion* and an unbelievable ending, but it's reasonable up until then.

1948. Directed by Fritz Lang.
Starring Joan Bennett, Michael Redgrave, Anne Revere, Barbara O'Neil, Natalie Schaefer, Paul Cavanagh. Black and White.
98 minutes.

Intervision

The Secret Policeman's Ball

Filmed version of the third Amnesty International Charity Comedy Gala staged at Her Majesty's Theatre in London in 1979. Some bright moments, some not so bright. Among the highlights: Rowan Atkinson's solo numbers; the ribaldry of Billy Connolly; and Peter Cook's lampooning of the Jeremy Thorpe trial. But that's only a personal selection. If your humour lies in other directions there are plenty of other contributors (see below).

1980. Directed by Roger Graef.
Starring John Cleese, Peter Cook, Clive James, Eleanor Bron, Pete Townshend, Rowan Atkinson, John Williams, Billy Connolly, Tom Robinson, Michael Palin, Terry Jones, Ken Campbell. Colour.
94 minutes.

Hokushin

The Seduction Of Joe Tynan ★

Liberal senator Alan Alda comes face to face with his conscience when he is asked by his mentor to endorse a racist right-wing candidate for the Supreme Court. He also has to decide whether to stay with loyal wife Barbara Harris or shack up permanently with lovely lawyer mistress

Meryl Streep. Very slow-going, practically static. Another director might have made something out of the events but as it stands this is dullsville. Alda also penned the screenplay.

Box-office rental	$11,405,000
Average rental (79)	$31,964,775

1979. Directed by Jerry Schatzberg.
Starring Alan Alda, Barbara Harris, Meryl Streep, Rip Torn, Melvyn Douglas. Colour.
107 minutes.

CIC Video

Semi-Tough

Pro-football players and longtime pals Burt Reynolds and Kris Kristofferson find themselves in competition for the hand of the much-married daughter of the boss of their football team. Reynolds wins by a whisker when he snatches Miss Clayburgh at the wedding ceremony – of Clayburgh and Kristofferson! A semi-success, boisterous and easygoing but not amounting to very much. Robert Preston supplies an entertaining cameo as the Miami football boss "Big Ed".

Box-office rental	$22,807,962
Average rental (77)	$36,913,348

1977. Directed by Michael Ritchie.
Starring Burt Reynolds, Kris Kristofferson, Jill Clayburgh, Robert Preston, Bert Convy, Roger E. Mosley, Lotte Lenya. Colour.
107 minutes.

Intervision

The Servant

Director Joseph Losey and screenwriter Harold Pinter explore the class war by concentrating on one basic situation – the relationship between a spoiled, indolent young aristocrat (James Fox) and his scheming lower-class manservant (Dirk Bogarde), who first cossets, then corrupts and finally usurps his employer as master of the house. Wendy Craig and Sarah Miles are the two women involved in the decadent and malevolent goings-on. An almost totally interior film that lends itself ideally to video viewing. Black entertainment indeed (in some ways reminiscent of the *Faust* legend) but film-making at its best.

1963. Directed by Joseph Losey.
Starring Dirk Bogarde, James Fox, Sarah Miles, Wendy Craig, Catherine Lacey, Richard Vernon. Black and White.
116 minutes.

Thorn EMI Video

The Seven Year Itch

This is the one in which Marilyn Monroe's skirt is blown high above her panties by the blast of the New York subway trains. The scene helped the movie become one of Marilyn's biggest financial successes, although today it seems dated and its jokes, many of which belong to their time, somewhat limited in scope. The whole piece revolves around a middle-aged publishing executive (Tom Ewell) who embarks on an affair with the girl in the upstairs apartment (MM) whilst his wife and son are away on summer vacation. Inferior DeLuxe colour and the CinemaScope process don't help video viewing. 2½ rating.

Box-office rental	$6,000,000
Average rental (55)	$7,239,750

1955. Directed by Billy Wilder.
Starring Marilyn Monroe, Tom Ewell, Evelyn Keyes, Sonny Tufts, Victor Moore, Oscar Homolka, Carolyn Jones. Colour.
105 minutes.

Twentieth Century-Fox Video

Shakespeare Wallah

The experiences of a poverty-ridden troupe of English actors as they travel across India scratching a living by bringing Shakespeare to the country's unenthusiastic provinces. A leisurely film that paints an interesting picture of India at a time when she was breaking away from British ideas, but still retaining traces of the old imperial rule. More a film of atmosphere and mood than content, it is quite fascinating if you're in the right mood. If you're not, you might find it hard going.

1965. Directed by James Ivory.
Starring Felicity Kendal, Shashi Kapoor, Geoffrey Kendal, Laura Liddell, Madhur Jaffrey, Utpal Dutt, Jim Tytler. Black and White.
115 minutes.

Home Video Productions

Shall We Dance

There was mention at the time this movie was made that Astaire and Rogers were on the downward slide, but there's not much evidence of it in retrospect. There's the usual flimsy plot – Russian ballet star Fred falls for famous hotcha dancer Ginger – and the usual outstanding score, this time by George Gershwin, whose contributions include "They Can't Take That Away From Me" and "Let's Call The Whole Thing Off", roller-skated by Astaire and Rogers against a Central Park setting.

Oscars	Nil
Oscar nominations (1)	Best Song ("They Can't Take That Away From Me")

1937. Directed by Mark Sandrich.
Starring Fred Astaire, Ginger Rogers, Edward Everett Horton, Eric Blore, Jerome Cowan. Black and White.
116 minutes.

Thorn EMI Video

Shane

For many, the greatest Western of them all and one that holds up remarkably well, as Alan Ladd rides once again into that little Wyoming
valley and guns down the baddies, led by greedy cattleman Emile Meyer
and treacherous gunfighter Jack Palance. A leisurely film, made with
much care and affection and boasting colour locations the like of which
have rarely been seen since. Shane's climactic ride into town is still a
stunner, and watch out for a gunfight photographed against the background of a distant storm. Almost thirty years old and worth every penny
of the asking price.

Box-office rental	$9,000,000
Average rental (53)	$6,098,850
Oscars (1)	Best Photography
Oscar nominations (5)	Best Film; Supporting Actor (Palance); Supporting Actor (de Wilde); Direction; Screenplay

1953. Directed by George Stevens.
Starring Alan Ladd, Jean Arthur, Van Heflin, Jack Palance, Brandon de
Wilde, Edgar Buchanan, Elisha Cook Jr. Colour.
116 minutes.

CIC Video

The Shape Of Things To Come ★

A long, long way from H. G. Wells. In fact, it starts some fifty years after
Wells' story ended and has something to do with a would-be-dictator of
the galaxy trying to take over a Moon colony. It's all really just an excuse
to make another science fiction fantasy. You could do worse. Can't see
how!

1979. Directed by George McCowan.
Starring Jack Palance, Carol Lynley, Barry Morse, John Ireland, Nicholas
Campbell. Colour.
98 minutes.

Intervision

Sherlock Holmes And The Voice Of Terror ★★

Holmes and Watson put an end to Nazi saboteurs operating in Britain and reveal the identity of the man behind a series of frightening radio broadcasts which foretell disaster. The first of the twelve double-feature Sherlock Holmes movies made by Universal in the 40s; updated to the war period, but enjoyable nonetheless, thanks to the icy calm of Mr. Rathbone and the bluff Nigel Bruce. Supports *The Adventures Of Sherlock Holmes* on a double-feature video tape.

1942. Directed by John Rawlins.
Starring Basil Rathbone, Nigel Bruce, Evelyn Ankers, Reginald Denny, Henry Daniell, Thomas Gomez, Mary Gordon. Black and White.
65 minutes.

MGM/CBS Home Video

Shivers

A medical researcher experiments by implanting parasites in humans to correct bodily imbalances. The parasites turn out to be a combination of aphrodisiac and venereal disease. When infected, males become raving sex maniacs. Need one go on? Loathsome cinema, thought up and directed by the man responsible for *The Brood*, *Scanners* and other masterpieces! Zero rating.

1974. Directed by David Cronenberg.
Starring Paul Hampton, Joe Silver, Lynn Lowry, Allan Migicovsky, Susan Petrie, Barbara Steele. Colour.
87 minutes.

Alpha Video
(distributed by Intervision)

Shock Corridor

Another very tough Sam Fuller movie about a go-ahead young journalist who sees the chance of a Pulitzer Prize if he can get himself admitted to an asylum where a murder has taken place. When he discovers that the murderer is one of the guards he goes berserk and is kept in the asylum as a catatonic. Ugh! A movie of dubious taste, crude and uncompromising but often highly imaginative. Not for the squeamish.

1963. Directed by Sam Fuller.
Starring Peter Breck, Constance Towers, Gene Evans, James Best, Hari Rhodes. Black and White.
101 minutes.

Video Unlimited

The Shout

The shout in question is a secret and fearsome yell perfected by the Australian aborigines so that it can kill instantly by the density of its sound. One who has learned the secret is asylum inmate Alan Bates, who gets himself mixed up with a composer of electronic music (John Hurt) and more sexily with the composer's wife (Susannah York), before meeting his doom in a thunderstorm. Another "make-of-it-what-you-will" movie jigsaw, a bit bizarre but powerful enough to hold the attention. And quite erotic at times. Set in the West Country. Adapted from a story by Robert Graves.

1978. Directed by Jerzy Skolimowski.
Starring Alan Bates, Susannah York, John Hurt, Robert Stephens, Tim Curry, Julian Hough, Carol Drinkwater. Colour.
86 minutes.

Rank Video

Shout At The Devil

Adventure in World War I Africa, with boozy ivory poacher Lee Marvin and old Etonian Roger Moore teaming up to become permanent thorns in the sides of the Germans. The sadism of German Commissioner Rene Kolldehoff, the beauty of Barbara Parkins and a huge fistfight between the two heroes keep things ticking over until the climax when Messrs Marvin and Moore destroy a camouflaged German battleship hidden away up an African river. Based on the novel by Wilbur Smith and cut to 108 minutes from its original length of 147.

1976. Directed by Peter Hunt.
Starring Lee Marvin, Roger Moore, Barbara Parkins, Ian Holm, Rene Kolldehoff, Gernot Endemann, Karl Michael Vogler. Colour.
108 minutes.

Videomedia

The Silent Partner

Bank cashier Elliott Gould outwits psychopathic robber Christopher Plummer when the latter tries to steal a fortune from his bank disguised as a department store Santa Claus. Mr. Gould, however, has dreams of his own and manages to transfer the money to his briefcase. Then comes double-cross, seduction and finally murder. Not a masterpiece but not half bad either, and a movie that keeps you on the go for much of the time. A nasty murder by Mr. Plummer will make your hair stand on end. 2½ video rating.

1978. Directed by Daryl Duke.
Starring Elliott Gould, Christopher Plummer, Susannah York, Celine Lomez, Michael Kirby, Sean Sullivan. Colour.
105 minutes.

IPC Video

Silver Dream Racer

Can London garage mechanic David Essex and his revolutionary new
motor bike defeat arrogant American golden boy Beau Bridges at the
world 500 cc. Championship at Silverstone? It takes 111 agonizing and
ear-splitting minutes before you find out. If you *want* to find out that is,
for this is surely one of the most inept British movies of recent times,
more like a synopsis on wheels than a movie with flesh and blood
characters. David Essex also composes and sings some of the songs
which are as monotonous as the action that unfolds on screen.

1980. Directed by David Wickes.
Starring David Essex, Beau Bridges, Cristina Raines, Clarke Peters, Harry
H. Corbett. Colour.
111 minutes.

Rank Video

Silver Streak

Comedy-thriller and a train movie with a difference. Mild-mannered hero
Gene Wilder spends as much time off the train as he does on it, as he
encounters first delicious Jill Clayburgh and then a rather less friendly
gang of crooks out to eliminate a distinguished art historian. Some pleasant scenery, daring stunts on train roof tops and a spectacular train crash
at Chicago station help make it all passable entertainment. Miss Clayburgh has the best line. When asked what she does for a living she
replies: "Nothing much. I can't do shorthand. I can't type. I'm a secretary".
2½ rating.

Box-office rental	$30,018,000
Average rental (76)	$22,752,350
Oscars	Nil
Oscar nominations (1)	Best Sound

1976. Directed by Arthur Hiller.
Starring Gene Wilder, Jill Clayburgh, Richard Pryor, Patrick McGoohan,
Ned Beatty, Clifton James, Ray Walston. Colour.
113 minutes.

Twentieth Century-Fox Video

Sinbad And The Eye Of The Tiger

Not the best of the Ray Harryhausen monster flicks with the heroic Sinbad travelling to a sacred shrine guarded by a sabre-tooth tiger, and Margaret Whiting conjuring up demons and transforming a prince into a baboon. Plods a bit at 113 minutes although the monsters will probably hold the kids' attention. Patrick Wayne – son of The Duke – is Sinbad.

Box-office rental	$7,700,000
Average rental (77)	$36,913,348

1977. Directed by Sam Wanamaker.
Starring Patrick Wayne, Taryn Power, Jane Seymour, Margaret Whiting, Patrick Troughton, Kurt Christian. Colour.
113 minutes.

RCA/Columbia International Video

Since You Went Away

Tears all round with this one, a sprawling Selznick tribute to the women who stayed behind and kept the homes going while the men were away during World War II. The picture centres on the experiences of one middle-class American family in the early 40s. Mum is Claudette Colbert, the two daughters are Jennifer Jones and Shirley Temple, the servant (inevitably) is Hattie McDaniel, the lodger is Monty Woolley ... the cast goes on and on in a movie that, although dated, still manages to leave a sizeable lump in the throat. If you think old movies are soft, forget it. If you like 'em, go out and get a copy of this right away. Lovely Max Steiner score. Perfect craftsmanship. Took nearly five million dollars in 1944.

Oscars (1)	Best Music Score
Oscar nominations (8)	Best Film; Actress (Colbert); Supporting Actor (Woolley); Supporting Actress (Jones); Photography; Art Direction; Editing; Special Effects

1944. Directed by John Cromwell.

Starring Claudette Colbert, Jennifer Jones, Joseph Cotten, Shirley Temple, Monty Woolley, Hattie McDaniel, Nazimova, Robert Walker, Lionel Barrymore. Black and White.
172 minutes.

Guild Home Video

Six Gun Gold

Tim Holt B-Western that supports the John Wayne movie *Tycoon* on a double-feature tape. Holt finds himself tracking down a fake marshal who has kidnapped his brother whilst pursuing a gold shipment. Routine stuff.

1942. Directed by David Howard.
Starring Tim Holt, Lane Chandler, Ray Whittey, LeRoy Mason, Jan Clayton. Black and White.
55 minutes.

Kingston Video

Sky Riders

The wife and children of rich American Robert Culp are kidnapped by a group of terrorists, who hide them away in a monastery high up in the Greek mountains. The ransom is five million dollars. How to get them out? Soldier of fortune James Coburn has the answer: a night attack by a team of hang-gliding daredevils. Indifferent.

1976. Directed by Douglas Hickox.
Starring James Coburn, Susannah York, Robert Culp, Charles Aznavour, Werner Pochath, Kenneth Griffith. Colour.
91 minutes.

Twentieth Century-Fox Video

The Sky's The Limit

Ask movie buffs to put together a list of Fred Astaire's dancing partners and they'll usually miss out Joan Leslie, who co-stars with the great man in this pleasant little movie about an Air Force flyer who spends a 10-day leave in New York. Joan dances with Fred in the number "I've Got A Lot In Common With You" but the highspot is the Astaire solo "One For My Baby". Available on the same tape as the Frank Sinatra movie *Step Lively*.

Oscars	Nil
Oscar Nominations (2)	Best Song ("My Shining Hour"); Scoring Of A Musical

1943. Directed by Edward H. Griffith.
Starring Fred Astaire, Joan Leslie, Robert Benchley, Robert Ryan, Elizabeth Patterson. Black and White.
89 minutes.

Kingston Video

Sleuth

A deadly game of cat-and-mouse between upper-class writer of detective stories Laurence Olivier and his wife's lover, lower-class young hairdresser Michael Caine. The setting is an English mansion, a veritable treasure house of games, toys and theatrical props. All are used in the game of trickery. But who is tricking whom? Burglary is part of the scheme of things. So too is murder. You don't know the answer 'til the final reel but it's worth the wait. And beneath the surface there are constant reminders of a class war still prevalent in English society. A civilized thriller with a chilling, unpleasant edge.

Box-office rental	$5,607,000
Average rental (72)	$17,543,950
Oscars	Nil
Oscar nominations (4)	Best Actor (Caine); Actor (Olivier); Direction; Original Music Score

1972. Directed by Joseph L. Mankiewicz.

Starring Laurence Olivier, Michael Caine, Alec Cawthorne, Margo Channing, John Matthews. Colour.
139 minutes.

Twentieth Century-Fox Video

The Slipper And The Rose ★★

The Cinderella fairy tale blown up into a huge 2½ hour musical extravaganza with songs by the Sherman brothers *(Mary Poppins)*, lovely European locations and a cast that includes Gemma Craven as Cinders, Richard Chamberlain as the handsome prince and Margaret Lockwood as the wicked stepmother. Could have done with some trimming but young gals will enjoy its unashamed innocence. Would have been a better bet if the songs had been up to standard.

Oscars	Nil
Oscar nominations (2)	Best Song Score; Best Song ("The Slipper And The Rose Waltz")

1976. Directed by Bryan Forbes.
Starring Richard Chamberlain, Gemma Craven, Annette Crosbie, Edith Evans, Christopher Gable, Michael Hordern, Margaret Lockwood, Kenneth More. Colour.
146 minutes.

Iver Films

Smokey And The Bandit ★★

King of the road trucker Burt Reynolds accepts a challenge to pick up a truckload of beer in Texas and bring it back to Atlanta in 28 hours. Chasing him every inch of the way: sheriff Jackie Gleason, who becomes obsessed with bringing Reynolds to justice when he teams up with his son's runaway bride Sally Field. The easygoing charm of Reynolds just about sees this one through, although the wild car chases and crashes, often brilliantly staged by stuntman Hal Needham, inevitably lose much of their effectiveness on video. The screenplay affords the best lines to

Gleason who finally gives up on his lanky, slow-witted son by exploding: "There is no way that you could come from my loins. First thing I'm going to do when I get home is punch your mamma on the jaw".

Box-office rental	$61,055,000
Average rental (77)	$36,913,348
Oscars	Nil
Oscar nominations (1)	Best Editing

1977. Directed by Hal Needham.
Starring Burt Reynolds, Sally Field, Jackie Gleason, Jerry Reed, Mike Henry. Colour.
96 minutes.

CIC Video

Soft Beds, Hard Battles

Peter Sellers tries out his "man of many faces" routine but even he can't save this dismal farce from hitting rock bottom. The story is about a Paris bordello being used by the Resistance in the fight against the Nazis in World War II. Sellers turns up in seven roles: an elderly French general, Hitler, a Gestapo chief, a Japanese prince, a British major, the President of France and a radio newsreader.

1973. Directed by Roy Boulting.
Starring Peter Sellers, Lila Kedrova, Curt Jurgens, Beatrice Romand, Jenny Hanley, Francoise Pascal, Rula Lenska. Colour.
107 minutes.

Rank Video

Soldier Blue

A run-of-the-mill Western for most of its length – a cavalry private and young woman flee across country after escaping an Indian attack – but one that turns into a movie of horrific proportions during its climax when the US Cavalry massacre Cheyenne men, women and children. The sequence, derived from the real-life incident at Sand Creek in 1864, made this one of the most talked about movies of the early 70s, and was meant to represent a parallel with the dreadful happenings in Vietnam. You need a strong stomach to keep looking; Donald Pleasence intrudes for a brief cameo as a gun-runner named Isaac Q. Cumber.

1970. Directed by Ralph Nelson.
Starring Candice Bergen, Peter Strauss, Donald Pleasence, Bob Carraway, Jorge Rivero, Dana Elcar, John Anderson. Colour.
114 minutes.

Twentieth Century-Fox Video

Somebody Killed Her Husband ★

Disastrous attempt to turn TV superstar Farrah Fawcett-Majors into a star of equivalent status on the big screen. The film sets out to be a comedy drama, with Farrah attempting to track down the killer of her hubby who is found slumped across the kitchen table with a knife in his back. Helping in the search: boyfriend Jeff Bridges. Neil Sedaka sings "Love Keeps Getting Stronger Every Day".

1978. Directed by Lamont Johnson.
Starring Farrah Fawcett-Majors, Jeff Bridges, John Wood, Tammy Grimes, John Glover. Colour.
97 minutes.

Guild Home Video

Son Of Kong

Kong Jr. is many feet shorter than his dad but he's rather more friendly, as he battles cheerfully with sea serpents, dragons and the like in the prehistoric forests of Skull Island. Helen Mack replaces Fay Wray as the lady in distress; Robert Armstrong repeats his role as the adventurer who encountered the mighty Kong in movie number one. But this picture is nowhere near as accomplished as the first film and often comes close to mediocrity. On the same video tape: *You'll Find Out*.

1933. Directed by Ernest B. Schoedsack.
Starring Robert Armstrong, Helen Mack, Victor Wong. Black and White.
70 minutes.

Kingston Video

Son Of Sinbad

Dale Robertson is the son in question – the usual devil-may-care adventurer who is imprisoned by a wicked Caliph but finds help at hand in the form of the legendary forty thieves – all played by harem girls! Vincent Price is the poet Omar Khayyam who accompanies him on his exploits. Rather dismal video fare, even though the skin-and-veil harem scenes with scantily clad girls caused the movie to fall foul of the American censors at the time of its first release. Supported on a 166-minute tape by the Tim Holt Western *Cyclone On Horseback* and the short *Pal's Return*.

1955. Directed by Ted Tetzlaff.
Starring Dale Robertson, Sally Forrest, Lili St. Cyr, Vincent Price, Mari Blanchard, Leon Askin, Jay Novello. Colour.
88 minutes.

Kingston Video

Sons Of The Musketeers

The sons and daughters of the original musketeers prove that loyalty is not dead when they come to the aid of the Queen of France, who suspects Robert Douglas of planning to take over the throne. The dialogue is soggy but the swordplay, organized by Fred Cavens, is scintillating and the appeal of red-haired, green-eyed Maureen O'Hara (as the daughter of Athos) as delightful as ever. Cornel Wilde features as the son of D'Artagnan. The film was shot on many of the original sets left over from Laughton's *Hunchback Of Notre Dame*. Not bad for kids and sharing a video tape with the Japanese sci-fi flick *The Mysterians!*

1952. Directed by Lewis Allen.

Starring Cornel Wilde, Maureen O'Hara, Robert Douglas, Dan O'Herlihy, Alan Hale Jr. Colour.
81 minutes.

Kingston Video

S. O. S. Titanic

Yet another version of the sinking of the poor old Titanic, a ship which has been to the bottom of the cinematic ocean more times than one cares to remember. Even so, the story *does* have drama and to make it dreary and boring demands a certain perversity of talent which the makers of this movie prove they have in abundance. Among those heading for that fateful iceberg: David Janssen (in his last screen role), Cloris Leachman and Captain Harry Andrews. As video entertainment this one doesn't even leave dry dock!

1980. Directed by Billy Hale.
Starring David Janssen, Cloris Leachman, Susan Saint James, David Warner, Ian Holm, Helen Mirren, Harry Andrews. Colour.
102 minutes.

Thorn EMI Video

The Sound Of Music

Julie Andrews as Maria von Trapp, the novice nun who renounces her vows to become governess of the seven von Trapp family in prewar Austria. Too sugary and sweet for most male tastes but there's no denying its durability and as family video entertainment it's difficult to top. The 'Do, Re, Mi' number is a *tour-de-force* of film editing although the opening mountain descent is a bit of a letdown on video. Based on the Broadway musical by Rogers and Hammerstein and eminently repeatable.

Box-office rental	$79,748,000
Average rental (65)	$13,881,050
Oscars (5)	Best Film; Direction; Sound; Editing; Scoring Of A Musical

Oscar nominations (5)	Best Actress (Andrews); Supporting Actress (Wood); Photography; Art Direction; Costume Design

1965. Directed by Robert Wise.
Starring Julie Andrews, Christopher Plummer, Eleanor Parker, Richard Haydn, Peggy Wood. Colour.
174 minutes.

Twentieth Century-Fox Video

Soylent Green

Cautionary, often quite frightening tale of what might happen if corporate enterprise was left to solve the problems of an over-populated world lacking the necessary food to survive. The solution? The Soylent Green of the title, an artificial wafer made from algae and fed as a staple diet to New York's forty million inhabitants. Its real content, however, is much more horrifying – human bodies broken down into food. The year is 2022 but it could be much closer. Charlton Heston is the one who stumbles on the terrifying secret; Edward G. Robinson (in his last film) plays a man who departs this world in a clinic to the strains of Beethoven.

1973. Directed by Richard Fleischer.
Starring Charlton Heston, Leigh Taylor-Young, Edward G. Robinson, Chuck Connors, Joseph Cotten, Brock Peters, Paula Kelly. Colour.
97 minutes.

MGM/CBS Home Video

The Spanish Main

On the face of it, no more than a routine Hollywood pirate adventure but, thanks to the expert hand of director Frank Borzage, a "cut above the average". Paul Henreid and Maureen O'Hara give a good account of themselves in the romantic leads, but the film belongs to Walter Slezak who features as a wicked Spanish viceroy and wanders from scene to scene, clad in silken robes with a monkey on his shoulder, idly dropping such phrases as: "Today, I have matters of state to attend to; papers to sign, people to hang." The movie is supported by three 17-minute shorts: *Motor Maniacs* with Edgar Kennedy, *My Pal* with Ted Donaldson and *Who's Zoo In Africa.*

Oscars	Nil
Oscar nominations (1)	Best Photography

1945. Directed by Frank Borzage.
Starring Paul Henreid, Maureen O'Hara, Binnie Barnes, Walter Slezak, John Emery, Barton MacLane. Colour.
101 minutes.

Kingston Video

Spellbound

This is the one in which a medical orderly bursts into the office of psychiatrist Ingrid Bergman and tells her that one of her patients has just cut his throat. To which she replies: "Is it serious?" After that nothing can really hold credulity, although Hitchcock's gradual unravelling of the mystery surrounding an amnesiac (Gregory Peck), who is convinced he is a murderer, is not without interest, especially in Salvador Dali's ingenious dream sequences. Nostalgic video viewing, not least when Miklos Rozsa's romantic score is going full tilt.

Box-office rental	$4,890,000
Average rental (45)	$4,841,666
Oscars (1)	Best Music Score
Oscar nominations (5)	Best Film; Supporting Actor (Chekhov); Direction; Photography; Special Effects

1945. Directed by Alfred Hitchcock.
Starring Ingrid Bergman, Gregory Peck, Leo G. Carroll, John Emery, Michael Chekhov, Rhonda Fleming. Black and White.
111 minutes.

Guild Home Video

The Spiral Staircase

German director Robert Siodmak pulls out all the stops in this eerie thriller about the activities of a homicidal maniac in a small New England town. The killer's victims are women with physical deformities, and, as Dorothy McGuire is dumb, and a storm is constantly raging outside the old mansion in which she lives, she's obviously next on the list. Shadowy staircases, close-ups of eyes peering through curtains and a murder above a nickelodeon all help to make this interesting late-night viewing, although time has deprived the film of much of its gothic, nightmarish quality. The camerawork of Nicholas Musuraca is still a *tour-de-force,* however. Rating: 2½

Oscars   Nil
Oscar nominations (1)   Best Supporting Actress (Barrymore)

1946. Directed by Robert Siodmak.
Starring Dorothy McGuire, George Brent, Ethel Barrymore, Kent Smith, Rhonda Fleming, Gordon Oliver, Elsa Lanchester, Sara Allgood, Rhys Williams. Black and White.
83 minutes.

Guild Home Video

Split Second

A "will-they, wont-they-make-it" movie – *they* being a group of hostages being held by an escaped killer and his gang in an old mining town in the Nevada desert. Bad enough in any case, but well nigh hopeless when a nuclear explosion is scheduled to take place in the area at 6 a.m. A cliff-hanging tension movie, efficiently directed by Dick Powell. Keith Andes and Alexis Smith are among the luckless hostages; Stephen McNally heads the baddies. Shares an above-average video tape with *Where Danger Lives.*

1953. Directed by Dick Powell.
Starring Stephen McNally, Alexis Smith, Jan Sterling, Keith Andes, Arthur Hunnicutt, Paul Kelly, Richard Egan. Black and White.
85 minutes.

Kingston Video

S. P. Y. S

Comedy-thriller made presumably on the premiss that if you can send up the army unmercifully in *M.A.S.H*, you can do the same to the spy business. Wrong, especially if you do it this way. *M.A.S.H* stars Donald Sutherland and Elliott Gould play a couple of CIA men who find themselves pursued by friend and foe alike when they come into possession of a list of KGB agents working in China. Miserably unfunny!

Box-office rental	$5,205,000
Average rental (74)	$18,456,150

1974. Directed by Irvin Kershner.
Starring Donald Sutherland, Elliott Gould, Zouzou, Joss Ackland, Shane Rimmer. Colour.
87 minutes.

Thorn EMI Video

Stagecoach

You only have to compare this picture with other Westerns of the 30s to realize just how important it was in the development of the *genre*. The trouble is that it is now *so* well known that audiences know every line of dialogue and every horse-fall off by heart, which rather decreases its video value. Still, if you haven't yet seen it, you have many pleasures in store, not least the performance of Thomas Mitchell as a drunken doctor, just one of the passengers travelling by stagecoach from Tonto to Lordsville, a route constantly threatened by bands of marauding Indians. Also along for the ride: Claire Trevor as a floozie with a heart of gold; John Carradine as a suave gambler; Andy Devine as the stagecoach driver; and John Wayne (in the role that made him famous) as The Ringo Kid. Supported on a double feature video tape by the 1946 whodunnit *Deadline At Dawn*.

Oscars (2)	Best Supporting Actor (Mitchell); Music Scoring
Oscar nominations (5)	Best Film; Direction; Photography; Art Direction; Editing

1939. Directed by John Ford.

Starring John Wayne, Claire Trevor, Thomas Mitchell, George Bancroft, Andy Devine, John Carradine, Berton Churchill, Donald Meek. Black and White.
99 minutes.

Kingston Video

Stage Struck

A remake of Katharine Hepburn's 1933 Oscar-winning *Morning Glory* about the rise to Broadway stardom of a young girl from the provinces. The dialogue (by Ruth and Augustus Goetz) sparkles, the direction of Sidney Lumet impresses. The trouble lies in the central performance of Susan Strasberg, who is a long way from being a substitute for Miss Hepburn. Still, the New York atmosphere is well caught and there are pleasing performances by Christopher Plummer (in his screen debut as a young playwright) and Henry Fonda who, as a world-weary producer, has probably the film's best line when he remarks about Miss Strasberg: "She's everything I don't have time for!" The movie shares a double tape with another remake, *The Girl Most Likely.*

1958. Directed by Sidney Lumet.
Starring Henry Fonda, Susan Strasberg, Joan Greenwood, Christopher Plummer, Herbert Marshall. Colour.
95 minutes.

Kingston Video

Starcrash

Space hero and space girlfriend are hired to track down and destroy an evil count who has plans to dominate the Universe. Yes, the same tired old plot, and no better in this mish-mash than when it was first used many moons ago. There are adventures on numerous planets, the inevitable robot and a police chief with a green face. There are also some rather dreadful special effects which are only partly compensated for by the fact that sexy Caroline Munro is seen for much of the time in a black leather bikini.

1979. Directed by Lewis Coates.
Starring Marjoe Gortner, Caroline Munro, Christopher Plummer, David Hasselhoff, Robert Tessier, Joe Spinell. Colour.
91 minutes.

VIPCO

Stardust

David Essex's drifter from *That'll Be The Day* a few years on as the lead singer of a Beatles-like rock group called "The Straycats". Success, however, is short-lived. After a brief spell at the top, he finishes up a recluse in a Spanish castle and dies from a drug overdose. Adam Faith emerges with most honours as the road manager who protests at Essex's death with the words: "Jim, you can't die, I own half of you!" If the theme of *That'll Be The Day* was frustration then that of this sequel is disillusionment. The end result, however, is the same: mediocre video entertainment.

1974. Directed by Michael Apted.
Starring David Essex, Adam Faith, Larry Hagman, Ines Des Longchamps, Rosalind Ayres, Marty Wilde. Colour.
111 minutes.

Thorn EMI Video

A Star Is Born

Third time out for this story of a fading movie actor who falls in love with a younger woman and helps her to the top whilst he rapidly disappears into drunken oblivion. This 1976 update transfers the whole thing to the rock scene, with Kris Kristofferson as the rock star on the way down and Barbra Streisand as the gal on the way up. The trouble is that Kristofferson is much too good to ever appear he's fading and Streisand is so dynamic that you wonder why she wasn't at the top in the first place. To be fully effective this one needs to be played loud, which may not make you terribly popular with the neighbours. Not at its best on video but a big hit in the cinemas in its year of release.

Box-office rental	$37,100,000
Average rental (76)	$22,752,350
Oscars (1)	Best Song ("Evergreen")
Oscar nominations (3)	Best Photography; Sound; Original Song Score

1976. Directed by Frank Pierson.
Starring Barbra Streisand, Kris Kristofferson, Paul Mazursky, Gary Busey, Oliver Clark. Colour.
140 minutes.

Warner Home Video

Star Trek – The Motion Picture ★

A huge malignant force, hidden in a cloud-like formation, heads straight for Earth. Captain Kirk, Mr. Spock and company are called in to investigate. Overblown tosh for nine-tenths of its tedious running time; imaginative only during its last few minutes. The whole thing could well have been told in a 50-minute TV episode of the series. On the cinema screen this one seemed long; on video it seems to go on forever. Mediocre effects.

Box-office rental	$56,000,000
Average rental (79)	$31,964,775
Oscars	Nil
Oscar nominations (3)	Best Art Direction; Music Score; Visual Effects

1979. Directed by Robert Wise.
Starring William Shatner, Leonard Nimoy, DeForest Kelley, Stephen Collins, Persis Khambatta. Colour.
132 minutes.

CIC Video

Steelyard Blues

Busy call-girl Jane Fonda, boyfriend and ex-jailbird Donald Sutherland and a guy called Eagle (Peter Boyle) live in a junkyard and decide to make an old aeroplane flightworthy in order to escape from it all. Sounds a bundle of laughs. Limp revolutionary protest movie, thin on plot and now very dated. Fonda rarely gives a bad performance and she's not bad here, she's just not that good. Nor is the film.

1973. Directed by Alan Myerson.
Starring Jane Fonda, Donald Sutherland, Peter Boyle, Garry Goodrow, Howard Hesseman, John Savage. Colour.
93 minutes.

Warner Home Video

Step Lively

Sinatra in his second starring role as a young country boy, who dreams of becoming a playwright but finds himself more successful in the crooning business, and finishing up saving a musical show from disaster. A remake of the hectic George Abbott Broadway hit *Room Service*, that includes four songs by Jule Styne and Sammy Cahn. Supports the Astaire musical *The Sky's The Limit* on an interesting double feature tape.

Oscars	Nil
Oscar nominations	Best Art Direction

1944. Directed by Tim Whelan.
Starring Frank Sinatra, George Murphy, Adolphe Menjou, Gloria De-Haven, Eugene Pallette, Anne Jeffreys, Walter Slezak. Black and White.
88 minutes.

Kingston Video

Steptoe And Son

Scriptwriters Ray Galton and Alan Simpson take Harold and his dad out of the confined world of the junkyard and the shabby house and send them on honeymoon to Spain when Harold gets married to a nightclub stripper. A crude, mediocre comedy that fails to transmit any of the pathos and warm humour that was so apparent in the long-running TV series. Sub-standard video.

1972. Directed by Cliff Owen.
Starring Wilfrid Brambell, Harry H. Corbett, Carolyn Seymour, Arthur Howard, Victor Maddern. Colour.
98 minutes.

Thorn EMI Video

Stevie

Glenda Jackson in top form as poet Stevie Smith in a straightforward adaptation of the London stage success by Hugh Whitmore. The film scarcely moves outdoors, and for the first twenty minutes (as Jackson frequently addresses the camera) seems as though it is not going to work. But it *does* work, and shortly thereafter has you firmly in its grip, both through the magic of the poetry and the performances of Miss Jackson and Mona Washbourne as the lovable aunt Stevie cares for in their terraced house in Palmers Green. Unusual, surprisingly rewarding video entertainment. Trevor Howard appears from time to time as a kind of male chorus.

1978. Directed by Robert Enders.
Starring Glenda Jackson, Mona Washbourne, Alec McCowen, Trevor Howard, Emma Louise Fox. Colour.
102 minutes.

Home Video Productions

Stiletto

Run-of-the-kill Mafia melodrama about a young playboy assassin (or stiletto man) who decides he wants to quit his bloodthirsty ways. But that's easier said than done, and shortly thereafter he finds himself on the other end of the line and a Mafia target himself. Alex Cord is the luckless hero, Britt Ekland his mistress. A good supporting cast includes Joseph Wiseman as a Mafia chief and John Dehner as a District Attorney, but they can do little with their material, which derives from a novel by Harold Robbins. Filmed in New York and Puerto Rico.

1969. Directed by Bernard Kowalski.
Starring Alex Cord, Britt Ekland, Patrick O'Neal, Joseph Wiseman, Barbara McNair, Roy Scheider, John Dehner. Colour.
98 minutes.

Twentieth Century-Fox Video

The Sting

A picture that was enormously popular back in 1973 – presumably because the public wanted more of the *Butch & Sundance* team – but that now looks exactly what it is: an inflated *soufflé* of a movie about a couple of con men who track down and put the sting on a big-time crook responsible for the death of one of their friends. And it all takes 129 minutes. The setting is Chicago in the mid-30s and the performances of Newman and Redford are more than capable, but this is one that depends on the element of surprise and once seen doesn't bear too much reviewing. Which makes it a dubious video prospect. Murky colour.

Box-office rental	$78,963,000
Average rental (73)	$22,271,150
Oscars (7)	Best Film; Direction; Story & Screenplay; Art Direction; Costume Design; Editing; Adaptation Music Score
Oscar nominations (3)	Best Actor (Redford); Photography; Sound

1973. Directed by George Roy Hill.

Starring Paul Newman, Robert Redford, Robert Shaw, Charles Durning, Ray Walston, Eileen Brennan. Colour.
129 minutes.

CIC Video

Stir Crazy

Whether you like this one or not depends on whether you enjoy the humour of Gene Wilder and Richard Pryor. If you do then you'll find it up to par as the two of them – Wilder, an aspiring playwright, Pryor, an aspiring black actor – wind up in jail serving a 125-year sentence for a bank hold-up they didn't commit. If you *don't* like them, and the evidence is that their humour is more popular on the other side of the Atlantic, then you'll find this a turn-off movie, zany but littered with a profusion of four letter words. A huge commercial success in the USA.

Box-office rental	$58,408,000
Average rental (80)	$30,086,027

1980. Directed by Sidney Poitier.
Starring Gene Wilder, Richard Pryor, George Stanford Brown, Jo Beth Williams, Miguelangel Suarez. Colour.
111 minutes.

RCA/Columbia International Video

Storm Over The Nile

The Four Feathers story under a different title but incorporating the same ingredients of the 1939 version, and even some of the same location sequences. Anthony Steel is coward Harry Faversham in this one; Laurence Harvey goes blind in the desert – still a fine scene. But less distinguished than its predecessor.

1955. Directed by Zoltan Korda and Terence Young.
Starring Anthony Steel, Laurence Harvey, James Robertson Justice, Mary

Ure, Geoffrey Keen, Ronald Lewis, Ian Carmichael, Michael Hordern.
Colour
107 minutes.

Twentieth Century-Fox Video

Stranger On The Third Floor ★★

Psychological melodrama of the low-budget variety about a newspaper
reporter whose circumstantial evidence condemns a boy to death for
murder, but who then has cause to doubt the wisdom of his testimony
when his neighbour is rubbed out in similar fashion. Nasty little maniac
Peter Lorre is at the back of it all. Highly regarded by *devotees* of B-
movies, the picture contains a terrific nightmare sequence and supports
The Thing From Another World on a double feature tape.

1940. Directed by Boris Ingster.
Starring Peter Lorre, John McGuire, Margaret Tallichet, Charles Waldron,
Elisha Cook, Jr. Black and White.
64 minutes.

Kingston Video

Straw Dogs

This one goes by the name of entertainment but was deservedly banned
by many authorities in Britain. A Sam Peckinpah movie, it relates the
misadventures (to put it mildly) that befall an American university graduate and his wife when they visit a village in Cornwall. There's a detailed
rape; a strangulation of a village girl (and a cat); and a vicious house
siege in which five men meet their deaths. It's the type of movie that gets
pages and pages of in-depth discussion in the posh film mags but which,
when you examine it closely, is worthless from first to last. Dustin Hoffman
and Susan George star. Advice: give it a miss.

Box-office rental	$4,000,000
Average rental (71)	$13,465,850
Oscars	Nil

Oscar nominations (1)   Best Music Score

1971. Directed by Sam Peckinpah.
Starring Dustin Hoffman, Susan George, David Warner, Peter Vaughan, T. P. McKenna, Del Henney, Ken Hutchison, Colin Welland. Colour.
118 minutes.

Guild Home Video

Strictly Dynamite

Very ancient (1934) Hollywood B-flick with Jimmy Durante as a temperamental radio star and Mexican fireball Lupe Velez as his bundle of trouble. Shares the same tape with the Sinatra vehicle *Higher and Higher*.

1934. Directed by Elliott Nugent.
Starring Jimmy Durante, Lupe Velez, Norman Foster, William Gargan, Marian Nixon, Eugene Pallette. Black and White.
71 minutes.

Kingston Video

The Stud

Joan Collins sheds her clothes and plunges with gusto into the mood of sister Jackie's best-selling novel about a spoilt millionaire's wife who installs her young lover as manager of a London discotheque. Love in a lift, a Parisian orgy and other erotica fail to compensate for the all-round inadequacy of this dross. A 20-song disco score is another drawback. That Joan Collins is still glorious to look at is small compensation. The sequel, *The Bitch*, is also available on video.

1978. Directed by Quentin Masters.
Starring Joan Collins, Oliver Tobias, Sue Lloyd, Mark Burns, Doug Fisher, Walter Gotell. Colour.
90 minutes.

Brent Walker Video
(distributed by Videospace)

A Study In Terror

Sherlock Holmes' first attempt at uncovering the identity of Jack The Ripper, who knifes his way through several East End prostitutes before meeting his doom. A box of surgical instruments minus a scalpel provides the first clue. Barry Jones (as a duke), John Fraser (as a lord) and Anthony Quayle (as a doctor who owns a Whitechapel clinic) line up as possible suspects. Effective and well made and with an exceptionally strong cast. See also *Murder By Decree*.

1965. Directed by James Hill.
Starring John Neville, Donald Houston, John Fraser, Anthony Quayle, Robert Morley, Barbara Windsor, Georgia Brown, Adrienne Corri, Frank Finlay, Judi Dench, Cecil Parker, Barry Jones, Kay Walsh. Colour.
95 minutes.

Vampix
(distributed by Videomedia)

The Stunt Man

Curiosity of a movie that becomes a kind of Kafka-type nightmare. An on-the-run Vietnam war veteran finds himself replacing a movie stunt man, whose death by drowning he has caused during an accident on a bridge. Thereafter the movie becomes a kind of game. What is truth? What is make-believe? In the end, despite some impressive sequences of stunt men at work, it emerges as a rather meaningless affair. Peter O'Toole dominates the proceedings with a tiresome portrayal of a God-like film director; a great music score by Dominic Frontiere helps you take your mind off the performance.

Oscars	Nil
Oscar nominations (3)	Best Actor (O'Toole); Direction; Screenplay

1980. Directed by Richard Rush.
Starring Peter O'Toole, Barbara Hershey, Steve Railsback, Sharon Farrell, John Garwood. Colour.
130 minutes.

Guild Home Video

Summer Of '42

Leisurely and evocative film about the sexual coming of age of a teenage boy during a golden 40s summer on a holiday island off New England. Corny? Oversentimental? Nostalgic? All these charges have been levelled at this movie but none of them is justified, for the film is possessed of a quiet beauty and a depth of feeling only too rarely found in contemporary movies. Gary Grimes is the 15-year-old adolescent hero; Jennifer O'Neill the young war bride who is the object of his adoration. Reflected in flashback and among the most romantic movies to be found on video. Enhanced considerably by Michel Legrand's lush music score.

Box-office rental	$20,500,000
Average rental (71)	$13,465,850
Oscars (1)	Best Music Score
Oscar nominations (3)	Best Story & Screenplay; Editing; Photography

1971. Directed by Robert Mulligan.
Starring Jennifer O'Neill, Gary Grimes, Jerry Houser, Oliver Conant, Katherine Allentuck. Colour.
102 minutes.

Warner Home Video

Sunday In The Country

Three dangerous bank robbers, on the run from the cops, decide to hole up in rural America. They choose the isolated farmhouse of Ernest Borgnine, and that's a mistake, for old Ernie is far more ruthless than any of 'em and they all get rather more than they bargained for. His granddaughter (home from college for the summer) looks on horrified as she witnesses grandad's brutality. So, I fear, will you if you take time off to glance at this spurious exercise in sadism and gratuitous violence. Michael J. Pollard from *Bonnie And Clyde* appears in similar vein as one of the gangsters.

1974. Directed by John Trent.

Starring Ernest Borgnine, Michael J. Pollard, Hollis McLaren, Louis Zorich, Cec Linder. Colour.
92 minutes.

Intervision

Superman

"You'll Believe A Man Can Fly" claimed the advertisements for this movie when it was released in the cinemas. Well, on video he flies just 23 inches, depending of course on the size of your television set. And that's not a great deal to get excited about in a movie so dependent on size and spectacle and special effects. Christopher Reeve plays the flying man of steel who works as a mild-mannered newspaper reporter by day; Margot Kidder is the gal who flies with him romantically above the lights of New York; and Gene Hackman is the megalomaniac bad guy. Goodish entertainment for the kids but one suspects that even they will be disappointed with the size of superguy's achievements on video.

Box-office rental	$82,500,000
Average rental (78)	$39,443,850
Oscars (1)	Best Visual Effects
Oscar nominations (3)	Best Editing; Sound; Music Score

1978. Directed by Richard Donner.
Starring Christopher Reeve, Margot Kidder, Marlon Brando, Gene Hackman, Ned Beatty, Jackie Cooper, Glenn Ford, Valerie Perrine. Colour.
143 minutes.

Warner Home Video

Suppose They Gave A War And Nobody Came?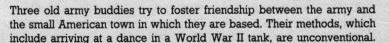

Three old army buddies try to foster friendship between the army and the small American town in which they are based. Their methods, which include arriving at a dance in a World War II tank, are unconventional.

Not so the movie, which is as ordinary as they come and one of those farce/satire mixtures which doesn't come off. A good comedy cast wasted. Poor video fare.

1970. Directed by Hy Averback.
Starring Brian Keith, Tony Curtis, Ernest Borgnine, Ivan Dixon, Suzanne Pleshette, Tom Ewell, Bradford Dillman, Arthur O'Connell, Don Ameche. Colour.
100 minutes.

Guild Home Video

Suspiria

To say that everything in this movie is over the top is an understatement. Director Dario Argento pulls out all the stops (and one means *all*) as he relates the adventures of an American girl student when she arrives at dead of night at a continental dance academy. She finds the house was originally owned by a notorious witch called "The Black Widow" and that the ghoulish goings-on are far from over. A bit of *The Exorcist*, a bit of *Rosemary's Baby*, in fact a bit of everything and as unsubtle as they come. But there's no denying the film is genuinely creepy and you certainly don't get bored. A deafening rock score is thrown in for good measure. You have been warned!

1976. Directed by Dario Argento.
Starring Jessica Harper, Alida Valli, Joan Bennett, Stefania Casini, Udo Kier. Colour.
97 minutes.

Thorn EMI Video

Swallows And Amazons

This one tries to do for Arthur Ransome what *The Railway Children* did for E. Nesbit. But although it falls some way short of that picture's standard, it's an acceptable enough adaptation. Virginia McKenna, as everybody's favourite mum, takes her four children on holiday to the Lake District where they gang up with rival children and play pirates all summer long. The period is 1929; the action enjoyable enough especially when Ronald Fraser as colourful Uncle Jim is around. Pleasing; should have been better.

1974. Directed by Claude Whatham.
Starring Virginia McKenna, Ronald Fraser, Simon West, Sophie Neville, Zanna Hamilton, Stephen Grendon. Colour,
92 minutes.

Thorn EMI Video

The Swarm

There *have* been worse movies than this one although, off-hand, it is difficult to think of them. It's about a swarm of African killer bees that penetrates an Air Force missile base in Texas then threatens to take over not only the State but also the USA. You'll enjoy a laugh a minute with this one until you realise you've paid out hard cash to watch it, whereupon, I assure you, the smile will quickly vanish from your face. Henry Fonda, Richard Widmark and good old cockney kid Michael Caine are among those involved. Heaven knows why.

Box-office rental	$7,700,000
Average rental (78)	$39,443,850
Oscar nominations (1)	Best Costume Design

1978. Directed by Irwin Allen.
Starring Michael Caine, Katharine Ross, Richard Widmark, Henry Fonda, Richard Chamberlain, Olivia de Havilland, Fred MacMurray. Colour.
116 minutes.

Warner Home Video

Sweeney

The small screen *Sweeney* blown up to the big cinema screen and now blown down again to video size. Sounds crazy, doesn't it, but that's what's happening to many of the TV spin-offs that were made by the British movie industry during the 70s. This 90-minute thriller has Scotland Yard's Flying Squad pair, Regan and Carter, up against the machinations of an international oil ring. There is blackmail, murder, prostitution, and it's as tough as it should be. But the plain truth of the matter is that the 60-minute TV dramas were better.

1976. Directed by David Wickes.
Starring John Thaw, Dennis Waterman, Barry Foster, Ian Bannen, Colin Welland. Colour.
90 minutes.

Thorn EMI Video

Sweeney 2 ★★

Here they come again and this time they're after a ruthless gang responsible for a long series of armed bank robberies. Formularised and tightly scripted, the only change from the first movie being that the pair now have a new chief, the last one being convicted of corruption!

1978. Directed by Tom Clegg.
Starring John Thaw, Dennis Waterman, Barry Stanton, John Flanagan, David Casey. Colour.
108 minutes.

Thorn EMI Video

The Swiss Family Robinson ★★★

A kind of Disney companion piece to *Treasure Island*, with pirates again as an all-important ingredient, but this time with John Mills, Dorothy McGuire and family as those up against them on a tropical island. Pirate chief Sessue Hayakawa heads the villainy; Janet Munro, James MacArthur, Tommy Kirk are among the younger cast members who enjoy what every video viewer would like to do – explore an uncharted island in the sun! A bit too long perhaps, but the scenery (the film was shot on the island of Tobago) is out of this world. Value-for-money escapist video.

| Box-office rental | $19,760,000 |
| Average rental (60) | $6,787,500 |

1960. Directed by Ken Annakin.
Starring John Mills, Dorothy McGuire, James MacArthur, Janet Munro, Sessue Hayakawa, Tommy Kirk, Kevin Corcoran, Cecil Parker. Colour. 128 minutes.

Note: the box-office figure of 19 million is made up of the original release rentals plus those of reissues.

Walt Disney Home Video

T

A Tale Of Two Cities

Sub-standard version of Charles Dickens' French Revolution tale about a dissolute young English lawyer who sacrifices his life on the guillotine to ensure the happiness of the woman he loves from afar. Fares badly when set alongside Lean's *Great Expectations,* although Dirk Bogarde makes a creditable attempt at lawyer Sydney Carton. Uninspired video, with Rosalie Crutchley going dangerously over the top as the fiery Madame Defarge.

1958. Directed by Ralph Thomas.
Starring Dirk Bogarde, Dorothy Tutin, Cecil Parker, Stephen Murray, Athene Seyler, Paul Guers, Ian Bannen, Alfie Bass, Ernest Clark, Rosalie Crutchley. Black and White.
117 minutes.

Rank Video

Tales Of Beatrix Potter

The only problem with this film (and it's a minor one) is its length. It goes on for just that wee bit too long; otherwise it's sheer enchantment. Members of the Royal Ballet Company dress up as Jeremy Fisher, Mrs.

Tiggy-Winkle, Squirrel Nutkin, Jemima Puddle-Duck and co. and dance out five of Beatrix Potter's most famous children's stories. Brilliantly lifelike animal masks (by Rotislav Doboujinsky) and the use of Lake District locations simply add to the pleasure, as does John Lanchbery's music, which is made up of a selection of Victorian melodies. Once you've caught sight of Mrs. Tiggy-Winkle scurrying along beside a stone wall you'll be hooked!

1971. Directed by Reginald Mills.
Starring Carole Anisworth, Sally Ashby, Frederick Ashton, Avril Bergen, Michael Coleman, Lesley Collier, Jill Cooke, Leslie Edwards, Graham Fletcher, Bridget Goodricke, Alexander Grant, Garry Grant, Ann Howard, Brenda Last, Keith Martin, Robert Mead, Suzanna Raymond, Wayne Sleep, Rosemary Taylor, Julie Wood, Anita Young. Colour.
90 minutes.

Thorn EMI Video

The Tamarind Seed

British Home Office widow Julie Andrews and Russian military attaché Omar Sharif fall in love while holidaying in Barbados, and find that their affair causes concern among the Intelligence Services of both East and West, and even results in the unmasking of a top British spy. An interesting theme – two innocents helplessly caught up in the Cold War – is muffed by director Blake Edwards although, to be frank, he is hampered by the unexciting personalities of his two stars, who fail to strike any sparks even though Miss Andrews dons a bikini for the Caribbean scenes. Dull, low-keyed stuff.

1974. Directed by Blake Edwards.
Starring Julie Andrews, Omar Sharif, Anthony Quayle, Daniel O'Herlihy, Sylvia Syms, Oscar Homolka. Colour.
125 minutes.

Precision Video

Target

Tim Holt and his sidekick ride to the aid of a young girl trying to outwit a crook who is selling land at low prices to the railroad. They succeed. 1952 B-Western; supports *The Naked And The Dead* on a double-bill video tape.

1952. Directed by Stuart Gilmore.
Starring Tim Holt, Richard Martin, Walter Reed, Linda Douglas. Black and White.
60 minutes.

Kingston Video

Target: Harry

First known as *How To Make It,* this was a TV pilot made back in 1969 and released on British screens ten years later. Its late arrival is indicative of its shabby status, for this is no more than a conveyor belt thriller about a flying soldier of fortune adventuring in Monte Carlo, Istanbul and the Greek Islands. The whole thing revolves around some plates stolen from the Royal Mint. Victor Buono as a Greenstreet-type international crook brings things to life occasionally, but this is poor video.

1969. Directed by Henry Neill.
Starring Vic Morrow, Suzanne Pleshette, Victor Buono, Cesar Romero, Stanley Holloway, Charlotte Rampling. Colour.
80 minutes.

Rank Video

Tarka The Otter

Handsomely photographed version of Henry Williamson's 1920s classic about the life of an otter and his mate in the rivers and countryside of North Devon. The humans don't come out of things very well, nor does the lead hound of an otter hunt which perishes after an underwater duel with the hero. Lovely scenery but a trifle long. Narrated by Peter Ustinov. 2½ rating.

1978. Directed by David Cobham.
Starring Peter Bennett, Edward Underdown, Brenda Cavendish, John Leeson, Reg Lye. Colour.
91 minutes.

Rank Video

Taxi Driver

Another example of a movie that was lauded to the skies when first released but which now looks even more repugnant and redundant than when it was first shown. Robert De Niro is a lonely Vietnam War veteran who becomes a New York taxi driver and finds the violence and squalor of the city turning him crazy and into an urban guerilla. Entertainment this is not. Nor, dare one suggest, is it even skilful cinema. Ugly sordid video but thoroughly representative of the so-called new wave American cinema of the 70s. Jodie Foster adds to the hell-on-earth vision with a portrait of a 12-year-old hooker.

Box-office rental	$11,600,000
Average rental (76)	$22,752,350
Oscars	Nil
Oscar nominations (4)	Best Film; Actor (De Niro); Supporting Actress (Foster); Original Music Score

1976. Directed by Martin Scorsese.
Starring Robert De Niro, Cybill Shepherd, Jodie Foster, Peter Boyle, Leonard Harris, Harvey Keitel, Martin Scorsese, Steven Prince. Colour.
114 minutes.

RCA/Columbia International Video

10 ★★

Dudley Moore superstar! That's what happened when this movie appeared in 1979. Dud's a 42-year-old songwriter hung up on sex. When he discovers the girl of his dreams – Bo Derek – he becomes even more hung up than usual and pursues her all the way to Mexico where she is on honeymoon. The result is disillusionment and a return to understanding girlfriend Julie Andrews. A sporadically amusing piece of video entertainment, although nowhere near as funny as some critics made it out to be at the time of its initial release. The title *10* is the top mark on Dud's 1 to 10 rating for girls he spies along the Californian beaches.

Box-office rental	$36,000,000
Average rental (79)	$31,964,775
Oscars	Nil
Oscar nominations (2)	Best Original Score; Best Song ("It's Easy To Say")

1979. Directed by Blake Edwards.
Starring Dudley Moore, Julie Andrews, Bo Derek, Robert Webber, Dee Wallace, Sam Jones. Colour.
122 minutes.

Warner Home Video

The Ten Commandments ★★★

Somehow, the parting of the Red Sea and the Exodus from Egypt don't seem quite the same on video as they did in the cinema. Certainly one wonders whether Cecil B. DeMille would have bothered to put so much effort into his retelling of the life of Moses (he took 82 assistant directors with him to Egypt) if he could have forseen it all finishing up on a 23-inch screen in your living room. Still, the lavish pictorial values and the magnificent costumes continue to serve the film well and the picture remains good video value, even though it does frequently sound like a biblical strip cartoon. Great music by Elmer Bernstein and just look at that box-office take!

Box-office rental	$43,000,000
Average rental (56)	$8,814,900
Oscars (1)	Best Special Effects
Oscar nominations (6)	Best Film; Photography; Art Direction; Costume Design; Sound Recording; Editing

1956. Directed by Cecil B. DeMille.
Starring Charlton Heston, Yul Brynner, Edward G. Robinson, Anne Baxter, Nina Foch, Yvonne DeCarlo, John Derek. Colour.
219 minutes.

CIC Video

Tension At Table Rock

Richard Egan, saddled with a reputation (unjustified naturally) of shooting his best pal in the back, regains his self-respect when he becomes the guardian of an orphan boy and backs up the attempts of timid sheriff Cameron Mitchell to restore law and order in town. After that he moves on to pastures new. Formula "stranger in town" western. Available on a double feature tape with *Revenge Is My Destiny*.

1956. Directed by Charles Marquis Warren.
Starring Richard Egan, Dorothy Malone, Cameron Mitchell, Angie Dickinson. Colour.
93 minutes.

Kingston Video

The Texas Chainsaw Massacre ★

Only for those who relish watching a masked man kill with a sledgehammer, impaling people on meat hooks, butchering victims with a motorized chain saw, etc. Based on a real case in Texas but not worth dwelling on despite claims that it is well made which it isn't. Cost just $300,000 and looks it. Close to zero rating.

1974. Directed by Tobe Hooper.

Starring Marilyn Burns, Allen Danziger, Paul A. Partain, William Vail, Teri McMinn. Colour.
81 minutes.

Iver Films

That Darn Cat

A Siamese cat known as D.C leads FBI man Dean Jones to the whereabouts of a woman bank teller being held hostage by two robbers. Sprightly Disney movie with slapstick and suspense as its two prime ingredients. The cat of course comes out streets ahead of the rest of the cast, although Hayley Mills (his owner), Elsa Lanchester (nosey neighbour), William Demarest (crabby husband), Ed Wynn (befuddled jeweller), do their best to keep pace with events. 116 minutes and not a moment too long. Excellent family video even if you do prefer dogs as pets.

| Box-office rental | $12,500,000 |
| Average rental (65) | $13,881,050 |

1965. Directed by Robert Stevenson.
Starring Hayley Mills, Dean Jones, Dorothy Provine, Roddy McDowall, Neville Brand, Elsa Lanchester, William Demarest, Frank Gorshin. Colour.
116 minutes.

Walt Disney Home Video

That'll Be The Day

Plenty of epithets were bandied around when this movie made its bow in 1973, presumably because it so successfully recreated the atmosphere of the age of pop in the late 50s. But a movie needs more than atmosphere and, after a reel or two, the adventures (erotic and otherwise) of David Essex's teenage drifter quickly become tedious and even his salvation through rock music is no more than mundane. Ringo Starr adds a bit of much-needed colour as a fellow drifter who's been around a bit, but this is a movie that now more than shows its age. Among the top-grossing British films of its year (see also *Stardust*).

1973. Directed by Claude Whatham.
Starring David Essex, Ringo Starr, Rosemary Leach, James Booth, Billy Fury, Keith Moon. Colour.
91 minutes.

Thorn EMI Video

That Riviera Touch

Morecambe and Wise, undaunted by the failure of their first movie venture, tried again with this one and once again the result was a flop. The pair are a couple of holidaymakers involved with a gang of jewel thieves on the Riviera. The film ends with a frantic chase by car, water skis and helicopter. But nothing can hide the fact that this is dismal entertainment.

1966. Directed by Cliff Owen.
Starring Eric Morecambe, Ernie Wise, Suzanne Lloyd, Paul Stassino, Armand Mestral. Colour.
98 minutes.

Rank Video

That's Carry On

Barbara Windsor and Kenneth Williams introduce extracts from the 28 Carry On films from *Carry On Sergeant* (58) to *Carry On England* (76). The result should perhaps have been the funniest of all the Carry Ons; that it is not simply emphasizes the dreadful sameness of this long series, although one has to admit that now the films have come to an end one almost misses the twice-yearly bout of double innuendo.

1978. Directed by Gerald Thomas.
With Barbara Windsor and Kenneth Williams and Carry On Extracts. Colour/Black and White.
95 minutes.

Rank Video

That's Entertainment!

When you bring together many of the best scenes from MGM's greatest musicals you can't really go far wrong and the title of this exhilarating movie just about sums it all up. For sheer value for money it's difficult to beat, and it's simply one dazzling sequence after another. Some highlights: Astaire dancing with the hat rack in *Royal Wedding;* dancing with Cyd Charisse in *The Band Wagon;* Gene Kelly splashing about to *Singin' In The Rain;* Judy Garland "Off To See The Wizard"; the Seven Brothers barn-dancing; and on and on and on. Delightful; one to watch over and over again. A must buy!

Box-office rental $12,020,000
Average rental (74) $18,456,150

1974. Directed by Jack Haley Jr.
Narrated by Fred Astaire, Bing Crosby, Gene Kelly, Peter Lawford, Liza Minnelli, Donald O'Connor, Debbie Reynolds, Mickey Rooney, Frank Sinatra, James Stewart, Elizabeth Taylor. Colour.
137 minutes.

MGM/CBS Home Video

That's Entertainment Part II

More of the same except that this time it's all hosted by Fred Astaire and Gene Kelly and one can't complain about that. Esther Williams skims through the water on skis; Lena Horne sings "The Lady Is A Tramp"; Doris Day renders "Ten Cents A Dance"; Bing Crosby croons and Louis Armstrong croaks "Now You Has Jazz"; Eleanor Powell taps "Fascinating Rhythm"; Astaire and Garland stroll down the avenue as "A Couple Of Swells." And plenty more including straight clips from *Boom Town, Gone With The Wind, The Philadelphia Story,* etc. As good as number one. Remarkable value to have both in your video library.

1976 Produced by Saul Chaplin and Daniel Melnick.
New sequences directed by Gene Kelly. Introduced by Fred Astaire and Gene Kelly. Colour.
126 minutes.

MGM/CBS Home Video

There Goes The Bride

Desperately unfunny movie about a neurotic advertising executive (Tom Smothers) who has to come up with an advertising slogan on the day of his daughter's wedding. A life-size cardboard cut-out of a 20s flapper gives him ideas and comes to life in the form of Twiggy. Martin Balsam is usually fairly astute about choosing his roles. Not on this occasion. He plays the groom's father and at one time during the proceedings screams: "It's a bad dream. Somebody tell me it's a bad dream". It isn't. It's for real!

1980. Directed by Terence Marcel.
Starring Tom Smothers, Twiggy, Martin Balsam, Sylvia Syms, Michael Whitney, Geoffrey Sumner, Graham Stark, Hermione Baddeley, Phil Silvers, Broderick Crawford, Jim Backus. Colour.
91 minutes.

Home Video Productions

There's A Girl In My Soup

Debonair, womanizing TV gourmet Peter Sellers meets his match in the person of zany kook Goldie Hawn. End of story although just how he meets his match takes 96 minutes to unfold and there are quite a few laughs along the way, not least when Miss Hawn declares herself to be unimpressed by Sellers' usually successful seduction technique. Adapted by Terence Frisby from his own London and Broadway stage hit. One of Sellers' few box-office successes of the period. Amiable but nothing special.

| Box-office rental | $4,500,000 |
| Average rental (70) | $16,881,800 |

1970. Directed by Roy Boulting.
Starring Peter Sellers, Goldie Hawn, Tony Britton, Nicky Henson, John Comer, Diana Dors, Gabrielle Drake. Colour.
96 minutes.

RCA/Columbia International Video

There's No Business Like Show Business ★★

Take the music of Irving Berlin, add a story of a show biz couple who bring up their three children in an act called The Five Donahues and there you have it – as corny an extravaganza as has ever come out of a Hollywood studio. *And* as predictable. *And* as mushy, especially when one of the kids grows up to be pop star Johnnie Ray who, by the end of the film has turned into a priest. Ugh! Mitzi Gaynor, Donald O'Connor and Marilyn Monroe, who wriggles her way through "Lazy" and "Heat Wave", partly compensate for the schmaltz. Ethel Merman and Dan Dailey are mom and pop who every now and then ask themselves: "Where did we go wrong?" Answer: by signing a contract to appear in this. The film's vigour just about gets it by; the DeLuxe colour is often variable.

Box-office rental	$5,000,000
Average rental (54)	$6,012,700
Oscars	Nil
Oscar nominations (3)	Best Story; Costume Design; Scoring Of A Musical

1954. Directed by Walter Lang.
Starring Ethel Merman, Donald O'Connor, Marilyn Monroe, Dan Dailey, Johnnie Ray, Mitzi Gaynor. Colour.
117 minutes.

Twentieth Century-Fox Video

They Shoot Horses, Don't They? ★★★★

This qualifies as one of the most harrowing movies to be found on video and if you want a couple of hours of lightweight entertainment forget it. But, if you want proof that contemporary American film-makers *can* make brilliant movies when the occasion demands, take a look. This is one of the most triumphant American films of the late 60s – a chilling look at the hopes, fears and disillusionments of the contestants in one of the dance marathons of the Depression 30s. Jane Fonda (in arguably her finest role) as a cynical loser, Susannah York as a Hollywood hopeful and Red Buttons

423

as an ageing sailor lead those contesting for the 1500 dollar prize. Gig Young is the master of ceremonies. Superb.

Box-office rental	$5,980,000
Average rental (69)	$13,660,950
Oscars (1)	Best Supporting Actor (Young)
Oscar nominations (8)	Best Actress (Fonda); Supporting Actress (York); Direction; Screenplay; Art Direction; Costume Design; Editing; Music Adaptation

1969. Directed by Sydney Pollack.
Starring Jane Fonda, Michael Sarrazin, Susannah York, Gig Young, Red Buttons, Bonnie Bedelia, Michael Conrad, Bruce Dern. Colour.
120 minutes.

Rank Video

The Thief Of Bagdad

Forty years old it may be, but the splendid special effects make this Arabian Nights fantasy as watchable and enjoyable as ever it was. Sabu plays the mischievous native boy who outwits the wicked Grand Vizier with the aid of a huge genie. The spectacular trick photography – flying horses, magic carpets, terrifying giants – and ravishing colourwork earned three Academy Awards and the whole thing was engineered by no less than six directors, three of them credited and three of them not – Alexander Korda, Zoltan Korda and William Cameron Menzies.

Oscars (3)	Best Photography; Art Direction; Special Effects
Oscar nominations (1)	Best Music Score

1940. Directed by Ludwig Berger, Michael Powell and Tim Whelan.
Starring Conrad Veidt, Sabu, June Duprez, John Justin, Rex Ingram, Miles Malleson, Morton Selten, Mary Morris. Colour.
106 minutes.

Spectrum
(distributed by Polygram)

The Thief Of Bagdad ★★★

Silent version with the same title but rather a different plot, as notorious thief Douglas Fairbanks battles with a fearsome dragon and defeats a Mongol army in order to prove he's worthy of a beautiful princess. Very long (137 minutes) but spectacular and with Fairbanks in top form, as he bounces out of three huge jars with the help of trampolenes concealed inside. Colour tints and an organ score by Lee Erwin. The film took seven months to shoot and used 4,000 extras on 6½ acres of sets.

1924. Directed by Raoul Walsh.
Starring Douglas Fairbanks, Snitz Edwards, Charles Belcher, Julanne Johnston, Anna May Wong, Brandon Hurst. Black and White.
137 minutes.

Spectrum
(distributed by Polygram)

The Thief Who Came To Dinner ★

This one looks as though it was made when the director was asleep. It's certainly enough to send most video viewers into slumberland, for Ryan O'Neal as a computer expert who gives up his job to become a jewel thief in the higher echelons of Texas society isn't exactly a riveting experience. In fact, he's downright tedious. A social satire? A slapstick farce? A comedy of manners? This movie tries for all three and fails on all counts. Jacqueline Bisset and Jill Clayburgh co-star.

1973. Directed by Bud Yorkin.
Starring Ryan O'Neal, Jacqueline Bisset, Warren Oates, Jill Clayburgh, Ned Beatty. Colour.
105 minutes.

Warner Home Video

The Thing From Another World

Before "the thing" of the title is actually seen, which is round about 40 minutes or so, this is a movie high on tension and high on craft. But after that it's all a bit of a letdown and becomes nothing more than a case of "let's hunt down James Arness", who plays the creature (an eight-foot intellectual carrot!) and looks no more frightening than a tall guy wearing elevator shoes. But those first few reels, set on a remote scientific outpost in the North Pole, are intriguing and lift this horror flick (produced by Howard Hawks) into the "must-see", three-star class. On the same tape: more fun and games in *Stranger On The Third Floor*.

1951. Directed by Christian Nyby.
Starring Robert Cornthwaite, Kenneth Tobey, Margaret Sheridan, Bill Self, Dewey Martin, James Arness. Black and White.
87 minutes.

Kingston Video

Things To Come

Alexander Korda at his most spectacular and ambitious; an adaptation by H. G. Wells of his own prophetic novel about the history of the world from the devastation of the World War of 1940 to the mechanized Utopia of 2036. Wells' war lasts thirty years otherwise he gets an awful lot of things right. Equate the Wandering Sickness that destroys half the world's population with nuclear fallout and you have a chilling movie. Over-talkative but Arthur Bliss' rousing score remains one of the most dramatic ever composed for a picture.

1936. Directed by William Cameron Menzies.
Starring Raymond Massey, Edward Chapman, Ralph Richardson, Margaretta Scott, Cedric Hardwicke. Black and White.
113 minutes.

Spectrum
(distributed by Polygram)

The Third Man

Still one of the best thrillers ever made, with Orson Welles lurking in the sewers of a bomb-shattered Vienna and best friend Joseph Cotten trying to discover why Orson's become involved in such a nasty racket as flogging watered-down penicillin. Highlights: Welles' first appearance in a doorway lit suddenly by a shaft of light (surely one of the great scenes in all cinema); the "cuckoo clock" speech on the giant ferris wheel; and the climactic chase through the sewers. A bleak masterpiece that was written especially for the screen by Graham Greene. Difficult to imagine it being done any better. Anton Karas' zither music haunts you long after the proceedings have come to an end. Superb video.

Oscars (1)   Best Photography
Oscar nominations (2)   Best Direction; Editing

1949. Directed by Carol Reed.
Starring Joseph Cotten, Alida Valli, Orson Welles, Trevor Howard, Bernard Lee, Paul Hoerbiger, Annie Rosar, Ernst Deutsch, Erich Ponto, Siegfried Breuer, Wilfrid Hyde-White. Black and White.
104 minutes.

Thorn EMI Video

The 39 Steps

Vintage Hitchcock and certainly more Hitchcock than John Buchan, from whose novel the film draws its source. Robert Donat is hero Richard Hannay who escapes the police in London to search for a spy leader operating in the wilds of Scotland. Basically, the movie is just another chase thriller, but it's topped and tailed by two skilful and exciting sequences in a theatre and includes one highly erotic moment when Donat and the lovely Madeleine Carroll are forced to spend the night together handcuffed by the wrist and she – willed on by the viewer – tries to unroll her stockings. Second only to *The Lady Vanishes* as the best prewar Hitchcock available on video.

1935. Directed by Alfred Hitchcock.

Starring Madeleine Carroll, Robert Donat, Lucie Mannheim, Godfrey Tearle, Peggy Ashcroft, John Laurie, Helen Haye, Frank Celier, Wylie Watson. Black and White.
87 minutes.

Rank Video

The 39 Steps

A not-to-be-despised remake, in fact considerably more faithful to Buchan than the Hitchcock film, correctly in period (1914) and this time with Robert Powell (Hannay) up against the spy network determined to bring about Britain's downfall. Attractive colour work and settings, a tense climax on the face of Big Ben and a neat cameo from John Mills as an undercover agent who finishes up with a knife in his back on the floor of St. Pancras station. Pacey; adapts well to the video screen.

1978. Directed by Don Sharp.
Starring Robert Powell, David Warner, Eric Porter, Karen Dotrice, John Mills, George Baker, Ronald Pickup. Colour.
102 minutes.

Rank Video

Those Magnificent Men In Their Flying Machines

They don't make 'em like this anymore – all-star comedy spectaculars that run for two to three hours and boast a new face every ten minutes or so. Too expensive probably, although another reason might well be that family audiences who used to go out for this type of movie now stay at home and watch the telly. Which makes this film – the story of the first international air race between London and Paris in 1910 – ideal video viewing. The scenes of old planes gliding majestically through blue skies have about them a gentle charm, and the delightful prologue plus the credits (enlivened by the drawings of Ronald Searle) are almost worth the price of the tape alone. Perfect viewing for rainy afternoons.

Box-office rental	$14,000,000
Average rental (65)	$13,881,050
Oscars	Nil
Oscar nominations (1)	Best Story And Screenplay

1965. Directed by Ken Annakin.
Starring Stuart Whitman, Sarah Miles, James Fox, Alberto Sordi, Robert Morley, Gert Frobe, Jean-Pierre Cassel, Eric Sykes, Terry-Thomas, Irina Demick, Tony Hancock, Benny Hill. Colour.
133 minutes.

Twentieth Century-Fox Video

The Three Musketeers

This is the 1935, and far from best version of the famous Dumas story about the young Gascon who joins the King's musketeers in the fight against the ambitions of the scheming Cardinal Richelieu. Walter Abel is D'Artagnan; Paul Lukas, Moroni Olsen and Onslow Stevens are Athos, Porthos and Aramis respectively; and Margot Grahame adds a dash of female treachery as Milady De Winter. Shows its age this one. On the same video tape as *Abbott And Costello Meet Captain Kidd*.

1935. Directed by Rowland V. Lee.
Starring Walter Abel, Paul Lukas, Ian Keith, Onslow Stevens, Ralph Forbes, Margot Grahame, Moroni Olsen. Black and White.
90 minutes.

Kingston Video

THX 1138

George Lucas a few years before his phenomenal success with *Star Wars*, still in the future but in much more sombre mood as he follows the attempts of Robert Duvall to break free from a hideous computerized society of the future where people are known only by numbers, dress completely in white, live in a subterranean city and are drugged on tranquillizers. Bleak clinical sci-fi, not dissimilar to Orwell's *1984*. Rarely seen so a good bet on video. 2½ rating.

1971. Directed by George Lucas.
Starring Robert Duvall, Donald Pleasence, Don Pedro Colley, Maggie McOmie, Ian Wolfe. Colour.
95 minutes.

Warner Home Video

Till The Clouds Roll By

All-star MGM biography of Jerome Kern, mundane for most of its length but saved by just about every musical star on the Metro lot chipping in with a song or two: Lena Horne sings "Can't Help Lovin' Dat Man"; Judy Garland does "Who?" and "Look For The Silver Lining"; Cyd Charisse and Gower Champion perform "Smoke Gets In Your Eyes"; Frank Sinatra climaxes the whole thing with "Ole Man River". Two dozen Kern numbers all told. Great music, mediocre movie.

Box-office rental	$4,500,000
Average rental (46)	$5,720,000

1946. Directed by Richard Whorf.
Starring Robert Walker, Van Heflin, Lucille Bremer, Dorothy Patrick, Paul Langton, Mary Nash, plus all-star cast. Colour.
137 minutes.

Mountain Video

Till Death Us Do Part

Enjoy a trip down memory lane and follow outrageous bigot Alf Garnett and family from 1939 to the late 60s. If you can stand the opinionated Mr. Garnett that is. And if you couldn't stand him on the telly you certainly won't like him in this film, which is even more coarse than the TV series, if that's possible. The film begins with the outbreak of World War II and finishes with Alf and family leaving their house in Wapping and heading for a housing estate in Essex.

1969. Directed by Norman Cohen.
Starring Warren Mitchell, Dandy Nichols, Anthony Booth, Una Stubbs, Liam Redmond, Bill Maynard, Brian Blessed. Colour.
100 minutes.

Thorn EMI Video

Time After Time

Cleverly plotted fantasy with H. G. Wells using his Time Machine to follow Jack The Ripper from Victorian London and trying to prevent him from carrying on his bloodthirsty trade in modern-day San Francisco. Not surprisingly Jack finds the sleazy night life of 'Frisco right up his street whilst H. G. is distinctly out of his element. Malcolm McDowell is Wells, David Warner a convincing Ripper and the special effects during the machine's journey are really something. Fabulous music score by Miklos Rozsa; good value.

Box-office rental	$6,300,000
Average rental (79)	$31,964,775

1979. Directed by Nicholas Meyer.
Starring Malcolm McDowell, David Warner, Mary Steenburgen, Charles Cioffi, Kent Williams. Colour.
112 minutes.

Warner Home Video

Tintorera

Jaws-type rip-off, following the mouth-watering experiences of a tiger shark off the coast of Mexico. Susan George shares the beds of the two leading men and survives; most of the rest of the cast perish, including the shark which gets a harpoon between the eyes. Routine eat-em-up stuff.

1977. Directed by Rene Cardona Jr.
Starring Susan George, Hugo Stiglitz, Andres Garcia, Fiona Lewis, Jennifer Ashley. Colour.
88 minutes.

Cinema Features
(distributed by VCL)

The Titfield Thunderbolt

Local inhabitants defying authority and taking matters into their own hands was a favourite Ealing theme in the late 40s and early 50s. In this movie, the theme is stressed yet again as an enthusiastic group of villagers decide to take over their Branch Railway line when the government decides to close it down as uneconomic. John Gregson provides the youthful vigour and George Relph, Stanley Holloway and Hugh Griffith (as vicar, benefactor and poacher respectively) all lend a useful hand. Naunton Wayne represents aloof officialdom but loses in the end, as officialdom always did at Ealing. Quiet and charming and nicely coloured. Not Ealing at the top of its form but quite passable nonetheless.

1953. Directed by Charles Crichton.
Starring Stanley Holloway, George Relph, Naunton Wayne, John Gregson, Godfrey Tearle, Hugh Griffith. Colour.
84 minutes.

Thorn EMI Video

To Beat The Band

Lightweight 1935 Hollywood comedy about a bachelor who inherits a fortune but only if he marries a widow. The trouble is she's already engaged to someone else. Includes several musical interludes and an appearance by songwriter Johnny Mercer. Supports the Alan Ladd Western *Drum Beat* on a double feature video tape.

1935. Directed by Ben Stoloff.

Starring Johnny Mercer, Hugh Herbert, Helen Broderick, Roger Pryor.
Black and White.
63 minutes.

Kingston Video

Tom Horn

The penultimate movie of Steve McQueen; an account of the last years of
famed Western gunman and ex-Cavalry scout Tom Horn when he is hired
by a Wyoming Ranchers Association to smash the rustlers in the community. Old-fashioned western and none the worse for that (there are
echoes of *Shane* in its theme) with some classical landscape photography
and some nice period touches including Horn's brief encounter with
boxer Gentleman Jim Corbett. Set in 1901.

Box-office rental	$4,300,000
Average rental (80)	$30,086,027

1980. Directed by William Wiard.
Starring Steve McQueen, Linda Evans, Richard Farnsworth, Billy Green
Bush, Slim Pickens, Peter Canon, Elisha Cook. Colour.
97 minutes.

Warner Home Video

Too Late The Hero

Naval lieutenant Cliff Robertson joins up with a 15-strong British patrol to
try to destroy a vital radio transmitter behind Japanese lines in World
War II. But it's a suicide mission from the word "go" and the men are
gradually destroyed by the Japanese until only two of them are left –
Robertson and cockney private Michael Caine. And then when *they* have
to make a dash for freedom only one of them makes it back to base. A
cynical, often harrowing Robert Aldrich anti-war movie set in the Philippines. Once its 133 minutes have come to an end you feel as though you
have been in the jungle all your life. Holds the attention, despite its length.

1970. Directed by Robert Aldrich.
Starring Michael Caine, Cliff Robertson, Ian Bannen, Harry Andrews, Denholm Elliott, Ronald Fraser, Lance Percival, Percy Herbert, Henry Fonda. Colour.
133 minutes.

Guild Home Video

Top Hat

Really, you can't do much better than this if you want to select just one of the Astaire-Rogers musicals available on video. Fred's a dancer who pursues the girl of his dreams from London to the Riviera, punctuating the action along the way with such Irving Berlin numbers as "Cheek To Cheek", "Isn't This A Lovely Day", "No Strings" and "The Piccolino". Totally unreal, of course, but of its kind practically flawless. Handsome sets by Van Nest Polglase.

Oscars	Nil
Oscar nominations (4)	Best Film; Art Direction; Song ("Cheek To Cheek"); Dance Direction

1935. Directed by Mark Sandrich.
Starring Fred Astaire, Ginger Rogers, Edward Everett Horton, Helen Broderick, Erik Rhodes, Eric Blore. Black and White.
100 minutes.

Thorn EMI Video

Tora! Tora! Tora!

The full story – the build up to and the attack on – Pearl Harbor in Hawaii on December 7, 1941, told from both the American and Japanese viewpoints. The action sequences are well-staged when they eventually occur, but long passages of inscrutable Japanese faces contemplating the effects of the attack don't exactly make riveting viewing. A long line-up of American character actors plays the various real-life personnel involved in the tragedy, although none of them really get the chance to show their paces. Moderate viewing.

Box-office rental	$14,530,000
Average rental (70)	$16,881,800
Oscars (1)	Best Special Visual Effects
Oscar nominations (4)	Best Photography; Art Direction; Sound; Editing

1970. Directed by Richard Fleischer.
Starring Martin Balsam, So Yamamura, Jason Robards, Joseph Cotten, Tatsuya Mihashi, E. G. Marshall, James Whitmore. Colour.
143 minutes.

Twentieth Century-Fox Video

Tourist Trap

There's this shut-down tourist museum with an adjacent house crammed with wax dummies. When a young guy calls in at a nearby diner he's done to death by a group of mysterious creatures. The dead boy's girlfriend starts a search for her missing mate and finds that she's stumbled not only into a world of telekinetic fantasy and madness but also into a pretty rotten movie. Don't make the same mistake!

1979. Directed by David Schmoeller.
Starring Chuck Connors, Jon Van Ness, Jocelyn Jones, Robin Sherwood, Tanya Roberts. Colour.
90 minutes.

Intervision

Tower Of Evil

A team of young archaeologists arrive on the deserted Snape Island to try to prove the innocence of a girl accused of butchering her three companions during a night on the island. A paste and scissors exploitation movie with nudity, a burning alive, a derelict lighthouse and a decaying corpse in a rocking chair as some of its ingredients. Paltry video, and unpleasant.

1972. Directed by Jim O'Connolly.
Starring Bryant Halliday, Jill Haworth, Anna Palk, William Lucas, Anthony Valentine, Jack Watson. Colour.
89 minutes.

Iver Films

The Train Robbers

This movie should have been made in the 40s as a double-feature with Randolph Scott. Instead, it was made in 1973 with John Wayne. He's just one of three gunmen whom Ann-Margret asks to recover the half-million in gold her late husband stole before departing this world. She wants the gold returned. You might want to return this tape after thirty minutes or so. Rod Taylor and Ben Johnson are also along for the unexciting ride.

1973. Directed by Burt Kennedy.
Starring John Wayne, Ann-Margret, Rod Taylor, Ben Johnson, Bobby Vinton, Christopher George. Colour.
92 minutes.

Warner Home Video

Treasure Island

Quite how Robert Newton managed to roll his eyes so effectively must remain a trade secret between ham actors. But he certainly let 'em go in this Walt Disney movie, so much so that his portrait of swaggering Long John Silver belongs with the screen's most famous performances. The rest of the playing is stilted and dull and the film itself disappoints, although an occasional "Ah, Jim lad" from Newton gives it a welcome shot in the arm!

1950. Directed by Byron Haskin.

Starring Robert Newton, Bobby Driscoll, Walter Fitzgerald, Basil Sydney, Denis O'Dea, Ralph Truman, Geoffrey Keen. Colour.
96 minutes.

Walt Disney Home Video

Treasure Island

Dreary remake, with Orson Welles taking over as Long John and Lionel Stander featuring as Billy Bones. Wolf Mankowitz and Welles himself (under the pseudonym of O. W. Jeeves) fashioned the script, which means that the result should have been better than this. That it is not is probably due to the fact that the cast is multi-lingual and that Britain, Spain, France and West Germany all had a hand in the film's production. A mess!

1972. Directed by John Hough.
Starring Orson Welles, Kim Burfield, Lionel Stander, Walter Slezak, Angel Del Pozo. Colour.
95 minutes.

Guild Home Video

The Treasure Of Pancho Villa

Hollywood actioner about an American adventurer (Rory Calhoun) who becomes involved with Villa's forces in Mexico in 1915. Standard conveyor-belt stuff, with a young Shelley Winters providing numerous voluptuous alternatives to the action. That excellent novelist and screen-writer Niven Busch wrote it all.

1955. Directed by George Sherman.
Starring Rory Calhoun, Shelley Winters, Gilbert Roland, Joseph Calleia. Colour.
96 minutes.

21st Century Video
(distributed by VCL)

The Triple Echo

A young army deserter (Brian Deacon) is persuaded by a lonely farm woman (Glenda Jackson) to pose as her sister and then finds the situation becomes even more complicated when a brutish oaf of a sergeant (Oliver Reed) becomes involved in things. A strange, complex little film, forcefully acted but totally implausible, and leaving you with another of those "What was *that* all about?" puzzles to sort out once it's all over. Set in the English countryside in mid-winter in 1942; based on a novel by H. E. Bates. Dubious video value.

1972. Directed by Michael Apted.
Starring Glenda Jackson, Oliver Reed, Brian Deacon, Anthony May, Gavin Richards, Jenny Lee Wright. Colour.
94 minutes.

Picture Time Video
(distributed by VCL)

True Grit

One-eyed US Marshal John Wayne, accompanied by a Texas Ranger and a young girl, gives chase to the killer who has murdered the girl's father. That's about it really, and that's about all you need to know, for this one's a beauty in every sense of the word and perhaps the last great example of the old-fashioned western, when the goodies chased the baddies across some of the most beautiful scenery imaginable. Bears viewing many many times, which makes it excellent value on video. Rousing Elmer Bernstein score.

Box-office rental	$14,250,000
Average rental (69)	$13,660,950
Oscars (1)	Best Actor (Wayne)
Oscar nominations (1)	Best Song ("True Grit")

1969. Directed by Henry Hathaway.
Starring John Wayne, Glen Campbell, Kim Darby, Jeremy Slate, Robert Duvall, Strother Martin, Dennis Hopper, Jeff Corey. Colour.
128 minutes.

CIC Video

The Turning Point

A kind of *All About Eve* of the ballet world, with ageing and lonely ballerina Anne Bancroft having to face the fact that she's on the downward slide, and Shirley MacLaine as a former dancer-turned-housewife who regrets giving it all up. MacLaine's "must-be-a-dancer" daughter brings Bancroft and MacLaine together again. And boy, do the sparks fly when they meet. Histrionic soap opera for the most part, although the two actresses occasionally manage to get the events up to a higher level. Plenty of ballet for dance fans. The pastel shaded colourwork doesn't come over too well on video. 2½ rating.

Box-office rental	$17,060,000
Average rental (77)	$36,913,348
Oscars	Nil
Oscar nominations (11)	Best Film; Actress (Bancroft); Actress (MacLaine); Supporting Actor (Baryshnikov); Supporting Actress (Browne); Direction; Screenplay; Photograph; Art Direction; Sound; Editing

1977. Directed by Herbert Ross.
Starring Shirley MacLaine, Anne Bancroft, Mikhail Baryshnikov, Leslie Browne, Tom Skerritt, Martha Scott. Colour.
119 minutes.

Twentieth Century-Fox Video

Twelve O'Clock High

There's only one combat sequence in this absorbing movie, but that's all one needs for this film is about the effects of war rather than war itself. Gregory Peck is the American general who has to take the strain of turning a shattered, battle-weary bomber group into a superior striking force once more. The result is an almost interior movie, but one that is so intelligently acted and written that it holds the attention throughout. Peck has never been better. Set in England in World War II and told in flashback. All-male cast; slow but satisfying video.

Oscars (2)	Best Supporting Actor (Jagger); Sound Recording

Oscar nominations (2)   Best Film; Actor (Peck)

1949. Directed by Henry King.
Starring Gregory Peck, Hugh Marlowe, Gary Merrill, Millard Mitchell, Dean Jagger, Robert Arthur, Paul Stewart, John Kellogg. Black and White. 132 minutes.

Twentieth Century-Fox Video

20,000 Leagues Under The Sea

Disney's first excursion into the really big league (no pun intended). An expensive version of Jules Verne's adventure tale about the mysterious Captain Nemo, who prowls along the ocean bed in the *Nautilus*, a huge underwater machine propelled by atomic energy. And all this in the 19th century! A giant squid, jolly sailor Kirk Douglas, French Professor Paul Lukas and cowardly little assistant Peter Lorre eventually help destroy everything he's worked for all his life. Great fun, although the smaller screen doesn't always do justice to the underwater scenes, especially the fight with the squid. James Mason features as Nemo.

Box-office rental $11,000,000
Average rental (54) $6,012,700
Oscars (2)   Best Art Direction; Special Effects
Oscar nominations (1)   Best Editing

1954. Directed by Richard Fleischer.
Starring Kirk Douglas, James Mason, Paul Lukas, Peter Lorre, Robert J. Wilke, Carleton Young, Ted de Corsia. Colour.
127 minutes.

Walt Disney Home Video

Twins Of Evil

Hammer scriptwriters ring the changes once again by involving not one girl but two – a pair of identical 19-year-old Austrian twins – in a nasty

440

bout of "bite-your-neck" vampirism. And for good measure there's also a bit of witch hunting into the bargain, led by ever-reliable Peter Cushing and his Puritan sect, The Brotherhood. The result is conventional horror fare with the statutory castle, statutory Pinewood locations and statutory lousy acting from the leads. Cushing apart of course.

1971. Directed by John Hough.
Starring Madeleine Collinson, Mary Collinson, Peter Cushing, Kathleen Byron, Dennis Price. Colour.
87 minutes.

Rank Video

2001: A Space Odyssey ★★★★

Just how much you are missing by watching this epic masterpiece on video will only be apparent to those who have seen Kubrick's visionary movie on the big screen. If you come to it first on video, I'm afraid it's a case of "You don't know what you're missing", because if ever a film demanded a wide canvas it is this one. On video the special effects, designs, camerawork and music lose about three-quarters of their power and effectiveness and one is left with just the shell of a great film about a gigantic space journey to Jupiter to find the true meaning of the Universe. The rating is four stars but in all truth it should be no more than two for video.

Box-office rental	$24,100,000
Average rental (68)	$14,411,950
Oscars (1)	Best Special Visual Effects
Oscar nominations (3)	Best Direction; Story & Screenplay; Art Direction

1968. Directed by Stanley Kubrick. Starring Keir Dullea, Gary Lockwood, William Sylvester, Leonard Rossiter, Margaret Tyzack, Robert Beatty, Daniel Richter. Colour.
141 minutes.

MGM/CBS Home Video

Note: The box-office take of *2001* is made up of several re-issues.

Two-Way Stretch

Or, "How To Make The Most Of Your Last Few Days In Prison And Become A Millionaire!" And how do you do that? Simple. You hop over the wall, rob a maharajah of jewels worth two million and then break in again to give yourself the perfect alibi. Peter Sellers, David Lodge and Bernard Cribbins are the three who think it all up; Lionel Jeffries is the guard who is supposed to keep an eye on them. Wonderful entertainment that has lasted more successfully than many a more famous comedy of its period. Sellers is in top form. So too is Jeffries. Worth the money!

1960. Directed by Robert Day.
Starring Peter Sellers, Wilfrid Hyde White, Maurice Denham, Irene Handl, David Lodge, Lionel Jeffries, Bernard Cribbins. Black and White.
87 minutes.

Thorn EMI Video

Tycoon

A mining picture which one critic summed up with the words: "Several tons of dynamite are exploded in this picture, none of it under the right people." Well, the people are John Wayne, Laraine Day, Cedric Hardwicke and Anthony Quinn, all of whom are at war with each other whilst building a mountain railroad that will link up with some valuable copper mines in South America. Dreary and old-fashioned, it shares a tape (and needs to) with the Tim Holt B-western *Six Gun Gold*.

1947. Directed by Richard Wallace.
Starring John Wayne, Laraine Day, Cedric Hardwicke, Judith Anderson, James Gleason, Anthony Quinn. Colour.
128 minutes.

Kingston Video

U

The Uncanny

Yet another horror omnibus movie, this time built around the menace of
cats who, according to poor old Peter Cushing, are about to dominate
the human race. Three nasty little stories go to prove his theory. Not for
cat lovers. Not for video purchasers either, despite the presence in the
cast of such veterans as Joan Greenwood who is devoured by her feline
pets, Donald Pleasence, who loses his tongue and Cushing himself who
ends up savaged to death.

1977. Directed by Denis Heroux.
Starring Peter Cushing, Ray Milland, Susan Penhaligon, Joan Greenwood,
Simon Williams, Roland Culver, Alexandra Stewart, Donald Pleasence,
Samantha Eggar, John Vernon. Colour.
85 minutes.

Rank Video

The Undefeated

Union colonel John Wayne rounds up some horses and agrees to sell
them to Emperor Maximilian in Mexico. Old enemy, embittered Confederate Rock Hudson, crosses his path during the trek and the pair finish
up teaming against the Mexicans. Post-Civil War Western; efficient, trad-
itional, passable – just! But poor colourwork.

Box-office rental	$4,000,000
Average rental (69)	$13,660,950

1969. Directed by Andrew V. McLaglen.
Starring John Wayne, Rock Hudson, Tony Aguilar, Roman Gabriel, Marian
McCargo. Colour.
118 minutes.

Twentieth Century-Fox Video

Underwater!

The most famous thing about this nonsensical adventure yarn is that its premiere, staged in Florida in 1955, was held in a specially built cinema 20 feet underwater. Otherwise, the bubbles that float from the diving gear of Jane Russell, Gilbert Roland and Richard Egan are distinctly more satisfying to the ear than the dialogue they have to deliver on dry land. They're all supposed to be after some treasure hidden in the wreck of a Spanish galleon in the Caribbean. Highspot for video viewers: Jane Russell, in clinging red bathing suit, swimming directly towards the camera. Shares a tape with the excellent Don Siegel thriller *The Big Steal*

1955. Directed by John Sturges.
Starring Jane Russell, Gilbert Roland, Richard Egan, Lori Nelson. Colour.
99 minutes.

Kingston Video

Union City

An accountant traps and kills a young thief who has been stealing his milk every morning. In a panic he hides the body behind a fold-up bed in an empty apartment. Slowly he becomes paranoiac, as he waits for the moment when the apartment is let and his crime discovered. But there's a twist ... A well-made, unsettling little thriller that hints at times of the work of Polanski and which builds up to a clever and ironic climax. Deborah Harry features as the killer's wife; the film is based on a story by Cornell Woolrich.

1980. Directed by Mark Reichert.
Starring Dennis Lipscomb, Deborah Harry, Irina Maleeva, Everett McGill, Sam McMurray. Colour.
87 minutes.

Intervision

An Unmarried Woman

A contented wife with a 15-year-old daughter suddenly finds that her marriage of many years has fallen apart and that her Wall Street husband has left her for a younger woman. A horribly topical theme although the fact that the wife is so well off and has nothing to do all day but talk to her similarly afflicted colleagues lessens one's sympathy for her plight somewhat. Great performance by Jill Clayburgh; an OK one from Alan Bates as the artist-lover who helps her try to pick up the pieces. No easy solutions, none given. Good video.

Oscars	Nil
Oscar nominations (3)	Best Film; Actress (Clayburgh); Screenplay

1978. Directed by Paul Mazursky.
Starring Jill Clayburgh, Alan Bates, Michael Murphy, Cliff Gorman, Pat Quinn. Colour.
124 minutes.

Twentieth Century-Fox Video

Up Pompeii

Spin-off from a TV series that seemed to have spun off from something else, although quite what is difficult to imagine. There's a plot to kill the Emperor Nero, a clumsy eruption of Vesuvius, Frankie Howerd as a wily slave and some pretty awful – and dirty – jokes. Patrick Cargill does manage to make something out of a bored Nero but need one go on . . .

1971. Directed by Bob Kellett.
Starring Frankie Howerd, Patrick Cargill, Michael Hordern, Barbara Murray, Lance Percival, Bill Fraser, Adrienne Posta, Julie Ege. Colour.
90 minutes.

Thorn EMI Video

V

Valley Of The Dolls

Three young gals try to break into show business in New York and find
that they finish up broken instead. Susan Hayward adds a bit of fire as an
ageing musical star, but this sour look at American show biz is so full of
clichés that even its unintentionally funny moments (of which there are
many) aren't funny. Three of the songs of Andre and Dory Previn perhaps
sum it up best: "Come Live With Me", "Give A Little More" and "It's
Impossible". Based on the novel by Jacqueline Susann.

Box-office rental	$20,000,000
Average rental (67)	$13,081,250
Oscars	Nil
Oscar nominations (1)	Best Scoring Of Music

1967. Directed by Mark Robson.
Starring Barbara Parkins, Patty Duke, Paul Burke, Sharon Tate, Susan
Hayward, Tony Scotti, Martin Milner, Charles Drake. Colour.
123 minutes.

Twentieth Century-Fox Video

Valley Of The Sun

Arizona in the 1860s. Government agent James Craig – out to protect the
Apaches and prevent them from going on the warpath – finds he has his
work cut out when he comes up against crooked Indian agent Dean
Jagger. That's basically it, although Lucille Ball is also in there somewhere
despite the fact that she's not everyone's idea of a frontier gal. Routine
stuff that supports the mountaineering drama *The White Tower* on a
double-feature video tape.

1942. Directed by George Marshall.

Starring James Craig, Lucille Ball, Dean Jagger, Billy Gilbert, Cedric Hardwicke. Black and White.
79 minutes.

Kingston Video

Vampire Circus

"The circus comes to town" takes on a new meaning with this movie, for it's run by the cousin of a vampire count who was staked to death by the townsfolk some 15 years earlier. And cousin Emil wants revenge, which he gets in a big way as his circus performers, in reality vampires, begin to change their form and knock off their victims. The usual Hammer House Of Horror stuff with some intriguing scenes, such as victims catching sight of their own death in a mirror maze and some pretty awful ones. Set in early 19th century Serbia and about par for the Hammer course.

1972. Directed by Robert Young.
Starring Adrienne Corri, Laurence Payne, Thorley Walters, John Moulder Brown, Lynne Frederick, Elizabeth Seal. Colour.
87 minutes.

Rank Video

Vampyres

Two lesbian lovers become vampires after being murdered in bed and lure unsuspecting victims to an old house where they feed off their blood. One young man is not killed outright because one of the girls fancies him. Small budget horror with plenty of blood and plenty of graphic sex. Just another reworking of the same old vampire theme.

1974. Directed by Joseph Larraz.
Starring Marianne Morris, Anulka, Murray Brown, Brian Deacon, Sally Faulkner, Michael Byrne. Colour.
84 minutes.

Rank Video

Vanishing Point

Ex-marine/ex-cop/ex-racing driver Barry Newman accepts an impossible bet to try and reach San Francisco from Denver by three o'clock the following afternoon. All of which makes for a good excuse for a car chase movie, in which Newman drives at breakneck speed along desert highways pursued by the cops. Blind disc-jockey Cleavon Little supports him on the radio and promotes him as "the last beautiful free soul on this planet". Good car sequences; full of pretentious *Easy Rider*-type clap trap for the rest of the time. Very much of its period and now dated.

| Box-office rental | $5,004,000 |
| Average rental (71) | $13,465,850 |

1971. Directed by Richard Sarafian.
Starring Barry Newman, Cleavon Little, Dean Jagger, Victoria Medlin, Paul Koslo, Bob Donner. Colour.
99 minutes.

Twentieth Century-Fox Video

Victoria The Great

Anna Neagle in her element, transcending 60 years with ease, as she takes us from the time the young Victoria took her place on the throne as a teenage girl to the period when she was known as the "Widow Of Windsor". The film centres on her love affair and marriage to Prince Albert and her matters of state with her various prime ministers. A Technicolor epilogue includes scenes of her proclamation as Empress Of India and the Diamond Jubilee of 1897. Tends to make you scoff a bit during its first twenty minutes or so, but then gradually gets hold of you and never lets go. Considering its age, more than passable. 2½ rating.

1937. Directed by Herbert Wilcox.
Starring Anna Neagle, Anton Walbrook, Walter Rilla, Mary Morris, H. B. Warner. Black and White/Colour.
112 minutes.

Thorn EMI Video

Villain

This movie is written by Dick Clement and Ian La Frenais, authors of *The Likely Lads*, but don't expect too many laughs along the way. The only likely lad in this grim little piece is a homosexual East End gangster who runs a large protection racket and has a mother fixation complex on the side. Shades of *White Heat* with James Cagney. But no Mr. Cagney this time. Instead, Richard Burton, who duly gets his come-uppance but not before plenty of stomach-churning events have unfolded themselves for your delight. Nasty this, very nasty, which is a pity, because it's also rather well made.

1971. Directed by Michael Tuchner.
Starring Richard Burton, Ian McShane, Nigel Davenport, Donald Sinden, Fiona Lewis, Joss Ackland. Colour.
98 minutes.

Thorn EMI Video

Von Ryan's Express

Part POW drama, part escape movie, with hard-hearted American colonel Frank Sinatra leading a raid on a German train and making for the safety of the Swiss border. Major Trevor Howard heads the British contingency who are also along for the ride. The script's a bit weak but that's not fatal in an adventure yarn such as this. Sinatra shoots an Italian girl in the back but makes amends by sacrificing his life for the others. Set in Italy in 1943; rousing, quite spirited video entertainment. 2½ rating.

Box-office rental	$7,700,000
Average rental (65)	$13,881,050
Oscars	Nil
Oscar nominations (1)	Best Sound Effects

1965. Directed by Mark Robson.
Starring Frank Sinatra, Trevor Howard, Raffaella Carra, Brad Dexter, Sergio Fantoni, John Leyton, Edward Mulhare, Wolfgang Preiss, James Brolin. Colour.
117 minutes.

Twentieth Century-Fox Video

Voyage Of The Damned

A thousand refugees, dispatched by boat from Hamburg as a propaganda exercise by Hitler, are refused admission to land in either Cuba or the United States but eventually find haven in European countries, when they are faced with the awful prospect of having to return to Nazi Germany. A powerful story (a true one) set in the spring of 1939, but too long for comfort and not enhanced by a cast made up of international all-stars, each of whom performs rather woodenly in the various shipboard vignettes that make up the screenplay. Max von Sydow as the ship's captain stands out from the rest. This should have been absorbing entertainment. Instead, it's just wearisome video.

Oscars	Nil
Oscar nominations (3)	Best Supporting Actress (Grant); Screenplay; Original Music Score

1976. Directed by Stuart Rosenberg.
Starring Faye Dunaway, Max von Sydow, Oskar Werner, Malcolm McDowell, James Mason, Orson Welles, Katharine Ross, Ben Gazzara, Lee Grant, Sam Wanamaker, Lynne Frederick, Julie Harris, Wendy Hiller, Maria Schell, Fernando Rey, Jose Ferrer. Colour.
137 minutes.

Precision Video

Voyage To The Bottom Of The Sea

Atomic submarine commander Walter Pidgeon, thought mad by the United Nations, decides to risk all as he heads towards the Polar ice-cap, where a flaming radiation belt is threatening the existence of mankind. His plan? To shoot a Polaris missile into the belt and cause it to explode backwards into space. No wonder they think he's nuts! Surprisingly, considering the danger of his situation, he gets more trouble from the crew than he does from the technological hazards of his mission. Passable video fare that relaxes through its sheer absurdity.

1961. Directed by Irwin Allen.

Starring Walter Pidgeon, Joan Fontaine, Barbara Eden, Peter Lorre, Robert Sterling, Frankie Avalon. Colour.
105 minutes.

Twentieth Century-Fox Video

W

Wagonmaster

A Mormon wagon train, guided by two young horse traders, finds itself menaced by Indians and outlaws as it makes its way across country to Utah in the 1870s. A film held in great affection by John Ford admirers, but despite its poetic qualities a little short on action and rather too leisurely to hold the attention for very long. In fact, when playing on video, it tends to give off a rather somnambulistic effect. Shares a tape with a 1951 opus *Double Dynamite* with Frank Sinatra, Jane Russell and Groucho Marx.

1950. Directed by John Ford.
Starring Ben Johnson, Joanne Dru, Harry Carey Jr, Ward Bond, Charles Kemper, Alan Mowbray, Jane Darwell, Russell Simpson. Black and White.
86 minutes.

Kingston Video

Walk Softly Stranger

Well-made little thriller revolving around a small-time crook (Joseph Cotten), who returns to his home town only to find his former heart-throb (Valli) crippled because of an accident. Determined to reform, he decides to pull off one last job before settling down but, as usual, that's one job too many. Little-known RKO movie of the early 50s, efficient in just about every department and well worth a look. The Western *The Half Breed* supports it on a double-feature video tape.

1950. Directed by Robert Stevenson.

Starring Joseph Cotten, Valli, Spring Byington, Paul Stewart, Jack Paar, Jeff Donnell, John McIntire. Black and White.
81 minutes.

Kingston Video

The Wanderers

Philip Kaufman "coming-of-age" movie about the experiences of a group of teenagers who make up a Bronx street gang in the early 60s. Out of *West Side Story* and other gangland movies and nothing very special, with the usual brawls, clashes over race, sex with girls, and so on. There's plenty of 60s pop music on the soundtrack but Kaufman's a talented director who can do much better work than this. Probably a cult movie of the future though. Better value for a younger video audience than an older one.

1979. Directed by Philip Kaufman.
Starring Ken Wahl, John Friedrich, Karen Allen, Toni Kalem, Alan Rosenberg, Jim Youngs, Tony Ganios, Linda Manz, William Andrews, Erland Van Lidth de Jeude. Colour.
112 minutes.

Picture Time Video
(distributed by VCL)

Warlords Of Atlantis

Victorian scientists discover a lost city beneath the sea and find that the place is overrun by prehistoric monsters and a race of dying Martians, whose wicked boss is planning to conquer the world. Muscular all-American Doug McClure stands in his way. A run-of-the-mill fantasy, although Martians under the sea instead of up in the skies is at least something new!

1978. Directed by Kevin Connor.

Starring Doug McClure, Cyd Charisse, Peter Gilmore, Shane Rimmer, Lea Brodie, Michael Gothard. Colour.
91 minutes.

Thorn EMI Video

The War Of The Worlds ★★★

Among the best, perhaps *the* best of the science-fiction extravaganzas produced in the early 50s when the "Watch the skies there might be a flying saucer about" scare was at its height. This one, of course, is based on H. G. Wells' novel of a Martian invasion of planet Earth, although Hollywood being Hollywood updates the whole thing to the 50s and transfers the invasion to Los Angeles. Nonetheless, George Pal's effects remain impressive and the Martians themselves all the more spine-chilling, in that you see only one (and then only for a few seconds) during the whole movie. But those few seconds stay with you.

Oscars (1)   Best Special Effects
Oscar nominations (2)   Best Editing; Sound Recording

1953. Directed by Byron Haskin.
Starring Gene Barry, Les Tremayne, Ann Robinson, Henry Brandon, Jack Kruschen. Colour.
85 minutes.

CIC Video

The Warriors

Nauseating piece of cinema about street gang warfare in New York and which was blamed for causing many imitative scenes of violence when it was first released in America. And one can well believe it. The "plot", if that is the correct word, is impossible to encapsulate. Suffice it to say that the violence ranges from Coney Island to Manhattan to the Bronx. Zero minus and close to dustbin corner. If to be watched at all certainly when all the children are abed!

| Box-office rental | $14,500,000 |
| Average rental (79) | $31,904,775 |

1979. Directed by Walter Hill.
Starring Michael Beck, James Remar, Thomas Waites, Dorsey Wright, Brian Tyler. Colour.
90 minutes.

CIC Video

Welcome To Blood City ★★

One of those "things are not quite what they seem" movies. Ostensibly, it's about a group of people who find themselves transported back to a Western-style town ruled over by cold-blooded sheriff Jack Palance. But are they really in the Old West, and what have computers to do with the town? That's as far as we go. If you like science-fiction or fantasy, or a mixture of both, you'll probably enjoy this although, to be frank, it's only a routine and sometimes confusing example of the *genre*.

1977. Directed by Peter Sasdy.
Starring Jack Palance, Keir Dullea, Samantha Eggar, Barry Morse. Colour.
96 minutes.

Thorn EMI Video

The Werewolf Of Washington ★★

Cross a spoof of the werewolf-type movie with a satire on American White House politics and you finish up with something like this, a rather curious fantasy that tries hard to come up with something new but never really delivers the goods. Journalist Dean Stockwell is the one who gets bitten and goes on the rampage around the capital. Some moments of genuine horror, some of genuine parody. But the mixture just doesn't gel.

1973. Directed by Milton Moses Ginsberg.

Starring Dean Stockwell, Biff McGuire, Clifton James, Beeson Carroll, Jane House, Michael Dunn, Barbara Spiegel. Colour.
90 minutes.

VIPCO

West Side Story

Time has not been too kind to this film which, when first released in 1961, was hailed by some critics as being the most innovative screen musical ever made. Certainly the opening helicopter shots of New York and the subsequent descent into the city (so effective in the cinema) count for little on video. And the exhilarating choreography of Jerome Robbins is also much less cogent on the small screen. What stands the film in good stead is the music score of Leonard Bernstein and Stephen Sondheim, especially the numbers "Something's Coming"; "Tonight"; "I Feel Pretty"; and "America", danced excitingly on a New York roof top by Rita Moreno and company. The story, an update of the Romeo And Juliet theme, concerns the conflict between two rival street gangs and the tragic American-Puerto Rican love affair that arises out of the gang warfare. Superb New York locations and camerawork.

Box-office rental	$19,450,000
Average rental (61)	$8,103,100
Oscars (10)	Best Film; Supporting Actor (Chakiris); Supporting Actress (Moreno); Direction; Photography; Art Direction; Costume Design; Sound; Editing; Scoring Of A Musical
Oscar nominations (1)	Best Screenplay

1961. Directed by Robert Wise and Jerome Robbins.
Starring Natalie Wood, Richard Beymer, Russ Tamblyn, Rita Moreno, George Chakiris, Simon Oakland, Ned Glass. Colour.
155 minutes.

Intervision

Westward Passage

An historical rarity; a David Selznick movie which is of interest mainly because it provides a fascinating glimpse of Laurence Olivier at work in early 30s Hollywood. He's an arrogant young novelist who marries wealthy Ann Harding and looks forward confidently to a bright future. But then poverty sets in, then divorce, then reunion and so on. A cliché tale of sorrow and sacrifice but still a rarity. Features on a somewhat peculiarly balanced double feature tape with *Enchanted Island.*

1932. Directed by Robert Milton.
Starring Ann Harding, Laurence Olivier, Zasu Pitts, Irving Pichel. Black and White.
73 minutes.

Kingston Video

What Ever Happened To Aunt Alice? ★★★

Geraldine Page, widowed and impoverished, decides on a unique way of keeping solvent. She hires a succession of housekeepers with few relatives but a lot of money and then bumps them off when the time is right. All goes well until the appearance of snoopy Ruth Gordon, who wants to know what happened to one of her friends who used to be in Miss Page's employ. If you like black comedy then you'll revel in this movie, for it's ghoulish humour at its very best. Miss Page and Miss Gordon enjoy themselves immensely. So, I suspect, will you.

1969. Directed by Lee H. Katzin.
Starring Geraldine Page, Ruth Gordon, Rosemary Forsyth, Robert Fuller, Mildred Dunnock, Joan Huntingdon. Colour.
101 minutes.

Rank Video

What Ever Happened To Baby Jane? ★★★

Bette Davis as a former vaudeville child star and Joan Crawford as her crippled, ex-film star sister locked together in a huge, decaying Hollywood mansion. Davis is mentally unstable and wants revenge on her sister; Crawford is terrified and helpless. Davis cackles, Crawford screams. It's all superior *Grand Guignol* and just about perfect for the small video screen, although if you have an aversion to rats watch out. You have been warned. Watch out too for the opening precredit sequence. There's more to it than meets the eye.

Box-office rental	$4,050,000
Average rental (62)	$7,477,500
Oscars (1)	Best Costume Design
Oscar nominations (4)	Best Actress (Davis); Supporting Actor (Buono); Photography; Sound

1962. Directed by Robert Aldrich.
Starring Bette Davis, Joan Crawford, Victor Buono, Marjorie Bennett, Anna Lee. Black and White.
132 minutes.

Warner Home Video

What's Up Doc? ★★

Peter Bogdanovich's attempt to revive the screwball comedies so popular in Hollywood during the 30s with Ryan O'Neal as a meek musicologist and Barbra Streisand as the talkative drifter who decides she will marry him as soon as she claps eyes on him! Sounds a bit like *Bringing Up Baby* but, needless to say, it's nowhere near as good. The events revolve around three identical suitcases containing (a) priceless jewellery (b) secret government papers and (c) Miss Streisand's underwear. All is resolved in a mad slapstick chase that ends in San Francisco bay. Streisand's fine; the rest of its a bit tame.

Box-office rental	$28,000,000

Average rental (72) $17,543,950

1972. Directed by Peter Bogdanovich.
Starring Barbra Streisand, Ryan O'Neal, Kenneth Mars, Austin Pendleton, Madeline Kahn, Sorrell Booke. Colour.
94 minutes.

Warner Home Video

When A Stranger Calls

A psychotic merchant seaman murders two children after terrorizing their young baby sitter. Seven years later he escapes from a mental institution and makes in the direction of the same woman, now married and with two children . . . The long opening sequence in this movie is quite frightening; after that it's strictly run-of-the-mill thriller stuff and rather unpleasant stuff at that. If you are a woman living alone this is about the last movie you will want to view on your video machine.

Box-office rental $11,400,000
Average rental (79) $31,964,775

1979. Directed by Fred Walton.
Starring Charles Durning, Carol Kane, Colleen Dewhurst, Tony Beckley, Rachel Roberts. Colour.
97 minutes.

Guild Home Video

Where Danger Lives

If you can accept sleepy-eyed Robert Mitchum as a talented young physician who becomes infatuated with one of his psychotic patients, then you may well find this little thriller to your taste. The bad gal Mitch gets mixed up with is dark-haired Faith Domergue, who does away with elderly hubby Claude Rains and then tries to do the same to Bob when she finally realizes the game is up. Goodish melodrama; set of course, like most RKO thrillers, in Mexico. On the same video double bill: *Split Second*.

1950. Directed by John Farrow.
Starring Faith Domergue, Robert Mitchum, Claude Rains, Maureen O'Sullivan, Charles Kemper. Black and White.
84 minutes.

Kingston Video

Whisky Galore

Compton Mackenzie's folksy tale of some Scottish islanders who bypass wartime rationing by raiding a wrecked cargo ship and smuggling 50,000 cases of whisky past the home guard. The almost child-like humour survives less well than that in other Ealing comedies of the period, but there's still the odd moment or two to savour, especially when pompous Basil Radford as a teetotal home guard officer is involved in things. Filmed entirely on the Isle Of Barra in the Outer Hebrides, which may account for the rather inferior camerawork and sound quality. Note author Mackenzie's cameo as a ship's captain.

1949. Directed by Alexander Mackendrick.
Starring Basil Radford, Joan Greenwood, James Robertson Justice, Gordon Jackson, Wylie Watson, Catherine Lacey, Jean Cadell, Bruce Seton. Black and White.
82 minutes.

Thorn EMI Video

Whistle Down The Wind

A bearded murderer on the run in the North Of England is sheltered by three farm children who believe him to be Jesus Christ returned to Earth. Allegorical tale treated simply but skilfully by director Bryan Forbes and although some twenty years old still a good viewing bet on video. Bleak Northern landscapes, haunting music score by Malcolm Arnold. Alan Bates as the murderer manages to hold his own against the awesome talents of the three kids – Hayley Mills, Diane Holgate and (especially effective) Alan Barnes.

1961. Directed by Bryan Forbes.
Starring Hayley Mills, Bernard Lee, Alan Bates, Diane Holgate, Alan Barnes, Norman Bird, Diane Clare. Black and White.
98 minutes.

Rank Video

The White Tower

Climb a Swiss mountain and sort out your troubles on the way up. That's basically what this one's all about, as six people risk their lives climbing a previously unscaled mountain peak. Heading the assault: Oscar Homolka as a Swiss guide. In close attendance: Lloyd Bridges as an ex-Nazi; Claude Rains as a boozy French writer; Cedric Hardwicke as an English scientist; Valli as the widow of a famous Italian climber; and Glenn Ford who seems to be around simply because he's American and because he's a star. Good Technicolor and filmed for the most part in and around Mont Blanc in Switzerland. *Valley Of The Sun* features on the same tape.

1950. Directed by Ted Tetzlaff.
Starring Glenn Ford, Claude Rains, Valli, Oscar Homolka, Cedric Hardwicke, Lloyd Bridges. Colour.
98 minutes.

Kingston Video

Who's Afraid Of Virginia Woolf?

A middle-aged college professor (Richard Burton) and his blowsy, shrewish wife (Elizabeth Taylor) trap and almost destroy two young campus innocents (George Segal and Sandy Dennis) during one of their vicious, no-holds-barred evenings of drunken fun and games. A bit remorseless to say the least, and certainly not everyone's cup of tea, but quite the most ferocious portrait of marital relationships ever put on screen. The intimacy of its subject suits the small screen perfectly; based on the award-winning play by Edward Albee.

Box-office rental	$14,500,000
Average rental (66)	$8,826,100
Oscars (5)	Best Actress (Taylor); Supporting Actress (Dennis); Photography; Art Direction; Costume Design
Oscar nominations (8)	Best Film; Actor (Burton); Supporting Actor (Segal); Direction; Screenplay; Sound; Editing; Music Score

1966. Directed by Mike Nichols.
Starring Richard Burton, Elizabeth Taylor, George Segal, Sandy Dennis.
Black and White.
129 minutes.

Warner Home Video

The Wicker Man

Rum occurrences on a small island off the west coast of Scotland, where a police sergeant investigates the disappearance of a 12-year-old girl and uncovers paganism, superstition and a form of sacrifice which entails being burnt alive on May Day! Edward Woodward is the unfortunate policeman; Christopher Lee, Ingrid Pitt and an "in-the-buff" Britt Ekland among the islanders. Held in very high regard in some quarters and although not measuring up to its inflated reputation, still a very effective piece of movie horror. Scripted by Anthony Shaffer who wrote *Sleuth*.

1973. Directed by Robin Hardy.
Starring Edward Woodward, Britt Ekland, Diane Cilento, Ingrid Pitt, Christopher Lee, Lesley Mackie, Walter Carr. Colour.
86 minutes.

Thorn EMI Video

The Wild Bunch

Sam Peckinpah's celebrated (for some notorious) homage to the last of the Western outlaws, set on the Texas-Mexico border in the year 1913 and following the last months of an outlaw gang as they offer their services to a Mexican general. It all ends in a huge bloodbath that in the first few seconds is impressive but which, after it has gone on for several minutes, becomes preposterous. *Butch Cassidy* told roughly the same story but more lyrically, although there *are* some quieter, elegaic moments in *The Wild Bunch* and these are among the best in the film. Still very violent and now rather dated.

Box-office rental	$5,300,000
Average rental (69)	$13,660,950
Oscars	Nil
Oscar nominations (2)	Best Story And Screenplay; Music Score

1969. Directed by Sam Peckinpah.
Starring William Holden, Ernest Borgnine, Robert Ryan, Edmond O'Brien, Ben Johnson, Warren Oates. Colour.
145 minutes.

Warner Home Video

The Wildcats Of St. Trinian's

The girls of St. Trinian's return but, alas, should have stayed in retirement. This one has them forming the first branch of the Union Of British School-girls and abducting the daughter of a wealthy Arab prince. Sheila Hancock is the headmistress, Joe Melia is "Flash Harry" and Frank Launder does what he can with the thin material. But Ronald Searle's wickedly funny drawings stubbornly refuse to come to cinematic life – just as they did during the earlier films in the series.

1980. Directed by Frank Launder.
Starring Sheila Hancock, Michael Hordern, Joe Melia, Thorley Walters, Rodney Bewes. Colour.
91 minutes.

Home Video Productions

The Wild Geese

The mercenaries in this movie are just too good to be true: Richard Burton is disillusioned but has noble motives; Roger Moore is a soldier of fortune; and Richard Harris does it all for the sake of his son at a private prep school. Between them they give the impression that mercenaries are no more than *Boy's Own Paper* adventurers. Their mission? To rescue a deposed leader from imprisonment in a central African state and deliver him to safety. Nasty double-crossing merchant banker Stewart Granger is behind it all. Routine bang-bang movie; topical, well made. A free-fall from 20,000 feet is a spectacular highlight.

1978. Directed by Andrew V. McLaglen.
Starring Richard Burton, Roger Moore, Richard Harris, Hardy Kruger, Stewart Granger, Jack Watson, Winston Ntshona, John Kani, Frank Finlay, Kenneth Griffith. Colour.
134 minutes.

Rank Video

The Wild Heart

One of the Powell/Pressburger efforts that didn't come off; an adaptation of Mary Webb's novel about a wild, romantic girl who finds passion, happiness and eventually an early death in the Shropshire countryside during the 1890s. Squire David Farrar is the one who lusts after her, gentle minister Cyril Cusack the one who tries to bring her comfort. The best thing in the film is the photography. A much butchered film that first ran to 110 minutes but was eventually cut to 86 by producer Selznick after extensive reshooting. Known also as *Gone To Earth.*

1950. Directed by Michael Powell and Emeric Pressburger.
Starring Jennifer Jones, David Farrar, Cyril Cusack, Sybil Thorndike, Edward Chapman, Esmond Knight. Colour.
86 minutes.

Guild Home Video

Willie & Phil

Paul Mazursky movie guaranteed to send you to sleep within half-an-hour of its opening credits; a disastrous attempt to do an American *Jules And Jim* with an English teacher (Michael Ontkean) and a photographer (Ray Sharkey) striking up a long lasting friendship both with each other and the Kentucky girl (Margot Kidder) who shares their beds in New York and California. Too cute by half. Worse, it's dull and at 116 minutes much too long. Advice: wait for Truffaut's film to be released on video.

1980. Directed by Paul Mazurksy.
Starring Michael Ontkean, Margot Kidder, Ray Sharkey, Jan Miner, Tom Brennan. Colour.
116 minutes.

Twentieth Century-Fox Video

The Winslow Boy

Film version of Terence Rattigan's play about a 12-year-old naval cadet who is charged with the theft of a postal order and whose father goes to the highest court in the land in order to prove his innocence. A superb performance by Robert Donat as the barrister hired to defend the boy; in fact beautifully crafted entertainment all round, a pleasure to listen to and intriguing in its glimpses of family life of the period (1912). Doesn't move around much, doesn't need to. One of the best oldies on EMI's list.

1948. Directed by Anthony Asquith.
Starring Robert Donat, Margaret Leighton, Cedric Hardwicke, Basil Radford, Kathleen Harrison, Francis L. Sullivan, Marie Lohr, Jack Watling. Black and White.
117 minutes.

Thorn EMI Video

Witchfinder General

Vincent Price in dastardly form as a sadistic lawyer, who assumes the role of a witchfinder during the days of Cromwell and roams the country inflicting torture on those unlucky enough to get in his way. Price might be in top form but there's no ham from him in this performance, just a portrait of malevolence that chills the blood. He gets his come-uppance when he is hacked to pieces by an axe. That could well turn your stomach, as might other sequences in this film which is, incidentally, very well made indeed. Good script, interesting period detail, subtle colour. And good video providing you don't think the sadism is overdone.

1968. Directed by Michael Reeves.
Starring Vincent Price, Ian Ogilvy, Hilary Dwyer, Rupert Davies, Robert Russell, Patrick Wymark, Wilfrid Brambell. Colour.
87 minutes.

Hokushin

Without Reservations

John Wayne in a romantic comedy? Well, yes, even he slipped out of type occasionally. In this one he's a marine flyer who meets up with authoress Claudette Colbert travelling by train to Hollywood, where her best-selling novel is to be filmed. Miss Colbert thinks Wayne would make an ideal hero for the film. He thinks otherwise. OK of its type and with some surprise guest appearances by Cary Grant, Jack Benny and gossip columnist Louella Parsons. Ladies watching the movie on video might well take exception to Wayne's chauvinistic attitudes: "I want a woman who needs me, who's helpless and cute – not one who wants to put the world right." Shares a tape with *Footlight Varieties*.

1946. Directed by Mervyn LeRoy.
Starring John Wayne, Claudette Colbert, Don DeFore. Black and White.
107 minutes.

Kingston Video

The Wizard Of Oz

The title says it all – although perhaps a reminder that Judy Garland sings "Over The Rainbow", that Ray Bolger (The Straw Man), Jack Haley (The Tin Man) and Bert Lahr (The Cowardly Lion) appear as her travelling companions, and that Margaret Hamilton nearly steals the picture as the Wicked Witch would not come amiss. The story, of course, is based on L. Frank Baum's tale of a Kansas farm girl who is transported during a cyclone to the magical land of Oz and then has to find her way home again. Perfect entertainment for younger members of the family and worth saving for future generations. Black and White in its opening and closing scenes; colour for most of its running time.

Box-office rental	$4,000,000
Oscars (2)	Best Song ("Over The Rainbow"); Original Music Score
Oscar nominations (3)	Best Film; Art Direction; Special Effects

1939. Directed by Victor Fleming.
Starring Judy Garland, Frank Morgan, Bert Lahr, Jack Haley, Ray Bolger, Billie Burke, Margaret Hamilton, Charley Grapewin. Colour.
101 minutes.

MGM/CBS Home Video

The Woman On Pier 13

This movie earned something of a reputation in the late 40s, for it was made when Hollywood's hysterical Communist witch-hunts were at their peak. Not that it's much of a movie – commie boss Thomas Gomez blackmails former commie-now-capitalist Robert Ryan in a tale of the San Francisco docks – but it does reflect the hysteria of the times. RKO studio head Howard Hughes had quite a hand in its production. Known also as *I Married A Communist*, it supports the excellent *Cornered* on a double feature tape.

1949. Directed by Robert Stevenson.
Starring Laraine Day, Robert Ryan, John Agar, Thomas Gomez, Janis Carter. Black and White.
73 minutes.

Kingston Video

Wombling Free

A well-intentioned movie but a miscalculation all the way along the line. Five television minutes of the fat and furry Wombles was one thing, 96 minutes of them in a feature film is quite another. David Tomlinson, Frances de la Tour and Bonnie Langford are some of the humans involved but, oh dear, what a mess. One star but only just!

1978. Directed by Lionel Jeffries.
Starring David Tomlinson, Frances de la Tour, Bonnie Langford, Bernard Spear, John Junkin. Colour.
96 minutes.

Rank Video

The Wooden Horse

Not only a wooden horse but wooden acting into the bargain, with familiar British players giving familiar impersonations of a whole range of familiar British POW types! Still, this *was* the first escape movie of the 50s and 60s and its first half tension just about sees it through. The story, a true one, concerns the ingenious escape from Stalag Luft 111 in 1943, when three British prisoners tunnelled their way to freedom by using a wooden vaulting horse to cover the underground passage dug daily during the physical exercise period in the camp. Leo Genn, David Tomlinson and Anthony Steel are the three who make it to safety. Among the top four box-office successes in Britain in 1950, but these days no more than average viewing.

1950. Directed by Jack Lee.
Starring Leo Genn, David Tomlinson, Anthony Steel, Bryan Forbes, Jacques Brunius. Black and White.
101 minutes.

Thorn EMI Video

Woodstock

Oscar-winning documentary of the historic four-day outdoor rock concert held in the small town of Bethel in up-state New York in August, 1969. All of which means three hours of vivid spectacle and shattering sound as Canned Heat, Richie Havens, Joan Baez, The Who, Joe Cocker, Country Joe and Fish, Jimi Hendrix, Stills and Nash and many more go through their paces. Probably the best film ever made for lovers of rock music; not, however, nearly as effective on video, for the stereophonic sound is lost and so are many of the multi-screen images and a host of other technical attributes. A fine documentary reduced to half a film.

Box-office rental	$16,200,000
Average rental (70)	$16,881,800
Oscars (1)	Best Documentary Feature
Oscar nominations (2)	Best Sound; Editing

1970. Directed by Michael Wadleigh. Colour.
184 minutes.

Warner Home Video

The World's Greatest Athlete ★★

Tepid Disney offering about a college sports coach who comes across a super Tarzan-type athlete while taking a safari to Africa, then takes him back to the good old US of A where he wins every event in sight. A witch-doctor-godfather, a touch of voodoo and an amusing miniaturisation sequence liven things up occasionally but *only* occasionally. Grade C Disney.

Box-office rental	$11,600,000
Average rental (73)	$22,271,150

1973. Directed by Robert Scheerer.
Starring Tim Conway, Jan-Michael Vincent, John Amos, Roscoe Lee Browne, Dayle Haddon, Billy De Wolfe, Nancy Walker. Colour.
92 minutes.

Walt Disney Home Video

X

Xanadu

Olivia Newton-John supposedly turned down many scripts before deciding on this one after her success in *Grease*. One can only ask: "What
were the other ones like?" In this she's a Muse who cannot experience
human feeling, but pops down to Earth now and then to have a good time
anyway. Bandleader Gene Kelly was her entertainment of the 40s, young
Michael Beck is her modern day attraction. But there's no point in going
any further. This one is a mish-mash of the most inept kind. It kind of
gives you the feeling that it was made to help sell the LP!

Box-office rental	$10,200,000
Average rental (80)	$30,086,027

1980. Directed by Robert Greenwald.
Starring Olivia Newton-John, Gene Kelly, Michael Beck, James Sloyan,
Dimitri Arliss. Colour.
96 minutes.

CIC Video

Y

You'll Find Out

And you will, once you've discovered what judge Boris Karloff, bogus
prince Bela Lugosi and psychologist Peter Lorre are doing in a spooky
mansion full of sliding panels, secret passageways and falling chande-
liers. The object of their attention is a young heiress celebrating her 21st
birthday. There's comedy as well, plus six musical numbers from the Kay
Kyser band. Available on a double tape with *Son Of Kong*.

Oscars	Nil
Oscar nominations (1)	Best Song ("I'd Know You Anywhere")

1940. Directed by David Butler.

Starring Kay Kyser, Boris Karloff, Peter Lorre, Bela Lugosi, Dennis O'Keefe, Helen Parrish. Black and White.
97 minutes.

Kingston Video

Young And Innocent

A man on the run accused of a crime he didn't commit; a young girl who reluctantly accompanies him on his search for the real criminal; and a villain with a twitching eye who is discovered in true Hitchcock style in a long tracking shot, that starts high in a hotel lounge and finishes in close-up on the eye of a black-faced dance band drummer. Now quaint and artificial and in any case rather minor Hitchcock.

1937. Directed by Alfred Hitchcock.
Starring Nova Pilbeam, Derrick de Marney, Mary Clare, Edward Rigby, Basil Radford. Black and White.
80 minutes.

Rank Video

Young Frankenstein

Mel Brooks in affectionate as well as zany mood, as he sends up the Frankenstein movies of the 30s, photographing all the goings-on in black and white and incorporating some of Kenneth Strickfaden's original designs for Frankenstein's laboratory equipment. Gene Wilder (as the grandson of the infamous Baron Victor) takes over as the mad doctor, Peter Boyle is his monster. Together they sing "Puttin' On The Ritz" in top hat, white tie and tails. Boyle also lights two cigarettes, *Now Voyager* style, after he has ravished Madeline Kahn. Sample joke. Wilder: "Pardon me boy, is this the Transylvania station?" Answer: "Ja, track twenty nine. Can I give you a shine?"

Box-office rental	$38,823,000
Average rental (74)	$18,456,150
Oscars	Nil

Oscar nominations (2)   Best Screenplay; Sound

1974. Directed by Mel Brooks.
Starring Gene Wilder, Peter Boyle, Marty Feldman, Madeline Kahn, Cloris
Leachman, Teri Garr, Kenneth Mars, Gene Hackman, Richard Haydn.
Black and White.
106 minutes.

Twentieth Century-Fox Video

The Young Lions

No one thought much of this version of Irwin Shaw's bestseller when it
first appeared back in 1958. Which is understandable because it turns
Shaw's story on its head. Instead of a young German being corrupted and
destroyed by Fascism, it offers a German being taken in and finally
sickened by Fascism. And that's not the same thing at all. Nonetheless,
as a war adventure this isn't too bad an effort, and the contrasting personalities of the three stars – Marlon Brando (blond German), Montgomery
Clift (persecuted Jew) and Dean Martin (wisecracking playboy) see it
through. Odd now to record that Martin comes over as the best of the
three. A superb Hugo Friedhofer music score is one of the film's plus
factors. 2½ star rating.

Box-office rental	$4,480,000
Average rental (58)	$5,306,500
Oscars	Nil
Oscar nominations (3)	Best Photography; Sound; Music Score

1958. Directed by Edward Dmytryk.
Starring Marlon Brando, Montgomery Clift, Dean Martin, Hope Lange,
Barbara Rush, Maximilian Schell, May Britt, Lee Van Cleef. Black and
White.
167 minutes.

Twentieth Century-Fox Video

The Young Ones

Cliff Richard musical about the son of a property magnate who gets together with his effervescent pals and tries to save their youth club, which is situated on some land about to be bought up by Cliff's dad – Robert Morley no less! A "Putting-on-the-show" finale in a battered old theatre eventually saves the day and also helped the movie become one of the biggest box-office hits of its year. The vigorous dance routines and songs ("All For One", "Nothing's Impossible", "Got A Funny Feeling", "Lessons In Love" and others, make it passable, if very dated entertainment.

1961. Directed by Sidney J. Furie.
Starring Cliff Richard, Robert Morley, Carole Gray, Richard O' Sullivan, Melvyn Hayes. Colour.
108 minutes.

Thorn EMI Video

Z

Zachariah

Morality play set in the Old West and centring on a young country boy, who rides off to become a gunfighter and experiences gunplay, sex with Belle Starr and the mysteries of the desert before settling down to a peaceful life. Sounds like a hundred other Westerns. What makes it different from all the rest is that it has a rock score, and that makes it *sound* very different indeed. But for rock fans rather than Western addicts.

1971. Directed by George Englund.
Starring John Rubinstein, Pat Quinn, Don Johnson, Country Joe & The Fish, Elvin Jones, Doug York Rock Ensemble. Colour.
93 minutes.

Rank Video

Zombie Flesh-Eaters

A strange disease causes people to become zombies and rise from the dead. An old cemetery on a mysterious island in the Antilles produces quite a few of them. What's afoot? Or, more to the point, how many zombies are afoot? Several people try to find out in this inferior Italian picture. None of them is very successful. Nor is the movie.

1979. Directed by Lucio Fulci.
Starring Tisa Farrow, Ian McCullough, Richard Johnson, Al Cliver, Auretta Gay. Colour.
89 minutes.

VIPCO

Zombies: Dawn Of The Dead ★★

More adventures with the zombies first resurrected by George Romero in *Night Of The Living Dead*. This time there are hundreds of them on the rampage through America, all of them eager to feed off any luckless person that gets in their way. A destruction of their brains is the only thing that will stop them. Four rather uninteresting actors do their best to make this overlong horror movie seem interesting, but all fail dismally to enliven the proceedings. Romero's ghouls are supposed to be symbolic and meant to represent the underprivileged of this world. So the picture has a deeper meaning? See what you think.

1979. Directed by George A. Romero.
Starring David Emge, Ken Foree, Scott H. Reininger, Gaylen Ross, David Crawford, David Early. Colour.
125 minutes.

Alpha Video
(distributed by Intervision)

Z. P. G.

1984-type tale of a bleak 21st century, when overpopulation and wholesale pollution have caused the world government to decree that no children be born for thirty years. Oliver Reed and Geraldine Chaplin, fed up with the substitute robot dolls, decide to risk death and have a child. Sci-fi melodrama, which starts promisingly with some interesting predictions of the future, then tails off badly. Average video. Z.P.G stands for Zero Population Growth.

1972. Directed by Michael Campus.
Starring Oliver Reed, Geraldine Chaplin, Diane Cilento, Don Gordon, Bill Nagy. Colour.
96 minutes.

Home Video Productions

Zulu Dawn

Sequel to the 1963 hit movie *Zulu;* the main difference being that this one deals with a battle the British lost – at Ulundi in 1879 – when 1300 British soldiers were overrun and massacred by Zulu warriors, despite possessing superior fire power. Otherwise it's much the same mixture as before, although not nearly as efficiently handled. Burt Lancaster (as the commander of a troop of African cavalry) and Denholm Elliott are among those who perish; Peter O'Toole as the blundering opportunist Lord Chelmsford is one of the survivors.

1979. Directed by Douglas Hickox.
Starring Burt Lancaster, Peter O'Toole, Simon Ward, John Mills, Nigel Davenport, Michael Jayston, Ronald Lacey, Denholm Elliott, Freddie Jones, Christopher Cazenove, Ronald Pickup. Colour.
117 minutes.

Intervision

VIDEO COMPANIES & DISTRIBUTORS

All films included in this book are distributed by Video Companies in this country. Any enquiries about films and tapes can be sent to them at the addresses listed below which, although correct at the time of going to press, are subject to change.

BRENT WALKER VIDEO CORPORATION LTD.
9, Chesterfield Street, London W1Z 7HP
(distributed by Videospace Ltd.)

CIC VIDEO
138, Piccadilly, London W1V 9FH.

CINEMA FEATURES
(distributed by VCL)

DERANN VIDEO
99, High Street, Dudley, West Midlands

GUILD HOME VIDEO LTD.
Woodston House, Oundle Road, Peterborough PE2

HOKUSHIN AUDIO VISUAL LTD.
2, Ambleside Avenue, London SW16 6AD

HOME VIDEO PRODUCTIONS
61–65 Conduit Street, London W1R 9FD

INTERVISION LTD.
Unit 1, McKay Trading Estate, London W10

IPC VIDEO LTD.
Surrey House, Throwley Way, Sutton SM1 4QQ

IVER FILMS.
Pinewood Studios, Iver, Bucks SL0 ONH

KINGSTON VIDEO
34, Windmill Street, London W1P 1HH

MEDIA VIDEO
(distributed by Video Programme Distributors)

MGM/CBS HOME VIDEO
Hammer House, 113–119 Wardour Street, London W1

MOUNTAIN VIDEO
West Central Street, London W1

PICTURE TIME VIDEO
(distributed by VCL)

POLYGRAM VIDEO
1, Rockley Road, London W14 OOL

PRECISION VIDEO LTD.
19, Upper Brook Street, London W1Y 1PD

RANK VIDEO LIBRARY
PO Box 70, Great West Road, Brentford, Middlesex TW8 911R

RCA/COLUMBIA INTERNATIONAL VIDEO
50, Curzon Street, London W1Y 8EU

SPECTRUM
(distributed by Polygram)

THORN-EMI VIDEO PROGRAMMES LTD.
Thorn-EMI House, Upper St. Martins Lane, London WC2H 9ED

TWENTIETH CENTURY-FOX VIDEO
Perivale Industrial Estate, Greenford, Middlesex UB6 7RU

21ST CENTURY VIDEO
(distributed by VCL)

VCL VIDEO SERVICES LTD.
58 Parker Street, London WC2

VIDEO INSTANT PICTURE COMPANY.
9, Sentinel House, Sentinel Square, Brent Street, London NW4 2XD

VIDEOMEDIA
68/70 Wardour Street, London W1

VIDEO PROGRAMME DISTRIBUTORS LTD.
Building No. 1, GEC Estate, East Lane, Wembley, Middlesex

VIDEOSPACE LTD.
272 London Road, Wallington, Surrey SM6 7DJ

VIDEO UNLIMITED
Patrick House, West Quay Road, Poole, Dorset BH15 1JF

VIDEOVIEW
(distributed by Videomedia)

VINTAGE CLASSICS
(distributed by VCL)

VIPCO
(distributed by Video Instant Picture Company)

WALT DISNEY HOME VIDEO
(distributed by Rank Video)

WARNER HOME VIDEO
PO Box 59, Alperton Lane, Wembley, Middlesex HAO 1FJ

INDEX OF 100 TOP STARS

Allen, Woody 26, 163
Andrews, Julie 392, 414, 417
Astaire, Fred 84, 123, 376, 380, 388, 421, 434

Bates, Alan 171, 192, 246, 347, 364, 383, 445, 460
Beatty, Warren 65, 209
Bergman, Ingrid 28, 33, 92, 230, 299, 314, 395
Bogarde, Dirk 12, 69, 122, 128, 139, 140, 379, 413
Bogart, Humphrey 15, 40, 92
Brando, Marlon 179, 193, 254, 322, 409, 471
Bronson, Charles 38, 66, 127, 130, 136, 219, 268, 367
Brooks, Mel 55, 213, 215, 297, 344, 471
Brynner, Yul 247, 418
Burton, Richard 12, 106, 165, 265, 284, 361, 449, 461, 463

Cagney, James 291
Caine, Michael 45, 69, 79, 151, 231, 232, 243, 255, 363, 389, 411, 433
Chaney, Lon 222, 335
Chaplin, Charles 102, 103, 194, 197, 243, 263, 292
Christie, Julie 50, 143, 171, 172, 192, 209
Clayburgh, Jill 378, 385, 425, 445
Clift, Montgomery 227, 471
Collins, Joan 18, 49, 51, 406

Connery, Sean 69, 299
Cotten, Joseph 17, 103, 150, 171, 183, 225, 339, 387, 394, 427, 435, 452
Cushing, Peter 24, 31, 32, 58, 115, 189, 233, 259, 308, 313, 441, 443

Davis, Bette 20, 128, 273, 457
Dean, James 152, 352,
De Niro, Robert 132, 416
Dietrich, Marlene 186, 242, 250
Douglas, Kirk 48, 96, 185, 255, 326, 371, 440
Dreyfuss, Richard 107, 237
Dunaway, Faye 65, 95, 100, 166, 305, 450

Eastwood, Clint 27, 71, 137, 159, 161, 163, 186, 194, 214, 276, 325

Finch, Peter 160, 171, 305
Fonda, Henry 29, 38, 66, 104, 180, 184, 265, 273, 291, 398, 411, 433
Fonda, Jane 36, 79, 93, 99, 110, 155, 241, 250, 310, 401, 424

Garland, Judy 285, 466
Grant, Cary 71, 289, 314
Guinness, Alec 168, 197, 245, 252, 256, 278, 298, 317, 348, 350

Hackman, Gene 65, 69, 142, 182, 281, 308, 340, 409, 471
Hawn, Goldie 149, 343, 422

Hepburn, Audrey 300
Hepburn, Katharine 15, 71, 264
Heston, Charlton 17, 27, 33, 42,
    154, 175, 337, 366, 394, 418
Hoffman, Dustin 23, 260, 405
Holden, William 122, 295, 305, 462
Hurt, John 20, 138, 153, 156, 189,
    286, 383

Jackson, Glenda 363, 402, 438

Karloff, Boris 94, 113, 120, 181, 201,
    234, 470
Keaton, Buster 108, 187, 263
Keaton, Diane 26, 193, 267, 270

Ladd, Alan 47, 148, 203, 211, 381
Lancaster, Burt 31, 92, 474
Lee, Christopher 28, 115, 120, 135,
    159, 167, 206, 235, 308, 313, 330,
    461
Lemmon, Jack 17, 99, 199, 251,
    291, 343
Loren, Sophia 92, 154, 168, 175

MacLaine, Shirley 21, 41, 81, 340,
    439
Marvin, Lee 48, 93, 127, 136, 210,
    384
Mason, James 32, 62, 67, 94, 116,
    168, 198, 209, 298, 312, 315, 330,
    440, 450
Matthau, Walter 79, 211, 247, 251
McQueen, Steve 56, 75, 222, 242,
    369, 433
Midler, Bette 138, 364
Minnelli, Liza 78, 421
Mitchum, Robert 49, 116, 170, 265,
    272, 282, 326, 376, 459
Monroe, Marilyn 76, 105, 188, 379,
    423
Moore, Dudley 417
Moore, Roger 161, 193, 312, 375,
    384, 463

Newman, Paul 76, 112, 216, 223, 403

Newton-John, Olivia 196, 469
Nicholson, Jack 85, 100, 154, 319,
    341
Niven, David 86, 129, 161, 175, 203,
    295, 298, 375

Olivier, Laurence 40, 67, 69, 105,
    146, 205, 212, 238, 251, 323, 351,
    389, 456
O'Neal, Ryan 69, 146, 200, 271, 277,
    307, 425, 458

Pacino, Al 118, 141, 193, 329
Peck, Gregory 67, 150, 203, 291,
    318, 329, 375, 395, 440
Presley, Elvis 60, 184, 190, 192,
    236, 247, 330, 365
Price, Vincent 37, 219, 256, 294,
    392, 418, 465

Redford, Robert 23, 69, 72, 76, 81,
    155, 218, 403
Reeve, Christopher 409
Reynolds, Burt 132, 163, 217, 283,
    307, 319, 378, 390
Rogers, Ginger 84, 380, 434
Russell, Jane 144, 183, 188, 325,
    444

Scheider, Roy 23, 182, 237, 238,
    250
Scott, George C. 46, 125, 179, 223,
    297, 331
Sellers, Peter 41, 174, 209, 226,
    252, 298, 321, 322, 336, 354, 355,
    390, 422, 441
Sinatra, Frank 81, 133, 144, 214,
    280, 401, 421, 449
Spacek, Sissy 35, 86
Stallone, Sylvester 129, 343, 361,
    362
Steiger, Rod 34, 249, 265, 268, 316,
    322, 332, 367
Stewart, James 17, 49, 421
Streep, Meryl 132, 378

Streisand, Barbra 211, 277, 327, 400, 458

Sutherland, Donald 59, 136, 138, 143, 151, 250, 278, 281, 298, 397, 401

Taylor, Elizabeth 29, 106, 288, 421, 461

Travolta, John 86, 196, 371

Ustinov, Peter 128, 199, 265, 416

Wayne, John 21, 34, 101, 102, 177, 180, 200, 265, 283, 357, 358, 375, 398, 435, 438, 442, 443, 465

Welch, Raquel 170, 206, 301, 319, 320

Welles, Orson 103, 272, 277, 291, 297, 427, 437, 450

Wilder, Gene 13, 55, 163, 344, 385, 404, 471

Wood, Natalie 63, 118, 199, 352, 375, 455

The Amazing Mr. Blunden ★★★

Lionel Jeffries proves that his success with *The Railway Children* was no fluke with this delightful tale of two children who are visited by an amiable ghost in the year 1918 and whisked back 100 years to help some orphaned children suffering all sorts of hardships in a country mansion. Clever photography, lots of period charm and an ingenious storyline help make this one of the best children's movies of the 70s. It's not up to *The Railway Children* but it's not far behind. Diana Dors steals the film with her portrait of the grotesque Mrs. Wickens; Laurence Naismith as the ghostly Mr. Blunden gives it charm. Based on the story *The Ghosts* by Antonia Barber.

1972. Directed by Lionel Jeffries.
Starring Laurence Naismith, Lynne Frederick, Garry Miller, Rosalyn Landor, Marc Granger, Diana Dors, James Villiers, Madeline Smith, David Lodge, Dorothy Alison. Colour.
99 minutes.

Family Video
(distributed by VCL)

The Andromeda Strain ★★★

How do you like your sci-fi? The *Star Wars* and *Close Encounters* variety? Then this one is not for you. If, on the other hand, you like to think about what you see, this is very definitely a 'must', the story of a deadly extra-terrestrial organism that descends to Earth aboard a returning American space satellite and kills all but two of the inhabitants of a remote desert village. Four scientists are called in to stop the micro-organism before it threatens the health of the world. A little on the slow side but with plenty of tension and scientific gadgetry and the 'Oh, God, this could really happen' thought stays with you all the way.

Box-office rental	$8,341,000
Average rental (71)	$13,465,850
Oscars	Nil
Oscar nominations (2)	Best Art Direction; Editing

1971. Directed by Robert Wise.
Starring Arthur Hill, David Wayne, James Olson, Kate Reid, Paula Kelly, George Mitchell. Colour.
131 minutes.

CIC Video

Assault ★★

Unsavoury thriller about a rapist turned killer who terrorises a girls' school. Now twelve years old but horribly topical as a subject and told in a 'whodunnit' format with the murders, etc being viewed through the subjective camera, and the killer's identity being saved until the final reel. Dour cop Frank Finlay investigates. Doctor James Laurenson, newspaper reporter Freddie Jones and hospital director Anthony Ainley are among the suspects. Lesley-Ann Down plays a schoolgirl. Routine.

1971. Directed by Sidney Hayers.
Starring Suzy Kendall, Frank Finlay, James Laurenson, Lesley-Ann Down, Freddie Jones. Tony Beckley, Anthony Ainley. Colour.
91 minutes.

Rank Video

Avalanche Express

Can American agent Lee Marvin get disillusioned KGB man Robert Shaw across Europe and to the safety of the West? The safest form of travel is the Atlantic Express. But there's a double agent on board. And Red terrorists are threatening to strike along the tracks. And there's an avalanche to watch out for in Switzerland . . . It sounds a tall order! Still, Lee Marvin's been through this type of thing before, and is just the right guy for the job. Rather a corny movie that starts off promisingly, tails off halfway through and finishes as a laughably bad botch-up. Director Mark Robson died halfway through shooting and it shows!

1979. Directed by Mark Robson.
Starring Robert Shaw, Lee Marvin, Linda Evans, Maximilian Schell, Mike Connors, Joe Namath, Horst Buchholz, David Hess. Colour.
88 minutes.

Twentieth Century-Fox Video

Battle Of Midway

Not really a movie for British audiences but passable for those who revel in reconstructions of real death events of World War II. This one tells how the Americans fought back against the Japanese at the 1942 naval battle of Midway. Henry Fonda pretends he's Admiral Nimitz, Robert Mitchum has a shot at Admiral Halsey and Toshiro Mifune makes an appearance as Yamamoto. There's also a lot of noise, model work and prodding about on maps. The action just got it by on the big screen. On video it's no more than routine.

Box-office rental	$22,329,000
Average rental (76)	$22,752,350

1976. Directed by Jack Smight.
Starring Charlton Heston, Henry Fonda, James Coburn, Glenn Ford, Hal Holbrook, Toshiro Mifune, Robert Mitchum, Cliff Robertson, Robert Wagner, Robert Webber. Colour.
131 minutes.

CIC Video

The Big Boss

Bruce Lee visits Bangkok and discovers that heroin smuggling is going on behind the front of an ice factory and that the factory contains the frozen bodies of those who have also stumbled on the deadly secret. Kick, grunt and groan rubbish. Of little entertainment value. Certainly of no artistic quality. Bruce Lee glowers and chops, especially in the film's second half, but it's all a waste of time, even from the very first jump/yell!

1971. Directed by Lo Wei.
Starring Bruce Lee, Maria Yi Yi, James Tien, Nora Miao, Han Ying-chieh. Colour.
98 minutes.

Rank Video

The Bounty Killer

Little known Western about a mild-mannered Easterner (Dan Duryea) who becomes a bounty hunter when he discovers that killing in the Old West can lead to profitable returns. Rather enjoyable little oater, of interest for its strong supporting cast which includes many old-timers in key roles – Fuzzy Knight as Duryea's partner-in-crime, Richard Arlen as a rancher, Buster Crabbe as an outlaw and Johnny Mack Brown as a sheriff. Supports *Macao* on a video double bill.

1965. Directed by Spencer Gordon Bennet.
Starring Dan Duryea, Rod Cameron, Audrey Dalton, Richard Arlen, Buster Crabbe, Fuzzy Knight, Johnny Mack Brown, Peter Duryea, Bob Steele. Colour.
92 minutes.

Kingston Video

Breaker Morant

Stark Australian movie about three Australian soldiers who are made scapegoats by the British during the Boer War and sacrificed in order to prevent the Germans entering the war on the side of the Boers. Looks with a somewhat less than enthusiastic eye at British diplomacy, army high command and politicians and bears a strong resemblance to *Paths of Glory* which dealt with a similar theme about the French Army in 1917. A mainly interior movie. Edward Woodward is the luckless Breaker Morant who goes to his death at dawn; Jack Thompson the defending counsel who tries to save him.

Box-office rental	$5,000,000
Average rental (80)	$30,086,027
Oscars	Nil
Oscar nominations (1)	Best Screenplay

1980. Directed by Bruce Beresford.
Starring Edward Woodward, Jack Thompson, John Waters, Bryan Brown, Charles Tingwell, Terence Donovan, Vincent Ball. Colour.
107 minutes.

Guild Home Video

Buffalo Bill And The Indians, Or Sitting Bull's History Lesson

Probably the slowest, dullest and yawniest 'western' ever made, set in 1885 when Buffalo Bill (Paul Newman) was taking his Wild West Show around America and having trouble in living up to his legendary image. Burt Lancaster offers a nice cameo as Ned Buntline, the dime novelist who helped create the legend but even Paul Newman fans will be hard put to find anything very entertaining in this film. Geraldine Chaplin features as Annie Oakley. Muted, rather murky camerawork doesn't help things along.

1976. Directed by Robert Altman.
Starring Paul Newman, Joel Grey, Burt Lancaster, Kevin McCarthy, Harvey Keitel, Allan Nicholls, Geraldine Chaplin, John Considine. Colour.
123 minutes.

Thorn EMI Video

Bundle of Joy

A big department store. A salesgirl finds an abandoned baby and is tagged as its unwed mother. A store owner's son falls in love with her. A song or two. Yes, 50s Hollywood conveyor belt stuff but although naive and hopelessly dated not without a little never-never-land charm. It's a remake of the 1939 classic *Bachelor Mother* with Ginger Rogers and David Niven. That was much better but as it's not yet available on video this one must suffice. On the same video double-bill: *Montana Belle*.

1956. Directed by Norman Taurog.
Starring Eddie Fisher, Debbie Reynolds, Adolphe Menjou, Tommy Noonan. Colour.
98 minutes.

Kingston Video

The Choirboys ★

The raucous goings-on of a group of Los Angeles cops who gather together in a park every Friday night to let off steam and search for wine, women and song. Little more than a series of vulgar revue sketches that presents the average American cop as a bully, a pervert, a nut-case and a few other things besides. Foul-mouthed and very definitely not director Robert Aldrich at his best. Charles Durning features as the 'choirboy' leader. Embarrassing video.

Box-office rental	$7,629,000
Average rental (77)	$36,913,348

1977. Directed by Robert Aldrich.
Starring Charles Durning, Louis Gossett Jr, Perry King, Clyde Kusatsu, Stephen Macht, Tim McIntire, Randy Quaid, Don Stroud, James Woods, Chuck Sacci, Robert Webber, Burt Young. Colour.
120 minutes.

MGM/CBS Home Video

The Cincinnati Kid ★★★

A kind of miniature *Hustler* (see page 223), rather more lightweight but with the same theme: young hopeful Steve McQueen determines to take on and beat reigning stud poker king Edward G. Robinson in a mammoth card game in New Orleans. You wouldn't think that a game of cards could create so much tension but it does. Even if you don't understand stud poker you'll find this one riveting stuff. McQueen is superb but it's Robinson's film, he's cool, polished, elegant, supremely confident as 'The Man'. Ann-Margret, Karl Malden, Tuesday Weld, Joan Blondell head the very strong supporting cast. *Note for movie buffs*: Spencer Tracy was originally set for the Robinson role. Edward G. took over when Spence became unwell. Sam Peckinpah began the film but was replaced after a few days by Norman Jewison.

1965. Directed by Norman Jewison.
Starring Steve McQueen, Edward G. Robinson, Ann-Margret, Karl Malden, Tuesday Weld, Joan Blondell, Rip Torn, Jack Weston, Cab Calloway, Jeff Corey. Colour. 113 minutes.

MGM/CBS Home Video

Conquest Of The Planet Of The Apes ★★

Number four in the Planet Of The Apes series. This one is set in the year 1991. North America is a police state and apes (not cats and dogs which have been wiped out by an endemic disease) are household pets. But not for long. Their day is to come once more. Par for the ape-movie course. Undemanding movie entertainment.

Box-office rental	$4,500,000
Average rental (72)	$17,543,950

1972. Directed by J. Lee Thompson.
Starring Roddy McDowall, Don Murray, Natalie Trundy, Ricardo Montalban, Hari Rhodes. John Randolph. Colour
85 minutes.

Twentieth Century-Fox Video

Dangerous Mission ★★

RKO programmer about a young woman (Piper Laurie) who witnesses a gangland murder in New York then flees to the safety of a remote tourist hotel in the Glacier National Park. Unbeknown to her, the law and a sinister underworld agent have tracked her down in the form of burly Victor Mature and sly Vincent Price. But who is the cop and who is the crook? Originally shot in 3-D which probably livened things up a bit. Average. On the same video double-bill: *Impact*.

1954. Directed by Louis King.
Starring Victor Mature, Piper Laurie, William Bendix, Vincent Price, Betta St. John, Steve Darrell. Colour.
75 minutes.

Kingston Video

Death Line

Not very nice movie about some students who discover a dying man in their local underground station then find that some cannibals are enjoying themselves in the tube tunnel and pop up now and then for new victims. Starts as a thriller, ends as a rather nauseating horror flick. Police detective Donald Pleasence and sergeant Norman Rossington do their best and are aided by MI5 man Christopher Lee. Unappetizing!

1972. Directed by Gary Sherman.
Starring Donald Pleasence, Norman Rossington, David Ladd, Sharon Gurney, Christopher Lee, Hugh Armstrong, Colour.
87 minutes.

Rank Video

The Desert Fox

Taught war drama about the career of Field Marshal Rommel during World War II, first as the brilliant commander of the crack Afrikan Korps in the desert, then as a member of the July 1944 plot to assassinate Hitler. James Mason is Rommel, Luther Adler features among the supporting players as Hitler. The actual assassination attempt and a brilliantly filmed precredit sequence of a commando raid on Rommel's headquarters are two of the film's highlights. Now over thirty years old but it never flags. Good video.

1951. Directed by Henry Hathaway.
Starring James Mason, Cedric Hardwicke, Jessica Tandy, Luther Adler, Everett Sloane, Leo G. Carroll, George Macready. Black and White.
88 minutes.

Twentieth Century-Fox Video

Dr. Jekyll And Sister Hyde

Yet another twist to Stevenson's tale of the young Doctor Jekyll and his search for the elixir of life. The setting is once again Victorian London but this time the good doctor (Ralph Bates) mixes a few female hormones into the potion and low and behold it turns into attractive Martine Beswick. Attractive but deadly for she kills at will and even makes passes at other men. Bodysnatchers Burke and Hare are also involved in events. Not bad.

1971. Directed by Roy Ward Baker.
Starring Ralph Bates, Martine Beswick, Gerald Sim, Lewis Fiander, Dorothy Alison, Neil Wilson, Ivor Dean, Paul Whitsun-Jones. Colour.
97 minutes.

Thorn EMI Video

Dr. Mabuse–The Gambler ★★★

A real treat for movie buffs and one of the most imaginative examples of video marketing yet to come from any distributor; the 1922 Fritz Lang drama about a power-mad master criminal who uses his secret organization of murderers and thieves (plus his hypnotic powers) to create his own personal criminal empire. Silent but wonderfully atmospheric and a real collector's item. Proves – if proof be needed – that Lang was truly one of the cinema's great directors. Rudolph Klein-Rogge is Mister Big; Carl Hoffmann in charge of the striking photography.

1922. Directed by Fritz Lang.
Starring Rudolph Klein-Rogge, Alfred Abel, Aud Egede Nissen, Gertrude Welcker, Bernhard Goetzke, Forster Larrinaga, Paul Richter. Black and White.
95 minutes.

Thorn EMI Video

Doctor Zhivago ★★★

One of the most famous movies of the 60s, made at a time when films boasted huge budgets and it actually showed on the screen. Omar Sharif is the Russian doctor/poet who finds himself in sympathy with the ideals of the Bolsheviks but unable to adjust to the new society when the revolution finally occurs; Julie Christie is his tragic love Lara, a name that became famous the world over thanks to the haunting theme tune of Maurice Jarre. Not as impressive as it once seemed and video doesn't really do it justice but some of the spectacular set pieces – a train speeding across the snow towards the Urals, a massacre in the Moscow streets and also in the brilliant gold of a wheatfield – are testament to David Lean's genius as a film-maker. A five-handkerchief spectacular.

Box-office rental	$46,550,000
Average rental (65)	$13,881,050
Oscars (5)	Best Screenplay; Photography; Art Direction; Costume Design; Music Score
Oscar Nominations (5)	Best Film; Supporting Actor (Courtenay); Direction; Sound; Editing

1965. Directed by David Lean.
Starring Geraldine Chaplin, Julie Christie, Tom Courtenay, Alec Guinness, Siobhan McKenna, Ralph Richardson, Omar Sharif, Rod Steiger, Rita Tushingham. Colour.
180 minutes.

MGM/CBS Home Video

Dressed to Kill ★★

A Brian De Palma exercise in gratuitous violence that owes so much to earlier Alfred Hitchcock films that it is almost impossible to regard it as an original work. Like Janet Leigh in *Psycho* before her, Angie Dickinson is the one who 'gets hers' when she is slashed to pieces by a man/woman wielding a razor in a lift. But who is he/she? The film keeps you guessing until the final reels although if you haven't twigged the identity of the culprit by then you must have been asleep. Cheap and slick and nasty and with a plot more full of holes than a Gruyere cheese. Not to be confused with the Sherlock Holmes film of the same name mentioned on page 146.

Box-office rental	$15,000,000
Average rental (80)	$30,086,027

1980. Directed by Brian De Palma.
Starring Michael Caine, Angie Dickinson, Nancy Allen, Keith Gordon, Dennis Franz, David Margulies, Ken Baker. Colour.
104 minutes.

Guild Home Video

The Dunwich Horror

Take a rare occult volume called *The Necronomicon.* Add a young man whose great grandfather was hanged in a New England village as a demon. Stir well, then thrown in an old mansion, a touch of Devil worship and Sandra Dee (yes, Sandra Dee!) as a young student. And what have you got? A right old mess? Surprisingly no, a not ineffective little piece of suggestive horror that relies more on Lewton-type atmosphere than monsters for its chills. Based on a short story by H. P. Lovecraft.

1970. Directed by Daniel Haller.
Starring Sandra Dee, Dean Stockwell, Ed Begley, Sam Jaffe, Donna Baccala, Lloyd Bochner, Joanna Moore Jordan, Colour.
86 minutes.

Guild Home Video

The Enemy Below

Above average Hollywood adventure drama exposing the futility of war. Robert Mitchum is the captain of an American destroyer; Curt Jurgens the commander of a German U-Boat. Together they play a deadly game of cat and mouse in the Atlantic but in the end prove nothing and succeed only in sending both of their vessels to the bottom of the ocean. Set during World War II; superior special effects.

Oscars (1)	Best Special Effects

1957. Directed by Dick Powell.
Starring Robert Mitchum, Curt Jurgens, Theodore Bikel, Doug McClure, Russell Collins, David Hedison. Colour.
98 minutes.

Twentieth Century-Fox Video

A Farewell To Arms

The first version of Ernest Hemingway's 1930 tale about the doomed romance between an American ambulance driver and the British nurse who cares for him when he is wounded in Italy in World War I. A good film from a great novel and tears aplenty at the tragic climax. Also something of a rarity, so well worth seeking out. Gary Cooper is the ambulance driver; Helen Hayes the nurse who dies in childbirth. Exquisite direction from Frank Borzage.

Oscars (2)	Best Photography; Sound Recording
Oscar nominations (2)	Best Film; Art Direction

1932. Directed by Frank Borzage.
Starring Gary Cooper, Helen Hayes, Adolphe Menjou, Mary Philips, Jack La Rue, Blanche Frederici. Black and White.
78 minutes

Vintage Classics
(distributed by VCL)

A Farewell To Arms

The same story remade twenty-five years later but nowhere near as effectively. Rock Hudson and Jennifer Jones are the ill-fated pair but are swamped by the huge production values of David O. Selznick whose last movie this was and who was determined to turn Hemingway's intimate tragedy into an epic. Hence the 157 minutes running time. John Huston might have made something out of it but was replaced by Charles Vidor after an argument with Selznick. Handsome photography; enjoyable performance from Vittorio De Sica as Major Rinaldi.

Box-office rental	$5,000,000
Average rental (57)	$5,760,550
Oscars	Nil
Oscar nominations (1):	Best Supporting Actor (De Sica)

1957. Directed by Charles Vidor.
Starring Rock Hudson, Jennifer Jones, Vittorio De Sica, Mercedes McCambridge, Alberto Sordi, Elaine Stritch, Oscar Homolka. Colour.
157 minutes.

Twentieth Century-Fox Video

The Final Programme

One of those 'end of the world is at hand' stories with a group of scientists based in Lapland trying to beat the odds by coming up with a form of self-reproducing human being – a hermaphrodite born of a man and a bisexual woman. They hope for a new kind of Messiah; they get (you guessed it) a misshapen monster. Par for the course for the misshapen monster-type movie.

1973. Directed by Robert Fuest.

Starring Jon Finch, Jenny Runacre, Sterling Hayden, Harry Andrews, Hugh Griffith, Julie Ege, Patrick Magee. Colour.
89 minutes.

Thorn EMI Video

The First Travelling Saleslady

Ginger Rogers pretends to sell corsets in the turn-of-the-century West but in reality sells barbed wire to the homesteaders. Carol Channing provides a few moments of humour and sings 'A Corset Can Do A Lot For A Lady'. And that's about it really. RKO was on its last legs when this was made and it looks like it. Of minor interest is that a young Clint Eastwood (sixth on the cast list) features as Channing's beau. Shares a comedy double-bill with *A Lady Takes A Chance*.

1956. Directed by Arthur Lubin.
Starring Ginger Rogers, Barry Nelson, Carol Channing, Brian Keith, James Arness, Clint Eastwood. Colour.
92 minutes.

Kingston Video

Fist Of Fury

Kung Fu pupil Bruce Lee goes on a revenge binge when he visits Shanghai and discovers that his old tutor has been murdered. Japanese, Russians, etc are among the victims of his wrath. Kung Fu codswallop with the usual slow-motion violence, boring karate fights and the unappealing personality of Chinese-American Bruce Lee. He was popular in the 70s but whether his lack of star quality has survived into the 80s is difficult to assess.

1972. Directed by Lo Wei.
Starring Bruce Lee, Nora Miao, James Tien, Robert Baker, Maria Yi. Colour.
106 minutes.

Rank Video

The Four Musketeers

As this movie was shot at the same time as *The Three Musketeers* it can hardly be called a sequel, more a continuation as director Richard Lester follows D'Artagnan and friends in their battles not so much with Richelieu as with the lustful Milady De Winter, revealed here as an unscrupulous whore who was once married to Athos. A ragbag of slapstick jokes, action and satirical comedy (a member of a firing squad has difficulty placing a blindfold over the patch of his one-eyed victim), it looks a bit like left-overs. Discerning video viewers will probably rather leave it than take it.

Box-office rental	$8,766,000
Average rental (75)	$27,300,250
Oscars	Nil

Oscar nominations (1)   Best Costume Design

1975. Directed by Richard Lester.
Starring Oliver Reed, Raquel Welch, Richard Chamberlain, Michael York, Frank Finlay, Simon Ward, Christopher Lee, Faye Dunaway, Charlton Heston, Geraldine Chaplin, Jean-Pierre Cassel. Colour.
103 minutes.

Intervision

Frenzy

Alfred Hitchcock returned to England to make this movie which is similiar in many ways to his prewar British thrillers and centres on a sex maniac who commits a series of necktie murders in London. It keeps you on the go but Hitch was beginning to go off the boil about this time and the overall unpleasantness of the theme (an extended rape and strangulation scene is especially repellent) leaves a rather nasty aftertaste. Plenty of "Cor what annuva murder" type dialogue and a blackly humorous moment in which Barry Foster enjoys a night ride with a body in a sack of spuds. But below par Hitchcock, and a particularly unsatisfactory ending.

Box-office rental $6,500,000
Average rental (72) $17,543,950

1972. Directed by Alfred Hitchcock.
Starring Jon Finch, Alec McCowen, Barry Foster, Barbara Leigh-Hunt, Anna Massey, Vivien Merchant, Bernard Cribbins, Billie Whitelaw, Michael Bates. Colour.
116 minutes.

CIC Video

Frogs

Nature revenges itself on the family of a crippled Southern patriarch (Ray Milland) living on a secluded island which has been forcibly reclaimed from nature by chemicals and insecticides. Pollution in this case doesn't cause monster mutation, just a vengeful intelligence as armies of normal sized creatures – snakes, lizards, leeches, scorpions and frogs – wipe out the family one by one, leaving to last the terrified Milland who is trapped in his wheelchair and gradually engulfed by hordes of frogs. Ugh! Tends to make you wake up in the middle of the night scratching and shuddering. But superior horror, and with a message!

1972. Directed by George McGowan.
Starring Ray Milland, Sam Elliott, Joan Van Ark, Adam Roarke, Judy Pace, Lynn Borden, Mae Mercer. Colour.
90 minutes.

Guild Home Video

Futureworld ★★

Sequel to *Westworld*, again set in Delos but this time with a rather tired plot of a mad scientist planning to take over the world by replacing all of its leaders with identical robots. Not a bad idea when you come to think of it but hardly the basis of an inspiring film. Reporters Peter Fonda and Blythe Danner put a stop to his plans and Yul Brynner reappears briefly in a dream sequence as the seemingly indestructible Gunslinger. Attractive Miss Danner is the best thing in the movie and worth resting your eyes on once you've got fed up with all the scientific gadgetry.

Box-office rental	$4,000,000
Average rental (76)	$22,752,350

1976. Directed by Richard T. Heffron.
Starring Peter Fonda, Blythe Danner, Arthur Hill, Yul Brynner, John Ryan, Stuart Margolin. Colour.
104 minutes.

Guild Home Video

Gentleman's Agreement ★★★

At one time this film was famed for its daring approach to a subject that had previously been taboo as movie material – anti-Semitism. Nowadays it looks not a little tame, inevitable perhaps considering the nature of its subject matter although *Crossfire* (see page 115) which was released the same year and dealt with the same theme has held up remarkably well. Gregory Peck stars as a magazine journalist who in order to probe into anti-Semitism in the States, poses as a Jew and finds that prejudice is rife, not only in hotels and country clubs but also among his own middle-class friends. The Zanuck-Kazan-Moss Hart combination proved to be a winning team at Oscar time although commercially the film didn't quite make the 4 million dollar mark, coming in at 3,900,000!

Oscars (3)	Best Film; Supporting Actress (Holm); Direction
Oscar nominations (4)	Best Actor (Peck); Actress (McGuire); Screenplay; Editing

1947. Directed by Elia Kazan.
Starring Gregory Peck, John Garfield, Dorothy McGuire Celeste Holme, Anne Revere, June Havoc, Albert Dekker, Jane Wyatt, Dean Stockwell. Black and White.
118 minutes.

Twentieth Century-Fox Video

The Godfather Part 11 ★★★★

More blood-splattered adventures of one of the best-known families in the States – the Don Corleone mob – this time following son Al Pacino's rise to supreme power after the death of Brando in part one (see page 192). It also takes time out to look at the young Brando (played by Robert De Niro) when he first arrives in New York at the beginning of the century. Confusing? Yes. Which is probably why this second movie didn't do as well commercially as the first. No matter, it's every bit as good, even superior in some sequences. A revenge murder in Sicily and the sudden bourgeois panic as the Castro Revolution takes hold are two scenes that are brilliantly realised. Not to be missed under any circumstances.

Box-office rental	$30,673,000
Average rental (74)	$18,456,150
Oscars (6)	Best Film; Supporting Actor (De Niro); Direction; Screenplay; Art Direction; Original Music Score
Oscar nominations (5)	Best Actor (Pacino); Supporting Actor (Gazzo); Supporting Actor (Strasberg); Supporting Actress (Shire); Costume Design

1974. Directed by Francis Ford Coppola.
Starring Al Pacino, Robert Duvall, Diane Keaton, Robert De Niro, John Cazale, Talia Shire, Lee Strasberg, Michael V. Gazzo. Colour.
200 minutes

CIC Video

The Heroes Of Telemark

How a group of brave Norwegians led an assault on, and destroyed, the vital Norsky-Hydro factory in occupied Norway in World War II, a factory producing 'heavy water' and vital to the Nazis hopes of putting together an atomic bomb before the Allies. Kirk Douglas and Richard Harris lead the team but this is a strangely lacklustre film that never quite comes to life as it should. It sounds as though it has been written by Alistair MacLean. In fact it is based on real-life events. Lovely sweeping vistas of Norway in winter. Director Anthony Mann's last complete film.

1965. Directed by Anthony Mann.
Starring Kirk Douglas, Richard Harris, Ulla Jacobsson, Michael Redgrave, David Weston, Sebastian Breaks, John Golightly. Colour.
131 minutes.

Rank Video

Honky Tonk Freeway

A disaster movie but of the wrong kind; a feeble tale of how the citizens of a small Florida resort take the law into their own hands and force an exit on the busy highway that is bypassing their town and ruining their livelihoods. Basically an Ealing type situation. Not in any way an Ealing type handling though. Most of it takes place on the road and includes some nuns, a couple of bumbling bank robbers, an elephant and some car crashes. If that makes it sound lousy then that's not the half of it. And believe it or not the man at the helm of this mish-mash was John Schlesinger.

1981. Directed by John Schlesinger.
Starring William Devane, Beau Bridges, Teri Garr, Beverly D'Angelo, Hume Cronyn, Jessica Tandy, Howard Hesseman, Paul Jabara, Daniel Stern. Colour.
107 minutes.

Thorn EMI Video

How To Marry A Millionaire

This was the second Twentieth Century-Fox movie to be filmed in CinemaScope and contains the famous line: "men don't make passes at girls who wear glasses." The girl in glasses in this one is none other than Marilyn Monroe, one of three models (Betty Grable and Lauren Bacall are her partners in crime) who pool their resources and rent a swank New York apartment in the hope of trapping millionaire husbands. Released in 1953, it was advertised as "Big As Life And A Million Times More Fun!" Well, it isn't quite that but thanks to Nunnally Johnson's script and the talents of the three stars, it'll do.

Box-office rental	$7,300,000
Average rental (53)	$6,098,850
Oscars	Nil
Oscar nominations (1)	Best Costume Design

1953. Directed by Jean Negulesco
Starring Marilyn Monroe, Betty Grable, David Wayne, William Powell, Rory Calhoun, Cameron Mitchell, Alex D'Arcy. Colour.
95 minutes.

Twentieth Century-Fox Video

Immoral Tales

One of those films that has pretensions to being a work of art but which, beneath all the surface gloss, is nothing more than a very dirty film indeed. All four stories are erotically motivated and have a 16-year-old girl discovering the delights of oral sex from her cousin, a countess bathing in the blood of village maidens, a French peasant girl masturbating with a cucumber and Lucretia Borgia enjoying sex with father and brother. It's all so beautifully photographed in rich colour that it almost seems like a clean movie. But it's not. After midnight video.

1974. Directed by Walerian Borowczyk.
Starring Lise Danvers, Fabrice Luchini, Charlotte Alexandra, Paloma Picasso, Pascale Christophe, Florence Bellamy, Jacopo Berinizi, Lorenzo Berinizi. Colour.
103 minutes.

Thorn EMI Video

Impact

Rarely seen Hollywood drama that begins as a routine thriller – wife and lover plan to murder the wife's millionaire industrialist husband – then takes a clever twist when the husband survives, pretends he's copped it and allows his wife to come to trial for his 'murder'. Brian Donlevy, Ella Raines and Charles Coburn make it all appear reasonably believable. Supports *Dangerous Mission* on a double-feature video tape.

1949. Directed by Arthur Lubin.

Starring Brian Donlevy, Ella Raines, Helen Walker, Charles Coburn, Anna May Wong. Black and White.
94 minutes (Originally 111).

Kingston Video

The Janitor ★★★

The *Breaking Away* team of director Peter Yates and writer Steve Tesich back together with a tale of a young janitor who witnesses the murder of a Vietnamese diamond importer and becomes obsessed with the young TV reporter covering the case. Gets a bit involved and complicated towards the end but as a thriller it's not bad and offers further proof that Yates is one of the best professional directors around. Sigourney Weaver (reporter) gladdens the eye if not quite matching the excellent William Hurt (janitor) in the acting stakes. Known as *Eyewitness* in the States.

1981. Directed by Peter Yates.
Starring William Hurt, Sigourney Weaver, Christopher Plummer, James Woods, Irene Worth, Kenneth McMillan, Pamela Reed. Colour.
108 minutes.

Twentieth Century-Fox Video

Kagemusha ★★

This is one of those movies the critics *tell* you to like, that you watch with great respect for close to three hours and then come away mumbling the words "masterpiece" and "brilliant." If you were honest, however, you would also add "boring" for this 159 minute Kurosawa film drags you wearily through life in warring 16th century Japan and asks you to concern yourself with a thief who is saved from crucifixion and masquerades as the double of a powerful clan leader. The battle scenes *are* well done but they're not that spectacular and one has to ask "Why all the acclaim?" Not that Kurosawa's not a great director. *Rashomon* and *Seven Samurai* more than prove that. This one (Japan's most expensive movie) doesn't. Overrated.

Oscars   Nil
Oscar Nominations (2)   Best Foreign Language Film; Art Direction

1980. Directed by Akira Kurosawa.
Starring Tatsuya Nakadai, Tsutomu Yamazaki, Kenichi Hagiwara, Kohta Yui, Hideji Otaki. Colour.
159 minutes.

Twentieth Century-Fox Video

King Kong ★★

The second version of the Kong story (see also page 248) and a pretty lamentable attempt to imitate its predecessor. The story remains the same although the death

495

venue has now been changed to the twin towers of the World Trade Centre in New York. Rotten special effects despite its controversial Oscar although Jessica Lange is infinitely more sexy than Fay Wray ("you goddam chauvinist pig ape!" she screams at one point) and Charles Grodin adds a touch of humour as the expedition leader. That's two plusses but that still only makes two out of ten!

Box-office rental	$36,915,000
Average rental (76)	$22,752,350
Oscars (1)	Best Visual Effects (Special Achievement)
Oscar nominations (2)	Best Photography; Sound

1976. Directed by John Guillermin.
Starring Jeff Bridges, Charles Grodin, Jessica Lange, John Randolph, Rene Auberjonois, Julius Harris, Jack O'Halloran. Colour.
135 minutes.

Thorn EMI Video

The Klansman

A glance at the writing credits of this movie – Sam Fuller and Millard Kaufman (who once wrote *Bad Day At Black Rock*) – raises one's hopes that it might amount to something above the norm. Alas, no. It's just a routine, rather ugly little movie about a small-town sheriff involved with the Ku Klux Klan and civil rights demonstrators in Alabama in the early 60s. Lee Marvin is the sheriff; Richard Burton offers a portrait of alcoholic cynicism as a weary recluse but it's all 'bang, bang, rape, rape, shoot, shoot' stuff that amounts to nothing more than the proverbial 'hill of beans'

1974. Directed by Terence Young.
Starring Lee Marvin, Richard Burton, Cameron Mitchell, O. J. Simpson, Lola Falana, David Huddleston, Lucianna Paluzzi, Linda Evans. Colour.
90 minutes.

Picture Time Video
(*distributed by VCL*)

A Lady Takes A Chance

Mild little comedy about a New York City gal who takes a 14-day holiday in the Wild West and falls for a no-nonsense no-marriage rodeo rider. Romance blossoms, the film does not. Dated wartime fare. Delicious Jean Arthur has her moments as always, co-star John Wayne has very few. Part of a video comedy double-bill. See also *The First Travelling Saleslady*.

1943. Directed by William A. Seiter.
Starring Jean Arthur, John Wayne, Charles Winninger, Phil Silvers, Mary Field, Don Costello. Black and White.
86 minutes.

Kingston Video

Lord Of The Rings ★★

Anyone trying to adapt Tolkien's famous trilogy to the screen deserves ten out of ten for trying. To pull it off successfully, however, is such a remote possibility that one wonders whether it was worth attempting in the first place. This 135-minute animated film delves into the first two books – *The Fellowship Of The Ring* and *The Two Towers* – and follows the adventures of two peace-loving Hobbits as they journey forth with the Ring which brings great power and corruption in the land of Middle Earth. The technique of over-drawing live action sequences is both fascinating and disconcerting; the whole piece, confusing, difficult to follow and dull. Ambitious but boring video.

Box-office rental	$13,791,043
Average rental (78)	$39,443,850

1978. Directed by Ralph Bakshi.
Colour.
135 minutes.

Thorn EMI Video

Macao ★★

A Howard Hughes production with voluptuous Jane Russell, sleepy-eyed Robert Mitchum and cheerful William Bendix all involved in murky goings on in the exotic port of Macao. The plot (undercover cop Bendix is seeking to bring gambler Brad Dexter to justice) is of little significance. But the handling is quite imaginative, not surprising perhaps since Josef von Sternberg was the original director and Nicholas Ray brought in to do extensive reshooting. Who filmed what? Dunno. But it's good fun trying to find out. Outstanding black and white photography; Jane Russell sings 'One For The Road'. Supported on a video double bill by *The Bounty Killer*.

1952. Directed by Josef von Sternberg (and, uncredited Nicholas Ray).
Starring Robert Mitchum, Jane Russell, William Bendix, Thomas Gomez, Gloria Grahame, Brad Dexter, Edward Ashley. Vladimir Sokoloff. Black and White.
80 minutes.

Kingston Video

Magic ★★★

Portrait of a disintegrating mind with Anthony Hopkins as a ventriloquist who finds himself being taken over by his foul-mouthed dummy 'Fats' and driven to commit a double murder. Luscious Ann-Margret is almost victim number three but manages to survive – just. A chilling, bleak little chamber thriller, adapted from his own novel by William Goldman and with several moments of spine-tingling terror not least when press agent Burgess Meredith bets Hopkins that he can't go a minute without talking in the voice of his dummy. Hopkins' 60-second Jekyll and Hyde type struggle is frightening to watch.

Box-office rental	$13,268,000
Average rental (78)	$39,443,850

1978. Directed by Richard Attenborough.
Starring Anthony Hopkins, Ann-Margret, Burgess Meredith, Ed Lauter, E. J. Andre, Jerry Houser. Colour.
107 minutes.

Intervision

The Man Who Haunted Himself ★

Conventional businessman Roger Moore crashes headlong in his car and finds that his other self (alike in looks but not in personality) emerges during the operation that follows and then proceeds to take over his job, wife and kids. Corny stuff hampered by atrocious special effects and colourwork and a plot that is so full of holes that it is hardly worth a second glance. Freddie Jones gives a few moments of pleasure as a twitching, pill-swallowing Scottish psychiatrist.

1970. Directed by Basil Dearden.
Starring Roger Moore, Hildegard Neil, Olga Georges-Picot, Anton Rodgers, Freddie Jones, Thorley Walters, John Carson. Colour.
94 minutes.

Thorn EMI Video

Master Of The World ★★

Run-of-the-mill fantasy from the American International stable with nasty old Vincent Price as a mad genius who thinks he can achieve world peace by bombing all hostile nations into submission from his giant 19th century flying ship. Wrong! Good young toughie Charles Bronson is up against him. Passable video fare for the kids but only occasionally does it rise above the comic book level. Based on two Jules Verne novels, *Robur The Conquerer* and *Master Of The World*.

1961. Directed by William Witney.
Starring Vincent Price, Charles Bronson, Henry Hull, Mary Webster, David Frankham, Richard Harrison. Colour.
104 minutes.

Guild Home Video

Monsieur Hulot's Holiday ★★★★

This is it, the one that should make just about everyone laugh, marking the first appearance of Jacques Tati's Monsieur Hulot as he takes off in his old car for an incident-packed and catastrophic holiday in a small seaside resort in Brittany. From the very first shot when the passengers run helplessly up and down station platforms unable to decipher the garbled instructions on a loudspeaker this is one of the funniest movies of all time. No more than a series of comic incidents strung together but a perfect example of Tati's genius with the art of mime. Lazy, charming, impeccably timed.

Oscars   Nil

Oscar nominations (1)   Best Story and Screenplay

1953. Directed by Jacques Tati
Starring Jacques Tati, Nathalie Pascaud, Louis Perrault, Michele Rolla, Suzy Willy,
Andre Dubois, Valentine Camax, Raymond Carl. Black and White.
91 minutes.

Zodiac Video
(distributed by Videomedia)

Montana Belle

Run-of-the-mill Western with Jane Russell as notorious outlaw Belle Starr having
several run-ins with the Dalton Brothers and setting her sights on gambler-saloon-
keeper George Brent. Filmed in the truly awful colour process of Trucolor, this
was a Republic picture made by Allan Dwan. But when Howard Hughes saw the
end result he purchased it for $600,000 and shelved it for four years. Perhaps he
wasn't so eccentric after all. Shares a video double-bill with the Debbie Reynolds/
Eddie Fisher comedy *Bundle Of Joy*.

1952. Directed by Allan Dwan.
Starring Jane Russell, George Brent, Scott Brady, Forrest Tucker, Andy Devine,
Jack Lambert, John Litel, Ray Teal. Colour.
81 minutes.

Kingston Video

Orca. . .Killer Whale

Or, let's try a *Jaws* rip-off with a whale and a very phoney looking whale at that.
The killer in question is a certain Orca Orcinus who takes revenge on captain
Richard Harris and his crew for killing his pregnant mate. Serves 'em right. They
deserve all they get. You don't deserve the mediocrity displayed on this tape
though. Bo Derek is in there somewhere but gets lost among all the corny action
stuff. Set off the coast of Newfoundland.

Box-office rental $9,430,000
Average rental (77) $36,913,348

1977. Directed by Michael Anderson.
Starring Richard Harris, Charlotte Rampling, Will Sampson, Bo Derek, Keenan
Wynn, Scott Walker, Robert Carradine. Colour.
92 minutes.

Thorn EMI Video

Ordinary People

The 1980 best picture Oscar winner, an intelligent, deeply felt drama of how an
upper middle-class Chicago family finds itself coming apart at the seams during
the aftermath of the death by drowning of the eldest son. Not a great movie and

not one that would have emerged as the best in a really good year but honest and well-made and quite riveting when Mary Tyler Moore is on screen. Her portrait of an all-American materialistic mother-bitch is a knockout. Adapts well to video because of its interior settings, etc. Robert Redford's first film as a director.

Box-office rental	$23,123,000
Average rental (80)	$30,086,027
Oscars (4)	Best Film; Supporting Actor (Hutton); Direction; Screenplay
Oscar nominations (2)	Best Actress (Moore); Supporting Actor (Hirsch)

1980. Directed by Robert Redford.
Starring Donald Sutherland, Mary Tyler Moore, Judd Hirsch, Timothy Hutton, M. Emmet Walsh, Elizabeth McGovern, Dinah Manoff. Colour.
124 minutes.

CIC Video

Players

Movies about sport have generally been box-office flops even if sometimes (see *The Hustler*) they have come off as works of art. This one is neither a work of art nor was it a success at the box-office. Ali MacGraw stars as a kept woman in her late 30s who seduces young tennis hustler Dean-Paul Martin down Mexico way. The setting is Wimbledon where Martin plays in the singles final against Vilas and remembers the whole dreary affair for our benefit. An unintentional laugh-a-minute whenever MacGraw is on the screen. Some interesting backstage glimpses of life on the modern day tennis circuit. Plus guest appearances of Pancho Gonzales, John McEnroe, Ilie Nastase, etc.

1979. Directed by Anthony Harvey
Starring Ali MacGraw, Dean-Paul Martin, Maximilian Schell, Pancho Gonzales, Steven Guttenberg. Colour.
120 minutes.

CIC Video

Puppet On A Chain

Alistair MacLean stuff about an American narcotics agent tracking down a gang of heroin smugglers in Amsterdam. Colourless performances don't help matters nor the sluggish direction nor a rather nasty surfeit of sadism not usually prevalent in films based on MacLean's work e.g. the 'hero' half blinding one of his victims by smashing his spectacles in his eyes. The only redeeming feature is the exciting speedboat chase (directed incidentally by Don Sharp) through the Zuyder Zee and Amsterdam canals. Routine.

1971. Directed by Geoffrey Reeve.
Starring Sven-Bertil Taube, Barbara Parkins, Alexander Knox, Patrick Allen, Vladek Sheybal, Ania Marson. Colour.
98 minutes.

Guild Home Video

Raid On Entebbe ★★

The Israeli commandos rescued the hi-jacked hostages at Entebbe, Uganda, on July 4, 1976. Just a few months later this movie was being shown on American TV and (in this country) in the cinemas. Fast work and perhaps a model for all those directors who take an age over their work for although it isn't great it's not bad either and made with a certain amount of expertise by director Irvin Kershner. A strong cast includes Charles Bronson as General Dan Shomrom in charge of the rescue operations and Yaphet Kotto as Idi Amin. Peter Finch (in his last movie) appears as Prime Minister Yitzhak Rabin.

1977. Directed by Irvin Kershner.
Starring Peter Finch, Martin Balsam, Horst Buchholz, John Saxon, Sylvia Sidney, Jack Warden, Yaphet Kotto, Charles Bronson, Tige Andrews, Eddie Constantine. Colour.
118 minutes

Thorn EMI Video

Scared To Death ★

Anything that was shot in the inferior colour process of Cinecolor used to produce groans of anguish from the audiences of the 40s and 50s. This is one such movie, a substandard horror tale set in a sanitarium occupied by a lot of very strange people. Bela Lugosi features as a stage magician who wears a Dracula-like cape and employs a dwarf to run his errands. There are also floating green masks that appear at windows. Sounds corny. Dead right.

1947. Directed by Christy Cabanne.
Starring Bela Lugosi, Douglas Fowley, Joyce Compton, George Zucco, Nat Pendleton. Colour.
65 minutes.

Vintage Classics
(distributed by VCL)

The Scars of Dracula ★★

Dracula i.e. Christopher Lee is alive and well as a group of young innocents discover to their cost when they visit his castle in good old Transylvania. The usual Hammer horror stuff, slightly below par in that it plods for most of its running time. Redeemed somewhat by Lee crawling crablike up his castle walls and being struck by lightning and consumed by fire during the climax. If only the rest had been up to standard. Dennis Waterman (in his pre-*Sweeney* and *Minder* days) is responsible for Mr. Lee's demise.

1970. Directed by Roy Ward Baker.
Starring Christopher Lee, Dennis Waterman, Jenny Hanley, Christopher Matthews, Patrick Troughton, Michael Gwynn, Wendy Hamilton. Colour.
96 minutes.

Thorn EMI Video

The Silver Bears

A good cast but a complicated story unless you're deep into high finance. Michael Caine is at the centre of it all as an international money man who eventually walks off with the Lugano bank he has always wanted to own. Making things difficult in a tale of cross and double-cross in the world silver market: London broker Charles Gray, gambling prince Louis Jourdan and Californian banker Tom Smothers. One of the film's virtues is that it's deft and non violent. One of its vices is that it's dull. Lovely locations. Too long at 113 minutes.

1977. Directed by Ivan Passer.
Starring Michael Caine, Cybill Shepherd, Louis Jourdan, Stephane Audran, David Warner, Tom Smothers, Martin Balsam, Charles Gray, Joss Ackland. Colour.
113 minutes.

Thorn EMI Video

Sinbad The Sailor

Douglas Fairbanks Jr sets out on the famous adventurer's mythical eighth voyage to search for the treasure of Alexander on the lost island of Deryabar. Sounds like fun especially when the movie's original advertising slogan blazed: 'He stormed a veiled beauty's boudoir. . .and made her love it!' It's doubtful, however, whether you'll love this naive and setbound swashbuckler even though the always excellent Walter Slezak and attractive Maureen O'Hara are on hand to help out. Try *The Spanish Main*, made by the same studio (RKO) about the same time. Much better value! Supporting *Sinbad*: three shorts – *The Adventurer* with Charlie Chaplin, *An Apple In His Eye* with Edgar Kennedy and *Pal, Fugitive Dog*.

1947. Directed by Richard Wallace.
Starring Douglas Fairbanks Jr., Maureen O'Hara, Walter Slezak, Anthony Quinn, George Tobias, Jane Greer, Mike Mazurki. Colour.
116 minutes.

Kingston Video

S.O.B.

A celebrated Hollywood film-maker is shaken to the core when his latest movie is taken apart by the critics and finishes up a financial disaster. Whilst contemplating suicide he hits on the idea of recutting it as a sex picture and joining the rat race of modern day Hollywood. After that, frenzied chaos all round. Top notch, often very bitter Blake Edwards comedy that looks with a jaundiced eye at the present day movie scene. Movie buffs will love it especially as many of the film's characters can be matched up with real life personalities. Julie Andrews appears topless in one brief scene; Bill Holden makes his final screen appearance. Fine cast.

Box-office rental	$6,003,822
Average rental (81)	$32,180,110

1981. Directed by Blake Edwards.
Starring Julie Andrews, William Holden, Richard Mulligan, Robert Vaughn, Robert

Webber, Robert Preston, Larry Hagman, Shelley Winters, Marisa Berenson, Loretta Swit. Colour.
121 minutes.

Guild Home Video

Something To Sing About

Manhattan bandleader James Cagney goes to Hollywood to star in a musical but finds that things don't quite work out as he had hoped. A Warner musical of the late 30s and a long, long way from Busby Berkeley but Cagney *is* Cagney and that counts for much. In this he both hoofs and sings. And when he's doing that the movie's very watchable. William Frawley supports as a studio press agent. Songs by Victor Schertzinger.

Oscars	Nil
Oscar nominations (1)	Best Music Score

1937. Directed by Victor Schertzinger.
Starring James Cagney, Evelyn Daw, William Frawley, Mona Barrie, Gene Lockhart, James Newill. Black and White.
84 minutes.

Vintage Classics
(distributed by VCL)

Song Of Norway

The life of composer Edvard Grieg as depicted in the stage musical by Milton Lazarus, Robert Wright and George Forrest. A trite script is the film's main drawback; the music and lovely Norwegian settings (old towns, snow-covered mountains, fjords) its prime attributes. Fans of *The Sound Of Music* will probably enjoy the escapism and, although its faults are legion, this one still has more to offer in terms of sheer entertainment than much of the garbage being served up by modern day film-makers. Corny but colourful.

Box-office rental	$4,450,000
Average rental (70)	$16,881,800

1970. Directed by Andrew L. Stone.
Starring Toralv Maurstad, Florence Henderson, Christina Schollin, Frank Poretta, Harry Secombe, Robert Morley, Edward G. Robinson, Elizabeth Larner, Oscar Homolka. Colour.
141 minutes.

Rank Video

Stromboli ★★

Roberto Rossellini movie about a young victim of war (Ingrid Bergman) who marries a fisherman to escape life in an internment camp and then finds herself spiritually isolated when she is unable to fit into his island community. Heavily criticised at the time of its first release (49), this one now looks considerably more interesting than it once did, its documentary scenes of life on the volcanic island of Stromboli being particularly rewarding. On the same tape: Fritz Lang's *While The City Sleeps*. Neither film is a vintage work but Rossellini and Lang on one tape cannot help but equate with value for money.

1949. Directed by Roberto Rossellini.
Starring Ingrid Bergman, Mario Vitale, Renzo Cesana, Mario Sponza, and the people of Stromboli. Black and White.
107 minutes.

Kingston Video

Sunburn

Insurance investigator Charles Grodin and lovely model Farrah Fawcett-Majors investigate a five million dollar insurance claim down Acapulco way. "Smile-a-lot" Farrah looks good. So does the scenery. The soundtrack, unfortunately, sounds dreary even though the producers try to hide the inept dialogue with 22 songs from Paul McCartney and Wings, Gladys Knight, Herbie Hancock, The Beachboys, etc. There's blackmail, murder and kidnapping but this is hardly a good buy. You can see better on TV just about any day of the week. Art Carney is a veteran private-eye and Joan Collins, Keenan Wynn (even Eleanor Parker) are all around. But it makes no difference.

1979. Directed by Richard C. Sarafian.
Starring Farrah Fawcett-Majors, Charles Grodin, Art Carney, Joan Collins, William Daniels, John Hillerman, Eleanor Parker, Keenan Wynn. Colour.
98 minutes.

Picture Time Video
(*distributed by VCL*)

Swing High, Swing Low

1937 movie with trumpeter Fred MacMurray finding himself on the way up when he meets and weds nightclub singer Carole Lombard but on the way down when alcohol and Dottie Lamour (fifth on the cast list as a high-living dancer) disrupt the music and the bliss. All comes right in the end, however. Mitchell Leisen's handling brings a glossy professionalism to strictly run-of-the-mill material. Based on the stage success *Burlesque*.

1937. Directed by Mitchell Leisen.
Starring Carole Lombard, Fred MacMurray, Charles Butterworth, Jean Dixon, Dorothy Lamour, Harvey Stephens, Anthony Quinn. Black and White.
95 minutes.

Vintage Classics
(*distributed by VCL*)

Tarzan, The Ape Man

'Jane, The Oomph Girl' would have been a more appropriate title for this crummy movie which dwells more on Bo Derek's physical attributes than the courageous escapades of Edgar Rice Burroughs' jungle apeman. Still, the attributes and the locations (Sri Lanka) are worth a gaze or two even if the rest of the film is not. Richard Harris features as Jane's Victorian explorer pa; Miles O'Keeffe (relegated to fourth on the cast list) is Tarzan. The dramatic incidents include a fight with a lion, near death from a snake bite and rescue from tribal sacrifice.

Box-office rental	$15,642,396
Average rental (81)	$32,180,110

1981. Directed by John Derek.
Starring Bo Derek, Richard Harris, John Phillip Law, Miles O'Keeffe, Akushula Selayah, Steven Strong, Wilfrid Hyde White. Colour.
112 minutes.

MGM/CBS Home Video

They Made Me A Criminal

1939 Warners melodrama with boxing champ John Garfield forced to flee the cops when he becomes involved in a false murder charge. He finishes up out West on a lonely ranch run by two young women and six young New York kids. Pursuing him all the way then eventually relenting is cop Claude Rains. No musical numbers despite the name of Busby Berkeley on the credits. The Dead End Kids are also featured. Efficient.

1939. Directed by Busby Berkeley.
Starring John Garfield, Claude Rains, Gloria Dickson, May Robson, Billy Halop, Huntz Hall, Barbara Pepper, Ward Bond, Ann Sheridan. Black and White.
92 minutes.

Vintage Classics
(distributed by VCL)

This Sporting Life

Lindsay Anderson's first feature and a movie that holds up remarkably well as it traces the life of a rebellious ex-miner turned rugby footballer and his tormented relationship with a lonely widow. Or, in verbal shorthand, a portrait of mutual self-destruction. A clever use of flashbacks and film technique help the movie look a good bet even today although it's a bit on the depressing side and the game of Rugby League certainly doesn't come out of things with much honour. Alan Badel (small town tycoon), Arthur Lowe (club director) and William Hartnell (talent scout) are among those supporting the two leads: Richard Harris and Rachel Roberts.

Oscars:	Nil
Oscar nominations (2)	Best Actor (Harris); Actress (Roberts)

1963. Directed by Lindsay Anderson.

Starring Richard Harris, Rachel Roberts, Alan Badel, William Hartnell, Colin Blakely, Vanda Godsell, Arthur Lowe, Jack Watson. Black and White. 134 minutes.

Rank Video

The Three Musketeers

Probably the most enjoyable of all the versions of Dumas' swashbuckling tale with D'Artagnan and his cronies defending the honour of Louis XIII against the evil machinations of Cardinal Richelieu. More spoofy and knockabout than previous versions and the brightness of the lighting photography betrays the fact that it was shot in Spain not France. Still, it's all passable enough entertainment with Faye Dunaway in especially good form as the wicked Milady De Winter, Michael York is D'Artagnan; Oliver Reed (excellent as Athos), Richard Chamberlain (Aramis) and Frank Finlay (Porthos) are his three swashbuckling companions. Elegant costumes, stirring music score by Michel Legrand.

Box-office rental $11,434,000
Average rental (74) $18,456,150

1974. Directed by Richard Lester.
Starring Michael York, Oliver Reed, Raquel Welch, Richard Chamberlain, Frank Finlay, Charlton Heston, Faye Dunaway, Christopher Lee, Geraldine Chaplin, Jean-Pierre Cassel. Colour.
107 minutes.

Intervision.

Time Bandits

Supreme being Ralph Richardson entrusts a group of dwarfs to put to rights what's wrong with the Creation so down they pop through various time holes in the cosmos, visiting Napoleon, the passengers on the Titanic, the Minotaur, etc. It all comes from the Monty Python gang so you can guess what's on the menu. Well, almost for this fantasy's not only zany but a bit fearsome as well with beheadings, impalings, burnings and biting off of rats' heads. It has its moments although it's a bit crude at times. One of the cinema's biggest financial successes of 1981.

Box-office rental $16,000,000
Average rental (81) $32,180,110

1981. Directed by Terry Gilliam
Starring John Cleese, Sean Connery, Shelley Duvall, Katherine Helmond, Ian Holm, Michael Palin, Ralph Richardson, Peter Vaughan, David Warner. Colour.
113 minutes.

Thorn EMI Video

Times Square ★

Two New York girls – one a slum kid from 42nd Street, the other the daughter of a politician – set up home on a derelict pier and find themselves the centre of a cult movement through their anti-establishment activities and rock act. A liberal sprinkling of four letter words adds to the general unpleasantness as do some twenty music numbers, one of which has the title 'Pissing In The River'. Cole Porter this is not.

1980. Directed by Alan Moyle.
Starring Tim Curry, Trini Alvarado, Robin Johnson, Peter Coffield, Herbert Berghof, David Margulies, Anna Maria Horsford. Colour.
111 minutes.

Thorn EMI Video

Tommy ★★

Elton John in big glasses as the Pinball Wizard, Ann-Margret rolling about in a lot of baked beans and Roger Daltrey, deaf, dumb and blind since witnessing a murder as a child, finding himself cured and a successful rock star. Mediocre stuff despite the reputation of Pete Townshend's celebrated rock opera. Ken Russell livens things up with some bizarre visual images which means it's never dull. Some cinemas played this in Quintophonic Sound when it was first released. Luckily that system has not yet reached home screens.

Box-office rental	$16,000,000
Average rental (75)	$27,300,250
Oscars	Nil
Oscar nominations (2)	Best Actress (Ann-Margret); Music Adaptation

1975. Directed by Ken Russell.
Starring Ann-Margret, Oliver Reed, Roger Daltrey, Elton John, Eric Clapton, Keith Moon, Jack Nicholson, Robert Powell, Paul Nicholas. Colour.
108 minutes.
Thorn EMI Video

To The Devil A Daughter ★★

One of the cinema's relatively few forays into Dennis Wheatley territory, made in the wake of the success of *The Exorcist* and centring on a bewildered American novelist (Richard Widmark) who finds himself trying to prevent a young woman from falling into the hands of diabolical priest Christopher Lee. For lovers of the rather nasty there's the birth of a convincing baby demon and plenty of black magic mumbo-jumbo; for those who enjoy a quiet night's sleep think carefully for there's enough here to keep you awake until the early hours. Strong cast.

1976. Directed by Peter Sykes.

Starring Richard Widmark, Christopher Lee, Honor Blackman, Denholm Elliott, Michael Goodliffe, Nastassja Kinski, Eva Maria Meineke, Anthony Valentine, Derek Francis. Colour.
93 minutes.

Thorn EMI Video

Traffic

Last time out for Jacques Tati's philosophical Monsieur Hulot. This time he finds himself driving a revolutionary new motor car from Paris to Amsterdam for a Deluxe Car Show. As you might expect, numerous mishaps befall him along the way although, to be frank, they are not as amusing as you might expect after the great man's escapades in his earlier films. The jokes are often too calculated to be really funny and although Tati's continuing message about the perils of the machine age is still hammered home forcibly the film is a bit of a letdown compared with other Tati exercises.

1970. Directed by Jacques Tati.
Starring Jacques Tati, Maria Kimberly, Marcel Fraval, Honore Bostel, Tony Kneppers, Francois Maisongrosse. Colour.
96 minutes.

Spectrum
(distributed by Polygram)

The Trial

Question: Why is Anthony Perkins as Joseph K awakened in the middle of the night by the police, taken to a secret trial in a giant courtroom and condemned for a crime that is never explained? Mr. Perkins doesn't seem to know what is going on. Neither, I'll wager, will you although Orson Welles' stimulating use of the camera often makes the bizarre proceedings enjoyable for *cineastes*. Helping to create the overall confusion: Jeanne Moreau as a seedy cabaret entertainer; Madeleine Robinson as Perkins' landlady and Welles himself as advocate Hassler. Based of course on Kafka's celebrated novel (about the individual suffering under bureaucracy) which somehow seemed to get its points across rather more successfully than the film. A pity. This could and perhaps should have been Welles' best film since *Ambersons*.

1962. Directed by Orson Welles.
Starring Anthony Perkins, Jeanne Moreau, Romy Schneider, Elsa Martinelli, Suzanne Flon, Orson Welles, Akim Tamiroff, Madeleine Robinson. Black and White.
118 minutes.

Intervision

Triple Kill

Curious movie that tells the last second thoughts of an American marine who dies by throwing himself on a grenade in the Vietnam War. In between is the story of

508

the destruction of a Mafia-controlled drugs ring in modern day Los Angeles. Telly Savalas is a narcotics agent; Robert Vaughn appears as the boss of the city's drug market. Routine. The 'last-seconds-before-death' angle has been done before and much more effectively in the 1961 American Civil War drama *Incident At Owl Creek*.

1971. Directed by Tom Stern and Lane Slate.
Starring Tom Stern, Telly Savalas, Robert Vaughn, Jeff Corey, Peter Lawford, Marilyn Akin, John Marley, Burgess Meredith. Colour.
91 minutes.

Picture Time Video
(*distributed by VCL*)

The Valachi Papers

A poor man's *Godfather*, based on fact but as dull as they come. Not only are the corpses stiff, so is the movie. Charles Bronson has the lead as Brooklyn-born mobster Joseph Valachi who turns informer and spills the beans on the Cosa Nostra while serving a life sentence. That excellent character actor Joseph Wiseman is in the cast as a Mafia boss but that isn't enough to make this one particularly engrossing. Spans a period of thirty years, from 1929 to 1962!

Box-office rental	$9,300,000
Average rental (72)	$17,543,950

1972. Directed by Terence Young
Starring Charles Bronson, Mario Pilar, Fred Valleca, Giacomino De Michelis, Amy Freeman, Gerald S. O'Loughlin, Lino Ventura, Joseph Wiseman. Colour.
127 minutes.

Thorn EMI Video

The Vampire Bat

Lionel Atwill completely bats (if you'll pardon the expression) as a professor who bumps off a number of people for their blood then feeds it into a parasite he has created in his laboratory. All set in a remote Bavarian village of course. Melvyn Douglas straightens things out and *King Kong* girl Fay Wray is saved at the last minute from a dose of Atwill's 'blood substitute.' Old and creaky. Not of any great quality even when it was first released some fifty years ago.

1933. Directed by Frank Strayer.
Starring Lionel Atwill, Melvyn Douglas, Fay Wray, Dwight Frye, Lionel Belmore. Black and White.
63 minutes.

Vintage Classics
(*distributed by VCL*)

Victim ★★★

Something of a watershed movie in that it was the first to treat the subject of homosexuality on screen and treat it (just as *Crossfire* had investigated anti-Semitism before it) within the format of a thriller. Dirk Bogarde plays an eminent barrister who puts his marriage and brilliant career at risk when he reveals his homosexual past after one of his former lovers – a victim of blackmail – commits suicide. Quite strong stuff even now; well acted and with a good number of London locations. A courageous film.

1961. Directed by Basil Dearden.
Starring Dirk Bogarde, Sylvia Syms, Dennis Price, Anthony Nicholls, Peter Copley, Norman Bird, Peter McEnery, Donald Churchill, Derren Nesbitt, John Barrie. Black and White.
100 minutes.

Rank Video

Voices ★★

Old house movie with a neat ending but which seems to go on forever. Failed writer David Hemmings and wife Gayle Hunnicutt go to stay at a large country mansion. They hear the voices of children. Could one of them be that of their son lost in a drowning accident years before? Or is it someone else? The last scene is genuinely surprising. But it's all very ordinary before that.

1973. Directed by Kevin Billington.
Starring David Hemmings, Gayle Hunnicutt, Lynn Farleigh, Russell Lewis, Eva Griffiths, Adam Bridge. Colour.
91 minutes.

Cinema Features
(distributed by VCL)

Watership Down ★★★

A long way from the cartoon world of Walt Disney with a group of rabbits leaving their about-to-be-destroyed warren to seek a safer place, far away from the murderous humans. Battles with other rabbits, attacks by rats and a hawk, trouble with cats, etc stand in the way of happiness and peace. Based on the novel by Richard Adams and not by any means a children's film although many will find it absorbing. And sad. John Hurt (Hazel); Richard Briers (the young Fiver); Ralph Richardson (Chief Rabbit); and Zero Mostel (the seagull Kehaar) are among the actors who lend their voices to the well known characters.

1978. Directed by Martin Rosen.
Colour.
92 minutes.

Thorn EMI Video

Westworld ★★

Two young Chicago businessmen pay a thousand dollars a day to enjoy a vacation in Delos, a futuristic holiday resort which offers them the chance to experience the delights of the past in three robot worlds – Roman World, Medieval World and Westworld. The latter allows guests to become gunslingers against lifelike robots who inhabit a pastiche western town. Sounds OK but when the robots go berserk and don't obey orders things become rather less than enjoyable. An ingenious idea that sounds better than it actually appears on screen. The sets and Yul Brynner's seemingly indestructible Gunslinger are the best things in a no more than average movie. Passable – just.

Box-office rental $7,000,000
Average rental (73) $22,271,150

1973. Directed by Michael Crichton.
Starring Yul Brynner, Richard Benjamin, James Brolin, Norman Bartold, Alan Oppenheimer, Victoria Shaw. Colour.
89 minutes.

MGM/CBS Home Video

Where Eagles Dare ★★

It's World War II. Richard Burton and Clint Eastwood head a commando unit parachuted into the Bavarian Alps to rescue a high-ranked Allied officer held by the Nazis in a supposedly impregnable prison. It all takes 158 minutes to unfold. And guess who wins? And guess who authored the novel on which this film is based? Right in one, Alistair MacLean! Straight down the line action adventure, ideal (often spoof-like) escapism for MacLean fans, boring as hell for those who tend to think they've seen all this kind of stuff before. Rather surprisingly, not as successful as one would have anticipated at the box-office.

Box-office rental $7,150,000
Average rental (69) $13,660,950

1969. Directed by Brian G. Hutton.
Starring Richard Burton, Clint Eastwood, Mary Ure, Patrick Wymark, Michael Hordern, Donald Houston, Peter Barkworth, Robert Beatty, Anton Diffring. Colour.
158 minutes.

MGM/CBS Home Video

While The City Sleeps ★★★

A sex murderer is on the loose in the streets of New York. Three members of the staff of *The Sentinel* are promised a key executive post if they can help nail the killer with an exclusive story. In the running for the job: ambitious George Sanders, nervy Thomas Mitchell, bland James Craig. Regular guy Dana Andrews is the one who sorts it all out however. One scene has you remembering that Rhonda Fleming had two of the best legs in the business. Above average Fritz Lang thriller, made on a tight budget but none the worse for that. Good newspaper atmosphere. *Stromboli* with Ingrid Bergman shares a video double bill.

1956. Directed by Fritz Lang.
Starring Dana Andrews, Rhonda Fleming, Sally Forrest, Thomas Mitchell, Vincent Price, Howard Duff, Ida Lupino, George Sanders, James Craig, John Barrymore, Jr. Black and White.
100 minutes.

Kingston Video

The Woman In Green

Some attractive girls are bumped off in the London streets by a killer who hacks off their right forefingers as a momento. Call for Sherlock Holmes for it's the worse case of mass murder since Jack The Ripper was at large. Lurking in the shadows are Henry Daniell as Moriarty and seductive *femme fatale* Hillary Brooke. No matter, Holmes defeats 'em both. Assisting in his usual bumbling manner, Nigel Bruce as Dr. Watson. Basil Rathbone, of course, is the famous sleuth.

1945. Directed by Roy William Neill.
Starring Basil Rathbone, Nigel Bruce, Hillary Brooke, Henry Daniell, Paul Cavanagh, Matthew Boulton. Black and White.
68 minutes.

Vintage Classics
(distributed by VCL)